ANNA SOKOLOW

Choreography and Dance Studies

A series of books edited by Robert P. Cohan, C.B.E.

Please see the back of this book for other titles in the Choreography and Dance Studies series

ANNA SOKOLOW
THE REBELLIOUS SPIRIT

Larry Warren

harwood academic publishers
Australia • Canada • China • France • Germany • India
Japan • Luxembourg • Malaysia • The Netherlands • Russia
Singapore • Switzerland • Thailand • United Kingdom

Copyright © 1998 OPA (Overseas Publishers Association) Amsterdam B.V.
Published in The Netherlands by Harwood Academic Publishers.

Amsteldijk 166
1st Floor
1079 LH Amsterdam
The Netherlands

British Library Cataloguing in Publication Data

Warren, Larry
    Anna Sokolow: the rebellious spirit. – 2nd ed. –
(Choreography and dance studies; v. 14)
    1. Sokolow, Anna   2. Choreographers – Biography
    I. Title
    792.8′2′092

    ISBN 90–5702–185–4

Cover photo: Anna Sokolow.

For my wife, Anne,
who has always been there with me

CONTENTS

INTRODUCTION TO THE SERIES

Choreography and Dance Studies is a book series of special interest to dancers, dance teachers and choreographers. Focusing on dance composition, its techniques and training, the series will also cover the relationship of choreography to other components of dance performance such as music, lighting and the training of dancers.

In addition, *Choreography and Dance Studies* will seek to publish new works and provide translations of works not previously published in English, as well as to publish reprints of currently unavailable books of outstanding value to the dance community.

Robert P. Cohan

LIST OF PLATES

AN APPRECIATION

Whenever I think of Anna, I have an immediate clear picture in my head.

I see her standing in space. Even if there is a crowd around her there is something separate, apart, whole and attractively arresting about her presence. She stands simply, her hands folded in front of her. She is composed, relaxed, or rather, ready. Her body exudes its uprightness, her spine straight, her head sitting proudly on a beautiful neck, poised, erect, calm, attentive. Most of all, I can see her wide, wonderful, observant eyes looking out, taking in, waiting, noting, seeing everything but not judging. She radiates warmth, strength, directness, interest, trust. And I think how like her work all of that is.

The body of her work is about the human experience. It unfolds with composure, strength, intuitiveness, and compassion. The spine of her work is uncompromising; the great intelligence of her work is infused with dignity, pride, deep humanity — it is about what she sees, through her choreography with tenderness and strength. What a gift she *is*, and what a *gift* she gives us.

Jerome Robbins

PREFACE

I once looked up Anna Sokolow in a few reference books and found that she was born in three different years and that her parents were from Poland except when they were from Russia. Her great work *Rooms,* I read, was premiered on Broadway in 1954, but I attended that premiere in 1955 and had saved the program. The year she first went to Mexico City varies almost as often as the government rank of the man who invited Anna and her company to dance there. And that was just the beginning.

Everyone who knows Anna Sokolow knows their own Anna, and in the nearly one hundred interviews I conducted for this book I seldom heard a significant incident described the same way twice. Even if several tellers of the tale had been present when the incident occurred, it made little difference. In the process of writing this book I have often been reminded of the key message of Akira Kurosawa's film *Rashomon*: An important happening may be perceived differently by each person who is there. Ultimately, we must draw our own conclusions after listening to the many sides.

I have given considerable effort to creating chronological narrative but the difficult yet delightful challenge of following Anna's trail has led me to feel that strict adherence to that format would be a futile attempt to domesticate a life that has defied convention and a career that has been largely nomadic. This book is, therefore, an episodic assessment of the life and work of Anna Sokolow. For many decades Anna has been split three ways — between Mexico, where she is known as the "founder of Mexican modern dance"; Israel, where she founded the first professional modern dance company; and New York, where her contributions have been numerous. And, of course, she has worked in many other cities in the U.S. and abroad. Assignments have taken her to England, the Netherlands, Canada, Japan, and New South Wales, to mention only a few of many countries. She has personally set her work on more than seventy groups, no doubt a modern dance record. Yet her fame has never quite kept pace with her accomplishments despite the fact that in her nomadic life her influence has spread far and wide.

The better-known pioneers of Anna's generation developed a technique that taught the vocabulary needed to prepare a dancer to dance in their works.

Some created schools and ongoing companies, but most important they produced a continuous sequence of dance events that critics and others writing about dance could follow. To accomplish this an artist needed to have roots in one place. "My roots are in New York," Anna once said, but her roots kept shifting. Her school was wherever she was teaching or choreographing at the moment, be it for the Ballet Independiente in Mexico, the Ballet Rambert in England, or for her most recent New York company, Players' Project. Later she would say, "Your roots are where you work. There you belong."

Yet this nomad has pioneered in the development of an unusually personal approach to movement that has become part of the language of contemporary dance. Using this approach, which employs a large variety of music from Teo Macero's jazz to the "mystic" chord and great rhythmic complexity of `Alexander Scriabin, Anna has created dances that explore the innermost feelings of men and women in reaction to the social and psychological pressures of contemporary life. Her deeply touching work, *Rooms,* dealing with loneliness and alienation, and her *Dreams,* which touches on the inner torment of victims of the Nazi Holocaust, are timeless, and like the "alienated youth ballets" that she started choreographing in the late 1950s, have been much imitated. But she was the originator.

She has also had a penetrating effect on the dancers who have learned to perform her works under her watchful and demanding eye. Anna insists that dancers transcend their technique to give expression to the deepest understanding they have garnered in their lives concerning the specific subject at hand, be it love, hate, fear, anger, or loneliness. To their astonishment, many dancers, especially younger ones, find that they are far more ready than they ever thought they could be to express those feelings in front of an audience. Many later remembered having no choice. The ferocity with which Anna attacks any perceived insincerity or placidity in rehearsals or classes has become legend. It has often led to the creation of an emotionally charged atmosphere in the studio, but the living sparks produced in the choreographer–dancer relationship may last the dancer for a lifetime. In later years most of the dancers and actors have spoken of her with deep love and appreciation. A sampling of some of their statements along with those of others whose lives have been touched by Anna are in the Testimonials section of the Appendixes.

For her concentration on the darker side of human experience in her work she has been referred to by dance critics as "the Kafka," "the Poe," and "the Solzhenitsyn" of the dance. One writer suggested that if Truman Capote had come up with an idea for a non-narrative ballet, Anna would surely have been the right choice for choreographer. Yet many critics have noted that even in the most wrenching of her works she somehow reminds her audience of the nobility and strength of the human spirit. Perhaps for some audience members, including this author, the deepest inspiration comes from Anna's unrelenting portrayal of the truth in life as she observes it.

After a performance by the Players' Project at the Kennedy Center's Terrace Theater in the fall of 1988 featuring *Dreams*, the Washington choreographer Pola Nirenska and her husband, Holocaust hero Jan Karski, approached Anna. Karski, who had entered the Warsaw ghetto and a Nazi death camp in 1942 to bear witness to the Holocaust, told Anna how deeply he had been moved by the performance.

"When you say that," she said quietly, "it gives me courage to go on."

"No," said Karski, "it is you who gives us courage."

ACKNOWLEDGMENTS

I want to start by thanking three special friends, Pamela Sommers, Kent Cartwright, and Charley Rutherford, who read sections of the manuscript and made valuable suggestions. I met all three of them at the University of Maryland at College Park, where I work, and it is to that university that I want to next express my appreciation. Through the years I have been allowed some invaluable free time to work on this project and received generous travel grants to support research work in Israel and Mexico. The dance department has been fully supportive since the project was started late in 1978.

Grateful acknowledgment is due to those I quote, whether from conversations, correspondence, or printed sources. Some supplied the missing pieces in a complex puzzle. Others brought the vividness and vibrancy of their personal experience to what would have otherwise been bare facts. Their names will be found in the text or in the Notes. Others who generously gave of their time to talk to me or answer my written inquiries include the following: Julie Arenal, Stephen Bank, Frank Brandt, Ethel Butler, Bruce Carter, Mary Chudick, Aaron Cohen, Jane Dudley, Eddy Effron, Erica Eigenberg Itzkowitz, Gerald Freedman, David Garfield, Rina Gluck, Zvi Gottheimer, Nellie Happee, Doris Hering, Sali Ann and Mike Kriegsman, Rose Levy, Daniel Lewis, David Lifson, Chris Mahon, Dorothy Madden, David Manion, Giora Manor, Sophie Maslow, Edna Ocho Meyers, Laurie Freedman Myers, Lisa Mitchell, Al Pischl, Sasha and David Pressman, Emma Pulido, Paul Sanasardo, Beatrice Seckler, Steven Siegel, Dora Sowden, Ernestine Stodelle, James Truitte, Barry Ulanov, Ofra Ben Zvi Seroussi, and Avraham Zouri.

Special thanks to Madeleine M. Nichols, curator of the Dance Collection of the Performing Arts Library at Lincoln Center, and to Genevieve Oswald, curator emeritus. Lacy McDearmon of the Dance Collection and Rod Bladel of the Theatre Collection were especially helpful in my quest, willing to go beyond the call of duty and to do so graciously. My appreciation for translation work (Spanish to English) to Susan Carnochan, José Coronado, Gabriel Houbard, Anadel Lynton and Anna Soler. Bruce Wyman and Stacie Bristow, both dance student recipients of Undergraduate Research Apprenticeships from the University of

Maryland, applied their skills at the word processor, and slowly, patiently, taught me to use the thing, too. They also displayed excellent judgement as they pored through a decade-long collection of files and audiotapes to find things this author needed "in the next ten or fifteen minutes, please!"

Many of the photographers whose work is represented here dug through their old files of negatives and generously gave me permission to include their work. "For Anna? Of course!" they said.

To Anna Sokolow, my thanks for welcoming me into her home when she was there, as well as when she was working abroad, thereby giving me complete access to programs, reviews, and photographs that she has collected through the years. We have had many fine talks together, talks in which we spanned the years from the late 1920s to the present. Anna is a private person, not given to intimate revelations; yet never, when I questioned her on a sensitive issue, did she insist that I exclude it from the book. Rather, she seemed to say to me by the look on her face and by her attitude: I have spent most of my career trying to express the truth, as I have seen it, in my work; why shouldn't you feel free to do the same in yours? Thank you, Anna.

The greatest support through this whole project has come from my wife, Anne. When it came time to put the years of research into finished form, gently and lovingly she gave me advice and editorial help as needed. Most important, when I wavered, she helped me to find the courage to keep going.

Anna Sokolow has been
called the rebel of the
contemporary dance world
throughout her career
because she has rebelled
against mediocrity, rebelled
against any dictum that
prevented the individual
artist from developing a
personal vision of the content
and form of his
or her art.
William Bales

Anna Sokolow, 1958. Photography by Lionel Freedman.
Anna Sokolow collection

Freight di Velt an Alte Kashe
"The World Asks an Old Question"

(Anna's favorite old Yiddish song)

Translated by Dorothy Bilik
From *Yidische Folkslieder* by Emil Sekuletz
(Bucharest, 1959)

The world asks an old question
Tra la tra di ri di dom
Tra di tra di di rom
So one answers
Tra di re di rey lom
Oy Oy
Di ra di ri di rom
And if one wants one can still say
Tray din tray din
The old question still remains
Tra la tra di ri di dom
Tra di tra di ra di rom.

1

BREAD AND ROSES

During a nine-week textile workers strike in Lawrence, Massachusetts, in 1912, the women strikers carried banners that read: "Bread and Roses." They were fighting not only for workers' rights, but for a quality of life. (Edith Fowke and Joe Glazer, Songs of Work and Freedom)

When Anna Sokolow's niece, Judy Kaplan, was asked why her grandparents had left Russia in the early 1900s, she answered, "Why does any Jew leave Russia?"

There is an old Jewish saying: Ask a Jew a question and he answers with a question. Both parties may well know the answer at the outset; the question is posed merely to emphasize the import of that which is already understood. (A better question might have been: Why would any Jew *not* want to leave Russia at that time?) Sarah and Samuel Sokolowski (later Sokolow) and their infant son Isadore were among the millions of Jews who left tsarist Russia in a tidal wave of Western migration between 1881 and 1914. These immigrants abandoned their homeland in droves to escape religious and economic persecution. Pogroms — those dreaded periodic attacks on the Jewish community — were on the rise in Russia and few Jews, the Sokolowskis included, regretted leaving.

The vast majority of these immigrants crowded into the steerage holds of steamships bound for the United States and what they hoped would be a new life. Few could afford to travel in a berth, where they could see the light and breathe the fresh air. But they could wait. America, the Promised Land, would be the light. Samuel came first, probably in 1905 or 1906, to find a job and to establish a home.

Samuel Sokolowski might have added to his reasons for wanting to leave tsarist Russia a desire to put some distance between himself and his in-laws, who made it no secret that they considered him a poor match for their pretty, lively, and intelligent daughter, Sarah Cohen. Sarah and the handsome Samuel (who bore a striking resemblance to Marcel Proust) had met, courted, and married in Pinsk, a Belorussian city known at the time for its railroad yards and steamship construction. Some of Sarah's relatives recalled that the Cohen family was in the lumber business and was involved in the building of the Pinsk streetcar system, but however they gained their superior financial status, they managed to make Samuel uncomfortable about his own, more meager, prospects.

Sarah and young Isadore (Izzy) arrived on Ellis Island in September 1907 with five dollars to declare at the immigration station. Their ultimate destination was Hartford, Connecticut, where Samuel and some of his relatives, who lived in nearby New Britain, would help the newcomers become accustomed to life in a strange new place. It was the usual pattern: immigrants would settle where there were relatives or *landsmen* to ease the shock of assimilation.

During his first year in America, Samuel had discovered that earning a good living was even more difficult for him here than it had been in Russia, where money problems had also plagued him. He took whatever job he could find. When a second child, Rose, was born in 1908, followed by Anna in 1910, the professions he listed on their birth certificates were merchant and laborer, respectively.

Many years later Anna Sokolow summed it up this way:

> In the European Jewish tradition, the man was really the scholar, and the woman he married and her family took care of him and their children. When they came here, a lot of them had to change and they did. They learned to cope with the system and realized that they had to earn a living. Well, my father was totally bewildered by it, and he could do nothing. Eventually my mother, with her great energy, stepped in and took over. I think this happened to quite a few of the families who came here.

In 1912, a fourth child, Gertie, was born. Unable to make ends meet in Hartford, the Sokolows decided to move to New York City, where work was available for men and women who could sew or were willing to learn. The family found affordable lodging on the top floor of an East 8th Street (now St. Mark's Place) tenement. After climbing six flights of stairs (the higher up one went, the cheaper the rents became) they reached their long, narrow, railroad apartment with a combination washtub/bathtub in the kitchen and a toilet in the hall. Compared to their previous housing situation in Hartford, this was a nightmare of windowless rooms, thin walls, insufferable heat and cold. But they were surrounded by people who, like themselves, were scraping for a living, and they adjusted to the new surroundings.

Soon after they settled in New York, Samuel began to suffer from disturbing symptoms that were eventually diagnosed as Parkinson's disease. When he was no longer capable of caring for himself, Sarah had no choice but to have him cared for in the charity hospital on Welfare Island in the East River, where he was to live out the rest of his life. Anna and Rose could not recall much about their father, who was ill for many years. On some of their Sunday visits he was barely able to speak with them.

In order to keep her family together, Sarah joined the ranks of the thousands of Russian-born Jews earning their living in the garment trade. Fortunately, a few blocks away from their apartment was a nursery school where Anna could be cared for while her older siblings were in public school. Gertie was simply too young to farm out during the day and was placed in a Jewish orphanage. It was not unusual for immigrant families facing tragedy of one kind or another to accept this alternative. Everyone had to make adjustments; Mama was now a working woman and Papa was too sick to earn a living.

After Samuel's departure from the household, Sarah's younger brother Harry, a bachelor, began to spend a good deal of time with her and the children, sometimes living with them and helping to pay the rent. Uncle Harry, who was a professional photographer and photo retoucher, took many photos of the Sokolows during this period. They show Sarah to be full-figured —not a conventionally attractive woman, but one who radiated vitality. Anna seems small for her age, thin, pretty, and wistful-looking. Rose appears more robust, looking like their mother as Anna did their father. Harry was the official photographer at the International Ladies Garment Workers Union (ILGWU)-run Unity House camp in Pennsylvania's Pocono Mountains, where Sarah spent her summer vacations in later years. One summer Sarah sent the girls to Unity House summer camp for children, with disastrous results. The mysteries of the country frightened Anna, especially at night when she was troubled by the darkness and strange sounds. She cried and sulked until they returned to the noise and bustle of the city, where she felt secure and comfortable. Anna was a city girl and always would be.

In order to help his family survive, Isadore dropped out of high school and worked at a succession of jobs: newspaper hawker, delivery boy, lamplighter. Eventually he enrolled in night school, finished college, and became a successful real estate attorney. By her own example, Sarah encouraged her daughters to become free souls while they were growing up; Isadore chose a more conventional direction for his life, and his mother's sometimes flamboyant and unconventional behavior was an embarrassment to him. Nevertheless, he continued to look after her and made sure that she was properly provided for.

In the Jewish family structure, a woman was supposed to marry, bear children, make sacrifices to educate those children, and then settle down to a few years of enjoying her offsprings' accomplishments, perenially subservient to her husband. Sarah decided on a different course. She was going to have some genuine pleasure in her existence, unhampered by the stereotypical role of a relentlessly committed mother or a grieving wife. She insisted that this land fulfill some of its golden promises to her within her lifetime. Had Samuel been well and able to support the family she might possibly have accepted the lot of the good, compliant Jewish wife, but out of necessity and predisposition, she became aggressive and outspoken. Being physically strong and high-spirited, she sought out male companions and lovers. Zelda Blackman, a cousin, remembers Sarah as a bright, outgoing woman whose magnetic quality attracted men to her without her seeming to encourage them:

> Once when she was visiting us in New Britain, we took her to see my father . . . My brother's father-in-law, a staid and proper gentleman, paid Sarah a great deal of attention. In the presence of all the family, including his wife, he asked her if she would like to go to the movies with him. Everyone gasped because he had never made a pass at another woman. (I don't remember the outcome of his proposal.)

Her independence of spirit was no doubt enhanced by her interest in the Socialist Party and her trade-union activities. In both of those arenas women were treated as equals to their male peers. Here she found herself at home. In the language of her time, she had chosen to be "a person," not a charity case dependent on handouts from public welfare or her family. There were three other brothers besides Harry, and, as the only sister, Sarah was the object of much affection and good-natured teasing. They could and would have helped her financially, but she had her own ideas about how she wanted to live her life and these required independence. She chose to fight for her own survival and that of her children.

Not one to express affection openly, Sarah showed her love for her children by dressing and feeding them well, by spending as much time with them as she could, and by doing everything in her power to give them some semblance of a Jewish upbringing. The Sokolow home was kept kosher, High Holidays were observed, and Sabbath candles were lit every Friday night.

Care was taken that the children were never left without supervision during the day. Rose picked up Anna at the nursery school after her own school-day was over and, when he could, Isadore kept an eye on them until Sarah returned home to make dinner. With Sarah's skills at the sewing machine and an investment of a dollar or two in fabric remnants (which were easily obtained in the garment district where she worked), she created an enviable wardrobe for her young daughters. Rose remembered the precise fitting sessions in which their mother pinned and repinned their dresses until they reached her exacting standards. She remembered, too, how impatient Mama was when she or Anna fidgetted during these sessions. They had to stand perfectly still or they would hear about it. Mama was short-tempered, a trait that she passed along to her children.

The usually undemonstrative Sarah, walking with a daughter's hand in each of hers, would merrily swing them out in front of her to change places as they paraded together down the street in their new outfits. Each special-occasion dress had a matching cape; the girls were sometimes mistaken for twins. Sarah took them with her to Workman's Circle dances, to the Yiddish Theater, and wherever else she could, not only to show them off but also to make it possible for her to go herself. Baby-sitters were an indulgence of the well-to-do. They often went to Central Park together, and in the warm weather there were frequent trips to Coney Island. Sarah took them to the movies on Saturdays. On Sundays they went for a short visit to Papa and then off on an outing of one kind or another.

The girls felt that they were closer in some ways to their mother than other children were whose mothers were home all the time, and they were probably right. They also knew that Mama was different, and that gave them license to be different themselves. The fact that Yiddish was Sarah's first language created something of a barrier to her understanding of the world in which her children were growing up and to some of the values that they were developing. But there was a bond of love and trust between them that made such things seem less important.

"My mother was a real working-class woman," Anna proudly recalled in later years. "She was a member of the ILGWU and a staunch Socialist. Her idea of a great man was Eugene Debs. People like my mother really fought for the proper conditions for workers in those days."

In such worldly movements as Zionism, socialism, and combinations of the two, many Eastern European Jews who settled in America transformed their old world religious zeal into energy to fight for social change. It was a period of extreme restlessness and ideological ferment. Everywhere, it seemed, there were new movements, parties, and associations for benevolent and social action, many of which grew into major forces in Jewish public life. In the next generation, Anna's, it would lead to a fierce intensity and independence. Many young people felt deeply committed both to social change and to the arts. In author Irving Howe's words, " . . . every idea was expressed in absolute and extreme terms."

Jewish socialism, central to Sarah's life, did not fulfill its goals — the creation of a new society in which all men and women would live without want — but it did help to raise the consciousness of the Jews themselves. Rather than continue to be victims, they became first-rate fighters.

The grim circumstances of the 1911 Triangle Shirtwaist Company fire, in which 141 women and 5 men who were locked into an eighth-story loft during working hours died, brought clearly into focus the fact that working people were often treated little better than slaves. Important and sometimes bloody battles had already been fought and won by the ILGWU by the time Sarah became a member in the early 1920s.

But there was much work left to be done. Workers in nonunion shops still had to put up with crowded, unventilated workrooms and filthy bathroom facilities; lunch areas were often nonexistent; work hours could begin at daybreak and last until nine at night; wages were barely higher than those paid to street clean-ers.

Angered by the conditions she observed all around her, Sarah began to take an active interest in politics. She avidly read the Yiddish-language news-papers, *Freiheit* and *Forward*, which reported the growing involvement of Rus-sian-Jewish immigrants like herself in socialist causes and political activities. Soon she began to attend meetings and participate in solidarity marches, occa-sionally taking her daughters along to these stirring events. Sarah could not be-come overtly involved in organizing union shops because of her family responsibilities and the fear of being blacklisted. Years later, however, she re-vealed to Rose how she had managed to do her part to further the cause of her beloved ILGWU.

A fast and clean sewing-machine operator, Sarah had no trouble finding work in nonunion shops as a pieceworker (one who was paid for each garment or portion of a garment sewn). After laboring in a shop for a while, she slowly and skillfully interested her fellow workers in taking the necessary steps to become unionized. This usually meant going on strike. When things were close to the boil-ing point she would ease herself out of that situation, confident that it would take the desired course, and move on to the next sweatshop.

When Anna was seven or eight years old, the family moved to the top floor of an East 12th Street tenement building, remembered by both Anna and Rose as the site of an incident that was frightening at the time, but fun to recall later. The two girls were avid readers, and one warm summer morning as they lay sprawled on the fire escape, their library books propped up under their chins, Anna leaned back too far and fell into the stair opening. Rose, imagining her sister a broken heap on the street below, looked over the railing with terror, only to dis-cover Anna on the fire escape directly below. "Not a scratch — like a bird!" the survivor proudly recalled sixty-five years later. (Anna was pleased, years later, to find out that *sokolow* is the Russian word for falcon, an association that she rather liked.)

An unusually close bond developed between the sisters in those days. They were together constantly and had much in common, including a love of reading, a fascination with learning, and a mischievousness of spirit. Envy was not an issue between them: what was good for either one of them was good for both. (When asked, in 1986, if they had been streetwise kids, a smile passed be-tween them. How could they have survived in those days with their self-respect intact if they had not been street—wise?)

Around 1919–20 Sarah once again packed up her brood and resettled, this time uptown on East 80th Street. They were to remain there for about five years. The girls attended an elementary school across the street from their apartment and spent their lunch and after-school hours at the Emanuel Sister—hood of Personal Service located on 82nd Street between First and Second Avenues. Such fine nonsectarian settlement houses were built and maintained by prosperous Jews to help look after the youngsters of working mothers and to perform other invaluable services for the community. This particular one — which offered classes in music, drama, the visual arts, sewing, embroidery, cooking, sports, and dance — rapidly became the central focus of the Sokolow sisters' lives. Often, when Sarah came home from work, her daughters would still be so involved in some activity at the Sisterhood that she would have difficulty coaxing them to come home.

"That place had an important influence on us," Rose recalled. "It taught us a way of looking at things. It made us curious. There were people there with fine backgrounds who wanted to give us everything they could. We never thought of ourselves as deprived kids. We were having a good time."

After a few years there, they were the old-timers, with matching status. In Rose's words, they became "king-pins" and they loved it! In 1980 she remembered the Sisterhood vividly:

> They had something going on every day after school. The woman who ran the place, Celia Strakosh, was quite a person. She had a vision about how fine such places could be. Elsa Pohl was the dance instructor. She was tall and very impressive, and everybody loved her. We never missed a class — we listened to her as if she were a goddess. She could infuse us with a delirium about dance. When she left to go home, we would follow her down the street, fighting for who walked closest to her.
>
> She was strongly against ballet; she told us it was artificial, that people didn't normally stand on their toes. She was giving us interpretive dancing à la Isadora Duncan. We danced barefoot. Music would be played on the piano and we were told to "dance to the music."
>
> Years later, when Anna Pavlova came to New York, Anna and I decided to go but felt like we were doing something we shouldn't do. Miss Pohl had made ballet sound so wrong. But we went anyway to the Met and sat way at the top. Pavlova looked so tiny from up there. She did *The Dying Swan* and we were astonished, mesmerized.

Of the two Sokolow sisters, it was Anna who truly found her niche in the dance classes at the Emanuel Sisterhood; Rose favored sports activities and crafts. (She later became a highly skilled weaver and teacher of weaving.) Anna was around ten years old when she started her dance classes and was soon receiving special attention. "She was different from the others," Rose recalled. "There was a poise, an independence, a 'person' there, even at that age." Anna described her introduction to dance classes in this way: "One day, I remember just looking in the room and seeing them dance around, and I liked it. So I asked, 'Could I join?' They said yes, of course, and that was it. I joined the class and fell madly in love with dancing."

Anna was perfectly at home in the activities at the Emanuel Sisterhood, but she had little interest in public school:

> I hated it. I hated to be told what to learn and what not to learn. When I got older I used to play hookey. But in playing hookey I found my way to the Metropolitan Museum, which was close by. I remember once the truant officer came to our house and, of course, my mother was horrified. He asked me: "Where do you go when you play hookey?" I said: "I go to the museum." He didn't believe it, but it was true. But then that's the story of my life. I've never done what I'm told to do. I've done what I felt was right. Even then.

By the time she had reached her mid-teens, Anna's negative feelings about school had intensified to the point that she dropped out, never to return. Most young people who abandoned their schooling in those years did so out of financial necessity. Anna, on the other hand, did it for her own reasons. Lithe, musical, and serious, she had come to be recognized as a promising professional dancer by the instructors at Emanuel Sisterhood. One of her dance teachers, Emily Hewlitt, a student of Bird Larson, formed a small performance group and Anna was the undisputed star, according to Olga Guariglia Vermandois, who was in the group as well. When Anna was fifteen, the teachers at the Sisterhood agreed that they had taken her about as far as they could in her dance training. Mrs. Strakosh arranged that she continue her dance education at the Henry Street Settlement House, the original home of the Neighborhood Playhouse. Thus it was that Anna returned to the Lower East Side.

Though basically liberal in her outlook, Sarah Sokolow was appalled at Anna's announcement that she was leaving school to pursue a career as a professional dancer. As with many of her generation, when she did not understand something on her own terms, her automatic response was to take a dim view of it. Basing their prejudices on their ultraconservative upbringing, "nice Jewish people" generally presumed that any woman performing in the theater was a woman of doubtful morals. About dancers, there was no doubt: they were little better than prostitutes, if, indeed, a difference could be drawn. Sarah's deep love for the theater did not confuse the issue for her at all. "You mean," Anna remembers Sarah saying, "you are going to be a *kurvah* (whore)." "No, Mama," she replied. "I mean, I am going to be a dancer." Anna likes to tell that at this point her mother ordered her out of the apartment and she began life on her own at the age of fifteen. That may be how it happened. More likely, the two arrived at a truce for a few years and Sarah, without liking it, came to accept her daughter's odd choice of career.

At the time, few people knew of the existence of the emerging dance form later to be known as modern dance. It would be many years before Sarah would have the slightest notion of what had so captured Anna's interest that it would cause her to leave public school and all of the opportunities made possible by a formal education.

In 1925 Samuel Sokolow died and a few years later Sarah remarried and took up residence in New Jersey with her new husband, Kalman Kravitz. The girls remained for a while in the Bronx with Uncle Harry, and it was there that Rose met and married the artist Arnold Bank. (Izzy, too, was married by this time, and so was Gertie, who had joined the family for a few years and was now off on her own.) The lively old household, with Sarah in command, was now a thing of the past. When Anna, Rose, and Arnold decided to move to Manhattan, they lived at first with six other young artists in a loft. Anna remembers that there were not enough blankets to go around and, as the smallest person in the group, she was given the laundry bag to sleep in.

Anna was on her own and had to earn her own living. She spent some time working in a factory tying teabags and took whatever odd jobs an unskilled young woman could find at a time when labor could be bought so cheaply. Concealed behind the small frame and seeming fragility was a forceful and demanding young woman, one who would make up many of her own rules as she went along. If the profession she wanted did not exist, she would create it. At a time when serious, nonballetic professional dancing scarcely existed as a means of earning a living, Anna made that her career choice. There were no parents to rely on. There was no one, for that matter, who was willing or able to subsidize her career. She planned to fulfill her potential and be self-sufficient in the process.

2

NEIGHBORHOOD PLAYHOUSE KID

Emotion, like a stream, must find an outlet; and through the temperament of an artist that emotion will find its natural form. (Irene Lewisohn, Program notes; Neighborhood Playhouse, 1930)[1]

Irene and Alice Lewisohn, two wealthy and cultured young Jewish women, were the founders of the Neighborhood Playhouse at the Henry Street Settlement House on New York's Lower East Side. The Settlement had been created through the efforts of the pioneering nurse, Lillian D. Wald, famous for her work in the tenements and earlier the founder of the Visiting Nurse Services. The original purpose of the Settlement was to help immigrants from Central and Eastern Europe improve their lot through language lessons, briefings on union activities, and medical care. Coaching was also available to prepare them for citizenship examinations. Later, recreation clubs were organized for many diverse interests and all ages.

The Lewisohns first worked at Henry Street as volunteers in club activities. Alice was an amateur actress of some accomplishment; Irene had studied expressive gesture with Delsarte-disciple Genevieve Stebbins. Both wanted to perform on the professional stage, but were strictly forbidden to do so by their Orthodox father. They complied with his wishes, for to do otherwise would have cost them their family and their inheritance. They were allowed, however, to participate in philanthropic activities of their choice. Their activities at the Henry Street Settlement provided what was at the time a reasonable alternative to the personal theatrical ambitions they had to put aside. Both sisters brought to their work considerable intelligence, taste, and an almost religious zeal. Their initial goal was to develop a synthesis of all of the performing arts and the crafts of theater production. Alice formed a dramatic group, while Irene concentrated on dance presentations. They were known to their youngsters as Miss Alice and Miss Irene. The early productions of the dance group were festivals featuring authentic European folk dances in the costumes of the region. Miss Irene's avowed personal goal in her work was to develop in the young participants a pride in and inspiration from their ethnic backgrounds. Something vital, she felt, was being lost in the passion for assimilation.

The first of these presentations, in 1913, was an outdoor pageant with dances celebrating the coming of springtime in many of the old-world cultures represented in the neighborhood. The response was overwhelming: the activity is reported to have drawn an audience of more than ten thousand. Dozens of children participated as performers.

In 1914, the sisters decided that the Settlement needed more space for classes, scenery, costume construction, and performance. A new building, which was to be their gift, was planned (their uncle, Adolph Lewisohn, likewise a philanthropist, was soon to be the donor of the stadium named for him at City College in NewYork). They traveled to Germany to study the most recent developments in theater and lighting design, and on their return hired the architect Harry Ingalls to design the new facility. A year later the Neighborhood Playhouse was completed and within months it was in constant use.

In the next few years, along with the folk dance presentations, festivals were developed featuring traditional Jewish rites and ceremonials with texts from the Psalms and the Prophets of the Old Testament. Alice directed, with Irene taking responsibility for everything pertaining to dance. In these early productions, the emphasis was on ritualistic posturings, mass movements, and processionals, which reflected the sisters' interest in the work of Dalcroze: they had visited his school in Hellerau, observed his experiments in mass and free movements and incorporated those ideas into their work. Their many trips abroad to gather ideas and costumes for their productions included travel to Japan, Egypt, India, Palestine, and Russia. They were looking for not only authenticity, but also emotional depth. Contemporary descriptions reveal that various moods of joy, grief, and exaltation were portrayed in danced and mimed sections of their most serious works. The style of movement was what was then referred to as "interpretive." Not wishing to be confused with the legion of Isadora Duncan imitators, Irene described her work as experiments in coordinating images and music.

Many of the performers continued to be neighborhood youngsters, but with the passage of time and the increasing sophistication of the productions, more and more professionals were invited to participate. Productions in the new Playhouse on Grand Street ran the gamut from amateur theatricals, festival celebrations, and experimental dance to fully professional theater offerings. The building helped to pay for itself by serving also as a neighborhood movie house for the first five years of its existence. Live performances of professional-caliber theater and dance were given between films — a variation on combining films and vaudeville.

In 1920, a professional performing company was installed at the Playhouse and over the next several years the wide-ranging repertory included Galsworthy's *The Mob*; *The Little Clay Cart*, a Hindu drama with dance; Sheridan's *The Critic*; and Ansky's *The Dybbuk*. Four highly successful seasons of satirical revues, *The Grand Street Follies*, added to the Playhouse's popularity with audi-

ences. As one of only three Off-Broadway houses at the time, the Neighborhood
Playhouse was providing a place for venturesome productions that were not
completely dependent on commercial success. Dance, some of it experimental,
was prominent in the *Follies* and in some of the dramas. An acclaimed dance satire, *Sooner and Later*, presented in the 1924–25 season, was, according to the critic
Anne Sprague MacDonald, "the first to explore the modernistic in dancing." One
year later, Martha Graham and Michio Ito appeared as a much publicized team in
the *Follies*.

The highest production and performance standards were adhered to, and
audiences and critics responded accordingly. John Galsworthy referred to the
Playhouse as "the house where magic has come to stay." Moss Hart said that he
learned more about his craft there than anywhere else. Because ticket prices were
quite reasonable, the 325-seat theater could not be self-sustaining, even with full
houses. To help keep the enterprise financially solvent, sympathetic stars such as
Ethel Barrymore, Yvette Guilbert, and Minnie Maddern Fiske gave benefit performances.

As a newcomer to the Playhouse, probably in 1925, Anna was admitted at
the junior level (for students age six to eighteen), which met Monday afternoons
and Saturday mornings. There were classes in dance and pantomime, diction and
voice — one hour of each weekly. The stated object of this nonprofessionally oriented instruction was "to train East Side youngsters to sing, dance, speak and
mime, in order to transcend their environment by exercising their imagination."
These classes, which had been taught at the Neighborhood Playhouse in one version or another for about ten years before Anna's arrival, became the center of her
life. Her only unhappiness there was that classes were not held more frequently.
Her appetite for learning was voracious; her energy and need to be recognized
and to succeed was boundless.

Anna's principal dance teacher, Blanche Talmud, had worked with the
Lewisohns for over a decade. Talmud had studied Dalcroze eurhythmics in New
York and Paris and had been exposed to the work of the pioneering teacher, Bird
Larson, but her most important influence had been Irene Lewisohn, who passed
along the Delsarte training she had received from Genevieve Stebbins. It was, to
say the least, an eclectic background and probably the best training a teacher of
interpretive dancing could find in those days. Talmud's was a softer style than the
intense and emotionally demanding one Martha Graham would soon be exploring, closer to the work of Isadora Duncan as seen in a performance by Irma
Duncan and a group of her Russian students at the Manhattan Opera House in
December 1928. After their visit, flowing scarves and movements beckoning to
the wind were very much in evidence in Playhouse dance classes.

In her years with the Lewisohns, Blanche Talmud became highly valued
by them as a teacher, performer-choreographer, and rehearsal director. She was

especially valuable to Irene Lewisohn during choreographic sessions; Miss Lewisohn, though often inspired in her conceptualizations, was not a choreographer to whom ideas came quickly and easily. When she stood, idea-less, at a rehearsal, knowing she wanted something to happen at this point or that, often it was Talmud who figured out what that something would be.

Lewisohn worked in her street clothes, her sable coat carelessly draped over a chair or the radiator, sometimes nibbling on a finger sandwich brought to her by her maid — a sight that could not have been overly endearing to the young dancers who were not always sure where their next meal was coming from. Sometimes Miss Irene preferred to work at home. She would gather together the lovely young dancers of The Junior Players in her lavish Park Avenue living room, describe her current project to them, and then, in her slow deliberate manner of speaking, say, "Now, be creative." Anna's profound aversion in later years to wealthy art patrons may well have had its roots in these awkward and painful sessions. For a time the Lewisohns bestowed the princely sum of fifteen dollars weekly on the young dancers who were studying, rehearsing, and performing with them. It was hardly enough for them to live on, even in those years.

As a teacher Blanche Talmud was more successful with the children than with the older girls, who took no pains to conceal their discontent with her versions of the Dalcroze and Delsarte work. It all seemed hopelessly old-fashioned to them. The training simply did not match the restless energy of the late 1920s and the young dancers must have recognized this without necessarily being able to articulate it. Fellow Playhouse student, Bessie Schönberg, like Anna a Junior Player at the time, commented: "Blanche must have been very ambitious or needed the income, or she couldn't possibly have survived the agonies we put her through." Bessie had a vague memory of Anna speaking up for Talmud when the complaints became unreasonable.

Blanche obviously adored Anna. In 1987 (at the age of ninety-four) she recalled: "Anna had beautiful hands and feet and used them gracefully. I used to call her my Botticelli dancer with the Botticelli feet. Anna loved dancing and would go any place where she had a chance to perform." The affection was mutual. Anna appreciated what she learned from her first significant teacher after Elsa Pohl. In later years she took time out from her demanding schedule to dance for Talmud occasionally. She must have understood on some level that Blanche Talmud had taught her a great deal about sensitively and thoughtfully articulated gesture, knowledge that served her well in later years.

Whenever the Lewisohns invited outside professional teachers to work at the Neighborhood Playhouse, they chose the best. Thus it was that Anna came into contact with the now legendary Bird Larson, one of the early experimenters in American dance. Neither a dancer nor a choreographer herself, she was one of the first teachers of movement in the United States to concern herself primarily with the development of a physiologically sound approach to dance training.

Among the areas she explored in her classes were "The tread, or full-use action of the feet; the mechanics of back and side falls, and the spiral, or controlled flow of movement through every successive vertebra of the spine." Deeply concerned also with aesthetic values, Larson wrote in a 1927 school brochure:

> The mastery of the body is not limited to the performance of physical feats but to understanding and feeling movement in relation to the emotions. Movement should be beautiful, beautiful in the sense that it is adequate, suitable in its quality, that it is the physical expression of a state of mind or emotion and that it conveys to the audience what the performer feels.

A few years after her tragically early death in 1927, John Martin referred to Bird Larson in his writing as "the first technician of the American dance."

How much of this Anna was able to absorb in her mid-teens can be only a matter of conjecture; she herself has no clear recollection of her classes with Larson. The concentration on the use of the trunk of the body surely must have contributed to her beautiful body carriage. The improvisations Larson employed in her teaching methods may well have been significant in Anna's readiness for the classes in choreography that Louis Horst inaugurated at the Playhouse the year after Larson's death.

With the continued success of the professional theater presentations at the Playhouse, the directors began to think in terms of extending their instructional program to suit the needs of their more ambitious and advanced students. For some time there had been a gradual shift from serving the needs of non-professionally oriented neighborhood children and young adults toward professionalism, and it was becoming increasingly evident that the connection with the Henry Street Settlement was no longer an appropriate one.

Moreover, tension between the Lewisohn sisters had been growing for some time. Irene, who appears to have been the more aggressive of the two, needed recognition for her artistic endeavors and was willing to make her work the center of her life. Doris Fox Benardete wrote about Irene Lewisohn, "It seems that she wanted to prove that she had larger talents than had been appreciated; that she could not only create aesthetically satisfying symbolic/lyric dramas, but also produce the largest theatre programs ever conceived or, if not the largest, grandiose enough to express beauty and aspiration on a heroic scale." She had the financial resources and the stamina to do it. Alice, who was far less driven than Irene, had somewhat different goals in mind for her life. She eventually married and eased herself out of the Playhouse's activities.

Irene and her good friend and co-worker at the Playhouse School, Rita Morgenthau (of the wealthy Morgenthau clan, whose cousin Henry was later

President Roosevelt's Secretary of the Treasury), decided to move to a new location and open a school specifically for the training of professionals. The Course in Arts Related to the Theater was launched at the new location on West 46th Street. The 1927 school brochure states: "It is intended primarily to put the students more in touch with their own capacities and to give them a broader, keener vision of the road they wish to travel, rather than necessarily to fit them to perform, as that depends entirely on individual creative ability." Statements like this notwithstanding, the new Neighborhood Playhouse School was run in a rigorously professional manner. Students were scheduled for annual review, and only those who were approved unanimously by the faculty were invited to return the next year.

When the school was officially opened in 1928, the new brochure stated: "We offer you a stern apprenticeship of two years under teachers each of whom is an artist in his field and therefore an exacting taskmaster. Come here only if you are willing to work with the intensity necessary to meet the standards which these teachers will hold for you." Anna was given a full scholarship and invited to join the special rehearsal classes of the Junior Festival Players.

Eventually, Irene Lewisohn's desire to continually improve the school's teaching staff, combined with the older dancers' impatience with their principal teacher Blanche Talmud, led Lewisohn to seek more advanced training for them. Martha Graham, the well-known proponent of the new dance, seemed the most likely choice. Along with Graham came her accompanist and composer, Louis Horst. It was with the Neighborhood Playhouse students that Graham explored, developed, and tested many of her new ideas. Some of her earliest cues and images were remembered years later by Gertrude Shurr (who danced with Graham at the same time as Anna): "Carve a place for yourself in space . . . focus through space, not just up and down . . . the hip bone must move as the jewel in a watch movement . . . contraction is ecstasy as well as despair." The new movement vocabulary was asymmetrical, the arms thrust out in whipping motions, angular and taut, gestures simple, elemental, and done with a blunt percussive thrust. Legs shot out to strike the air uncompromisingly. The dancers were told that they were not to be pretty for the audience, a highly radical idea at the time. Graham was searching for and finding a technical vocabulary that would adequately serve her expressive needs, and Anna was there soaking it all up.

In addition to her classes with Talmud, Larson, and Graham, Anna studied movement with Michio Ito and Benjamin Zemach, singing with Frances Brundage and Madame Dessoff, and diction with Laura Elliot, all well-known and respected performers and teachers. There were courses in theatre craft with equally distinguished faculty, whom she could often watch at work in Playhouse productions. Among her teachers was the gifted scenic designer, Aline Bernstein, who was enjoying enormous success on Broadway. (She was the true-life model for Thomas Wolfe's wealthy lover in his autobiographical *Look Homeward Angel*.) In the same building where theatre craft was taught, Anna could see Bernstein's designs for the Lewisohn's productions being executed. Other professionals were at work there too, designing and executing costumes and developing lighting plots. Anna was receiving what was doubtless the only comprehensive education in dance and related arts — because the focus in dance was on the emerging modern form — available in the United States or anywhere at that time. That dance techniques were studied not in isolation from other theatre-art forms, but rather in combination with them was to affect her entire career.

This artistically lively yet highly structured environment in which schedules were tightly designed and strictly adhered to was a nearly perfect one for Anna. Although in public school she had demonstrated an unwillingness to stay with work that did not interest her, she liked discipline. At the Playhouse she felt highly motivated and so applied herself to classes with great seriousness. When productions were mounted, she was dependable, focused, and diligent. This self-discipline, combined with her special dance talents, won her special attention at the school.

The first major theatrical event in which Anna participated was a presentation at the Manhattan Opera House in May 1928. Irene Lewisohn had put together an impressive program in conjunction with conductor Nikolai Sokoloff and his Cleveland Orchestra, which was brought in for the occasion. One of the works on the program was Ernest Bloch's *Israel Symphony*, with Martha Graham importantly featured in the cast of twenty-two dancers. "It was a very grand, sumptuous work," Sophie Maslow remembered. "In one scene everyone was at the Wailing Wall beating their breasts. Martha was standing still. You didn't look at anybody but her." This was followed by *Nuages and Fêtes*, in which Michio Ito played "A Fawn-like Creature"; Graham "A Passing Cloud Form"; Blanche Talmud, Sophie Bernsohn, and Anna Sokolow "Other Cloud Forms"; and Benjamin Zemach "A Storm Cloud." These works were closely related to Ruth St. Denis' music visualizations: somewhat literal interpretations of the music through dance. But in the serious orchestral dramas, such as *Israel*, Irene Lewisohn was trying with some success to create an exalted form of dance/drama dealing with universal symbols.

In the program notes for the production, Lewisohn wrote, "The human race when profoundly moved has always sought release in melody and rhythm. Emotion, like a stream, must find an outlet; and through the temperament of an artist that emotion will find its natural form." It was with these lofty concepts that she went forward with her milestone productions, and it was in this 1928 season that Anna's name first appeared in a program as a professional dancer.

This program, the first of the three spectacular yearly productions staged by Irene Lewisohn in large uptown theaters, can be seen as a further development of the work she had been doing on Grand Street with her sister Alice. Now, however, she was on her own, making all the major decisions, and she made some good ones. Her best idea was to use Martha Graham, Charles Weidman, and Doris Humphrey as principal performers. In addition to adding lustre to the enterprise as dancers, these most gifted artists did invaluable work by choreographing their own roles within the overall structure Lewisohn designed.

The following year, Graham and Weidman danced the leads in Strauss' *Ein Heldenleben*, again with the Cleveland Orchestra conducted by Sokoloff and with Irene Lewisohn directing. It must have worked well: the dance and pantomime were described by one reviewer (Louis Horst) as "unforgettably beautiful." Anna did not appear in this work, but Charles Weidman remembered that she acted as stand-in for Graham, who was assisting Miss Lewisohn with the choreography. Her name does appear on the program as a performer in Enesco's *Romanian Rhapsody No. 1*. Also included in this cast were other familiar names in the early days of modern dance: Betty Macdonald, Mary Rivoire, Felicia Sorel, Gluck-Sandor, and Ronny Johansson.

The last of the three major enterprises with the Cleveland Orchestra in which Anna was involved was a staging of Loeffler's *A Pagan Poem*, with a hopelessly old-fashioned scenario by Irene Lewisohn based on the writings of Virgil. Anna played one of several temple priestesses. Graham and Weidman were once again featured. Sophie Maslow, another priestess, remembered how Weidman gleefully told off-color jokes to the young women as they held him aloft in one scene. They had to mask their merriment from the watchful eye of Miss Irene and, at the same time, be careful not to drop their precious cargo, the protagonist, Narcissus. Many years later Weidman remembered Anna's participation in the 1930 *Pagan Poem*: "She was adorable, so quiet and nice."

Others remember a somewhat different Anna. Bessie Schönberg recalled a time when Anna coldly removed her from the cast of her student choreography because Bessie was not getting the movement just right. Another time, during a performance, Anna accidentally slammed her powerful little body into Bessie so hard that she almost knocked her into the orchestra pit. Anna apparently did so without even noticing. Certainly she was not always the adorable, quiet, and nice young woman Weidman remembered, nor did she try to pass herself off as anything of the kind.

In the epilogue to her book on this richly creative period, Alice Lewisohn Crowley wrote: "Louis Horst has said that '. . . these orchestral dramas gave dancers the necessary push to express dramatic and emotional values which up to that time had been conceived more or less abstractly.' "The Lewisohn productions appear to be among the first important foundation stones on which American modern dance was built.

It was Irene Lewisohn who first suggested to Louis Horst that he teach choreography to dance students at the Playhouse. At the time the only way one could learn to create dances was by performing in, or studying, the works of others; there were no recognized basic principles of composition for modern dance. What better way to start than to work with principles evolved over the centuries for the teaching of musical composition? It was Horst's inspiration to frame the study in the context of pre-classic dance forms, the highly stylized court dances of the sixteenth and seventeenth centuries.

Horst believed that dance must be formal in structure and at the same time imaginative in conception. His classes were intended to develop in his students a sense of form, for which he believed the colorful and energetic court dances were the perfect medium. But the challenge was always there for his students to combine the unique with the familiar in their assignments; that uniqueness was referred to by Horst as a quality of strangeness. In his evaluations, the portly, heavy-jowled Horst was exacting and demanding. His terse comments or bored yawns could eviscerate his young students, but just as often he was supportive and encouraging. His students feared, admired, and respected him and used what he taught them for the rest of their professional lives. Sophie Maslow commented: "We all studied choreography with Louis. It never occurred to us not to. If we wanted to dance away from the Graham company, what would we dance if we didn't create the dances ourselves? There were no solos to be learned like a variation from *Swan Lake*, and we certainly were not going to do excerpts from Martha's works."

When Horst took his young students out with him to do dance lecture-demonstrations — a form he helped to pioneer — he used the best of their studies as examples of basic choreographic concepts. For the dancers, it was an invaluable opportunity to perform their own short creations for discriminating audiences and, by doing so, to develop confidence in their creative abilities. Their maestro was taking their efforts seriously; they were encouraged to do the same. Besides Anna and Sophie Maslow, other gifted students in these classes included Bessie Schönberg, Ethel Butler, and Martha Hill, all of whom danced with Graham.

Anna gives credit to Horst for teaching her more than dance composition:

> He was a fantastic teacher. If he introduced the music of Satie, for instance, and I didn't even know how to spell the name, when I asked he would say "Well, you just go and find out." So I went to the library and found out who Erik Satie was, and then to the museum to look at the Greek and Etruscan works, and then I started to understand what Satie meant when he called a piece a "Gymnopédie." In this way I think I became a genuine student. He introduced me to a world I never knew before and apparently I was born with an appetite for that kind of learning, not for the kind public school offered.

While working with Horst, Anna may have found some version of the support and fatherly guidance she had been deprived of by Samuel Sokolow's devastating illness. Her love and respect for Horst bordered on adoration, even as she spoke of him fifty years after this period of apprenticeship. There was another, less well-known aspect to their professional relationship. Gertrude Shurr comments:

> A great deal of credit should be given to Anna for her contributions to Louis Horst's classes in pre-classic and modern dance forms. I don't think these forms would have been completed without her. For every suggestion, every problem Louis had, Anna was the one to bring in a solution. She always had a dance to demonstrate what Louis wanted. . . . Two have remained with me all of these years; her "Crown of Thorns," choreographed for the Medieval period, and her opening movement of the earth primitive study. I still see them quite vividly.

All who remember Anna in those classes acknowledge that she was Horst's outstanding composition student. After several years she became his assistant and was paid the magnificent sum of twenty-five dollars weekly for the job, which included helping students with their assignments. She apparently took this position to heart, becoming so adept at it that she became known as "Louis' Whip."

Choreography for Actors was one of the classes for which Anna was an assistant. David Pressman, later a successful theater and television director, remembers:

> In the first year we did pre-classic stuff, in the second it was to the music of Malipiero, Prokofiev — difficult music to play. Anna was very dynamic, a demanding disciplinarian. She couldn't stand people who didn't bring in the assignments they were supposed to. And she had no patience for the dumb ones. Yet if we wanted to work at night she would come there to help us. She also had no patience with people with rhythmic problems or, for her own reasons, rich ones. We had one perfectly lovely girl whose father was a bank president. Anna was not overly kind to her . . . .
>
> [Anna] was not quite skin and bones, but hard. The guys used to joke about how skinny and hard she was. I remember Anna in Martha's *Celebration* and *Course*. Both were different from *Primitive Mysteries* and Martha's other dour works. There were very bright colors and running themes. Anna was wonderful in these. *Celebration* was odd for us because it was like classroom exercises strung together. I had done that movement in class. I remember Anna as being unsentimental but deeply emotional. She made it plain to us that she thought ballet was bourgeois crap, sentimental claptrap, and certainly not part of the revolutionary world.

Anna worked with Louis Horst until 1938 and later spoke of him as her most important teacher. He had not only introduced a world of new music to her (she first heard Gershwin, Poulenc, and Scriabin among many others from his keyboard) but he had also led her, through music, to an understanding of some of the most basic tools of her craft. At the same time he encouraged her by his continuing recognition of her abilities and talents.

Anna must have been invited to join Graham's professional company in the late months of 1929 because her name appears in the program for the first performance of *Prelude to a Dance* (later retitled *Salutation*) on January 8, 1930. It was a professional relationship that was to last eight years (ten if the two years of student apprenticeship at the Playhouse are included). Graham accepted nothing less than perfection from her dancers. All rehearsals were done at full performance level. Marking would have been unthinkable. When Graham was upset with a dancer she was known to fly into an uncontrolled rage. Those who learned to put up with this — and most did — knew they had to get what Martha wanted quickly and without discussion or the next attack would be even more painful for everyone present. Anna was to develop her own version of this style a few years later.

As Graham worked toward this level of perfection from the dancers in her group, she made only slight use of them in the actual dances: often they were only elements of design. In *Heretic*, for example, they acted primarily as an opposing force to the energies of the solo figure. Nevertheless, the choreography demanded deep understanding of Graham's intentions as well as enormous concentration. *Celebration* was an early exception to this tendency. A poem of rejoicing, in which Martha did not perform, it gave some of the younger dancers an opportunity to explode on stage. David Pressman remembered Anna leaping through space so fast that she was almost a blur. Horst, who sometimes conducted rehearsals for Graham, often used Anna as a model. "I could jump and I could turn," Anna recalled fifty years later. "I should have been a ballet dancer."

During the earliest years of the Graham company, Martha's choreography seemed to emerge easily and naturally. The epoch-making *Heretic* (1929) was created in one evening, but by 1932 the process had become a slow and painful one. Much has been written about the legendary work sessions in the years that followed. Martha, seated at the far end of the studio, became quietly introspective in order to find the inspiration to proceed. The dancers were expected to sit or stand quietly wherever she had last placed them. They waited, sometimes for hours, while their brilliant leader sought the truth that only she would recognize. Only occasionally did the work seem to emerge easily and without the slow, painful process most of her choreography appeared to require. Never very patient, Anna must have gone through her own despair, immobilized, for what had to seem like endless periods of time.

For many years Anna's innate rebelliousness did not manifest itself in rehearsal or performances. There was one notable exception. The group was preparing for a lecture-demonstration and Graham proceeded to give long, slow, painful stretches — the kind Anna's tightly knit body could not easily handle. Without saying a word, Anna went to the dressing room and began to change into her street clothes. Martha followed and asked where she was going. "I can't do that," Anna said, gesturing toward the warm-up area. "You don't have to," was the reply. Four words from each of them and the problem was stated and resolved.

With a compassion and indulgence she exhibited only rarely, Martha was known to adjust her choreography to accommodate Anna's physical tightness. Sometimes those adjustments amounted to little solo variations. Graham was taken with the combination of passion and simplicity in the dancing of the lovely young woman whom she had been nurturing since the Neighborhood Playhouse days. A special bond, seldom if ever expressed outwardly, had developed between them.

Another well-remembered story, which Anna particularly enjoyed recalling in later years, involved an incident at a reception for the Graham Company given by a wealthy patron. Making polite conversation, one of the guests asked Anna what she had done before becoming a dancer. "I was a prostitute," she answered, straight-faced. Later, somewhat recovered, the lady asked Martha, glancing in Anna's direction, "Isn't it terrible about that poor young lady?" In answer to Martha's quizzical look she added, "About her being a prostitute before she became a dancer." Martha somehow managed a smile and said, "Anna has a lively imagination." For some time afterward Anna was asked to stay close to Martha's side at such occasions.

From the time she was a young woman, or earlier perhaps, Anna enjoyed being naughty from time to time. Or, to put it another way, she liked to find out where the limits were and push them just a bit further. Years later, in a nostalgic visit with Ethel Butler, the dancers were talking about those early years. Anna asked, with obvious relish, "Was I really awfully bad?" Ethel's reply was to smile broadly.

3

DANCE AS A WEAPON

In our dances we do not chase a butterfly across the stage. (Miriam Blecher, quoted by Joseph Mitchell, World Telegram *December 13, 1934)*

One of the highlights of Anna's early career was her participation in the now-legendary production of an early twentieth-century masterpiece. The flamboyant conductor of the Philadelphia Orchestra, Leopold Stokowski, had a passion for the contemporary. He also loved controversy and the attention it brought. In 1930 he invited choreographer Léonide Massine to Philadelphia to revive his 1920 staging of *The Rite of Spring* to the then infamous score by Igor Stravinsky. The original ballet by Nijinsky, together with the wildly original score, had caused a furor at its 1913 Pairs premiere. Nicholas Roerich, who designed the original sets, was recruited for the revival.

To ensure some fireworks in the production, Stokowski insisted on having Martha Graham dance the leading female part of the Chosen One. Interesting temperaments to combine, Massine's and Graham's. Massine was successfully producing extravaganzas at the Roxy Theater in New York and was very used to having people do things the way he wanted them done. Graham, however, made it clear from the beginning that she considered herself his equal as an artist and had no intention of bending to his will. She must have been aware that working with internationally known figures such as Stokowski and Massine could only enhance her reputation, but by then she had built too much of an authoritative persona to start playing the role of compliant dancer to Massine's great choreographer. In any case, she had her own growing reputation and following to bolster her confidence. Fireworks did fly, but the collaboration ultimately proved successful.

Anna was among the Graham dancers who auditioned for and was accepted into the corps. Among the thirty-nine other dancers in the group were Louise Creston, Mary Rivoire, and Eleanor King as well as Harold (or as he sometimes preferred, Felix) Kolb, who had danced with Graham in 1926 when she worked briefly in Rochester, New York. In Eleanor King's autobiography, *Transformations*, she describes some of the choreography in detail as well as the illustrious conductor's participation:

> Stokowski came to rehearsals periodically. Each time, drastic changes were made for the better. If there were no visitors, he was all to the point, cogent, explaining

verbally to the dancers the emotions behind the music. This was much heeded since on principal, Massine, like classical ballet masters in general, never gave one word of interpretation to the dancers, who are taught steps as abstractly as mathematics. You did as you were told, no questions asked. Stokowski saw at once that we were moving like automatons, with no feeling for what we were doing. Disregarding the choreographer, he pulled me from the line, made me kneel, raise a bent arm, and vibrate it to demonstrate a prayer gesture to the Earth Spirit. If members of the board of the League of Composers — wealthy lady patrons of the arts — [and sponsors of the event] were attending, Stokowski would put on pyrotechnic displays. However, his theater instinct was always right. While Massine looked on, Stokowski changed the final lift of the Virgin, rearranged the spacing of the ensemble for the ending, and in other ways tightened up the mass designs.

Anna watched all of this and learned. And so, according to her biographers, did Martha Graham. A choreographer with a less creative sense would have been deeply upset by Stokowski's visits. Massine, however, wisely accepted the conductor's input, knowing it would make his work look better. He chose to vent whatever frustrations he had on his leading dancer, who nonetheless held her own by remaining aloof. At one point, Massine even suggested replacing the obdurate Miss Graham. She maintained her composure and continued to work as she wished; when necessary, Stokowski intervened on her behalf. In performances she surprised everyone by delivering everything her choreographer had asked of her including some spectacular un-Graham-like split leaps. Among the things Anna was learning were the prerogatives of excellence.

Philadelphia audiences were impressed by the production and the press there was generous. In New York it fared even better. *New York Times* music critic, Olin Downes, gave the work high praise. John Martin, writing in his regular *Times* dance column, proclaimed it a "noteworthy contribution to the movement for a synthetic theatre art [an art form of synthesis] which shall include all the contributory arts on equal terms. Massine covered himself with glory with his endlessly inventive movement filled with the same pagan fire and rapture as the music."

The following summer Anna performed at the famed Woodstock Playhouse with "Felix Kolb and His Concert Dance Group," which included Graham dancer Mary Rivoire and Anna's good friend Sophie Maslow, who whimsically chose to become Sophie Maslova for the summer. Anna was featured with Felix on the first program in a minuet, a tango, and a czardas. She also did a solo to the music of Ravel. Jean Rosenthal, who was later to have a distinguished career as a lighting designer, was involved both as a performer and as technical director. On a second program, titled "Vaudeville by Woodstock Artists," Anna and Felix performed "The Original French Can-Can Music Hall Dance." Such a lighthearted summer must have provided welcome relief from the intensity of Anna's life in New York, although being in the country was never a particular treat for her.

There is some suggestion that a serious romance blossomed between Felix and Anna that summer, but in 1987 she said she honestly could not recall.

Her sister Rose remembers going up to Woodstock for a visit and being drafted immediately into service as a curtain-puller. From the start, her involvement in Anna's career was an active one. She was intelligent, quick-witted, and willing — and she sewed extremely well. Working closely, the sisters developed the designs for most of the costumes Anna and her dancers wore from the earliest days onward. For her hundreds of hours of work as a seamstress during the years that followed, Rose received program credit and Anna's undying appreciation. There was also the pleasure of seeing her adored sister blossoming into a first-rate artist and being there to help when help was needed. Rose was destined never to have a dull moment during those years.

The talent Anna displayed in Louis Horst's classes at the Neighborhood Playhouse was by this time bringing her so much positive feedback that she decided to make some solos for herself. Subject matter was not a problem. The economic and social crises of the time, combined with profound concern over the acceleration of Fascism in Germany and Italy, affected every aspect of the lives of Anna's generation of dancers. It was natural that much of the dancing of that period focused on those issues, since content — dancing about something — was the primary raison d'être of modern dance. And of course the influence of the Communist Party was ever-present in artistic circles.

The young modern dancers of the 1930s came primarily from working class families. Those who aspired to professional standing in the dance world came to think of themselves less as artists than as workers: dance was their work. They had been attracted by the social content of the choreography that was being done at the time and by the notion of dance as a potential agent of change. The concept that group action was necessary for change was reiterated daily in conversations of young people, in the speeches of reformers, and in the radical press of the day — most notably in the *Daily Worker.* The slogan one often encountered, particularly in that paper, was some version of "Workers of the world, unite! You have nothing to lose but your chains. The old order is crumbling and a brave new world is at hand." Many young dancers, as workers, heeded the cry. Some of Anna's earliest solos, with titles like *Derision, Histrionics,* and *Homage to Lenin,* addressed themselves to the need for change and the building of a new order.

In the years between the stock-market crash of 1929 and 1932, when Anna gave her first solo performances, discontent had been growing and making itself known among the rank and file of the American work force. Social injustices that had been long-tolerated or overlooked were held up to public scrutiny. In the South, lynchings were still very much a fact of life. The infamous Scottsboro case, in which nine young Alabama blacks were unfairly tried for the rape of two white girls and convicted on insufficient evidence, was still a burning issue; it had become symbolic of the appalling miscarriages of justice that were commonplace in the courts. National attention was focused on grievances that, until then, had been largely ignored. Labor was on the move and strike followed strike, finally making headlines when police in some cities aided strike-breakers or acted in their stead.

But it was not only discontent and angry indignation in the air; change was there too and unions were to play an essential role, not only with strikes but also with educational and cultural programs. Anna remembered in 1975:

> The unions were really my first audience. They would present programs where poets or writers would read their work and singers and dancers would perform in their halls. I remember going on a tour sponsored by the Jewish Fraternal Order with a singer, an actor, and musician. We toured up to Montreal, over to Chicago, and down to Washington. It was about a two-month tour and we got fifty dollars a week, a lot of money in those days. We traveled on slow trains and buses, but that was part of it. Nobody complained about things like that. As I remember, it was a wonderful audience. They understood us.

In those years unions were often more that bargaining agencies: their meeting halls served as centers for the social and cultural lives of their member-ship. All artists were welcomed, particularly by those unions whose membership was predominantly Jewish. A hunger for the arts seems to have been a part of the ethos of that people.

In the Depression years, radical American political groups were deeply involved in organizing the estimated fourteen million unemployed. In many cases, they helped to launch the unions and to make them work. They were also willing and ready to organize dancers and actors who would dramatize political ideologies, but the dancers got a head start. After a young organizer named Harry Simms was slain by New Jersey police at a rally of the unemployed, a mass funeral was held in New York City on February 17, 1932. Young dance students Miriam Blecher and Nadia Chilkovsky, walking in the parade, were inspired by the experi-ence to launch a working-class organization for dance. The dancers founded the New Dance Group with the slogan: "Dance is a weapon in the class struggle."

The founders began to teach classes for both aspiring young artists and workers in white-collar and industrial jobs. For a fee of ten cents, students re-ceived one hour of Hanya Holm technique, one hour of creative work, and one hour of reading and discussion of revolutionary literature. Contests were held to promote dances meaningful to their worker audience and prizes like the entire *Little Lenin Library* were awarded.

By November 1932 ten such groups had joined to form the Workers Dance League, a cooperative organization with the avowed purpose of pooling their resources for production and various other activities, including the dis-semination of information on the emergence of the new radical dance. Besides

Blecher and Chilkovsky's New Dance Group, there were Edith Segal's Red Danc-ers, The Workers Dance Group, The Office Workers Union, The Needle Trades Workers, The Industrial Union, The Jack London Club, Nature Friends, and the Harlem and American Youth Federation Dance Groups. They gave classes for their comrades, discussed Marxist philosophy, and held mass folk-dance assem-blies. The League later defined itself in the January 1935 issue of the magazine *New Dance* as

> an organization of dance groups and dancers interested in making the dance a vital part of our present era. It was organized in the midst of the crisis at which time the modern dance world, steeped in pessimism, mysticism, exoticism, di-versified abstractions, and other flights from reality, was suddenly projected sharply against the background of the increasing misery of millions of people. The League decided that dancers, to be significant, should serve the artistic de-sires and needs of the broad masses of people.

From the first issue in 1933 of the influential leftist *New Theatre* magazine, it was clear that the radical dance would figure prominently in its pages. As un-signed editorial presented a clear mandate for positive recognition of the Workers Dance League: "At the same time when bourgeois dancers are concentrating on being 'arty' and original, groups of younger artists, repelled by the stagnation of theory and practice in this 'modern' dance, have formed groups for the purpose of expressing feelings and ideas common to all, to do something to better the present woeful condition of the masses."

What, we must wonder, did the dances on the early Workers Dance League programs look like? We may be enlightened by some of the extremely sharp criticisms of these works that appeared in the radical press, which was ever quick to criticize its own. Emmanuel Eisenberg wrote of a June 2, 1934, perfor-mance at New York's Town Hall:

> Out of twelve conceptions only the "Van der Lubbe's Head" of the New Dance Group, the "Comintern" of the Red Dancers, and the "Pioneer March" of the Junior Red Dancers did not follow the pattern of the evening.
>
> This pattern, broadly speaking, was along the following lines: Six or ten young women, clothed in long and wholly unrepresentative black dresses, would be discovered lying around the stage in various states of collapse. Soon, to the rhythm of dreary and monotonous music, they would begin to sway in atti-tudes of misery, despair and defeat. The wondering observer in every case was brought to the choiceless, if tired, realization that this must be the proletariat in the grip of oppression: not because the program gave titles indicating both theme and contents — and the groups performing were known to have a revolutionary intent.
>
> The swaying would continue for a couple of minutes in the rhythm of utter resignation . . . and then, a vision. Uprising. Revolt. Sometimes it came in the form of a light flooding suddenly from the wings of the balcony; sometimes in

the form of sheer music intensity; sometimes as a dynamic figure in red, running passionately among the startled tragedians; once it was in the incredible person of a soap-box orator who moved both hands and mouth in an appallingly inept realistic parody. And always the group would respond with victory: hope had arisen, strength had come, freedom was won, the revolution had arrived. There was never any basis for the introduction of the new motif. Deadly swaying and intolerable oppression had gone on long enough, so a revivifier entered the scene and turned it from grave to gray. No problem of method. No transition. Break from your chains and go forth to the open world.

A kinder way of describing these dances would be to say that in conforming to the agitprop style, each dance focused on a single issue to which workers could relate: unemployment, hunger, employer injustice, or unionism. The presentations were short, the movements staccato with many raised fists, and they often ended with the performers coming downstage holding hands to sing or move to the strains of the "Internationale." The technical level of the dancing was often very low, high and passionate involvement notwithstanding. "In our dances we do not chase a butterfly across the stage," said Miriam Blecher in a *World-Telegram* interview.

Late in 1931, Harold(Felix) Kolb decided to move to the West Coast. Anna, with all of her New York involvements, could not have been less interested in such a move. Although their relationship was a pleasant one, she did not regard him as a great love in her life and chose to stay behind. A few months later, the twenty-two-year-old dancer, imbued with the fervor of the times and already embarked on a career as soloist, met Alex North, a gifted musician who was studying at the Juilliard School of Music. "He was a shy pianist when we met," Anna recalled. "I don't remember how I met him. I asked him if he would play for me and he did. The discovery that he could compose came from my asking, 'Why don't you do this?' or my saying 'I think you can write this.' I took him to the theater for the first time in his life. I think he was aghast. I had been going since I was a child. I'm sure he must have found *me* naive in many ways."

She was slim, almost to the point of being bony; pretty, with an oval face, piercing blue-gray eyes, a high forehead, and light brown hair that could look blonde under stage lighting. It was the long, graceful neck and the proud bearing of the head that one remembered most — those and the slim, expressive hands of a working-woman who is also an artist. What was prettiness in person became beauty on the stage. There was a special kind of alertness to her dancing — a listening quality and quicksilver response. She was a regal performer whose diminutive size made for a courageous, even heroic presence.

For Alex, intellectually keen and somewhat reserved, it must have been Anna's boundless energy that proved the most vital attraction. She was acutely alive and responsive to the social issues of the times and this, too, appealed to him. She responded to injustice with uninhibited anger and fierce indignation, responses that the more controlled Alex had difficulty expressing. After a year or two with Anna he became known for his quick barbs and sardonic wit. Most often, however, he was charming and ingratiating: Anna could be angry enough for both of them. It was he who calmed her down when her impatient behavior at rehearsals ceased to be effective for anything but building further tension in her dancers. In addition to being a peacemaker, it was he who provided Anna with a reading list, literally and figuratively, concerning the issues of the day.

In 1982 he remembered:

> Yes, in some ways she was very naive. Her ideas about what was going on — the problems in society — were emotional rather than intellectual. Whatever was concretized, whatever came into clear focus for her regarding the so-called "movement" of the period came because of her contact with me, my brother, and friends who were active in the struggle of that time. She was not involved enough in the dynamics of the period to read up on stories in the *New Masses,* the *New Republic,* or the *Nation* on her own. A lot of it seeped in through social contacts. There have been few other periods like that in the history of our country in terms of a sense of belonging. Remember, this was a period in which there were eight newspapers in New York, not just the few that exist now. They were left of center, right of center — only the *Daily Worker* was communistic. But people were informed. It came through your pores. With Anna, I would say that it was 75 percent emotional and 25 percent knowing in an intellectual sense exactly what was going on. Part of that feeling of belonging came from the fact that all of us felt that we were trying to do our part to improve the domestic situation during the Depression. We wanted to give some hope. By reflecting the period in our work, we were trying to do positive things, lifting the spirit of the so-called "masses." Anna performed wherever and whenever she could. She was the most dedicated person in that field. She was brave and she was a rebel — the first in the Graham Company to do things on her own.

Anna never had a good head for the business details associated with her work. Here, Alex was able to provide invaluable support. Although the amounts were trifling by any standards, money had to be there for promoting her budding career — for photographs, costume fabric, and sometimes for rehearsal studio rentals. There was so little money, in fact, that their first home together was a loft they shared with ten or twelve other people on West 12th Street. With so many businesses failing in those days, lofts were plentiful and cheap. After many months of living on a shoestring they were able to pool their resources and rent a tiny apartment on 13th Street between Second and Third avenues, which they shared for a time with Ethel Butler.

Anna's sister Rose remembered it as "a time when nobody had any money; nobody had any work. . . . I don't know how many apartments we had during that time. We would move in, knowing we could pay a month's rent and a deposit — so that was good for two months. It took the landlord four months to get us dispossessed; we were good for six months. A lot of people lived like that . . . we were lucky that we were young. Sometimes it was difficult to get enough food. One night we were visited by some neighbors. We had some bananas. Did you ever see anyone eat banana peels? That was what I saw that night. Somehow we managed, but it was not a nice time."

The 13th Street apartment offered luxurious privacy after communal life in the loft. Ethel Butler remembered: "When I lived with them they seemed to be getting along very well. They had some wild fights but nothing out of the ordinary. They both have volatile personalities, but he seemed very open to me — in a way more so than Anna. He was a fun-loving guy."

If Anna had been primed for the dance of social protest by her upbringing, it could be said that Alex had been radicalized by his. The son of a blacksmith and a seamstress, the young musician was much influenced by his journalist brother, Joseph, who was to become a founder and one of the editors of the left-leaning weekly *New Masses*. Among the distinguished contributors were Maxwell Bodenheim, Kenneth Patchen, Muriel Rukeyser, James Agee, and Federico García Lorca; it was here that Richard Wright was first published. Other well-known authors included William Saroyan, John Dos Passos, Dorothy Parker, Theodore Dreiser, and Ernest Hemingway. *New Masses* served as an outlet for some of the best social-protest writing of the period.

Anna first became a part of this world of brilliant writers and thinkers in her years with Alex. Here she made many new friends, some of whom eventually helped her in her career. They soon recognized in her a kindred spirit, and a talented one. Bessie Schönberg remembered Anna and Alex at that time:

> For many years when they were working together, when you saw one you saw the other. They were very much in love. Alex is a delightful, warm human being, crazy in many ways. They were a marvelous pair. Anna hasn't a great deal of humor, Alex has a lot. He would tease her. She would get very annoyed with him and everybody would laugh. Then she would realize that she had been "had" again and laugh with us. There relationship was a serious and, at the same time, a lighthearted one. The empathy they had for each other was extraordinary. I think they were very important to each other in the formulation of their artistic beings in their early years. One of the great things about the relationship was that there were two artists in it.

Anna and Alex gave each other courage, support, warmth, and sometimes an ongoing reason to work when encouragement from the outside world was in short supply.

4

RADICAL THEATER/RADICAL DANCE

How the stock-market crash, a disrupted economy, tightened belts, and the Forgotten Man abruptly remembered caused the theatre to change its tune, and sing an angry song of social significance in the thirties. (John Mason Brown, Dramatis Personae)

In 1927, the millionaire art patron Otto Kahn created a sizable endowment for the establishment of the New Playwrights' Theatre. Five young writers were involved: John Howard Lawson, Michael Gold (the pseudonym of Ira Granich), Francis Farragoh, Emjo Basshe, and John Dos Passos. The Depression had yet to cast its shadow, so that the concern of the New Playwrights' Theatre group for the plights of the underprivileged and the downtrodden went largely unnoticed. It appears that neither the downtrodden nor their oppressors were much interested in what these sympathetic intellectuals had to say. The radical theater of the thirties was to have other forebears.

The most dynamic early impetus toward the development of a radical theater for working-class audiences was actually to come from the amateur stages of foreign-language workers' groups that presented plays in German, Italian, Yiddish, Finnish, Russian, Swedish, Hungarian, and a half-dozen other languages. Cut off from the mainstream of American theater, these amateur groups kept alive the social values of the naturalistic theater, all but forgotten on Broadway during the Roaring Twenties.

Some of the more radical groups adopted that fighting slogan of the Soviet drama, "Theatre is a weapon," and labeled themselves agitprop troupes. One of the most successful of these was the Prolet-Bühne, born of New York City's German working-class population. They produced plays that were crude in plot and characterization and full of revolutionary labor clichés, but the performance had an immediacy and directness that often inspired and energized their working-class audiences. The following lines from *Unemployment*, produced by an English-speaking agitprop troupe in the fall of 1930, illustrate just how crude the new agitational technique could be in its early years:

> 5 WORKERS [*chanting*]: Won't somebody give me a job?
> 1 WORKER: I am hungry, why can't I have food?
> I see lots of food in restaurants. I am

                              cold, why can't I have a coat?
                              I see many in clothing stores. . . .
               CAPITALIST: There isn't anyone can have a better
                              yacht than I. I've got to have the best
                              little yacht in the world. . . .

Presentations of so naïve and controversial a nature were bound to arouse criticism and hostility in some quarters. Certainly no more Otto Kahns came forward with endowments. The form died out, but it left a legacy of vitality and presence that was to surface again in the Federal Theatre Project's "Living Newspaper." Professional actors who were interested in having protest theater of a more articulate and subtler nature organized the New Theatre League, which adopted a liberal rather than a radical program, calling for "a mass development of the American Theatre to its highest artistic and social level; for a theatre devoted to the struggle against war, fascism, and censorship."

Another step that advanced the growth of the theater of protest in the United States, one that was to affect Anna Sokolow's career considerably, was the opening of the Theatre Union in 1933. For its home, the group leased the Civic Repertory Theatre on West 14th Street (formerly Eva Le Gallienne's Playhouse) and produced plays of social significance with fine actors and an excellent production staff. The Theatre Union attracted a large working-class audience, the largest in the history of American theater. Somehow they managed to put on professional performances with very low admission fees and to build an audience of proletarian and middle-class organizations, including labor unions and other groups affiliated with the Socialist and Communist parties. The unemployed were given free seats. It was a truly nonexclusive theater and the most successful of its kind.

The Theatre Union fared remarkably well with the critics, but even the productions that received lukewarm reviews were kept running by the recommendations of appreciative audiences. Tickets were scaled to the Depression pocketbook (around thirty-five cents) and audiences came by the hundreds. One of the most successful early plays was *Stevedore*, written to protest the way black people were being treated in general, and in the maritime professions in particular. More than ten thousand people came to see this play. The Theatre Union survived and flourished for several years because, unlike most of the other agitprop groups that were concerned more with the message than the medium, they maintained high professional standards. First-rate professional playwrights, such as Albert Maltz and George Sklar, and actors of the caliber of George Tobias and Howard Da Silva were involved. The company's most significant artistic contributions lay in enriching and deepening the earlier agitational plays while bringing to the radical stage some of the stored-up experience of older theater.

Following the success of their very first production, *Peace on Earth,* the Theatre Union's board of directors decided to add a dance group to the organization. They saw Anna's impassioned dancing and choreography at a performance sponsored by the Workers Dance League (shown in their theater) and invited her to form such a group. It was to be a subsidiary of the Theatre Union, performing in their productions as needed and representing them in performances in the community in a repertory of socially significant dances. Ethel Butler recalled the fateful day in the early summer of 1933 when Anna's group was first launched:

> I was riding on the Sixth Avenue "El" [elevated train] with Anna, the sun blazing in the window, and she turned to me and said, "I am going to start a company, would you like to be in it?" I said yes, and for a couple of days I was the only member of her company. Actually, Anna and I were already a group of sorts. We had been doing performances for a lot of Socialist and Communist organizations together. Most of the dances dealt with the conflict between workers and their capitalist bosses.

Ethel remembered the choreography as somewhat simplistic — not very impressive, but moving to the audiences who saw their convictions eloquently expressed through dance by two tiny but dynamic young women.

In addition to Ethel, Anna's first group included Marie Marchowsky, Anita Alvarez, Ronya Chernin, Celia Dembroe, Ruth Freedman, Eleanor Lapidus, Florence Schneider, and Ethel Solitar, all young dancers from the Graham school. A few were in their early teens, the others not much older. The name given to the group, "Dance Group of the Theatre Union," was later changed to "The Theatre Union Dancers" and still later to "Dance Unit."

Aza (Cefkin) Bard McKenzie, who joined the group a year later, remembered these early times:

> When I started with Anna, I was about twelve or twelve and a half. Anita Alvarez could not have been much older — maybe twelve or fourteen. Marie Marchowsky was sort of my sponsor. We had been at a children's camp together, Camp Kinderland. It spawned many dancers. I had been dancing for a while. I lived in a housing development that was cooperatively owned — it was left-wing and had a Jewish *shule* [school] attached to it. If you went to that kind of school you got lessons in music, dance, and choral singing. It was very cultural. I was a serious dancer by the age of eight. It was Duncan-style dance and such wonderful exposure. By the time I came to Anna, I was a committed dancer.
>
> Anna was dancing with Martha, but there were no rehearsal conflicts. Martha kept a proper schedule and Anna didn't care how late rehearsals were. I remember doing a lot of homework on the subway when I was in high school. Some of the other dancers were in college. She worked us like a martinet and she got worse as her frustrations built. I remember one rough rehearsal in later years when Gertrude Shurr happened to be there. She couldn't bear the hollering and practically had tears in her eyes. But we all loved Anna, so we heard it a different way. She was so good to me. I adored her. What can I say? I can't imagine any of her contemporaries carrying on that way. But, on the other hand, she was always that demanding of herself, too. I don't know whether I sensed it as a kid, or if I'm seeing it in retrospect, but her standards were always a little higher than other similar groups.

Anna grew up with an intense inner anger smoldering in her personality, which may have sprung from the early disappearance of her father from her life or from the fact that Sarah had to be away from home so much and, when she was there, was not particularly warm or loving — and quick to lose her temper. She was, after all, Anna's first model and a powerful one.

Anna taught herself to draw on that well of powerful emotion in her dancing and choreography, but when it burst forth in awesome displays of fury in rehearsals it could be frightening to anyone who was not accustomed to it. She may have unconsciously cultivated this side of herself because, being small in stature, she felt that her statement had to be more powerful than anyone else's so that people would pay attention, so that she would be taken seriously. She was the little brown wren who would make such a big noise that she would be perceived as being bigger than she really was. By the sheer force of her personality, she would be a wren who lived up to the Russian word *sokolow* when she felt she had to.

In line with the leftist thinking of the time, Anna's name was not mentioned in the title of the group or in the earliest publicity and programs of the Dance Unit. It was the collective effort that was significant; no individual was to be seen as important. Of course the choreography was hers exclusively and she was responsible for recruiting and rehearsing the dancers. Yet for a time she shouldered a great deal of responsibility with little recognition to go with it.

For her commitment to the Theatre Union, Anna received a tiny salary and whatever fees the group was paid when it performed publicly (most frequently for unions) — usually five or ten dollars. She saw nothing extraordinary in this arrangement at the time or even when reflecting on it many years later. It actually was a fair one by Depression-era standards. Even the Theater Union's most successful productions did not relieve the stress of financial problems. There was literally no money to pay her beyond this pittance.

Anna was a twenty-three-year-old dancer and choreographer whose reputation until this time had been based almost exclusively on her association with Martha Graham's company. Her new association with the extremely popular and fast-growing Theatre Union was a boon to her career, one that helped to put her ahead of several of her struggling contemporaries. She had become the youngest choreographer in America to be leading a professional dance group of her own. As the group began to prove its value, Anna requested and received permission to use her name in publicity and programs — "Directed by Anna Sokolow" after the name of the group — so that she could accept responsibility if things went poorly and receive recognition if the work went well.

Anna was right at home dancing for unions and their Jewish working-class groups. Like their members she was impatient and unwilling to accept a life of fear and poverty reminiscent of what they or their parents had left behind in Europe. She grew up understanding how that generation had banded together to fight nearly insurmountable odds, how they had won their heroic victories by standing up and being counted. A famous song of the period asked the question, "Which side are you on?" These people had answered that question through their actions. Some had endured near starvation as they marched in picket lines in freezing cold temperatures. Some had been beaten up. All had paid dearly for their right to some dignity as a part of the American work force.

The people Anna and her small group danced for were together largely because of the realization that permanent organizations such as the ILGWU were a necessity if their painful and costly battles were to have lasting results. Memories of what nonunion shop conditions had been like were still fresh in their minds; indeed, survivors of the Triangle Shirtwaist factory fire were part of that work force. Yet nonunionized shops were still very much in evidence, if not prevalent. More work remained to be done.

Some garment workers took home no more than three or four dollars for a week's work after paying for their needles, electricity consumed, and various supplies. They were taxed for the chairs they sat on, made to pay for clothes lockers, and fined if they came to work five minutes late. Conditions were improved by the strikes and membership in the ILGWU had greatly increased, but there was still much room for progress. Anna had observed her mother as heir to less tangible, but no less important gains from those strikes, in which Anna had sometimes walked side by side with her mother. In picket lines, thousands of people had discovered the strength in their unity — that they were capable of creating a force whose efforts could lead to change. As part of her upbringing, Anna learned to be a fighter and to join with others in the struggle for respect and dignity and for what the immigrant community came to refer to as a normal life.

The Theatre Union Dance Group was never given an opportunity to appear in a theater production of their parent organization. The impetus to make their first dance appearance grew out of an invitation to perform at the First Anti-War Congress at the St. Nicholas Arena in late August 1933. The sponsoring group, the American League Against War and Fascism, nearly filled the enormous hall, and Anna's first major group piece, the *Anti-War Trilogy* (later performed as the *Anti-War Cycle*), was hailed as a great success.

The work was performed in three sections: "Depression — Starvation," "Diplomacy — War," and "Protest" (later changed to "Defiance"). It was the first major work for Anna and also for Alex, who composed the equally successful score. *New Theatre* critic, Leonard Dal Negro, wrote of the piece:

> They took the entire canvas of imperialist war and diplomacy and translated it into a three-partitioned dance. . . . There was no vulgarization of the mechanics of dance, no recession into the mimic gestures of the drama, no need for literary props. *Anti-War Trilogy* was performed at concerts, mass meetings, workers' clubs, everywhere with singular acclaim; its appeal was immediate and direct. True, the theme is rather

generalized (a fault with much dancing of the Left) but what difficulties its reception had are chargeable to the unfamiliarity of the audience with the technique used (which is pure and unabashed Graham). The sharply stylized movements, always direct and aggressive, came as a shock to the unaccustomed observer.

Dal Negro, writing from an enlightened Marxist point of view, states that although the choreography was not created through the party-preferred process of collective thought, this piece proved that the individual creator could produce work of a high quality. After a while this criticism of Anna's dances would disappear from the radical press; in her case the individual artist was recognized because the choreography was so fine. Anna could no more have worked in a choreography-by-committee situation than she could have created a classical ballet.

A more seasoned commentator on dance, *New York Times* critic John Martin, wrote in his *America Dancing*, "While it was in spots fairly literary, in the tradition of the 'social content' agitation of the time, it showed a real feeling for creative movement and for group choreography." This was praise from Caesar. Ralph Tayler wrote in *Dance Observer* (after listing numerous complaints about the program of tiresome protest dances he had just seen):

> The outstanding exception of the evening, however, was the performance of *Anti-War Cycle* by the Theatre Union Dancers, under the direction of Anna Sokolow. This trilogy exhibited commendable choreography and a fine sense of interpretive balance, despite its avowed purpose of propaganda. It was danced with excellent style and verve, the participants demonstrating a superior command of the technical problems involved. The pianist, Paul Creston, accompanied with impeccable precision. . . .
>
> The Worker's Dance League as a whole projects a strong sense of enthusiasm and energy and if it is able to break away from the over-generalizations which so often cause Communist art groups to bite off more than they can chew, we can look forward to the establishment of what may develop into a vital center of dance activity.

The Theatre Union, with its own organizational problems, was paying scant attention to the Dance Group and its needs. They provided some help with the cost of rehearsal space and some incidental expenses, but most of the company's income came from the bookings the Workman's Circle and similar groups offered them. They were kept busy performing on one tiny union-hall stage after another. Once, to gain a few feet of performance space, they rolled a piano out of the way. As they turned to go, they heard a crash — it had rolled clear off the stage! The dancers hid until Alex assured them that they were safe and still welcome.

If there had ever been talk of the Theatre Union sponsoring a major public presentation of their dance group it was soon forgotten; they had been given a name and an identity and little else. Quite the opposite was true of the treatment they received when they performed for The New Dance League, formerly the Workers Dance League. Proud of the participation of the professional-level Dance

Unit and the New Dance Group in their concert events, the League put time, money, and sincere effort into their support of these fledgling companies. They also put Anna under some gentle pressure to become more fully involved in the organization. The League was expanding its membership to groups in large cities throughout the United States and wanted to make the point that it embraced professionals as well as amateurs. Finally, her patience with the Theatre Union lost, Anna separated herself and her dancers from the organization in February 1935. They continued to call themselves the Dance Unit, but their primary alliance now was with the New Dance League, which regarded them as standard-bearers.

Leonard Dal Negro wrote in the August issue of *New Theatre:*

> Six months ago the Dance Unit severed their connection with the Theatre Union and became an official unit of the New Dance League. This divorce from the parent organization brought with it serious problems. The Dance Unit with its stalwart dozen performers now had the weighty problems before them of maintaining a studio, paying an accompanist, buying and making costumes, etc. The revenues are slight enough. No group can long exist on the small fees (usually from $5 to $10 for the entire group for an evening's performance) they are paid by the working class organizations they dance before. Consequently for a long period they were never sure where they would rehearse next. The problem was partially solved through the generosity of Sophia Delza, sincere and valuable friend of the new dance movement, who put her studio at the disposal of the Unit.
>
> Structurally the Dance Unit differs in many ways from the other groups in the New Dance League. What differentiates it most is that its small membership is made up of young women whose exclusive occupation, often at great sacrifice, is the dance. The majority of the other groups are workers in industry and in offices, who dance as an avocation, though one that plays an important part in their lives.

Dal Negro's article was misleading on a few points. Many of Anna's dancers were still in school; dance was not quite their exclusive occupation. What did differentiate them from most of the other groups is that they were rehearsed to the bone by their gifted director/choreographer: Anna's standards for excellence were no less severe than those Martha Graham imposed on her company. As for rehearsal space, they had had to scramble before, so that was not new to them. Now at least they had Sophia Delza's long and narrow, but well-located studio on West 16th Street to work in. Alex played for them occasionally, but mostly they did without music unless they were rehearsing for a performance with him or with their friend, the pianist/composer Paul Creston, whose wife, Louise, was also in the Graham Company. Classes were most often accompanied by the teacher on a hand-held drum.

To make up for lost income from the Theatre Union, Anna applied to the Art Student's League for modeling work. They turned her down, inviting her to come back again when she had some meat on her bones. She did, and added a short but successful career as a model to her accomplishments — successful, that is, considering the buying power in those days of the thirty-five cents an hour she was paid for her work.

5

ANNA IN THE PROMISED LAND: RUSSIA

The artist is better at unmasking than convincing. (Unidentified article, Soviet Art, July 14, 1934)

Alex's busy schedule in the early months of 1934 — studying at Juilliard, accompanying classes at the Neighborhood Playhouse, composing and playing for Anna, and working at Western Union — was beginning to tell on his health. He needed a change of schedule and environment and opted for a dramatic one. He applied for and received permission to study musical composition at the Moscow Conservatory for Music. His connection with Joseph North opened the door partially for him; his skill as a telegraph operator opened it the rest of the way.

Once settled in Moscow, he invited Anna to join him for a while. He wrote to her rhapsodically in March of 1934 (after admitting to her that he had downed a few stiff vodkas), "When you receive this, April will be here and then, and then, and then! MOSCOW the birthplace of civilization! The kernel of the new Renaissance — where millions are struggling to make for themselves a decent society. And you and I shall witness it together. We shall go south to Odessa, to the Black Sea, and spend time there observing, and taking part in this new life."

Anna was not sure that she agreed about Moscow being the birthplace of civilization, but she wanted very much to be with Alex and to see for herself. Somehow she managed to be released from her commitments to the Theatre Union and Graham, and to get a bank loan for the boat trip to the land her parents had fled thirty years earlier.

A few weeks before Anna arrived in Russia, *Dance Observer* printed an article by Alex North in which he complained about the stagnant condition of dance there: "With all the progressive strides made in the fields of theatre, cinema, music, and painting, the art of the dance in the Soviet Union lags behind." About the revolutionary ballet *Flames of Paris* he wrote: "When one attends [this ballet] with some understanding of the revolutionary dance, he will be astounded at the incongruity. The attempt to instill revolutionary content in the ballet form fails completely and one leaves impressed only with the excellent execution of the dances."

At the age of twenty-four Anna was a valued member of an outstanding modern dance company in the United States, a choreographer of rising stature, the director of her own group, and on her way to becoming one of the first modern dancers to visit and perform in Russia since Isadora Duncan. Her presence there might serve to change any notions the Russians had about how dance could fit into the revolution.

She sailed the last week in May on the *Ile de France*. It was the first period of sustained inactivity in her adult life and she spent most of the Atlantic crossing reading and looking at the ocean. She arrived in England and although her visit was brief her impressions of London were so memorable that she resolved to return one day. The Russian ship, the *Smolney*, which she boarded for the rest of her journey, was more appealing to her than the massive and impersonal *Ile de France*. The *Smolney* was small and intimate, with no distinction of classes except in sleeping quarters, which she described as horrible; however, the food was excellent. The crew of young Russians who wanted to learn jazz dancing and to speak English made good company.

When the ship passed through Germany's Kiel Canal, Anna watched a group of German youths being drilled, military style, and heard them shouting "Heil Hilter!" in cadence. It was a chilling sight, one that she would never forget.

Alex met her in front of Leningrad's Hotel Europa as arranged and sightseeing commenced almost immediately. That first night, as they were walking through the streets of the city, they passed the Maryinsky Theatre and noticed that a ballet performance was in progress. Anna approached the doorman and asked to be admitted. He at first refused. With characteristic boldness she challenged him with a few Russian words she knew: "why not? I am a dancer!" He shrugged and let them enter. It was a performance of *Swan Lake*, and the ballerina was the brilliant Galina Ulanova. Anna wrote to her friend Ronya Chernin, "I enjoyed the dancing very much but the production was old-fashioned, elaborate and sentimental, and so banal that it sickened. The pure ballet dancing I enjoyed tremendously. They had some very fine dancers."

Anna spent two days in Leningrad, enthralled by the beauty of the city. Then it was off to Moscow.

The visit started out auspiciously. Alex's uncle, a Muscovite, was there to meet them at the entry to the city, but the customs officials were slow to clear Anna, suspecting some mischief. She had only about thirty dollars to declare — far too little for an American traveler, according to the Russian's perceptions. Alex motioned the uncle over when it was clear that there was a problem. Uncle quickly smothered Anna with kisses and Russian terms of endearment. The officials passed her through.

Anna went to live with Alex in an apartment he shared with a friend on Karaka Street. Their large sunlit room had a piano and familiar home comforts, such as a bathroom and the use of a kitchen. From the apartment windows, Anna could see the city and some of the spectacular sights it had to offer its visitors.

Homes, factories, and theaters were under construction everywhere, or so it seemed to her from the bustle of the building activity she observed in the city. To give Rose some idea of the vitality of theater and dance in the city, she wrote that the official (although possibly somewhat exaggerated) figure for nightly attendance at dance, music, and theatre events was two hundred thousand.

Throughout her stay in Moscow, Anna wrote to Rose weekly, beginning on June 14:

> Well I'm in Moscow and sometimes I have to pinch myself to realize it. But all I have to do is look out the window from our really lovely, large room with huge French windows, and I see wonderful oriental churches and the round tops of St. Basil's with gold crosses. It has been so hectic for the first few days. This is the first chance I've had to write. Alex met me in Leningrad and I sure was glad to see him in front of the Hotel Europa. I had no trouble with any of my baggage — No difficulty in bringing in any of my stuff. I could have brought more — especially groceries.
>
> Most people do not eat at home very much because attached to every theater and factory of any kind there is a restaurant. The members get cards to eat there for very little money. Alex has a card to the Bolshoi Theatre, the largest in Moscow where all the famous actors and actresses eat.
>
> Alex also has a membership at an excellent theater club where we have midnight suppers. So we only have breakfast at home. All this would not be possible except that Alex has an excellent friend, Grisha Schneerson, who is head of the dance in the International Bureau of Music. He is a very nice young man and likes Alex very much. Last night he, Alex, I and some other friends went to the Park of Culture and Rest to see an open air opera and ballet. We saw "Prince Igor." It was marvelous in spite of the fact that I hardly understood what they were speaking about. Alex speaks Russian very well. They were so nice that I had a wonderful time anyway.
>
> Everything I've seen so far is very elaborate and spectacular. They don't seem to understand simplicity in ballet but everything is interesting and exciting. About my own dancing, I think I'll be able to give a few concerts and appear on certain programs. Right now, I'm arranging for a place to rehearse. By the first of July, or perhaps sooner I will be ready to show my dances to the concert bureau and then a contract will be arranged for me. But they already know about me through publicity and Alex and Grisha so now it is a question of getting ready.

In spite of the exciting and challenging new environment, Anna was preoccupied with thoughts of her young group back home. Her departure date for Russia had made it impossible for her to be at an important performance on June 2 at Town Hall in New York. The letter she wrote to Ronya Chernin on June 28 reveals some of her strong concerns and convictions:

> I kept wondering how rehearsals were going and how the performance went and these last few days I could hardly wait for news. I feel that the group's performance at Town Hall was great proof of fine spirit and solidarity. I feel very responsible now toward the group and shall always do my best to create dances of importance and significance. But as I said before I left, the most important thing

now is for the group to work especially hard on pure dance technique because we must do the "March of the Pioneers" [premiered as *Two Pioneer Marches*] with a brilliance and technical assurance that it needs. Of course in comparison to the other groups ours has quotes, excellent technique, endquote, but we know our own technical shortcomings and the *March* shows them too obviously. So try to work together as much as possible. Next fall we must do bigger things and advance.

About the comments about our being "abstract," that will be a problem always and I am so sure that we will finally convince them that our approach is the only approach as far as using the art as a weapon of propaganda, and that art and propaganda are too closely related to make such distinctions. I really feel that our performance at City College [January 7, 1934], being the first real one, had quite an effect on the other dance groups, more than they are willing to admit. They are very anxious here to know more about the Workers Dance League and its different groups. They know about the New Dance Group and Edith Segal's [Red Dancers] group. But about us, just this year's publicity, and they feel that we are a little different, but some pictures will help.

She follows this with detailed instructions for a session with the photographer Alfredo Valente. Rose was to be in charge.

Anna stayed in close touch also with her mother, who thought it most odd that her daughter would travel to Russia, of all places.

We have been having terrible heat here and Alex and I go swimming almost every day. They have beautiful outdoor pools along the Moscow River and you should see how sunburned I am. There are many Americans coming over now and every day I meet someone I know. There is much to see in Moscow — model factories, nurseries where mothers who work leave their children in excellent care and there are wonderful museums and art galleries. We have many American friends who have been here a few years and they all like it very much. Some of them don't want to go back to the States . . . . I'm giving a concert on August 12 in a very large theater. There will be announcements all over Moscow. I have to take picture with a Russian photographer. I'll have some to give you when I come back. I leave Moscow August 20 and will be back in early September. You will meet me at the boat, yes?

Your loving daughter,
Anna

Anna and Alex were given permission to use the Foreign Workers Club facilities, where they rehearsed together daily for two to three hours. They spent their remaining free time using his pass to the Bolshoi Theater, touring the city, and taking midnight suppers at the exclusive Theatre Club. Anna was asked to do a lecture-demonstration in Graham technique for the director and other authorities of the Park of Culture and Rest and invited guests, including people from the concert bureau who were to audition her for other public performances and the possibility of a short tour. The Culture and Rest people strongly suggested that she change her name for this and other performances. How could they interest an audience in an American Artist with a Russian name like Sokolow? Smith or Smee would serve her much better, they argued. Anna refused. Her presentors finally chose to refer to her as "Anna Sokolova" in publicity — an odd decision, which certainly could not have helped matters any. To avoid confusion (they said) they would print that name in English on posters and in ads.

Leonard Dal Negro questioned her about her performance activities in Russia for the October 1934 edition of *New Theatre:*

> My performance had something of the effect usually attributed only to gentlemen who pull rabbits out of hats. For two hours I gave an exhibition of the Graham technique; no dances, simply bare framework, the basic principles of a modern art.
>
> The audience had never seen anything like it before. It was entirely outside of their experience. They sat mentally agape. Unheard of dancing! No pretty curved movements! No acrobatic pirouettes! They were amazed, bewildered, as any group of people must be who are steeped to their eyes in traditions of 400 years of "pretty" dancing.
>
> After the performance they asked question after question (via interpreter). Bewildered, they were greedy to know more of this strange art. Why did I never point my toe? Why was my face so expressionless? (Russians like clearly shown emotions in their dancing.) For hours after my tiring performance I sat and answered questions. The audience was not satisfied — they had to see more of my work.

Anna gave another performance a short time later at the Foreign Workers Club. Her audience again consisted of the same professional dance and theater people plus a number of American friends and well-wishers. At this performance she exhausted her repertoire of solo dances. When it was over, the audience, in characteristically Russian style, insisted on a meeting to discuss the performance. Anna described the event to Dal Negro:

> "Off the whole group trouped to ask interminable questions, way into the morning." Imagine [wrote Dal Negro], if you can, a like happening after an American dance recital. . . . "My solo dances were not so bewildering to some of the audience as the exhibit of plain technique had been. Some of my dances were decadent they thought. I must admit I think so also. I do not feel I have created satisfactory revolutionary solos up to date, not because of the lack of desire to do so, but because I feel I haven't developed to a point where I'm capable of doing revolutionary solos possessing complete identification with the class struggle."

The Russians invited her to return. "We must see how your technique looks in group work. Come back and we will give you as many girls as you need to work with and all the assistance that you want. Work for a year — then show us." It was a generous offer, but she felt she had to refuse — her home was in the United States.

The unnamed critic who reviewed her performance in the July 14, 1934, issue of *Soviet Art* shared some of her audience's misgivings. Complaining that

Anna's style was far from original and suffered from the excessive influence of Western expressionism, the writer commented that her dance stemmed from traditions born at the start of the century with the modernist decadent school of dance — the school of Duncan and others:

> Followers of this school of dance including Sokolow explain their negative attitude toward classicism by condemning the restrictions it places on their expression, but the sum of' technical skills displayed by Anna Sokolova [sic] is not great either. Her face, when she dances, remains frozen; she does not mime; her style is somewhat cold and static. She is actually limited to a degree by conventions proper to abstract dance. The revolutionary themes calling for revolutionary struggle and self-sacrifice leading to new victories suffer from artificial and forced expression. The music of Scriabin, Franck, and Hindemith can hardly be regarded as convincing vehicles for the call to revolutionary struggle. The artist is better at unmasking than convincing.

Having expressed party-line misgivings, the critic then warmed up to Anna's strengths, at times contradicting earlier pronouncements:

> She is unquestionably a talented dancer with great taste; an artist who meticulously perfects each movement of her dance, achieving in this area great technical excellence. She builds her dance with restraint, concentrating mainly on content in spite of the fact that she sees it in somewhat abstract terms. Her dance does not have the element of misleading exterior dynamics; it is concentrated and creates one unified image. Her dance is simple and extremely well-organized. A. Sokolova directs the best dance collective in New York, part of the Workers Dance League. As A. Sokolova continues to work with proletarian avant-garde groups, perfecting her art, she can expect to grow even stronger in her field of artistic endeavor.

Anna auditioned for the Soviet concert bureau, with the hope of securing a short tour. This never materialized, probably because of delays due to red tape. She had found, much to her dismay, that Russia seemed to lack the incisive efficiency she was accustomed to as a New Yorker. One had to wait interminably for everything in Moscow. Her disappointment at not being booked was compounded by the fact that she had hoped to earn enough to buy a few gifts and to have some pocket money for her return voyage. Instead, she had to write to Rose for a small loan to see her through.

She kept busy rehearsing her dances with Alex, going to theatres and museums, and taking frequent walks through Red Square. She and Alex were there for one of Moscow's magnificent parades — this one in honor of the first successful Soviet stratosphere flyers. "The whole city marched with red flags, flowers and song," she wrote to Rose. "The Red Army is stunning. They sing while they march. I can't describe the marvelous spirit with which the people greeted the flyers. The workers marched too. Many groups of physical culturists — children, tanks. Something we never witness in New York."

There were many parties to attend and a host of Russians to meet: friends of Alex from the conservatory as well as other artists. Anna found herself smiling and nodding a great deal. Her grasp of the Russian language was limited to expressions she had learned from her mother and a few new ones acquired while there. Language barriers notwithstanding, she found the Russian people pleasant and hospitable. If she grew homesick, she could call on some of the Americans she knew who were visiting Moscow or making their homes there.

Although thoroughly taken by the splendor of Moscow, Anna appears to have found her experience there somewhat unsettling. She had come to Russia with good reason to believe that in this great revolutionary country she would encounter a superior revolutionary dance movement, one that would make the work being done in the United States by proletariat dancers seem pallid by comparison. What she found instead was a classical ballet tradition that was as much a favorite with the Communist hierarchy as it had been with the tsar and his court, regardless of the fact that it reflected the values of the deposed monarchy. What was called "the Peoples Dance" or "Plastique" was a kind of athleticized folk dancing combined with ballet movements, done, according to Anna, by groups in every factory, every collective, and every school. In her letters she explained that it was part of the cultural activities and health programs. For special events, groups of these dancers were banded together for performances of mass dancing, which were filmed in order to be shown throughout Russia and to be released for international consumption. What, she wondered, did any of this have to do with the art of dance?

Anna wrote to one of her friends that she would never want to remain in Russia, even though there were some temptations. The invitation to stay had intrigued her: "We could make a great dancer out of you," she had been told, but she knew in her heart it could never be. She would never make Russia her home.

Much that she and Alex had planned, including the trips to Odessa and the Black Sea that Alex had dreamed of in his letter, never happened, for lack of money. But the experience of being there at that particular time proved a richly rewarding one for both of them. It took Anna many years to absorb the sobering new insights about the revolutionary country that was so idealized in her circle at home:

> We were still a couple of kids, and very idealistic. I found that a tremendous amount of conformity was necessary there and I never could have done that. Their idea of Revolutionary Dance was to wave a red flag at the audience as they balanced in their toe shoes. It didn't interest me at all. I just knew instinctively that it was wrong for me.

Upon her return from Russia, although Anna continued to create dances on Russian themes, only one, *Dances of All Nations,* a pageant performed in

Madison Square Garden to commemorate the fourteenth anniversary of Lenin's death, had anything resembling a revolutionary quality. Her passion for Soviet causes had cooled considerably by that time.

For Alex, the professional training had been invaluable. When his composition teachers, Anton Weprik and Victor Belyi, discovered in due course that he had considerable talent, they paid him the great compliment of recommending him for admission to the League of Soviet Composers, the only American ever to have been so honored.

Sarah Sokolow, Samuel Sokolow,
circa 1903.
Photographer unknown.
Courtesy of Stephen Bank.

Anna, Sarah, and Rose Sokolow, circa 1922.
Photograph by Uncle Harry.
Courtesy of Stephen Bank.

Anna Sokolow, 1926.
Photograph by Uncle Harry.
Courtesy of Zelda Blackman.

Gertie, Anna, and Rose Sokolow, circa
1925. Photograph by Uncle Harry.
Courtesy of Stephen Bank.

Anna Sokolow, Elsa Pohl and unknown dancer
as Beauty, Reason and Folly at the Emanuel
Sisterhood, 1922. Photograph by Hiram Myers,
Social Welfare Photography.
Anna Sokolow collection.

Anna Sokolow, 1927.
Photograph by Uncle Harry.
Courtesy of David Lifson.

Flyer for International Labor Defense
program, December 15, 1935.
Courtesy of Rose Levy.

Martha Graham (center), Anna Sokolow (to her
right) and others in "Hymn to the Virgin" section
of *Primitive Mysteries*, 1931. Photograph by
Edward Moeller. Courtesy of Rose Levy.

Florence Schneider, Celia Dembroe, Marie Marchowsky, Rose Levy, and Eleanor Lazurus, the
Dance Unit, *Anti-War Trilogy*, 1934. Photograph by Alfredo Valente. Courtesy of Rose Levy.

Anna Sokolow with Alex North,
Triuna Island, Lake George, 1936.
Photographer unknown.
Anna Sokolow collection.

Ignacio ("Nacho") Aguirre, 1939.
Photographer unknown.
Courtesy of Rose Levy.

Anna Sokolow, pen and ink drawing
by Ignacio Aguirre, New York, 1944.
Anna Sokolow collection.

Anna Sokolow, "The beast is in the garden . . ." section of *The Exile*, 1939. Copyright © Barbara Morgan.

Paloma Azul class, Mexico City, 1940.
Photograph by Mayo.
Anna Sokolow Collection.

Raquel Gutiérrez, Rosa Reyna, and Anna Sokolow in Paloma Azul class, Mexico City, 1940.
Photograph by Mayo.
Anna Sokolow collection.

Anna Sokolow in unknown
choreography of the late
1940s. Photograph by Marthe
Krueger. Courtesy of Vivian
Nathan.

Anna Sokolow in
Kaddish, 1945.
Photographer unknown.
Anna Sokolow collection.

Johnny White, 1952.
Photographer unknown.
Anna Sokolow collection.

Anna Sokolow, Margalit Oved (in left foreground), Inbal class, Tel Aviv, circa 1955.
Photographer unknown. Anna Sokolow collection.

Jane Lowe and Richard Caceres,
Juilliard Dance Ensemble, "Largo Desolato"
from *Lyric Suite*, 1972.
Photograph by Milton Oleaga.

Anna Sokolow Dance Company, "Desire" section from *Rooms*, 1966.
Photograph by Edward Effron. Courtesy of the photographer.

Netherlands Dance Theater,
Rooms rehearsal,
Amsterdam, 1967. Photograph by
Hans Van Den Busken.
Anna Sokolow collecton.

Jeff Duncan (Ray Cook in the
background), "Panic" section
from *Rooms*, 1967.
Photograph by Edward Effron.
Courtesy of the photographer.

6

LANDMARKS

The house was crowded to the guards [guardrails], and enthusiasm was everywhere in evidence. If the cheering began as a gesture of friendliness, it soon became quite obviously more than that as the young dancer's simplicity of manner and fine integrity took hold. (John Martin, Review of Anna's Broadway debut at the Guild Theater: New York Times, November 15, 1937)

In 1935, Anna became involved in several theater and dance events that were to become landmarks in her career and in dance history as well. It all started with a program that included *Waiting for Lefty,* Clifford Odets' first effort at playwriting for the Group Theatre. *Lefty,* based on the taxi-drivers' strike of the previous year, was destined to become one of the most famous agitprop works of its time.

The powerful and violent one-act play was premièred on January 6, 1935, at the Guild Theater as part of a Sunday-night benefit performance for *New Theatre Magazine.* Actors were seated in chairs on an otherwise bare stage with a few of them, including Odets and Elia Kazan, placed in the audience as voices of the people, responding aloud to what was happening on stage. The only other work presented on the incendiary program was Anna's *Anti-War Cycle* — a work with its own considerable impact. Fortunately, Odets insisted that his play, which rocked the theater like an exploding bomb, be last on the program, threatening to withdraw the work unless he had his way. Considering the exhilaration and excitement generated by this première, anything that followed would have seemed pallid by comparison.

According to one eye-witness account, "The first scene of *Lefty* had not played two minutes when a shock of delighted recognition struck the audience like a tidal wave. Deep laughter, hot assent, a kind of joyous fervor seemed to sweep the audience toward the stage. The actors no longer performed; they were being carried along as if by an exultancy of communication such as I had never witnessed in the theatre before. Audience and actors had become one."

Anna and the Dance Unit enjoyed the association with this milestone play. They had, in effect, warmed up the audience for what was to be the main attraction and received a considerable ovation of their own in the process. Anna's participation in the program helped to identify her as the dancer/choreographer most closely associated with the Group Theatre and won new friends for her on the staff of *New Theatre,* the official organ of both the New Theatre and New Dance Leagues. It also led to an association with another significant and more mainstream theater organization, the Theatre Guild.

In the program for the 1935 Theatre Guild Broadway production of André Obey's *Noah* there is a curious credit: "Dances directed by Anna Sokolow and Louis Horst." Other program credits include Louis Horst, composer; special visual effects, Ludwig Bemelmans; animal masks and costumes, Remo Bufano. (Among the nine dancers portraying animals in the production was Georgia Graham, Martha's sister.) Press clippings indicate that the production was a huge artistic success, in part because of an understanding and polished performance by the renowned actor, Pierre Fresnay, and an extraordinarily handsome staging. Sadly, reviews fail to comment on the dances or the unique Sokolow/Horst collaboration. In 1936, Anna assisted Martha Graham in staging the movement for the Guild's production of *Valley Forge.* Little is written about it, but it appears that although Anna did a good deal of the work she received scant credit for her labors.

Her first association with Bennington College came in the summer of 1935 when, as a dancer in Graham's company, she participated in a seminal dance workshop. Graham had been invited by Martha Hill, a former dancer in her company, to teach at this idyllic campus nestled in the Vermont hills and to bring her entire group along to participate in an adventurous project. She was commissioned to create a group piece, using twelve company members and twenty-four students from the Bennington Summer School of the Dance, most of whom were physical-education teachers. The objective was to demonstrate how such a production is built from the ground up, giving the teachers practical ideas that they could later apply to their own work. She had six weeks to form the motley group into a professional-looking ensemble.

Martha worked with extremely gifted young collaborators in this first venture. Alexander Calder designed mobiles, Norman Lloyd composed the music, and the set and lighting designs were by Arch Lauterer. The finished work, *Panorama,* was a sparkling success and, in the midst of the excitement generated by the production, it was announced that the following year Bennington would host the first annual American Dance Festival.

It was also during this summer at Bennington that Anna met Muriel Stuart, who, according to Don McDonagh, was attending the session as a "spy" for Lincoln Kirstein. Kirstein wanted to know what the troublesome modernists were up to and Stuart (who would one day become a renowned ballet teacher) was to report back. Balanchine's brilliant and wealthy sponsor had a curious fascination with Graham and a great respect for her artistry. Although known for a lifelong and often vitriolic disdain for modern dance, in those days Kirstein routinely sent cases of first-rate spirits to the Graham studio with his compliments.

It was during that summer, in *Panorama* rehearsals, that Muriel and Anna got to know each other and became good friends. Although they worked in very different areas of dance, each appreciated and admired the other's dedication and talent. Years later, Stuart described Anna's dancing as being "like quicksilver."

Reviews of Anna's work in New York during this period reveal that she was gaining a fine reputation not only for the superior craftsmanship of her agit-prop dances like *Anti-War Cycle,* but also for pungent satire in works such as the two solos, *Romantic Dances* and *Histrionics,* all from 1933. These, along with the biting 1934 trio *Death of a Tradition* (which she performed with Sophie Maslow and Lili Mehlman), were among the most successful pieces in her repertoire in the mid-1930s.

In *Histrionics,* Anna portrayed a Shakespearean actor, in Hamlet-style garb, making a mockery of overstated and insincere performance in the commercial theater. About this parody of acting and dancing styles, one critic wrote, "Anna Sokolov's [*sic*] *Histrionics* . . . revealed one of the cleverest dance wits that it has ever been my fortune to see. What humor she had — what cruel cutting humor! . . . How expertly she cut to the heart of both the pathos and rottenness in the Broadway dance arena." It was an intense work, powerfully performed by a gifted young artist, who was sometimes referred to in the press as "The Little Queen of Satire."

In late 1934, these dances were presented on a New Dance League joint program titled "Revolutionary Solo Dances." John Martin singled Anna out in his review:

> [The revolutionary dancers] are learning that there is a difference between militancy and blatancy, between the force of the accurately directed logic of art and that of the stuffed club bludgeoning the air. . . .
>
> Miss Sokolov [*sic*], especially, appears now as an artist of great gifts. Her dancing covers an unusually wide range and is characterized throughout by fine integrity and imagination. Her wit is devastating and in her current solos she turns it full blast upon certain romantic insincerities. Of all the young dancers in the field there is none who seems more completely ready to come forth on her own or more likely to make a great career when she finally elects to do so.

Anna's next major group work, *Strange American Funeral,* was based on a poem by Michael Gold, author of the widely read novel *Jews Without Money* and a frequent contributor to *New Masses.* Anna knew Gold through Alex's brother Joseph, who was a close friend of Gold. When she read the searing *A Strange Funeral in Braddock* (see Appendix) and learned that Elie Siegmeister had created music based on the text, she knew she had to make a dance that would attempt to capture its tragic essence. Siegmeister approved the project and enjoyed coming to watch rehearsals.

The poem tells the true story of a well-liked Bohemian immigrant steel-worker, who was killed when he fell into a vat of the molten metal. It contrasts his simple, loving nature with the brutality of the industrial steel mill where he worked. One reviewer wrote of the dance, "His death emerges as a poignant metaphor for the destruction of the individual in an industrial society that cares little for personal safety or well-being." The social issues were made personal and concrete by vivid characterization, a growing element in her choreography.

Anna did not appear in the work. She wanted to concentrate on the considerable challenge she had undertaken — to combine dance and poetry successfully. It was a time when leading modern dance critics such as John Martin and *The Christian Science Monitor's* Margaret Lloyd let it be known that they felt a blending of words and dance could only operate to the detriment of both. Typically, Anna did what interested her, warnings notwithstanding. Audiences sided with her. The work was a resounding success wherever it was performed.

The poem is almost filmlike in design, moving backward and forward in time and interweaving the protagonist's internal world with external reality. Anna chose not to mirror the poem in her dance, but to reinforce it with complementary imagery, finding movement themes in poetic images such as the resolve of the widow to make herself "harder than steel." The work was characterized by strong linear formations and potent motifs. In one section a dancer was held aloft as a grim funeral cortege slowly crossed the stage. John Martin's reactions were as expected:

> When Anna Sokolow recently presented her new group composition, "Strange American Funeral," at the Park Theatre in performances by the Dance Unit, she made two facts increasingly clear. One is that she is an exceptionally gifted composer with complete authority in the handling of a group, and the other is that it is impossible to dance to poetry, however excellent, which was not written especially for dancing. The first of these facts served only to emphasize the second.

Perhaps the most important champion of modern dance of his time, and one whose words were taken very seriously by artists in the field, Martin sometimes used his reviews as a sermon for his flock of eager readers. After complimenting the work for passages "superb not only for their integrity of feeling but for their boldness of imagination," he stated that he found the dance as a whole inchoate and pointless:

> When our poets learn to dance or our dancers to write, we can look for the emergence of a great theatre of such heroic calibre as that of Aeschylus and Sophocles. Until such an exchange of learning takes place, however, it would be well for our poets not to try to "restore" dancing to the theatre and for dancers to quit "interpreting" poetry.

The radical press disagreed. The critic for *New Theatre* described *Strange American Funeral* as "a major work in creation, [which] glows sharply and distinctly as one of the most magnificent compositions in contemporary dance."

It might be said that Anna had the last word with Martin on the subject. When he needed an example of dance as propaganda for his now-famous lecture-demonstration series, it was to Anna he turned, and it was *Strange American Funeral* that she gave him. Whatever differences may have existed between the spunky twenty-six-year-old choreographer and America's most influential dance critic, he openly expressed his admiration for her in his writing. In describing the second generation of modern dancers in *America Dancing,* he wrote, "Certainly there is no more conspicuous talent among them than that of Anna Sokolow ... [who] appears to be destined for the front rank of the next generation of dancers."

There were some complaints by other writers that *Funeral* was a bit heavy-handed in spots, but they were consistently qualified by some mention of the fact that Anna's messages were presented in clear movement terms. Unlike many of her contemporaries who were sometimes guilty of presenting clumsily danced diatribes as choreography, Anna did not idealize the people and situations she danced about by extolling the virtues of the working class and deploring their plight. Rather, she worked toward an expression that sensitive and intelligent working people could understand in terms of their own experience and she did it through choreography that was original and striking. The emphasis was on dance. Margaret Lloyd wrote: "Anna always managed to be more the artist than the agitator. The urgency of her message never displaced her from the realm of dance." Nevertheless, she was claimed by the left as one of their own and began to be characterized in the radical press by phrases such as "first in the esteem of the workers and intellectuals who comprise left dance audiences." It was a position she would hold until the end of the decade.

It was not until April 5, 1936, five years after she made her first dances, that Anna showed a full evening of her own work in concert. It was presented at the Y.M.H.A. on Lexington Avenue at 92nd Street (popularly known as the "Y"). Under the inspired and sympathetic leadership of its educational director, Dr. William Kolodney, the "Y" was almost the only home that modern dancers could call their own in the late 1930s. No fee was charged for use of the building and most of the essential publicity was done by the "Y". Admission fees were kept to an absolute minimum: a subscription series of ten recitals could be seen for three dollars.

Anna was one of the artists whose work eventually came to be identified with the place. The stage was too small and the dressing facilities practically non-existent, but everyone had a good view of the stage in the 660-seat house and modern dancers were treated with respect and understanding. For the many artists who were leading a hand-to-mouth existence, the "Y" was something of a gift from heaven.

It was a double gift for Anna because she earned a substantial part of her living by teaching beginning Graham technique classes there. The faculty included Martha Graham, Doris Humphrey, and Hanya Holm, among others. The invitation to teach alongside the top-ranking artists of this older generation indicates how highly regarded she was as a teacher, although still in her twenties.

The curtain-raiser for Anna's April 5, 1936, program on the prestigious Major Subscription Series at the "Y" was the premiere of *Opening Dance,* a vibrant solo to music by Shebalin (later reworked for soloist and group to a composition by Alex). According to numerous accounts, the work fairly burst with an energy and rhythmic excitement seldom seen in modern dance in the mid-1930s. (For the performers in the later group version, it was an endurance trial comparable to the one Martha Graham had created for her dancers in *Celebration,* a work in which Anna shone.) She followed *Opening Dance* with *Romantic Dances, Histrionics, Speaker,* and *Strange American Funeral.*

After intermission she presented another premiere, *Inquisition '36* (North), a raw antivigilante piece (it fared poorly and was never shown again), and *Four Little Salon Pieces* (Shostakovitch), described by John Martin as a "delightful satire of social affectation." In this work and *Speaker,* in which she walked to the footlights and harangued the audience, looking directly at them, she best displayed her unusual flair for presenting bitter comment in a humorous guise.

Ballad (in a Popular Style) that followed was a wistful, lyrical excursion into jazz, danced to piano and whistled obbligato composed and performed by Alex. Anna felt a strong affinity for jazz, which grew out of her love for and end-less fascination with New York, a city that pulsated with its rhythms. She had been exploring Manhattan and been nourished by its richness and diversity since her childhood, when she and Rose walked for hours, peering into hallways and shop windows, absorbing the sounds and smells of a place abounding in both. *Ballad* was by no means the first time a modern dancer had ventured into jazz, but no one had done it better. It was a stunning dance, at once subtle and exuberant, pure dance with no reason for being other than its rhythm and beauty of motion. *Ballad* became something of a trademark for Anna.

She closed the evening with *Suite of Soviet Songs* (Adomian). Considering that the program started at nine p.m. and consisted of nine works, one wonders what time the audience went home that Sunday night.

Over the next three years she presented at least six more full evening performances (three of them at the "Y"), gaining further public and critical acclaim with each major presentation. One of her most significant works during that period was *Excerpts from a War Poem* (February 28, 1937), a large group piece based on the poem. "War is Beautiful" by the Italian Futurist/Fascist F. T. Marinetti, who was known in Europe and the United States for his piercing statement, "War is the only world hygiene." The poem was excerpted in the Dance Unit program:

> War is Beautiful, / . . . because it fuses in Strength, Harmony, and Kindness, /
> . . . because it realizes the long dreamed of metalization of the human body, /

> . . . because it symphonizes pauses choked by silence, the perfumes and odors of putrification and creates the spiral smoke of burning villages, / . . . because it serves the greatness of our great Fascist Italy.

Marjorie Church wrote about Anna's work in *Excerpts* that "she has taken the essence of fascism, embodied in a poem extolling the beauties of war, and has plucked this expression of an ideology mercilessly apart, line by line, exposing a ruthlessness, a savagery, and a masochistic blindness underlying this viewpoint which are appalling in their implications."

The costumes for *War Poem* were designed by Anton Refregier, whom Anna had met the previous summer while participating in a unique workshop called "Arts in the Theatre." It was funded by a grant from Yaddo, one of the most prestigious American writer's colonies. Triuna Island on Lake George, which Yaddo owned, was converted from a baronial summer home into theater spaces and workshops in which artists could live and create. (The writer John Cheever ran the boat back and forth to the island that summer.) The program was designed to explore the arts of music, dance, and design. Resident artists and student interns were encouraged to be open-minded to art forms other than their own and, at the same time, "to avoid art as social activism," as the published director's report for the summer program read. It pointed out that

> among large groups of artists the conviction has become strong that only by infusing an art with the force of a social cause can the art be made to justify itself. When, however, the motivations of revolution, of specific change in social organization, become the driving forces of the art itself, that organic quality is lost that is the identifying mark of art.

One wonders how Anna and Alex were selected for the project, considering that specific change in social organization was intrinsic to their work. It might have been a naive attempt at their conversion or they had simply been lucky applicants. They were pampered with beautiful living quarters, food prepared by cooks who had worked in Roosevelt's White House, and an idyllic setting in which to do their work. In the ample time allowed between teaching classes, Alex improved his tennis game; Anna swam and got a suntan — rare for her. Blissfully, there were no financial worries for a while; Yaddo even provided a small stipend.

A group project, *Dog Beneath the Skin*, by W. H. Auden, involved the entire faculty for a while, but it came to no finished form. The Yaddo administrators were not upset; their emphasis was on collaborative process rather than on finished product. A warm friendship developed between Anna and Alex and Anton Refregier and his wife, which resulted in his designs for *War Poem*.

The distinguished poet and translator, Ben Belitt, wrote about his first contact with modern dance, a performance of Anna's solo work at Yaddo. He epitomized what many may have felt on encountering the renegade art form for the first time:

> I saw her perform her whole repertory, such as it was then — and the top of my head came off! I felt a great affinity for it, didn't question its oddity. It seemed to me to be mysteriously compatible with the things that mattered to me and with what I was doing and feeling as a poet. It was the live phenomenon of a very gifted dancer suddenly tumbling a whole repertory in front of a person who was ready to be touched in new ways and had seen nothing resembling it. . . . I paid great attention. Everything was pristine, unprecedented, ingenuous.

In the winter of 1937 Anna premiered a new solo, starker in social content than anything she had done for a while. *Case History No.* — was a work in which she vividly projected the gestures and what was later to be called the body language of a young delinquent who falls into a life of crime. Calling it "a burning indictment against society and the first great revolutionary dance characterization," the *Daily Worker*'s Louise Mitchell wrote, "Anna Sokolow depicts the lifetime of thousands of youths who roam this country as vagrants and petty criminals, who live in the slums of New York, Chicago, or Detroit. She dances, with boyish bravado, their willfulness, frustration, desperation, the hunted suspect, the third degree, the cringing crying boy killers, the last mile." It was a bitter, angry characterization, frightening in its intensity. Nearly twenty years passed before she fully understood, developed, and applied the gold mine of expression she had uncovered to *Rooms*. No one had ever done a dance quite like *Case History No.* — before. It was revolutionary in a way that Louise Mitchell could not have fully understood in 1937, when the word seemed to have only one meaning, strictly political, that everyone recognized.

Slaughter of the Innocents was another fine work of the period. Inspired by Herbert Kline's pro-Loyalist documentary film *Heart of Spain,* with its wrenching footage of the bombing of Spanish civilians, the dance depicted the suffering of innocent women and children during wartime. In this compelling solo, Anna turned continuously, a full skirt swirling about her, arms and upper body expressing the anguish of loss. The sculptor Santos Balmori, who saw the work in Mexico, later described it as "a dance of perpetual motion."

The dancer/poet Edith Segal witnessed an extraordinary scene after one of the highly charged concert performances in the late 1930s. She was visiting with Anna in her dressing room when Dorothy Parker knocked on the door. Without saying a word, the famous wit kneeled down, kissed the hem of Anna's skirt, and exited, leaving behind a bewildered Anna Sokolow, for once rendered speechless.

Segal, herself a Communist Party member and quite proud of it, recalled another revealing incident that took place around the same time. She had convinced Anna to attend a Party meeting with her, hoping, perhaps, that at last her friend would join. The speaker focused his presentation on the importance of recruitment, particularly of those in the public eye. Soon it became obvious that he was addressing many of his remarks to Anna. By then she was something of a celebrity in the New York art world and would make a good catch. According to Segal, Anna met his stare and went home unaffiliated. She had work to do and wanted to be free to proceed in her own way.

For her February 28, 1937, concert at the "Y," Anna added four men to the Dance Unit, her first male dancers, for the premiere of *Excerpts from a War Poem.* (Graham incorporated men into her company more than a year later.) They were Alex Berg, Milton Feher, Lew Rosen, and Allen Wayne. The women in the group were Aza Cefkin, Ronya Chernin, Ruth Freedman, Rose Levy, Grusha Mark, Mary Monroe, Ruth Nissenson, Florence Schneider, June Sokolow (a cousin), and Sascha Spector. Later in that season, she recruited a dancer whose name appears on her programs as Michael Grey; he later came to be known as Michael Kidd, the Broadway and film choreographer.

In 1937, *New Masses* sponsored Anna's official Broadway debut. John Martin wrote of that highly successful performance in the *New York Times* on November 15, 1937, that "Miss Sokolow ... has a wide and true emotional range, which can sound the depths of feeling and dash off straightway to the most delicate spoofing. That much of her style derives directly from Martha Graham is not surprising, but there is beneath it a personal note that marks her beyond any mistaking as an individual artist with genuine creative powers." Martin also praised Alex North, who was responsible for the majority of the musical settings, describing him as an invaluable collaborator whose music possesses vitality and imagination and that "rarest of attributes, a feeling for movement."

It was also at this performance that Leonard Bernstein met Aaron Copland, and they became lifelong friends. Bernstein marked the event of Copland's eightieth birthday with an acrostic that began, "Anna Sokolow, bless her golden soul" (see Appendix). Bernstein's biographer, Joan Peyser, refers to a crush that the brilliant musician had on Anna and to music he was writing for her. Anna has no memory of either.

The esteemed critic Edwin Denby described Anna as a performer during this early high point of her career:

> Her figure, with the small head, the solid neck, the small sloping shoulders and elongated limbs was immediately touching. Her hands and wrists were lovely, her arms, light. Her dancing had the directness of a child's motions. When she lifted her forearm, when she ran and leapt, you watched the action itself, it was the action in itself that moved you.

In January 1937, Anna was included in New Dance League — sponsored performances in Detroit and Chicago, on one leg of an East Coast tour. Billed as "Soloists from New Dance League," Jane Dudley, Sophie Maslow, Anna Sokolow, and William Matons appeared at Detroit's Art Institute. Their performance, which included Anna's *Death of a Tradition* and *War Monger,* was very well received in both the radical and mainstream press. This tour and others during the middle and late 1930s, sponsored by organizations such as the Workman's Circle, took Anna to dozens of cities as far north as Toronto and as far south as Washington, D.C.

She traveled considerably farther that spring when Martha Graham toured with a company of fifteen dancers to thirteen cities, including Chicago, Vancouver, San Francisco, Los Angeles, and Tallahassee. They finished with a gala performance in New York. On tour, Anna, Sophie Maslow, and Dorothy Bird were singled out for their humorous dancing in *Victorian Generalities* (later renamed *Four Casual Developments*). Anna's most vivid memory of those weeks was of hearing the adventurous radical journalist Anna Louise Strong speak in Seattle on the tragedy of the Spanish Civil War. A few months later, she made one of her most important works of the period, *Slaughter of the Innocents,* on that subject. Although Anna enjoyed her first glimpses of the West Coast, she had not yet acquired a taste for travel. "It has been fun seeing different cities," she wrote home, "but there is no place like New York."

The highlight of this eventful year was to come that summer: the Bennington School of the Dance, in its fourth summer session, awarded fellowships to Esther Junger, José Limón, and Anna Sokolow that provided them with room and board, studio space, and the technical support needed to produce their own work. In founder/director Martha Hill's words, "You had a summer scot-free of any expense — but you were not paid beyond that." The choreographers were given six weeks to prepare both their solos and the group dances that were to be performed by dancers selected from the students enrolled in the summer course. Anna wrote to Rose, "I have a beautiful suite for myself, excellent food, and everything I need to work well — so I'd better deliver the goods." The new work, *Façade — Exposizione Italiana* (North), was described by Margaret Lloyd:

> [In] an exposition or exposé of fascism that could be called a sequel to *War is Beautiful,* Anna, symbolizing the people (good, of course) was the Citizen, silently, but not inactively, observing the bad, bellicose ones proceed to heap ruin on all their heads. "Spectacle" illustrated the pomp and pageantry of Mussolini's nefarious régime . . . "Belle Arte," the pride in nationalistic culture; "Giovanezza" vainglory in athletic skills as ingredient to martial glory; "Prix Femina" maternal awards for woman, breeder of soldiers, sacrificing her wedding ring *en masse* to war; and "Phantasmagoria" the nice mess all this got the simple Italian people into. It was, like its companion piece, a little heavy going choreographically.

Anna's performance in this impassioned work was remembered especially for a frenzied moment in which she literally ran up the wall.

As she had been in *Anti-War Cycle,* Anna was among the vanguard of those who condemned the dangerous political developments in Italy and Nazi Germany. She had joined leading dance figures like Graham, Humphrey, Kirstein, Tamiris, and Weidman the previous year in boycotting the International Dance

Festival (part of the Olympics) held in Berlin. In his announcement of the boycott in the May 1936 *New Theatre,* Emmanuel Eisenberg had commented tersely, "Let the German Ministry of Culture and Propaganda perform its own *danse macabre* in utter solitude before the entire agonized cultural world."

For a brief time that year, Anna joined forces with Sophie Maslow, Miriam Blecher, Jane Dudley, Si-Lan Chen, and Lily Mehlman in what was to be a chamber dance group. The dancers, all of soloist calibre, wanted the opportunity to work with other accomplished artists in a cooperative situation. Although the efforts never came to complete fruition, one can only marvel at the fact that these young women, who held a variety of survival jobs and usually danced every night and on weekends as well, found the time and the energy to work together.

Alex, now recognized by modern dancers as an important collaborator, was kept busy accompanying classes, rehearsals, and performances for other dancers as well as Anna. He toured sometimes with Hanya Holm. To continue his growth as a composer, he studied with Aaron Copland and Ernst Toch. In 1937 he was asked by Martha Graham to create a score for her large group piece, *American Lyric.* Not one of her enduring works, it was nonetheless an important credit for him.

In an undated souvenir program (probably 1937) for Martha Graham and Dance Group, in the description of the company, the only group member who appears to have rated a paragraph-long biographical sketch was Anna Sokolow. She is described as the leading figure in the New Dance League " ... whose choreography is an important feature in their programs." Yet as 1937 drew to a close, it was more and more obvious to the dancers in the Graham company that Anna and Martha were becoming dissatisfied with each other. As Anna's own artistic reputation increased, she became more self-assured and her relationship with Martha, once very warm, grew strained. One evening Anna arrived late at a rehearsal in which Martha was lost in concentrated thought. The dancers stood waiting; it was a scene Anna knew well. "It's like a morgue in here," she commented in her clear, strong voice. Graham came out of her reverie long enough to say, "If you don't like it, there's the door." Anna shrugged and stayed.

The problem was an obvious one, but not one that was ever to be resolved. Martha's unique way of working required unquestioning dedication. For many years Anna had, quite against her nature, been a model of compliant behavior. But along with her growing reputation, she was developing a personal style that precluded reverence toward anyone. Anna, in fact, enjoyed ruffling people's feathers, sometimes even Martha's.

Although Martha appears to have seriously encouraged her dancers to try their own wings and become involved in their own choreographic projects (she even encouraged some of her promising students to audition for Anna's group), she probably had not anticipated that one of them might come into her own with as

much distinction as Anna had. After one of Anna's concerts, Martha condescend-
ingly let the young choreographer know that she felt that excursions into jazz were
a bit vulgar, and when Anna started to explore Jewish themes in her choreography
the older artist coolly suggested that she seek inspiration in the Bible, rather than in
everyday life. Anna remembers thanking her for the advice and deciding on the
spot to continue doing exactly what she was doing. "What Martha was saying to
me, really, was 'Be nice. Be polite.' I was never an obedient disciple."

On January 28, 1938, at the Hippodrome Theatre, the Dance Unit appeared in a *Dance for Spain* benefit along with Lincoln Kirstein's Ballet Caravan
and the companies of Tamiris, Graham, and Holm. Anna's group performed *Excerpts from a War Poem* and received a thunderous ovation. It was plainly time for
Anna to concentrate solely on her own creative talents. Her last performances
with Martha Graham were in late 1937 on the program featuring *American Lyric.*

There is little doubt that the parting of the ways was not overly amicable
and left wounds. In the mid-1960s, when *Primitive Mysteries* was restaged for a
memorial performance in honor of its composer Louis Horst, Anna was the only
available dancer from the original cast who was not invited to participate in the
reconstruction work. This must have saddened her, for there was certainly no
professional whom she regarded with greater love and respect than Horst and his
fondness for her had been no less profound. She inevitably gives credit to Horst as
having been her most important teacher, minimizing the influence of Martha Graham on her work. Yet on one occasion in the 1940s, when asked what it was like
working with Graham during all of those years, she revealed her ambivalence by
responding that "It was like being inspired seven days a week." (In 1988 Anna and
Martha were able to greet each other warmly backstage at the "Celebration of
Sixty Years of Graham Technique" in New York, and that afternoon Anna was
pleased by an invitation to be a guest teacher at the Graham School.)

A photograph of Anna by William Stone appeared on the cover of the
March 1938 issue of *Dance Observer,* her second cover for that influential magazine, which had been conceived of and was nurtured by Louis Horst. In the photograph she seems painfully thin; her left hand casts a mysterious shadow on her
costume and her face glows with a luminous beauty.

The same year, Anna created the dances for the Lenin pageant at Madison
Square Garden. Another interesting assignment in 1938 was the "Filibuster Bal-
let" for the musical revue *The Bourbons Got the Blues,* which included Duke
Ellington in the cast. According to the May 16 *Time* magazine:

> The review [sic] got its chief bounce from a satiric ballet summarizing the Senate fili-
> buster against the Anti-Lynching Bill. Blaring out, through a loudspeaker, verbatim
> excerpts from the speeches of Senators Ellender and Bilbo, prancing about in a good
> deal of pantomimic horseplay, *Filibuster* slid now and then into a fancy-tickling mo-
> ment, as when as whole stageful of senators suddenly started playing with toys.

For Alex as well 1938 was an interesting year. Elia Kazan, who met Alex through Anna, had been invited to direct a film, *People of the Cumberland,* a documentary based on the restoration of economic security to the Tennessee mountain region. Kazan asked Alex to compose the score. The success of this collaboration led to several others and eventually to a distinguished career for Alex as a film composer. Nearly fifty years later, Alex spoke about his work as a composer for Anna and how it affected his later career:

> She was very instrumental in my putting notes down on paper. I really have to give her a lot of credit for where I am today. I had the opportunity — the privilege of working with her and it was invaluable to me later when I was writing film scores. The dancer does the dance first. The film is shot first. You have to tailor the music to the dance as music is tailored to a film. This skill I first learned working with Anna. Through her I met people connected with the theater and this led to my work in films.

One of Anna's most important and memorable solos was created as the decade drew to a close. *The Exile,* her poignant reaction to the terrifying situation in Nazi Germany, was performed to a poem written for her by Sol Funaroff and set to music by Alex. The baritone, Arno Tanney, with whom Anna frequently worked, sang and spoke the piece. On occasion Anna chose instead to speak the words while Alex played and Tanney sang. By dividing the work into two sections, "I had a garden . . . " and "The beast is in the garden . . . ," she first depicted the sweetness of Jewish life in pre-Nazi Europe and then, with searing intensity, the arrival of the beast in the garden, the beast of Nazism. A photograph of Anna in the second section, taken by Barbara Morgan, gives us some indication of her intensity as a performer.

In tracing Anna's artistic development through this era, John Martin continued to applaud her as a young artist "from whom brilliant things are yet to come." Interestingly, he identified her firmly and clearly as a practitioner in the romantic tradition: "Though her interest was and is centered in the immediate present . . . her stand automatically aligns her with an ancient and honorable tradition, romanticism, distinguished by a release of the imagination to soar into any field that invited, and by a freeing of the passions to re-experience or enjoy synthetically high moments of feeling or excitement."

During the height of the Depression, President Roosevelt had courted financially stricken artists when their support was needed for his policies. To reciprocate, he threw them a bone in the form of arts projects administered by the Works Projects Administration (W.P.A.). Artists who qualified to work on special projects were paid only a trifle more than they would have received in relief checks had they applied. But with the dignity of support from the government, they created magnificent murals, photographs, novels, plays, and poems, some of which are today regarded as classic Americana, documenting the era as no previous era in American history had ever before been chronicled. It led to an unprecedented burst of creativity and provided employment for writers such as Saul Bellow, Ralph Ellison, and Richard Wright and to painters the caliber of Willem de Kooning, Arshile Gorky, and William Gropper.

When the W.P.A.'s Federal Theatre Project finally got around to establishing a Dance Project in 1936, Anna was earning a living, though barely, through her teaching, performing, and some modeling work. As long as she and Alex could scrape together enough to live on, they did not want or need welfare. The W.P.A. was a formal organization with a hierarchy; there were rules to be followed and red tape to wade through. That was enough to keep her away. It was also well known that the Dance Project was beset by problems, many of them precipitated by the political appointment of an ill-qualified director, whose myopic vision included the proposal of a uniform modern dance technique that everyone would use. Needless to say, this unique idea neither increased his popularity nor was it given much attention. A great cry arose, however, when after many months of promises and delays only a few concerts were presented and red tape tied up the others.

Helen Tamiris, a strong and verbally articulate fighter for political causes, was a leader in the battle to make the Dance Project a workable enterprise and later became one of its mainstay choreographers. This activism on Tamiris' part led people to identify her along with Anna as the two outstanding figures of the radical-dance era.

In 1938 George Kondolf, director of the Federal Theatre Project in New York, approved the idea of presenting a revue designed to put as many unemployed professional singers, actors, and dancers to work as possible. Anna was invited to do the choreography for this project, *Sing for Your Supper,* and accepted. By regulation, her cast had to be chosen from those who were bona fide relief recipients.

The whole production was troubled from the start: it was too big, tried to accomplish too much, and lacked a strong director. As month after month of rehearsal went by, many of the performers lost patience with the delays. When other opportunities came along they left the show, which then had to be rewritten to accommodate new talent. This caused further delays. *Supper* became an object of ridicule in theater circles as it limped along toward completion in the middle of the second year of rehearsals.

Although Anna choreographed several numbers for the show, by the time it was trimmed down to a manageable size only one of her numbers, *The Last Waltz* — built on the idea of a last waltz in Vienna before the Nazis took over — survived to opening night. There were other dances in the production (termed "Dance Routines" in the program), staged by Ned McGurn, but Anna's group provided the class dance act. Surprisingly, according to the reviews, the whole evening came off like a well-produced if not sparkling variety show, with the focus of many of the numbers on social and political satire. In one typical skit, "Leaning On A Shovel," the characters were five not-too-productive W.P.A. workers and a "Dream Girl." The evening did include more pungent works but was hardly designed to incite a riot or even to change any strong opinions. That, however, was not the way everyone chose to perceive it.

In her 1940 book, *Arena*, Hallie Flanagan, the director of the Federal Theatre Project, details the politically motivated destruction of that organization. She relates how *Sing for Your Supper* was singled out for some of the most violent attacks in 1939 meetings of the House Committee to Investigate Un-American Activities. To discredit Roosevelt's New Deal policies, the chairman Martin Dies and other archconservatives claimed that the Theatre Project was dominated by Communists and that all of its output was tainted by party propaganda. One may well wonder why suspected Communists had been allowed to participate in W.P.A. projects in the first place, when they were so feared and hated by these people. It seems that Republican Party stalwarts, witnessing the full-scale adoption of the Democrat's New Deal projects, had insisted early on as a self-protective device that *nobody* could be excluded because of party affiliation. By 1939, with the New Deal losing impetus, they were ready to counterattack.

Sing for Your Supper was chosen as a prime target by the House Committee (none of whom had seen it) and was never allowed to finish its run. Every night the audience for this allegedly subversive review had stood to cheer the *Ballad of Uncle Sam* number which, later renamed *Ballad for Americans*, became the theme song of the 1940 Republican National Convention and a few years later one of the great patriotic songs of World War II.

Yet with the end of the Depression imminent and drums of war sounding in Europe, it was too much of a nuisance for Roosevelt to stand by those theater artists in the face of these loud and vicious accusations. By giving in to the Dies Committee's accusations, he not only discredited the work of thousands of individuals and cost them their jobs, but helped to set the stage for the witch hunts a decade later.

Anna was present neither for the long-awaited opening of *Sing for Your Supper* nor for the anguish caused by its closing. By this time she had immersed herself in another world completely.

7

MEXICO

She was like a drop of ink in a glass of water — that small drop will color all of the water in the glass. (Ignacio Aguirre, personal interview, May 15, 1981, Mexico City)

In March of 1939 Anna's friend and neighbor, Emilio Amero, brought the Mexican painter Carlos Mérida to see her work at the New School for Social Research in a performance sponsored by the Theater Arts Committee (TAC).* It was a benefit to raise money for the wavering W.P.A. Arts Project.

Mérida, who was in New York to study "the rhythms of the city," had a deep personal interest in dance and often incorporated dancing figures into his cubist paintings. He had been the first director of the Dance Department in Mexico City's Instituto Nacional de Bellas Artes (School of Fine Arts) and his teenage daughter was studying to be a professional dancer. The painter was deeply moved by Anna's work. Recognizing in her a social consciousness and a fighting spirit very close to his own and that of many of his fellow artists in Mexico, he wanted them to see her expression of that spirit in the language of dance. After the performance, he made his way backstage. Anna vividly remembered the encounter forty years later: "He asked if I would like to come to Mexico. I said of course I would. I thought he was kidding me. A short time later I received an invitation from the Department of Fine Arts of the Mexican government to perform with my group in Mexico City. He was serious!"

The letter explained that the offer could not include transportation to the Mexican border, but if the dancers could get themselves to that point, they would be transported the rest of the way and cared for during their stay. Several of the performances would be scheduled for the Palacio de Bellas Artes (Palace of Fine Arts), Mexico City's greatest performance center. No formal contract was offered, only a stipulation in the letter that the dancers would share in the profits.

---

* Political cabaret was an established tradition in Europe when it was first tried in New York in 1938. TAC was the first group in this country to take social satire out of the theater and endow it with the immediacy and informality of a cabaret setting. In its first year, participants in the popular Cabaret TAC reviews included theater celebrities such as Frances Farmer, Will Geer, Robert Benchley, Gypsy Rose Lee, and Marc Blitzstein.

At the time, the company included Alex, the singer Mordecai Baumann, and the stage manager, Allen Wayne, as well as Anna and nine other dancers. There was no money for such a luxury as travel — especially for that many people — in those late Depression years. Most of the dancers were still supported by their families; some by tiny incomes from part-time jobs. Anna had only rarely been able to pay honoraria; certainly no one either expected money from her or counted on it. Help was needed if the trip to Mexico were to become a reality. She took the letter of invitation to Rita Morgenthau at the Neighborhood Playhouse. Morgenthau, who had taken a special interest and pride in Anna's progress through the years, felt that it was too important an offer to pass up and agreed to pay for round-trip coach tickets to the border city of Laredo, Texas.

Early on a lovely April morning, bleary-eyed from the previous night's performance in Boston, the dancers pulled out of Grand Central Station laden with food for the four days and nights of their journey to Laredo. One of them, Rebecca (Rowen) Kramer, remembered, "Our mothers packed roast chicken and other food to eat on the train . . . food for several days. At 125th Street someone said, 'I'm famished, let's eat!' That was it for the chicken." When they finally reached the Mexican border, hungry and achingly tired, they were chagrined to find that arrangements for proper visitors' permits had yet to be made. Until the matter was cleared up, they had to stay in Laredo. This was decidedly not in the budget. After several nights of napping on each other's shoulders on the train, they had to crowd into a few rooms in a run-down hotel for one more sleepless night. When at last they received clearance from the immigration authorities, they were taken aboard a rickety Mexican train, on which they were at least properly fed and looked after. Things were beginning to look up. Now they were the official guests of the Mexican government.

When they arrived in Mexico City a few days later, exhausted and disheveled, they were met by a contingent of artists and dancers who greeted them with cheers and flowers. Spirits newly raised, they proceeded to their hotel. On the way they were startled to see large billboards announcing the upcoming performances of "Anna Sokolow, La Gran Bailarina Rusa." Some overzealous publicist had neglected to find out just what kind of dancing Anna was bringing to Mexico City. Her Russian name had led him to assume that it was Russian ballet. Mérida had apparently neglected to keep track of what was going on. The group was driven past the majestic Palacio de Bellas Artes and there, indeed, were lights spelling out "Anna Sokolow y Su Cuerpo de Ballet." Ticket sales at the Bellas Artes were going well, and for whatever reason the publicity was never altered to indicate that this was in fact a modern dance company and not a troupe of Russian ballerinas. The dancers were too busy trying to adjust to the food and the altitude to pay much attention. Jumping turned out to be easier in Mexico City; breathing was not. They gasped and choked and sometimes fainted, but eventually became accustomed to dancing in thin air.

From the moment they set foot on Mexican soil, a comedy of errors unfolded. "From the start there was no money for us and, to the best of our knowledge, no accounting to Anna either," Aza Bard McKenzie remembered. Neither Anna nor Alex had ever been expert in business matters; certainly they had never had any experience with negotiations involving foreign currency and thinking. They had naively assumed that their share of box-office profits would be at least adequate to cover their expenses. They were in for some surprises.

Originally, there had been some half-dozen performances scheduled over a period of four weeks. Only two weeks were to be in the Bellas Artes. Due to popular demand, the number of performances was increased to twelve, and then to twenty-three, and all of them presented in that grand theater. Many of the performances were free to students and to the general public as part of the government's program of cultural activities for workers. What was not made clear to the dancers was that they were expected to contribute gratis these additional performances.

Even more confusing was the lack of income from the paying audiences. It appears that a major part of the problem lay with the impresario, who was quite vexed to find that his Russian ballerina had turned out to be a barefoot social reformer. "As it happened, he was very right-wing," recalled McKenzie. "In fact, some people who were in a position to know referred to him as a Fascist. We had good reason to believe it was so when, after the first performance of the decidedly anti-Fascist *Esposizione Italiana,* he stood up and yelled loudly, 'Viva Benito Mussolini!' We were ruining his reputation! The whole thing was very funny. We laughed and cried a great deal in those days." At times the dancers vented their frustration by throwing things at the huge posters that announced their Bellas Artes appearances.

They should have targeted the impresario for some of their anger. When an interviewer asked Anna about the rumor that he had attempted to coerce her into removing *Slaughter of the Innocents* from the program, she laughed it off. Neither he nor anyone else could tell her what she could or could not put on the stage. His revenge appears to have been to withhold most of whatever funds she and the group were entitled to.

One night during the season, part of the electric sign in front of the Bellas Artes went out and the remaining portion read "Anna Sokolow y Su Cuerpo" (Anna Sokolow and her body). It might well have been a nasty bit of sabotage by the unwilling impresario. He would have been disappointed by the dancers' reactions; they found it wonderfully amusing.

Regardless of the financial stress they faced, the dancers were enjoying their overnight celebrity. Across the top of one article in Mexico City's popular press was a large publicity photograph of Anna with the handwritten words, "Greetings to the Mexican People," with her signature below. The feature article that followed offered nothing but praise:

> *Slaughter of the Innocents* is a living poem about the Spanish war and a marvelous
> expression of human pain and agony. All of the dances that were presented open-
> ing night are vibrant and deal with current problems. Yet they are full of beauty
> and grace. . . . This work is for those who do not need to take refuge in an evening
> of classical works or an exaggeration of folkloric values. Anna Sokolow is neither
> classical nor folkloric. She is, rather, the true expression of modern art. . . . It is an
> art of refinement and of the masses. An expression of our century which takes a
> noble and loyal stance, celebrating life itself.

The lengthy program that Anna presented at the Bellas Artes was a retro-
spective of the best of her work in recent years: *Dance Overture, Ballad in a Popular
Style, Case History No. — , Studies in Jazz Time, Slaughter of the Innocents, Strange
American Funeral, Suite from a War Poem, The Exile,* and *Façade — Exposizione
Italiana.* Fortunately, the Mexican sense of time was far different from our own.
Most North American audiences would have been overcome by a program of this
length and substance; the Mexicans loved it.

In a letter to John Martin, which was reprinted in the *New York Times,* the
writer Emmanuel Eisenberg, who was visiting Mexico City at the time, marveled
at the ease with which the work was accepted. "What was amazing," he wrote,
"was that nothing seemed amazing. Mexican audiences seemed to be able to accept this kind of dancing without effort and without adjustment."

The critics in Mexico City were quick to recognize Anna's uniqueness.
Lya Kostakowsky wrote in *El Popular* on April 27, 1939:

> If, in Mexico City, the majority of attempts at modern dance have failed, it is be-
> cause those dancers think, foolishly, that a revolutionary ballet consists of putting
> on the stage a group of people who must react in a revolutionary fashion — with
> red flags and chants. The artistic manifestation of something truly revolutionary
> should be, above all, art. All of this has been demonstrated to us very clearly in the
> art of Anna Sokolow . . . in the intelligence, sensibility, and in the unique beauty
> — the enormous tragic expression she possesses.

Anna and her dancers were pleased with the diversity of their audiences,
which included all classes of people from high-level professionals to barefoot
peasants. "Everyone from the peasants to the intellectual circle of the city took
to us," dancer Rebecca Kramer remembered. "The women, especially, were astounded. It's easy to understand when you think of their role in society at the
time. Suddenly there we were, big, strong, independent women, dancing barefoot! The members of the Taller Graphica were particularly drawn to us, partially,
I think, because they were social realists and recognized that we were too. They
wined and dined us." The group of radical graphic artists who comprised Le
Taller de Grafica Popular (People's Graphics Workshop) seemed always to be
there after performances, waiting with gifts of flowers and drawings and invitations to lunch. There were flirtations and pairings off.

The dancers, it seems, were in demand on a personal level. They found themselves much sought after by young and not-so-young gentlemen admirers. Anna received special attention from Francisco (Paco) Iturbi, a wealthy and cultured older gentleman, who apparently adored her from the outset. She was equally taken with him and a relationship developed that, at first, went unnoticed by Alex, who had himself become interested in a young Mexican lady. No one who was there at the time could quite remember which infatuation came first, nor does it matter. Their personal relationship, it seems, had run its full course by then. Alex was ready to develop an artistic identity independent of his association with Anna. She needed some time to explore other relationships. They had been together for seven years.

Before Mexico, some sides of Anna — both as a woman and as an artist — had gone largely unexplored. The relationship between Anna and Alex had been primarily one of loving comrades. His personality had provided a flinty stimulus to her creativity, and of course there was the marvelous music he had tailored to her needs — music for which he was by then well known in New York dance circles. They had been lovers and at the same time co-workers, on an equal footing artistically. Young and inexperienced when they met, they fell easily into certain roles and played out those roles for many years. Anna was the tough, streetwise fighter, the angry and impatient one. Alex, more sophisticated and controlled, was a natural charmer. Aza McKenzie, who knew them well during this period, remarked, "Anna was a street kid, Alex, a grace note." Charm notwithstanding, he was not above having a good laugh at her expense in front of their friends — and he was known to have a wandering eye. She doubtless knew more of this than she acknowledged openly. In public, at least, they were still a much admired and envied couple — a younger version of the Martha Graham–Louis Horst relationship in some ways.

But Mexico opened Anna's eyes to a different view of herself. Iturbi, with his elegant European manners, treated her as an alluring and desirable woman. She also discovered that artists are given a special kind of respect in Mexico. This was new to her and she wanted to experience more of it. When Sophie Maslow and her husband, Ben Blatt, came to Mexico to visit with Anna and Alex near the end of the Bellas Artes season, they were saddened to find that their longtime friends had to be seen separately.

Just as the Bellas Artes engagement neared completion, the unsettling news of the nonaggression pact signed between Russia and Fascist Germany (up to that point sworn enemies) hit the headlines, and in a burst of patriotic indignation Alex decided to return immediately to the United States. Most of Anna's dancers — tired, broke, and homesick — followed quickly on his heels, anxious to resume their lives in the States. (They had so little money among them on the return trip that, as they approached New York, they rejoiced when one found a stray penny in her purse. It was used to buy a water cup so that they could brush their teeth properly.) Anna chose to stay behind; the separation from Alex was complete.

The affair with Iturbi did not last long. It seemed that he had some rather old-fashioned ideas, with which Anna did not agree. He wished to marry, and promised her a large allowance plus her own theaters in Mexico City and New York. He would see her weekly, or live with her at his convenience, a not unheard of marriage arrangement among the wealthy at the time. Anna would of course be free to continue to dance and choreograph; it was, after all, Anna the dancer with whom he was infatuated. She, on the other hand, was interested in a relationship of equals (such as she was used to with Alex) and would consider nothing less. The proposed arrangement smacked of the sexism that she and others of her generation had learned to despise. Iturbi told her she was a fool for turning him down. She responded, "If I did it, it wouldn't be me any more."

Ignacio (Nacho) Aguirre was waiting in the wings for Anna when the Iturbi affair came to an end. Handsome and easygoing, Aguirre was a gifted artist with a colorful past. In his early teens he had fought against Pancho Villa as one of the youngest members of the famous Venustiano Carranza troops. Later, after studying art, he worked as an assistant to David Siqueiros in the creation of one of the great muralist's major works. So captivating a figure was Nacho that years later Marlon Brando, who met Nacho through Elia Kazan shortly before filming started, may well have used him as a model for his characterization of the protagonist in the film *Viva Zapata*.

A few weeks after the close of the season at the Palace of Fine Arts, Anna was invited by the secretary of public education, Gonzalo Vasquez Vela, to remain in Mexico City to teach and work toward the foundation of a government-sponsored Mexican modern dance company. The potential was so enormous that she could not resist. And she was in love. She agreed to an eight-month commitment to work with young dancers at the Casa del Artista. Fifteen were chosen at an open audition. Most of them were graduates of the government's Fine Arts School of the Dance and many were teenagers.

A newspaper announcement stated:

> Miss Sokolow will not attempt to impose a particular, predetermined foreign style on our dancers, but rather will try to develop a means by which they can, themselves, creatively solve the problems of evolving an indigenous Mexican dance form. From this, it is hoped, a style will develop that will take full advantage of the folkloric fountains, which are of incomparable richness and value.

What actually happened is that Anna went to work teaching her modified version of Graham technique along with some basic ballet. The intensity with which she taught and the imagery she used transformed these techniques into something uniquely hers. Many of the dancers had studied ballet with Nellie Campobello, the principal teacher at the Bellas Artes school. Some had also worked with Hypolite Zybin, who had been with the Ballet Russe de Monte Carlo before settling in Mexico City. Both were solid teachers and had provided a good foundation for the young women. They had learned to work hard and the preparation served them well; Anna was, as always, a hard and demanding taskmaster.

The salary she received was minimal and the work difficult, but she felt quite content, for something was happening to her in this new country that affected her very deeply. Many years later, she remembered this period:

> I was introduced to all the great artists — Rivera, Orozco, Siqueiros — and they accepted me as a fellow artist and were interested in my work. Somehow, what they felt was important to put in painting related very much to what I was doing in dance. And the experience of living in Mexico and coming to understand a totally different kind of life. . . . I was fascinated to watch simple Indian people approach the great murals in the Bellas Artes theater. They took off their hats and looked at the work with the same respect they would have if they were in a church. They have a tradition of respecting art and whoever is involved in art is respected there. For the first time in my life I knew what it felt like to be an artist.

Less pleasing was the fact that she had to learn to contend with a considerably different sense of time from the one she was accustomed to. She has always prided herself on the fact that she was rarely a moment late for an appointment or a rehearsal. She had to learn to wait and be patient about it, and this was not easy for her. But she was inspired by the exuberance and dedication of her new collaborators. It was such a joy to be with them; they felt the same about her. She learned to put up with the problems inherent in dealing with people whose temperament was sometimes diametrically opposed to her own. Her spirit was fed by the quality of their work and by their appreciation of her artistic accomplishment.

As the months went by a gradual softening in her creative work occurred, a lyricism she had scarcely taken time to explore before. Perhaps it was the slower pace of the country, the insistence of her new friends that she allow time for relaxation and pleasure in her schedule. The unqualified love of Nacho Aguirre, perhaps the first of that kind of love she had ever known, must have made a difference, too. He accepted her, as she was, on every level. A modest but confident man, neither demanding of her nor jealous of her friends or her career, he made her feel beautiful and desirable in a way that she had never quite known before. He liked to compare her to the central dancing figure in Botticelli's *Primavera*; to him she was the equal of that matchless beauty of Renaissance Florence. Fifty years later, he still had a photograph of Anna in his living room, adjacent to a print of the painting, with auburn-tressed Simonetta Vespucci in her diaphanous white dress.

In the Sokolow tradition, the classes at the Casa del Artista were grueling; sometimes, during intense rehearsal periods, they lasted from late afternoon until well into the evening. More than one pair of watchful parental eyes scrutinized her every move at rehearsals. With the exception of Carlos Mérida's daughter, Ana, who had been accepted into the group, most of the girls were from conservative middle-class Catholic families. It was not that the parents did not trust Anna; she was, in fact, very well liked. It was the whole business of modern dance, so different from ballet and folk dancing, that worried them more than a little. But their daughters were devoted to the North American *maestra* and the parents soon came to trust and respect her. A feature article in one of the large Mexico City newspapers referred to the diligent workers as "Las Sokolovas," and the name stuck. To this day, some of them still proudly say, "I am a Sokolova" meaning, "I am one of the original ones."

Anna learned Spanish rapidly, but her primary means of communication with her Mexican dancers in the early months was through the tone of her voice, through her eyes and, of course, through her body. Nacho was frequently there to interpret. In 1981 several Sokolovas remembered:

> At first we could only understand a few words. We followed what she did — watched her body and gestures. Then a few more words. Finally, we understood. She spoke of "light" and "force." She was telling us that there is a light here [she points to the area of the chest above the sternum] that lights the whole face. You must never hold your head in such a way to cut off that light. Each time you must try to put more energy into that light. It comes from deep inside. The arms are a continuation of this energy. She told us that you have to feel your whole body, all of your energy, your blood, flow through your pores, through your fingers, through space, and project into the atmosphere, filling it with your way of being, with your personality. These concepts were very novel for us. We were a little frightened but we had strong personalities and were dying to be dancers. It was the most important thing in our lives at that time. Anna found a group that was well prepared for her and one with fire inside.

Frequently, Anna's new artist friends from the Taller Grafica would come to watch classes, bringing others with them. In this way she met the writers José Bergamin and Constancia de la Mora, who were to become good friends. Other visitors to the classes included the composers Silvestre Revueltas and Carlos Chavez. Within a year she was involved in artistic collaborations with Bergamin, Chávez, and Revueltas.

As Anna prepared her group of young professionals for performances in the summer of 1939, Mexico City bristled with a wealth of artistic activity. The great painters and muralists Rivera, Orozco, and Siqueiros adorned canvases and murals with their brilliant colors and forms. The composers Chávez, Revueltas, and Blas Galindo strove to create a Mexican sound in contemporary music, and writers and filmmakers worked in collaboration to create a twentieth-century culture out of the ashes of centuries of colonialism and despotic leadership.

And there was an infusion of new energy. Many Spanish artists, writers, and composers, who had spoken out openly against Franco and knew their lives were endangered when the Loyalist cause was lost, fled to political asylum in Mexico. It was Spain's loss and Mexico's gain, for those gifted expatriates included José Bergamin and the composer Rodolfo Halffter. (Bergamin had been a close friend of the playwright and poet Federico Garcia Lorca, who was executed by the Spanish Civil Guard when Franco came to power.)

A few years earlier, in Spain, Bergamin and Halffter had collaborated on the creation of a ballet, *Don Lindo de Almería*, inspired by scenes of Andalusian life. Pablo Picasso agreed to do the sets and Joan Miró expressed interest in doing costumes for the work, but because of the political turmoil in Spain it was never staged. The scenario treated Andalusian life without sentiment or the obligatory exaggeration of ethnic charm so prevalent in ballet scenarios at the time. The librettist later explained, in fact, that "the scenes are traced with a decided anti-color, anti-local-customs approach." Years earlier, Lorca had read the scenario and praised it highly. On his recommendation, Bergamin chose Halffter as composer, rather than Manuel de Falla as he had originally intended. In a letter to Bergamin, Lorca wrote that "[you need] music for the eyes with a few beats of the kettledrum that will vaguely resound in the innards."

Halffter heard about Anna's work and after watching several of her classes told her about his dream of producing *Don Lindo* in Mexico. When he found that she knew little of Spanish and flamenco dancing, he was delighted. The collaborators had envisioned an approach untainted by preconceptions about Spanish art, music, or dance. Anna agreed enthusiastically to do the choreography. The gifted artist Antonio Ruiz was enlisted for scenery and costumes.

The major obstacle facing the production was lack of an available and affordable theater, what with the city's bursting theatrical activity. Helping Anna and her expatriate friends find a stage for their production of *Don Lindo de Almería* became something of a cause in the artistic community. Finally, Antonio Palacios, director of the Spanish Lyric Art Company, agreed to allow the work to be staged at the Teatro Fabregas on the evening of January 9, 1940, between two of his zarzuela performances. It was a resounding success, with a slightly inebriated Silvestre Revueltas raucously leading the enthusiastic, cheering audience. One reviewer wrote that, "such an effort should not be lost among the multitude of good intentions that a city such as Mexico knows almost daily. With this stupendous seed a magnificent fruit can be attained, but it must be planted and cared for with strict attention."

Anna's efforts as a teacher also did not go unnoticed. In October, the dancers were presented in a lecture-demonstration and received high praise from the music critic Adolfo Salazar:

> In a room of the Palace of Fine Arts a few days ago, Anna Sokolow, the dancer and dance teacher, gave a performance by a group of her disciples who are working with her toward the development of a ballet group. . . . From basic techniques they developed the materials into something more modern than academic in quality. The dances are structured in such a way that a beautiful effect is produced . . . the talented dancers have the discipline, the disposition, and the enthusiasm . . . the girls have precision and great facility. The boys, an agility and incredible elasticity.

Anna's contract with the Ministry of Public Education expired in January and, after an absence of over nine months, she returned to the United States, having promised to return to Mexico for at least one more season. Before leaving, she created two works for her newly christened Ballet Bellas Artes (Fine Arts Ballet): *Los Pies de Pluma* (Feathered Feet), a suite of pre-classic dances, and *Entre Sombres Anda el Fuego* (The Fire Walks Between Shadows), a technique demonstration performed to the music of Blas Galindo.

In March of 1940, a group of close associates felt confident enough in the work Sokolow had left behind to present the formal debut of the Ballet Bellas Artes at the Palace of Fine Arts. The program, which was performed to live music, included a repeat of *Don Lindo* and the two new dances. The program notes contain a dedication to Anna Sokolow for her contributions to the development of modern dance in Mexico, the first formal acknowledgment of this work. Many more were to come.

The short season was highly successful, so successful in fact that it led to the formation of a new group, which included not only dancers but also artists and musicians. The plan was to embrace all of the arts, with dance as the primary focus. The artistic collaborators on the project were Anna, Halffter, and Bergamin, with the painters Manuel Lozano and Antonio Ruiz. Help was sought from the socialite Adela Fomoso de Obregon Santacilia and her husband, Carlos, a successful architect. In addition to having wealth and connections, they were known for their sincere interest in developing new vistas in the arts. The Santacilias agreed to be sponsors.

The name chosen for the new group, La Paloma Azul (The Blue Dove), is the title of a popular traditional Mexican folk song and was also the name of the *cantina* where the artists involved in the project liked to meet. It was a good choice: Paloma Azul was a title that people in Mexico City knew and loved. A motto was chosen to appear on all programs and advertisements with words from a poem by Lope de Vega: *Las Artes Hice Magicas Volando* (loose translation: The Arts Make Magic Wings). The dancers chosen for Paloma Azul were Raquel Gutiérrez Lejarza, Carmen Gutiérrez Lejarza, Ana Maria Mérida, Isabel Gutiérrez Lejarza, Alicia Ceballos, Delia Ruiz, Josefina Luna, Alicia Reyna, Rosa Reyna, Alba Estela Garfias, Martha Bracho, Emma Ruiz, Aurora Aristi, Delia Gonzalez, Antonio Cordova, Alejandro Martinez, Mario Camberos, Ramon Rivero, Augusto Fernandez, and Gustavo Salas.

In the three months between Anna's return to Mexico in the summer of 1940 and the first performance of Paloma Azul in September, she created a total of four new works for the company. The surreal *Lluvia de Toros*, based on the drawings of Goya, was subtitled "Scenes of caprice, disaster and madness." It is remembered as having a genuinely bizarre quality, odd both for its imagery and sequencing. It certainly was a departure for Anna, but one that she made apparently without much thought or fanfare. The work, originally titled *Balcon de España o Enterrar y Callar y Lluvia de Toros* (Spanish Balcony or To Bury and to Keep Silence and Rain of Bulls) was described by Antonio Luna Arroyo in his biography of his wife, the dancer Ana Mérida:

> Landscapes of Goya evoke the fantasy: an enormous gorge and a balcony are seen. Two ladies from Madrid appear, then two black bulls. Enter a military man, a friar, and a magistrate. They are carrying large umbrellas, which they use to defend themselves against the bulls, as if the latter were wind and rain. They are able to escape. The ladies from Madrid leave. Three figures in grotesque masks enter. They are the carnivorous vulture, the burro, and the manly goat, all in the manner of Goya. They dance and act out scenes from Goya etchings.

La Madrugada del Panadero (The Dawn of the Baker), another collaboration between Bergamin and Halffter, was similar in character to *Don Lindo*. *El Renacuajo Paseador* (The Wandering Tadpole), set to music by Revueltas, was adapted from a popular children's story. Carlos Mérida designed highly imaginative costumes, settings, and masks for this production. Sadly, Revueltas was destined never to see the final results of the collaboration; he died of a lung infection on the very evening that the work was premiered, October 5, 1940. The dancers observed several minutes of silence backstage that night upon learning of the death of this man who had so wholeheartedly supported their endeavors.

The most ambitious undertaking of the season was a staging of Carlos Chávez' 1933 *Sinfonia de Antigona* (Antigone Symphony), with Anna dancing the lead. Carlos Santacilia designed costumes and a majestic set for the work and the composer conducted the National Symphony. The critic Carlos Gonzalez Pena wrote, "The stately beauty of Chavez' music and the choreography of Anna Sokolow left a deep impression of grandeur. It is very simple, without rigidity, noble, without opulence, eloquent, and full of emotion. It is an accomplishment of uncommon mastery." The piece was shown only a few times and little is known about it, but it is interesting to note that *Antigona* anticipated Martha Graham's characterizations of tragic Greek heroines by several years.

The entire season received the highest praise from Mexico City's critics. Reviewers in *El Nacional, El Universal Grafico, Redondel,* and *Jueves de Excelsior* wrote that Anna Sokolow and La Paloma Azul deserved the fine ovations they had received, that high expectations had been exceeded, and that "this fine company must not be allowed to fall apart and disappear into thin air." It was a brief but triumphant season.

Despite such auspicious beginnings, the group did not continue beyond its first venture. Problems had developed between some of the painters, which made it impossible for them to continue to work together. Also around this time Adela Santacilia decided to direct her resources and energy toward the foundation of a university for women in Mexico City, and she and her husband withdrew their patronage. La Paloma Azul was disbanded when it was clear that the underpinnings had slipped away.

Anna was faced with an important decision. She was torn between her love for Nacho and the need to stay connected to the New York dance world. It was clear that in order to sustain a group in Mexico she would have to become a full-time teacher and choreographer there. This she was unwilling to do, although she was sorely tempted. She had come to love Mexico but her roots were in New York, and it was that city she depended on for the renewal of her creative spirit. Reluctantly, she decided that she could spend only a part of each year in Mexico City. Nacho actually encouraged Anna to stick to that decision when she wavered a few times. He feared that her creative energies would be dissipated, not only by the necessity of teaching but by government red tape as well. He knew that she should be concentrating primarily on her creative work. So it was that Anna's nomadic life began.

Nacho made one attempt, in 1944, to spend some time with Anna in New York. Her friends were immediately taken with his warmth, honesty, and good nature, and with his talent as an artist. Sarah, however, disapproved. She wondered why her beautiful daughter had given up her fine musician in Mexico and brought home a swarthy foreigner whose English was no better than her own; but she was too busy to spend much time troubling herself about it. She had buried her second husband several years earlier and was once again earning her own living, actively involved in Workman's Circle activities, and dating regularly. Nacho eventually won Sarah over as he had everyone else. He was not charmed by New York, however, and it became clear that if Anna wanted to be with him, it would have to be during her visits to Mexico City. Though very much in love, they found it necessary to continue to endure long periods of separation.

8

FINDING A FULLER EXPRESSION

"Why?" Anna asked José Bergamin, pointing toward a piously rendered painting of a saint hanging on the wall of his home in Mexico City. "Why not?" replied Bergamin. (Anna Sokolow, personal interview, November 10, 1979, New York)

For the next several years, whenever Anna would visit Mexico to choreograph and teach, Las Sokolovas worked with her in any space they could rent or borrow. It was not easy. As the artistic and national politics shifted, so did the amount of official support she received on her visits. Only occasionally were they offered the luxury of the fine studios at the Bellas Artes. One time, when the winds were blowing in the wrong direction, Nacho was asked by the Bellas Artes officials to financially guarantee a performance Anna was to present with her Mexican group in the grand theater. He happily agreed to do so, knowing full well that he could never afford to cover the expenses if money problems arose. He expected the concert to pay for itself and it did. Anna gave little attention to such matters. Even in those lean years, there was usually enough money to get her to Mexico and back home again, and that was all that concerned her. When she was with Nacho she required very little.

The professional situation in Mexico was further complicated by the creation of a rival company. A few months after the last performances of La Paloma Azul in 1940, Waldeen Falkenstein — an American expatriate known professionally by her first name only — made contact with many of the same dancers and artists who had come together to work with Anna. She decided to settle in Mexico and quickly made a fine name for herself with a few outstanding choreographic works, most notably *La Coronela* (The Colonel's Wife). Now Anna had competition both for dancing talent and resources from a full-time resident of the country. The Sokolovas, those who remained loyal to Anna, now had rivals. Waldeen's followers came to be known as "Waldeenas," a designation made partially in jest, and partially in earnestness; they were the other team.

Over the next several years, the lines were clearly drawn, and not merely by personality. Waldeen clearly favored Mexican subject matter in her works; Anna chose a more universal approach, believing that Mexico would, in time, take its place as an international dance center. She disdainfully described the work of some of Waldeen's followers as the "Welcome-to-sunny-Mexico" approach. Their popularity, however, could not be denied.

The Sokolovas continued to perform together on an irregular basis and in a variety of circumstances. In 1944 Anna created a dance version of the opera *Carmen* for the opening of an elegant nightclub, the Sans Souci. Nacho designed the costumes. A year later, she choreographed and Sokolovas danced in the film *The Court of the Pharoah*, directed by Julio Bracho and starring the well-known actress Mapy Cortes. The film as a whole did not fare well with the critics, but Anna's work on this, her only major commercial film, was highly praised. The next season she and her dancers presented a major concert at the Bellas Artes. The highlight of the evening was the premiere of her later famous solo *Kaddish*, to the music of Ravel. A few years later, Anna was the choreographer for the 1948–49 Bellas Artes opera season, and again many of the Sokolovas were there in the productions.

As they matured, many of the young women built independent careers for themselves as teachers and choreographers. Several went on to become important figures in the field, not only in Mexico City but throughout the country. In later years, whenever Anna was invited to choreograph in Mexico, she continued to invite these dancers to perform for her and they made certain that they would be available as often as possible.

However frequently they performed in those difficult but productive years, they never again used the name La Paloma Azul. But like Las Sokolovas, the name was associated with many of their undertakings by those who spoke or wrote of them. They had become a part of Mexican dance history. Sokolovas figured in the creation of two of Anna's masterworks: *Lyric Suite* (1953) and the large-group version of *Dreams* (1961), both of which were given their first professional performances in Mexico. Anna's influence on the dancing and artistic works of that generation of performers and choreographers and that of succeeding generations is undisputed. Ana Mérida, who chose to join forces with Waldeen, later said, "I knew when I did this that I gave up working with a genius of twentieth-century dance."

More significant, perhaps, than her accomplishment of training a generation of dancers in a new idiom, is the fact the La Paloma Azul and the modest groups that had preceded it in 1940 showed the Mexican people that they had the talent and the wherewithal to create first-rate indigenous modern dance. A prototype had been established, one of very high quality.

Nacho Aguirre described it this way in 1981:

> Her collaboration with important writers, painters and musicians set an important precedent which was to be followed almost immediately by other artists in the dance profession. Her "all or nothing" teaching style set a model which is reflected in the way dance is taught in Mexico today. She was like a drop of ink in a glass of water. That small drop will color all of the water in the glass.

Today, when Anna makes one of her frequent trips to Mexico City to work or to visit with friends, she receives a warm welcome from the press, and "La Gran Bailarina Rusa" of 1939 is now referred to as "La Fundadora de la Danza Moderna de Mexico" (the founder of Mexican modern dance).

Time would prove that the continuing contact with Mexico was invaluable to Anna's growth as an artist. Yet in the 1940s, whenever she returned to the States, the opposite seemed true. The New York critics found both the old and the new works to be uneven and they let her know it. This letdown seems to have happened because she had interrupted a pattern of many years. Her creative energy, with its roots in the life-flow of New York, had most often come from the passionate involvement, which she shared with her contemporaries, in the searing experiences of living through the Depression. She was also keenly and painfully aware of the rise of Fascism in Germany and Italy. Her language of movement and her reasons for making dances grew out of the emotional energy that was generated all around her.

Mexico had certainly opened new doors and had allowed her to explore a softer, more lyrical approach to movement. Just as she began these explorations, the United States was embarking on a period of sweeping change. Europe was on fire and a new patriotism was in the air; war was coming. Lyrical, lighter works, some based on folk themes such as those she had created in Mexico, seemed like frivolities when shown in a New York now focused on the shattering developments in Europe.

The Wandering Tadpole, with its cheerful Revueltas score and stunning Carlos Mérida sets, did not amuse or delight audiences in New York as it had in Mexico. *Vision Fantastica* (*Lluvia de Toros* in Mexico), based on Goya etchings, although likewise a success there, proved a near disaster when transplanted. The light and pleasant *Songs for Children* (Lorca poetry set to music by Revueltas) was well received, but hardly regarded as a major work. There is no question that the absence of the full symphony orchestra and the majestic stage of the Bellas Artes for which these works were created made a considerable difference.

Curiously, even though Anna continued to perform some solo works from her old repertoire, these poignant cries against war that had been among her finest works of the previous decade and that should have been especially relevant to the present were regarded by some as outworn. Perhaps her dancing, reinforced by ballet classes in the past several years, was beginning to change, too, to become softer. To her New York critics, the choreography lacked the focused passion and power of her pre-Mexican period. *Dance Observer* critic Lois Balcom wrote in January 1942: "While attaining a more vivid lyricism than the earlier group works, the work still seems reminiscent of a stage which modern dance once passed through but has now for the most part emerged from — the stage of fixed gaze and unrelieved persuasive movement when tenseness in body pattern was made to serve for high emotional tension in the dancers themselves."

Another problem stemmed from the fact that most of the dancers in the old group were gone, some to new careers and some to the business of raising a family. A few continued to work with Anna on and off during the next few years. For a while there was a trio consisting of Clara Nezin, Aza Cefkin, and Frances Sunstein. She just was not in any one place long enough to shape a sizable group to the standards she had set during the 1930s.

Another *Dance Observer* critic, Mary O'Donnell, described a Sokolow performance at the "Y," to which a throng of well-wishers had come with high-spirited anticipation. The first half of the program consisted of familiar solos: *Ballad in a Popular Style, Case History No. — , Slaughter of the Innocents,* and *The Exile.* O'Donnell wrote that "Even in these seasoned dances there was a lack of the dynamic impact of execution that usually characterizes Miss Sokolow's performance. [Her] new work, *Songs for Children,* . . . was very charming and pleasant to watch. This is scarcely adequate praise for a mature artist after an absence of many months from the concert stage."

A harsher review came from Walter Terry in the *Herald-Tribune*, following a concert in 1941 at the Mansfield Theater. Allowing that she was, in his opinion, "destined to become an important figure in the American dance," he found her group choreography still to be in the formative stages. Her newer pieces from Mexico were "muddled — designs were not clear and movements seemed to have little bearing on the theme at hand." Curiously, a few weeks later, the same critic wrote, "Anna Sokolow . . . is the only young dancer to emerge from the modern dance [of the thirties] with a personal style, an ability to stand on her own and with recognizable promise in her work."

In December 1943, Edwin Denby tried to analyze what was going wrong in Anna's concert work by comparing a recent performance to others he had seen in the late 1930s:

> Miss Sokolow's present adult subjective fervor no longer suits the girlish simplicity of her former compositions; the more intense she becomes the more she hides their real character. And so the old numbers dealing with such themes as slum childhood, juvenile delinquency or Loyalist Madrid — numbers that once seemed natural as adolescent reflections — now, seen in an adult atmosphere, look artificial and false to their terrible themes.

The *Christian Science Monitor's* Margaret Lloyd, an admirer of Anna's work since the late 1930s, was later able to see this time for what it was: a period of transition. She wrote in *The Borzoi Book of Modern Dance:*

> Apart from the Mexican products, in which she had not yet found herself, this was a changing Anna. The social comment was sweeter. She did not look so fighting mad about it. The acerb harangues of *Mill Doors, Speaker, Inquisition* were far in the past. . . . There was a new spirit in her costumes (still by Rose Bank), a new light-

ness of mood and manner in her dancing (lifted by ballet techniques), a new outlook, an expanded internationalism. . . . But the best was yet to be.

The disappointing concerts of the early 1940s were hard for Anna to live down. A new group of artists doing work that was perceived as more timely basked in the limelight now. Although her work began to glow again by 1946, it took several more years for her to reestablish herself as a force in the New York modern dance scene. In his 1946 book, *The Dance*, John Martin does not even mention her name, a glaring omission considering the enthusiastic predictions about her career that he had penned a decade earlier in his *America Dancing*.

Even during this difficult time, several of her shorter works won high praise, notably *Lament for the Death of a Bullfighter*, an excerpt from *Homage to García Lorca* (which predated Doris Humphrey's *Lament for Ignacio Sánchez Mejías* by several years), and *Mama Beautiful*. In her *Lament*, to stirring music by Revueltas, Anna danced in turn the Spanish Lady, the bullfighter hero, and then a figure responding to Lorca's tragic death. The skirt of her somber black dress, when held open, became a blood-red cape, which she manipulated with matador-like concentration. It was then, and remains today, a strong, gripping work. *Lament* was to become one of Anna's signature solos. A short film, *Bullfight*, with similar material, was made by Shirley Clarke in 1957; it is the only record we have of Anna as a performer.

Mama Beautiful was danced to music by Alex North, while a poem written for Anna by Mike Quinn was read aloud. It was a brief reprise of her social-commentary works, described as "a haunting song of the tenements, showing through a child's responses the brave and lovely mother who tries to make her see butterflies where cockroaches are, and brownies in place of rats."

As her first decade-and-a-half as a dancer/choreographer drew to a close, in spite of the setbacks of the early 1940s, Anna could look back on a period of extraordinary accomplishment. She had been recognized as a first-rate dancer and her choreography had brought her to the forefront of her generation. Moreover, she had tackled one of the hardest jobs an artist can take on — use of her medium to express a need for change in society — and she had done so without losing sight of the art form itself in pursuing that goal.

She was one of the few who had fulfilled another of John Martin's predictions, when he wrote in 1934, "The Workers Dance League is aiming to produce propaganda under the guise of art, but it seems very likely that one of these days it will find that it has produced art under the guise of propaganda."

After World War II, it was necessary for artists in all fields to find more personal modes of expression. The social consciousness of the 1930s had been replaced by the patriotic Americana that had blossomed forth to support the war effort. Now neither was in vogue. The economy was in an upward spiral and most members of contemporary society were looking forward to a well-earned period of peace and prosperity.

Anna was well into a period of deep personal exploration that would soon place her work securely at the heart of its time. The late 1940s were important years of growth for her in many ways. Her movement range broadened, her dances increasingly opened out into space, her world-view was expanding, and introspection had begun to play a greater role in her work.

She was also a teacher of established reputation, working in a number of studios around the city. One of her more interesting affiliations was with Wilson Williams, who invited her to teach ballet and modern dance to his Negro Dance Company in their Carnegie Hall studio. She sometimes also performed for him as a guest artist.

In the progressive New York world of the 1930s, religion had come to be regarded in Marxist circles as the "opiate of the masses." Anna was quite proud of her Jewish background, but it was more a pride in a cultural heritage than religious awe. In *The Exile* (1939), she had made her first and only significant reference to Jewish roots. That those roots could provide a source of continuing inspiration had not yet occurred to her. Oddly enough, it was in Mexico that she gained new insights that would help her to integrate her religious background into her art. She often spoke in later years of an incident in the mid-1940s that she regarded as a turning point in her artistic life. During dinner with José Bergamin in his home in Mexico City, she noticed a piously rendered painting of a saint such as only a practicing Catholic would display. She gestured toward it and asked, "Why?" His simple reply was, "Why not?" Such moments could make a deep and lasting impression on Anna.

Within a year she choreographed *Mexican Retablo*. The work, which was divided into two scenes, is described here by Margaret Lloyd:

> "Our Lady" of the paisano, as depicted in native paintings, stands on her pedestal with fixed outward arms, moving with stiff gestures like an animated doll, gently, metronomically tapping one foot to the native air. She is half musical toy, half holy image, until in one unbelievable moment she bends toward the worshipper in an attitude of infinite tenderness, and becomes a living image of love. . . .
>
> The second part . . . dramatizes an emotional attitude toward the Virgin, in dark, impassioned contrast to the serene luster of "Our Lady." Anna is a shawled and anguished supplicant kneeling before the image (now of course invisible), appealing for the life of the man she loves.

This touching solo, remembered by many viewers forty years later, was one of Anna's first steps toward finding a fuller expression of her own religious background.

In 1945, she chose Mexico City for the premiere of her memorable and enduring *Kaddish* (Ravel), in which she wrapped Orthodox Jewish prayer boxes, *tefillin*, around her arm and head — a daily prayer ritual observed by highly religious Jewish men. Perhaps she chose to show the work there first because her experiences in Mexico had encouraged her to look into her own heritage. By returning to Judaism for inspiration she reestablished continuity with the world of her childhood through her art. With the exception of *Mama Beautiful*, that continuity had been broken for several years. Now the process of turning her life experiences into the expressive language of dance was once again unfolding.

Another memorable solo, *The Bride*, performed to traditional music, derived its material from Orthodox Jewish wedding customs. The wedding canopy, or *chuppah*, and a chair served as decor. A tremulous young woman, wearing a simple white wedding dress and headdress, is about to be married to a man she has never met. Frightened and bewildered one moment, curious, alert, and cautiously happy the next, she finds a bit of comfort in her mother's assurances, represented by a soprano singing from offstage. Anna's young bride plaintively captured for the audience that irretrievable moment of passage into young womanhood.

In the spring of 1946, Anna dazzled audiences and critics alike with a tightly conceived and stunningly executed program, performed with a new warmth, generosity, delicacy, and grace. After years of trial and error she had mastered her Mexican material — assimilated it so that it could work anywhere. She had looked deeply into Jewish traditions and found what she, alone, could say about them. One critic wrote, "It was a solo program, presented with the artistry of a song recital, Anna, like a lieder-singer, projecting each number with jewel clarity, creating and sustaining a mood."

Reviews were splendid — even from Walter Terry:

> Anna Sokolow . . . has improved enormously over these past few seasons. Her concert at the YMHA last Sunday was distinguished not only by her dancing skill but by fine choreography and excellent programming. . . . Miss Sokolow, who used to appear as a rather ungracious and defiant performer and a rather remote dancer, now fills her dances with warmth and, when the occasion demands, gentleness as well as conviction.

In the 1940s Anna frequently worked with Alex, sometimes sharing a program on which he played his own music. He continued to compose for her, but their professional relationship was stormy and frequently punctuated with intense arguments. It was difficult for these two strong personalities, now living separate lives, to arrive at the kind of healthy compromises that had been possible when they were romantically involved. In spite of the upheavals, they collaborated until Alex moved to California to launch his career as a composer for Hollywood films.

During these years Anna supported herself by teaching once a week in Boston and in various studios in New York. In the spring of 1942, Margaret Lloyd wrote a two-part series about the Boston classes called, "Dance Is One; Dance Is for People."

> "Puncture the air! Puncture the air!" The command came from a trim little figure
> in long black ballet tights, bright jersey socks, and soft black practice shoes, teach-
> ing a class in modern dance, attaching weight to ballet techniques and instilling
> lightness into modern movement. Miss Sokolow is . . . an inspiring teacher as
> well as a dynamic dancer . . . she expresses that latent strength that is never
> wasted in idle gesture, that calm self-possession, derived, like her great teachers',
> from inner stillness . . . she taught that little class in Boston as if the future of
> dance depended upon it.

She took ballet classes at the Metropolitan Opera Ballet School with Margaret
Curtis and later with Edward Caton. It was still a period in which the modern
dancers who studied ballet were a rare phenomenon, but Anna had been doing it
for a decade. "I loved the work," she remembered forty years later. "I was a wonderful jumper and leaper. I should have been a ballet dancer."

One year the Jewish Fraternal Order sent her on an extended tour for several weeks, with a singer, an actor, and pianist. The pay was good: fifty dollars
weekly. They performed in dozens of cities, as far north as Canada and as far west
as Chicago. She sometimes mounted productions outside of New York, such as the
1944 biblical extravaganza *Revelations* in Montreal and a concert in her home town
of Hartford, sponsored by an enterprising young dance teacher there named
Alwin Nikolais.

9

THE UPS AND DOWNS OF BROADWAY

In "Moon-Faced, Starry Eyed" Miss Sokolow has designed an outstanding dance for Sheila Bond and Danny Daniels. It is vulgar, honest and extremely ingenious. . . . The grass-roots American ballet looks like a going concern. (John Martin, New York Times, December 21, 1947)

Anna had begun to show an interest in broadening her association with the theater in the early 1940s. She had appeared in the American Youth Theatre's *You Can't Sleep Here* in May 1941, at the Barbizon Theater. It was a socially conscious revue that also featured Earl Robinson and the singer-comedienne, Betty Garrett. Anna danced *The Exile*. It was an ambitious attempt to bring together divergent mediums such as modern dance, poetry, and street vaudeville. The show did not fare well with the critics, but Anna's work was a notable exception.

When Elia Kazan heard that Elmer Rice's 1929 Pulitzer Prize play, *Street Scene*, was being made into a musical, he suggested to Anna that she contact the producers to express interest in doing the choreography. It clearly had the makings of a first-rate production: music by Kurt Weill, lyrics by Langston Hughes, and settings by Jo Mielziner. Anna took Kazan's advice and got the job.

The play, which was set in a crowded tenement section of the Lower East Side of Manhattan, was a natural for her. It burst with a volatile energy that struck chords of recognition in its first audiences in 1929, and again in 1947 when those tenements were physically virtually unchanged. The scenario searingly brought to life that hot and humid time in a New York summer when people's lives spill out onto the sidewalk and become everybody's business.

The collaborators, Weill and Hughes, clearly captured the atmosphere, the tensions, and the theatrical values of the play, a story of star-crossed lovers imprisoned by poverty and eventually caught up in tragedy.

Although the production was largely successful with audiences, critics varied considerably in opinion, particularly in their response to Weill's work. Some were lukewarm, others hailed it as a brilliant folk opera. Brooks Atkinson, writing for the *New York Times*, called it "a musical play of magnificence and glory." What everyone did seem to agree on was that Anna's work had contributed greatly to the overall effectiveness of the production. In addition to staging the songs, she was asked to choreograph a street game for children and a duet —

both in a pitifully small space for dancing. In the children's dance, "Catch Me If You Can," she created choreography so alive with childlike energy that few in the audience noticed that it was danced by adults: in compliance with child labor laws, although children could be there to watch, they could not perform.

In the steamy duet, "Moon-Faced and Starry-Eyed," Anna broke fresh ground on Broadway and literally stopped the show. Sheila Bond and Danny Daniels, the dancing counterparts of the leads, performed what was described as a wildly sensuous duet, in which Anna used the vernacular — jitterbug — as her medium, scoring choreographic points by using the heat of this popular dance to communicate the passionate feelings of the protagonists. The vocabulary did not have to be translated, it was urgently felt. In *Oklahoma!* and *On the Town*, Agnes de Mille and Jerome Robbins had pioneered in the use of dance to further the plot of a musical, but their language was based on a ballet vocabulary. In *Street Scene* Anna proved that social-dance forms have an inherent dramatic power when they are artfully used as an expression of the society that created them. Ten years later, Robbins used his genius to bring this concept to its fullest expression on Broadway in *West Side Story*.

Brooks Atkinson, not given to lavish praise, wrote that "Moon-Faced" outranked any other musical number then on Broadway, but even he missed the broader implications of her accomplishment. Langston Hughes, however, was impressed enough with Anna's work to inscribe a book of his poetry to her with a warm note of appreciation.

Suddenly, Anna became a celebrity in theatrical circles. Asked in an interview by the popular and highly influential columnist Walter Winchell how she could have "so vividly captured the flavor of squalid city streets in her wonderful dance which highlights *Street Scene's* theme," she replied in her characteristically sparse interview style: "It's simple, when you've been part of them." She might also have mentioned that she had been making dances expressing the deep emotional currents that underlie the surface explosiveness of New York since 1937.

Anna never liked to say much in interviews. She once explained her reticence to elaborate on her ideas — a trait that has driven many interviewers to distraction — in this way: "A dancer's business is to express herself in movement rather than words. I do not have any particular theories because I am still in the process of developing." (That was in 1937. She made a similar remark in a conversation with her close friend Johnny White forty-five years later.)

A few months later, Anna joined forces with Alex, this time on a musical play produced by the Experimental Theatre of American National Theatre and Academy. Arnold Sundgaard's *The Great Campaign* was a peculiar mixture of political satire and surrealism, with music and dance sequences. It received a mixed reception, but Brooks Atkinson, who liked the show, singled out Anna and Alex for special praise. One of the dancers in the production, who later made a name for himself in the concert field, was the young Glen Tetley.

In the summer of 1947, during her yearly visit to Mexico City, Anna was invited once more to make Mexico her home. Carlos Chávez asked her to head the modern dance department of the newly formed Academy of Mexican Dance, which he directed. She declined, promising to return in 1948 to choreograph the opera season at the Bellas Artes. On the way home she stopped in Los Angeles for what promised to be a fascinating assignment.

She had been asked by Joseph Losey, director of *The Great Campaign* (and later an outstanding filmmaker), to stage the movement for the premier of Bertolt Brecht's *Galileo*, which was scheduled for production in the tiny Coronet Theater in West Los Angeles. The brilliant screen actor Charles Laughton was cast in the title role. When Anna arrived it was clear that sparks had been flying for some time. Orson Welles and Mike Todd, both originally involved in the production, had bowed out, leaving behind bitter feelings. Laughton was nervous about appearing on stage for the first time in over a decade, and Brecht, who attended all rehearsals, raged demonically as was his custom. He had complaints about the scenery, the costumes, Laughton's performance, and eventually about Anna's choreography.

After a week or two of rehearsals, Anna and Brecht were at odds. At their first meeting he had wanted to make quite sure she knew who he was, and presented her with some reading material describing his importance in the theater. This was not a good approach to take with Anna who, as an avid theatergoer, knew precisely who he was and had initially been delighted at the prospect of working with the distinguished playwright. Now she was losing patience. "In Germany," Brecht informed her, "I was known as emperor of the theater." "We don't have emperors here in America, Mr. Brecht," was her response.

The relationship reached the breaking point when he attended rehearsals of her staging of a carnival scene and announced that he did not want any of her tawdry Broadway tricks in his production. She informed him that she did not know any Broadway tricks, packed her bags, and returned to New York. (In a version of the story Anna told to an interviewer for *The Drama Review* in 1965 she remembered offering to rework her material until it pleased Brecht, but composer Norman Lloyd, a neutral observer, later said that Anna was simply unwilling to submit to the playwright's iron rule and quit.) Lotte Goslar, a German émigré and a fine dancer and mime, was enlisted to do the staging and the work proceeded without difficulty.

Far from being upset by the incident, Anna was pleased with herself for standing her ground and relished telling her version of the encounter for years afterward. She would not be put down. Not even by an "emperor."

In two very different productions of the Weill/Brecht *Seven Deadly Sins*, one for the Netherlands Dance Theater in 1967 and another in Detroit in 1976, Anna, in her role as director, was able to explore her own interpretation of Brecht's work, having in these productions far more artistic control than she had had when she was doing incidental dances for *Galileo*. Although neither production was particularly successful, the second, done at the Detroit Music Hall Center with Cleo Laine as the singing Anna and Mary Hinkson as her dancing counterpart (the lead character is called Anna), is worth a closer look. This version, conducted by Lane's husband, John Dankworth, gives a clear indication of Anna's unevenness as a theater director when literal, not abstract, ideas are the main substance of the communication.

Brecht's scenario is rather specific, calling for stage action that lends itself better to mime than to abstract dance. Anna decided not to follow his libretto to the letter. "The big problem for me was that I didn't just want to pantomime words. I wanted to try something that had more depth, that involved more imagination. If you stick to just translating words into pantomime, well, I don't think you'd be making an impact with this work: you wouldn't be exploring the depths which are possible." Anna abstracted the feeling imparted by the words and the music and gave the ballet her own characteristic stamp. Brecht's incident for each sin is very specific and at the end of the demoralizing episodes she experiences, the lead character is devoid of human feelings.

Anna sees the character as a testament to the human spirit bowed down by the many compromises she makes, but left with the components of her humanity. Brecht's rhetoric is undermined by Anna's "larger and more compassionate understanding that most of our lives are spent traveling through the great gray areas which lie somewhere between the absolutes of right and wrong," Richard Philp wrote in the May 1976 *Dance Magazine*.[*] The article continued: "Many in the audience were confused by the complex ballet, seeking to understand the meaning of a libretto so obviously didactic, a score so tunefully pungent, while so much takes place on stage. The abundance of impressions and images seemed to lead to a diffusion — rather than a focusing — of attention." Anna explained to Philp that she felt that Brecht and Weill represented an era that is totally strange to people today. They were Germans projecting ideas about an America they had never yet seen. She projected her own philosophy into her interpretation.

> It is possible for some people to do certain things and not necessarily change for the worse. I'm referring to the dancing Anna, who prostitutes herself because she needs to build that little house on the Mississippi in Louisiana for her family. . . .
> But they don't return to Louisiana doing hitch kicks . . . That is the price she must pay: sadness. If you want all of that, you pay, and the price is exacted in

---

[*] Copyright © 1997 *Dance Magazine*.

many ways. Some people lose everything except the money they've earned. Anna is a whore, but she's an innocent whore. After seven years of earning money, she goes back to her family and that house with innocence.

Mary Hinkson — like Anna an ex-Graham dancer, but of a much later era — gave her role a luminous performance. Philp wrote:

> As a dancing actress, Hinkson is in command of the gestural, movement language to a degree seldom seen in American theater. She embraced the role so completely that the Brecht-Weill didacticism, which threatens to overwhelm other performance elements, succumbs to the lyrical world of tenderness, understanding and romanticism which Hinkson embodies. In its special way, hers is a major victory.*

For several years after the 1947 *Street Scene* and *The Great Campaign*, Anna was frequently called on to stage dances and movement for plays on and off Broadway. At that time, the use of movement in a show that was not technically a musical almost always signaled a noncommercial or experimental theatrical venture. As a result, many of the productions with which Anna was associated paid her very little and ran only a short while. She did not care. For most of her professional life her attitude has been: "I don't eat much, I don't care for expensive clothes, and I don't pay a lot for rent. What do I need money for? I want to work, and I want work that is stimulating and keeps me growing."

Her name and her theater and dance talents were well known by this time. She had earned a fine reputation and, successes and failures notwithstanding, she was identified as an artist with considerable talent and unimpeachable integrity. In her lexicon, that was enough.

Anna's next venture into commercial theater, the 1948 musical *Sleepy Hollow*, failed to bring her even the satisfaction of a *succès d'estime*. Pleasant music by George Lessner, handsome sets by Jo Mielziner, and a few rather good dances by Anna could not save a show that seems to have lived up to its name. (Dorothy Bird, Anna's friend from the Graham company who frequently danced for her, was partnered in the production by James Starbuck, who went on to choreograph the legendary television program *Your Show of Shows*.) *Sleepy Hollow* took a lot of ribbing from the critics. In the June 4, 1948, *New York Post*, Richard Watts, Jr., with tongue in cheek, listed several new things the production taught him about the famous Washington Irving story; one of them involved Anna's work:

> An important discovery [I made] is that Ichabod was really chased from Sleepy Hollow by a ballet, which makes him an additionally sympathetic figure. It happens that the dance which Anna Sokolow staged to represent the joke played on the schoolmaster is one of the livelier items of an otherwise listless show. Indeed,

all of Miss Sokolow's choreography brightens up the evening noticeably. But somehow the idea of a musical comedy hero being put to flight by a pirouette had an ominous and symbolic ring to it, I thought.

Anna's dances, along with the costumes by David Ffolkes and sets by Jo Mielziner, were all the critics could find to praise in the production. To visualize the many details of the story, Mielziner had chosen to fill the stage with scenery, severely limiting the available space for dance. With years of experience in adapting her work to whatever performance area she was given, Anna somehow found space for dances that were described by Brooks Atkinson as fresh and striking.

In 1949 she did dances for *Regina*, a musical version of *The Little Foxes*, with music by Marc Blitzstein and direction by Robert Lewis, a close friend from the Actors Studio days. Cheryl Crawford was the producer and the popular radio singer, Jane Pickens, admirably portrayed the title role. Critics were especially complimentary to Lewis for his deft combination of music, theater, and dance in a strikingly integrated whole. In the *New York Times*, Atkinson wrote about the performers: "Under Mr. Lewis' direction, they act with complete understanding of the characters they are playing and with the ability to project and move and express points of view.... The characters are developed from the inside out."

As a young man, Bobby Lewis used to do hilarious satires on the modern dancers of the time for his friends. He loved them and could laugh at them (and help them enjoy a laugh at themselves), but he also had a deep understanding of the importance of movement in the theater. Associated with him, Anna was able to do some of her best work for Broadway. The rich potential of integrating the arts in the theater became something of an obsession for Anna in those years and still remains a fascinating challenge forty years later. Although *Regina*, successful in every way but commercially, closed after only two months, to Anna it was an unqualified success because it met her own artistic goals.

Neither the acting and directing talents of Burgess Meredith nor the sets and costumes by the famed Motleys could save *Happy as Larry* (1950) from being what critic John Chapman described as "an overdose." There were too many leprechauns and too many witches; there was too much of an attempt to make a startlingly original musical score. Chapman wrote about the music: "Sometimes it was blues, and again boogie woogie, and again, violently and grimly modern." The show did not stand a chance.

10

THE ACTORS STUDIO

I remember one brisk fall day walking down Fifth Avenue right after taking her class and I started to sing. I think it was one of the greatest moments of my life. I thought: I've got it all now. My body feels good, my brain feels good. I feel alive. I'm going places. (John Silvester White, personal interview, January 9, 1981, Sherman Oaks, California)

In the spring of 1947, Elia Kazan told Anna about plans for an exciting new acting laboratory and asked if she would be interested in participating. Kazan, after his dance studies with Anna at the Group Theatre in the 1930s, believed that the actor's body needed training and that such training should be integrated into the ater studies. Actors Studio was the name given to the new enterprise, and Anna Sokolow was to be the dance teacher.

The Studio has close historical ties to the Stanislavsky-based work of the Group Theatre during the 1930s, when Lee Strasberg, Harold Clurman, and Cheryl Crawford joined forces to create an extraordinarily fine production unit with first-rate ensemble acting. Anna had taught dance classes to actors in their studio for a time during those years. The major focus of the Group Theatre's work had been on the social, political, and economic problems of the time and on the conflicts of the individual in his struggle for a better life. Elia Kazan, Robert Lewis, and Clifford Odets were among the talented artists to emerge from the enterprise. From 1931 to its demise ten years later, the Group championed a fresh, naturalistic style of acting that was to have a profound influence on the development of the theater of its time. It was, in effect, the beginning of the end of artificial and affected acting that had carried over from the nineteenth century.

In 1947, after a six-year hiatus, some key figures from the Group Theatre — Kazan, Crawford, and Lewis — directed their energy toward the formation of the Actors Studio. Their excitement was renewed by the prospect of having an artistic home base once more, ensuring some continuity in their work. They would develop a pool of actors with a common understanding of the art who would be used in future productions, but the primary focus was to be on training actors, rather than on production, as it had been with the Group.

Anna was pleased to be asked to participate in the venture. When her instincts told her that the time was right for a new direction she did not deliberate. The fact that Studio teachers would be working without pay was not important to

her; teaching dance to highly talented young actors would be a fascinating challenge once again. The opportunity to work again with her good friend "Gadge"
(Kazan's nickname because he always seemed to be tinkering with one gadget or
another) made the invitation more appealing.

The approach to acting taught at the Studio, the "method," has its roots in
the work of Constantin Stanislavsky, who trained his actors to develop their characterizations by recalling and refining their own deepest personal experiences.
Anna was a natural choice for teaching these classes: the emotional honesty of her
own dancing and choreography matched perfectly the ideals of the Studio. Her
recent success as choreographer of *Street Scene* made her all the more attractive as
a faculty member. In a sense, she had been working with her own version of
Stanislavsky technique for many years without recognizing it as such. She called
it "looking for truth," but it was the same thing. Her early exposure by her mother
to the Yiddish theater — the vital and intense acting styles of stars such as Boris
Thomashefsky, Jacob Adler, and David Kessler — had been an inspiration to her
since her childhood. She could, in a sense, count these visceral performers among
her teachers. Now, actors would be learning from her once again.

The school's founders agreed that there would be two levels in the new
school, an advanced class for established Broadway actors already familiar with
some of the Group Theatre acting techniques, to be headed by Lewis, and Kazan's
beginners class, an introduction to the "method." In the original plan, class size
was to be severely limited, but so many gifted performers applied, that the numbers were soon increased. Kazan's class opened with twenty-six actors and
Lewis' with fifty-two. Among the original twenty-six in Kazan's group were
Jocelyn Brando, Joan Copeland, Betsy Drake, Lou Gilbert, Julie Harris, Steven
Hill, Cloris Leachman, Nehemiah Persoff, and James Whitmore. Martin Balsam,
Kim Hunter, and Vivian Nathan were added soon afterward. This was the class
that Anna taught.

At the Actors Studio, Anna was thrown into constant contact with superbly
gifted young artists who were open and malleable. They could, under her guidance,
gain fresh insights into the characters they portrayed through the process of movement exploration. She also participated in a fine workshop in which she could
explore the relationship between theater and dance — a relationship that had intrigued her since her early days as a performer in Irene Lewisohn's lyric dramas.

Dance classes were held on Monday and Thursday from 10:00 a.m. to
11:30 a.m. At 10:00 a.m. *sharp* the doors were closed. The actors quickly learned
that Anna expected them to be there right on time or they would not be allowed in
the door. Each class included floor warm-up exercises, based on Graham technique, and a modified ballet barre. As in a standard modern dance class, there
were center floor exercises and then movement through space (i.e., exercises
across the floor). John Silvester White, an actor in those original classes, recalled

his first: "I had never been put through such torture in my life. The next day my muscles ached so badly I could hardly walk. And she was tough. When she would spot somebody she thought was being a little lazy she would grab them in the rear and say, 'That's not a dead thing you're dragging around. Use it!' We learned how to use it. She was imposing!"

Julie Harris, who had already performed successfully on Broadway when she took classes with Anna at the Studio, remembered:

> I was doing an arm movement at the barre, thinking I had pretty good form (I had studied at Steamboat Springs, Colorado, three summers with Merce Cunningham and Valerie Bettis). Suddenly I felt a burning sensation on my hand. Anna had slapped me. "You look like a little old lady painting teacups," she told me. I think I cried, but it didn't take long for me to realize how much I had to learn from her. She helped me to understand I had to go outside of myself if I was to realize my full potential.
>
> Once, after I did a scene from *Miss Julie*, which opened when I ran into the room from out-of-doors, she asked me what Miss Julie had been doing before the scene began. I told her she had been out dancing with the peasants. Anna said, "I didn't see that when you began the scene. You should be flushed and out of breath if you've been dancing. You should show us that you need a drink of water." Of course, she was right.
>
> I loved to watch her dancing in her concerts. She was a brave and beautiful figure on stage. I can still see her lovely oval face.

Anna taught her actors how to walk with dignity and assurance and how to fall without hurting themselves. "The floor is your friend," she would tell them. And there was imagery — always imagery. "Walk as if you are listening to a bird singing." "Someone is following you. Walk faster . . . faster . . . run — your life depends on it. Run!" They ran and they fell and learned to scramble back to their feet, lightning fast. The demand for inner motivation was constant. She was looking for a direct flow from emotion to physical expression. In order for her students to achieve this, she needed to break down inhibitions about expressing deep feelings physically and replace "correct" responses with uncensored movement. In the process, she was helping them find the confidence to move in ways that they initially felt were beyond their capacities. They liked Anna and they trusted her. She spoke their language and did not let them get by with anything short of their best.

She sometimes lashed out in anger. Her choice of victim was almost predictable: any pampered-looking young actress who appeared to come from a privileged background was usually the type that took the brunt of it. Generally a good judge of character, here Anna could be way off base. The fragile, madonnalike beauty Eva-Marie Saint caught Anna's somewhat prejudiced eye one day; she seemed to lack physicality in her movement. Anna slapped her bottom and shouted, "What are you doing? That is nothing. You look awful!"

Vivian Nathan, one of Anna's earliest students at the Studio and later a personal friend, recalled the more usual, and often magical interaction Anna had with her students:

> There is an incident involving me that has become something of a legend at the Studio. Anna staged a fight, between Richard Boone and me, on a stage about twenty-two feet wide. I was leaning on the proscenium on one side of the stage. He was sitting on a chair by a table at the other. She told me to leap onto the table. That's an impossibility, right? Well, I did it. How, nobody knows. I never stopped to ask how I did it. Remember, I'm not a dancer. She never had any doubts. She expected things from you and you did them. Sometimes they were quite extraordinary.

Occasionally she worked with two or three couples, at other times with a solo figure. The images she gave the actors to work with were drawn from her lifetime as an insatiably curious observer in what may be the loneliest city in the world. Three women were told that they were looking out a window. "What do you see?" They explored movement ideas. Another time, Eli Wallach and Vivian Nathan were told to work on lifts. The lifts themselves were not important, what was important was that a mood, a city landscape, had to be created. One day she brought in some music — Stan Kenton's "The Nearness of You." Anne Hegira improvised under Anna's direction while the others watched. "How does it feel to be near someone who is not there?" she asked. Hegira was spellbinding.

Anna's masterpiece, *Rooms*, grew out of experiments nurtured by the willingness of those young actors and actresses to allow themselves to be physically and emotionally vulnerable during the process. They improvised with spoken lines as they did the movement improvisations. Aza Bard McKenzie, with whom Anna created "Escape," the stunning second solo in *Rooms*, remembered:

> As the months went by, the roles and characters would change or be moulded in one way or another. The ballet in its finished form didn't differ that much from what finally emerged from those sessions. The movements were later elaborated upon somewhat because very well-trained and skillful dancers eventually did them. Anna, of course, developed the movements, but it was in the evolution of the relationships, the inner content, that the actors were so valuable.
>
> What they came up with was the life that was going on inside of them. It was a give-and-take between her skill and what they could reveal of their inner life. There was no printed program when we did the work at the Studio for an invited audience. After we performed the work there was much discussion. Then they insisted that we do it again because they loved it so much. It was exhilarating!

In the early Actors Studio days, Anna often joined the actors for coffee and snacks. Soon, she and John Silvester White began to take a personal interest in each other (with the professional name of John Silvester, he is now best known for his portrayal of the crusty vice principal (then principal) in the television series *Welcome Back, Kotter*). In 1981 he remembered:

When I joined the Actors Studio in 1947, Elia Kazan told me he wanted me to take some movement classes with Anna Sokolow. I didn't stand very straight and he thought that I needed some work. I had never heard of Anna, but one of the actors warned me that she was "like a drill sergeant." Studying acting with Kazan and movement with Anna, I felt transformed. I remember one brisk fall day walking down 5th Avenue right after taking her class and I started to sing, I think it was one of the greatest moments of my life. I thought: I've got it all now. My body feels good, my brain feels good. I feel alive. I'm going places.

At around this time, Anna announced to Kazan that she wanted to participate more in the activities of the school. She wanted to experience acting so that she could get "inside" the process. Kazan suggested that she do some scenes with the actors. She did all right in the scenes I saw her do, but she hated having to learn the lines. For her third scene, she asked me to work with her. We did some John Howard Lawson thing with a Depression setting. It was terribly realistic and dry. We rehearsed in her studio on 73rd Street off Broadway. It was one of those buildings set aside for the use of performing artists in those days — full of concert singers and musicians. It was a big, long room full of Mexican art. She had paintings by Nacho Aguirre on the wall and told me very proudly about him.

One night, she invited me to have dinner with her. Fried chicken livers with onions was her specialty. That was about it for her cooking repertory. Soon we were doing more talking than rehearsing. We were fascinated with each other and one thing led to another. I don't remember how the acting scene turned out, but soon I sublet my apartment and was living with her. She was about ten years older than I, but that didn't matter.

Anna got permission to direct a modest production using students in the class. It was her own version of William Saroyan's *Razzle Dazzle*, which she called *Elmer and Lilly*. In this short one-act play she included dance, acting, and some little vaudevillelike sketches. John White described it:

> She cast me in one of the parts. We did this thing late at night for an invited audience. A lot of people lined the walls of the rehearsal studio where it was performed. It was wild. Actors were dancing, singing — taking chances they would not have taken without her. I don't know what it looked like because I was in the middle of it. I do remember that Julie Harris was very good and that we all worked very hard. Saroyan came to see it and liked it very much.

Nacho accepted the news of Anna's new relationship philosophically. On one level he must have known that their long separations would one day lead to this. It was something of a miracle that with people of their temperaments the relationship had lasted for close to eight years. There were some nonpersonal contributing circumstances. Several politically well-placed Mexican arts administrators had discovered José Limón, and for a few years they saw him as something of a messiah. It was not that they lost track of Anna — she was, in fact, still treated with the greatest respect — but the invitations for her to return to work were sparse. Without work, which was then and still is today the center of Anna's life, the appeal of being there diminished. Her friendship with Nacho continued to be strong. When she brought John White with her to meet him, the three of them got on very well. The photographs of Anna alongside the Botticelli *Primavera* stayed up on Nacho's wall.

Anna continued to teach at the Actors Studio until the mid-1950s, when a personality clash between her and Lee Strasberg, who was then leading the studio, provoked her to leave. Students implored him to try to coax her back, but to no avail. It was clear that Strasberg could bear to have only one very strong personality in the Studio at a time, his.

11

THE EARLY FIFTIES

I remember when I stopped dancing. One day I got ready to go to class. I put my stuff in a bag and was on my way down the street when the thought came to me: 'I don't want to be doing this any more.' I went right home and put the bag away. I didn't feel I had to dance. It wasn't important any more. (Lucille Rhodes and Margaret Murphy, outtakes from a film interview of Anna Sokolow, December 27, 1975)

The early and middle 1950s was an unsettling, even heart-breaking time for many of Anna's left-leaning contemporaries. Some stayed in hiding while Senator Joseph McCarthy and his House Un-American Activities Committee (HUAC) did their witch-hunting work. There were tragedies, careers cut short, blacklists, accusations, and betrayals. The social atmosphere was dense and oppressive and a state of general artistic inertia set in. The literary critic, Maxwell Geismer, described it as "a kind of self-induced immobility on the part of our artists and intellectuals, a self-repression, a type of do-it-yourself censorship." If the one-time Communists, Marxists, and fellow-travelers among these artists and intellectuals (and there were many of them) were not already under investigation by McCarthy and his committee, if their careers had not already been ruined, they were doing their best to lay low and avoid the now famous knock on the door.

The indictments brought about during this terrifying era were ludicrous in the light of historical reality. At the core of those indictments was the charge that those who had been involved in the fight for social change in the thirties — longshoremen and dancers, coal miners and film writers — had been guided solely by a fanatic loyalty to Marxism and in fact cared nothing about issues of unemployment and starvation. Artists were accused of putting a premium on any work that carried the party line no matter how crude the product, no matter how threadbare the quality.

The men and women under attack were the same ones whose unflagging commitment to social change had caused the government to respond at last to some of the needs of the American people. One of the most positive results of their passionate battles was the passage of the Social Security Act of 1935, which benefited the entire country.

But now they were the "Un-Americans."

Some of Anna's friends had continued party activities well into the 1940s. Some had been so involved in the activities of the earlier era that they became obvious targets for McCarthy and his minions, regardless of their current political beliefs and affiliations. And there were those who were simply baffled that the investigations were going on. In America? How could that be? It was a mess. A national tragedy.

In the mid-1930s Anna had been too occupied with her own numerous enterprises and too independent to cast her lot completely with one political organization. By refusing to identify with the purely political aspects of the movement, she avoided being a prime target in the investigations. She had inadvertently made herself less interesting to the witch-hunters. Investigators did come to her door at one point, but she refused to submit to any questioning before speaking to her attorney. Following his advice, she held her ground and refused to speak, whatever the risk. They did not bother her again.

When some of her friends felt compelled, for whatever reasons, to cooperate with the investigations, she was deeply pained but tried to forget it as soon as possible. She would not judge them. Johnny White saw things somewhat differently. He was furious at the investigations and the cowardice shown by many people in the film and television industries, who capitulated to red-baiting crusaders by blacklisting performers. So great was his anger with people in the industry that he refused to accept work on television for some time. In this matter, Anna proved the calm one.

The question once again arises: did Anna ever become a member of the Communist Party during the 1930s — even for the briefest time? The answer is easily arrived at by anyone who has known her and is aware of her need for elbow room, both for her talents and for her eccentricities. Anna has never liked being told what to do by anyone. She is a highly disciplined person, but the terms of that discipline are uniquely her own. In her lifetime she has often paid a high price to be able to follow those terms. Her dislike of any brand of authoritarianism is sincere and deep-rooted. Consistent only in her inconsistency in most areas of her personal life, she has never wavered from the belief that emotions as well as allegiances that do not spring from a deep well of personal feeling are worth nothing. Legislation from any level that tells her how to think or work would be not only intolerable for her, but also doubtless render her incapable of any work of any significance. In her own words:

> I was never a member, you see. What I felt, I felt very personally. It had nothing to do with a doctrine. I must say I believed in what the party could do. In principle, yes. Of course, later, it became shockingly disillusioning. But even then I never, for example, finished a dance with a fist up in the air, or took a red flag out and waved it. Never. There were people who did that.

Even then I tried to show people the truth, then let them make up their own minds. You don't shove it down their mouths. I didn't anyway. You see, I don't want to be labelled in that way or in any category. I was not even labelled in that day. I refused it.

Time would one day prove the genuineness of her commitment to the principles she believed in. Long after many of the joiners and recanters had gone in an easier, more comfortable direction, Anna continued to do battle for the things she valued in her own, always personal way.

Early in the fearful and suspicion-ridden McCarthy era, and perhaps as a small antidote to the environment it was creating in the world of the arts, Anna created a great dancing role for herself; one that dealt with possession and exorcism. It was the part of Leah in her dramatization of S. Ansky's *The Dybbuk*, which was presented at the Weidman Studio Theater in early March 1951.

The play is based on the Chassidic legend of Channon, a young student who dies when his beloved Leah is forced by her father to marry another man. The soul of Channon becomes a vagrant spirit, or dybbuk, and enters Leah's body. During the wedding she refuses to go through with the ceremony. The rabbi drives the dybbuk out, but Leah chooses death in order to be reunited with her love.

In this work, Anna made her first major attempt to combine the spoken word with mime and dance. Most of the performers in the cast were from the Actors Studio, including Lou Gilbert (who narrated), Richard Malek, Vivian Nathan, and Lucille Patton. It could have been seen as a Studio project but for the fact that it was produced entirely by Anna.

Although *The Dybbuk* had a strong, original score by Siegfried Landau, excellent costumes by her sister Rose, and a gifted cast of actors and dancers, there were some difficulties with the complex evening-long work. Doris Hering wrote in the May 1951 *Dance Magazine*:

> The very color and variety of the material and the fact that Miss Sokolow endeavored to give equal value to words, mime and dance, presented problems. Some sort of unified thread was needed so that one could be carried through the transitions from one medium to another. And that last thread should have been the character of Leah. Instead, the work was episodic, with Leah stepping in and out of focus.*

Problems notwithstanding, the production received mostly positive notices, such as this one in the March 18 *Herald-Tribune* from Walter Terry:

> The finest dramatic passage in "The Dybbuk" is that in which the spirit of Channon enters the body of Leah as she is participating in the wedding festivities. Miss Sokolow as the heroine, dances this section tellingly, communicating through emo-

---

* Copyright © 1997 *Dance Magazine*

tional gesture, body tensions or frenetic actions the rending passion which has stabbed her inner being. Here and in the ensuing passages dealing with the rabbi's exorcising of the invading spirit and with the final uniting of the lovers, Miss Sokolow has created dance-drama of a high order.

The role of Leah was described by several reviewers as a perfect one for Anna's mature performing talents. She must have danced it superbly. (Vivian Nathan remembered how, at one point, Anna as the possessed Leah burst into a dazzling and lightning-fast series of foot-stamping movements and just as suddenly stopped, leaving the audience breathless.) On the strength of that characterization her name became identified with the play, and a few years later she was called on to stage the movement for a highly successful television version of *The Dybbuk*, directed by Sydney Lumet, with Carol Lawrence in the role of Leah (a young designer named Jac Venza did the sets).

The Dybbuk was to be Anna's last major concert appearance as a performer.* The decision was arrived at simply and without fanfare:

> I remember when I stopped dancing. I got ready to go to class. I put my stuff in a bag and was on my way down the street when the thought came to me: 'I don't want to be doing this any more.' I went right home and put the bag away. I didn't feel I had to dance. It wasn't important any more.

A back injury that had been causing her considerable pain for several years may have contributed, but a desire to work exclusively as a choreographer was doubtless the stronger motivation. Anna's decision would, in time, help her to relinquish the vision of the single artist (herself) as the central figure on the stage and allow her imagination to split the dramatic images that came from within her into parts for other people. She had learned from *The Dybbuk* that linear dramatic development was not her forte. She would have to learn how to create her own form. That process took a while to evolve, but once it did, she created *Lyric Suite*; the most brilliant phase of her career was launched.

For the few years between her last performance as a soloist and *Lyric Suite* it is difficult to pinpoint where Anna was headed as an artist or, for that matter, just what she was doing. Now she was busy with her teaching at the Actors Studio, now off to Mexico, now staging an enormous Purim or Chanukah Festival in Madison Square Garden to raise money for Israel, or working out the movement for a Broadway or off-Broadway play.

---

* There was one more low-key appearance a year later, when Doris Hering convinced Anna to appear at the Museum of Natural History in a program of ethnic-inspired works in the "Around the World with Dance and Song" series. Anna performed *The [Jewish] Bride* and *Mexican Retablo* on a program that included Jane Dudley's *Cante Flamenco, Harmonica Breakdown*, and *Reel*; Martha Graham's *El Penitente*; and Donald McKayle's *Games*.

During the late 1930s and into the 1940s and 1950s Anna was frequently sought out for her skill in handling large numbers of dancers in pageants and festivals. These took place most often in New York, but she did pageants in Montreal, California, and Detroit as well. A good example of the genre was the lavishly produced *Purim Jubilee* at the old Madison Square Garden in March 1952.

The annual event, sponsored by the Greater New York Committee for State of Israel Bonds, was written by Norman Rosten and staged by John O'Shaughnessy. Film star Melvyn Douglas narrated the program and the noted actress Betty Field spoke the role of Queen Esther. The queen was danced by the petite and lovely Dorothy Bird. Several Actors Studio people were involved, including Aza Bard, Fred Sadoff, Vivian Nathan, and Lucille Patton. One of the dancers was an eighteen-year-old named Arthur Mitchell, who would later distinguish himself in the ballet world. In the 1953 version, Anna had her first contact with Jack Moore, who was to become one of the most important male dancers ever to work with her.

Anna did not deliberately set out to go in so many directions, but it was as a freelance choreographer that she had chosen to support herself. That was going to take time and a readiness to go wherever the opportunities were. To make ends meet, she taught children twice weekly in Great Neck, Long Island, sharing a studio with Dorothy Bird.

If anyone took her brief absence from the American modern dance limelight as a signal that she was finished with concert work, they just were not keeping track. In late 1952, she created an enduring spoof of lecture-demonstrations, *A Short Lecture and Demonstration on the Evolution of the Tiger Rag* (title later changed) for the virtuoso tap-dancer, Danny Daniels. Carmen Gutiérrez, a beautiful young "Sokolova" from Mexico City, was his partner.

Undaunted by previous difficulties, Anna chose to use the spoken word in this piece. A narrator and a pianist were on stage with two dancers. The narrator, a scholarly gentleman, educated the audience with direct quotes from Jelly Roll Morton, whose words and music had been the inspiration for the piece. All four played their roles with mock seriousness, and the audience understood and loved the joke. Agnes de Mille thought the work was good enough to include excerpts in the 1953 national tour of her Dance Theatre, with Daniels and the lovely Gemze De Lappe dancing and James Mitchell narrating. It was the first Sokolow choreography to be seen west of the Rockies.

That year, Anna had a brief contact with one of her few idols in the dance world, George Balanchine. At the instigation of her friend Muriel Stuart, Lincoln Kirstein had invited Anna to teach choreography and modern dance technique at the School of American Ballet in the spring of 1953. It was a short session, but the idea was unique enough to merit a story in the June issue of *Dance Magazine*. Unfortunately, Anna's hectic schedule made it difficult to bring her back on a regular basis and the experiment was never repeated.

Anna was seldom awed by the powerful, the wealthy, or the famous, but George Balanchine was an exception. Being on the faculty of the great choreographer's school gave her the courage to introduce herself to him one afternoon in a coffee shop. She told him how much she enjoyed his work and that she had, indeed, been inspired by it. He looked at her curiously, smiled, and asked her how she spelled her name. She told him. Another curious smile. "That's the wrong way to spell it," he replied in his charming Russian accent. Then he smiled a third time and went back to his conversation with Lincoln Kirstein. (Many Russian's prefer the "v" spelling when words that end with that sound are transliterated into English.) Rather than being offended by his odd manner, Anna found it very droll and enjoys recounting the incident.

From pageant, concert dance, and the ballet world, Anna returned to the theater. She was importantly involved in the premiere of the controversial Tennessee Williams play, *Camino Real*, which opened on Broadway in March 1953. The play grew out of a production of his *Ten Blocks on the Camino Real* at the Actors Studio. Williams had been so taken with Elia Kazan's insightful handling of the shorter work that he decided to develop it into a full-length play. Kazan was to direct and he chose Anna to stage the movement. The splendid cast included Eli Wallach, Jo Van Fleet, and Hurd Hatfield.

Camino Real takes place in a kind of limbo in which Don Quixote, Lord Byron, Casanova, Marguerite Gautier, and other well-known characters appear. The scene is set in a mythical Central American town full of decadence, violence, and cruelty. There is no clear story. Most of the characters are waiting to pass through to somewhere else — although it is not clear where. The characters have in common their brooding dreams of love, loneliness, and defeat. The production contained crowd scenes, a fiesta, and a mock fertility ritual, all of which Anna staged with images she drew from the macabre skeleton drawings of the Mexican printmaker José Guadaloupe Posada. She worked so closely with Kazan that she was referred to in the program as "Assistant to the Director" (she could not be credited as choreographer because, by the Broadway rulings of the day, that would have changed the classification of the show to a musical — *Camino* was hardly that.)

Wishing to explore new ground in this play, Williams dispensed with ordinary notions of theatrical form. No clear sense of time was established and his poetic images seemed to have no literal relationship to one another. It was a demanding play to sit through, one with so much contrapuntal movement and dialogue that the audience's attention was forced to shift constantly. Williams later wrote:

> My desire was to give these audiences my own sense of something wild and unrestricted that ran like water in the mountains or clouds changing shape in a gale, or

the continually dissolving and transforming images of a dream. . . . Elia Kazan was attracted to this work mainly, I believe, for the same reason — its freedom and mobility of form.

The play took a terrible beating from four of the major New York theater critics. Among them Richard Watts, Jr., felt that Williams "had set out willfully and purposely to be mannered, pretentious and difficult, and in this perverse task, he has been only too successful." Walter Kerr wrote, "Williams is thinking about poetry and the process of poetry rather than writing it. The play is calculated poetic manufacture, nearly without content and certainly without inspiration." Others found it incomparably beautiful and considerably ahead of its time. Perhaps the most important comment in the press came from Watts in a later review: "One thing I'll have to say about *Camino Real*. It has a rare capacity for arousing people to anger and that is a healthy state of affairs in any man's theater."

Camino Real played an essential part in helping to free contemporary American theater from realistic construction and now, over thirty-five years later, it is regarded as a milestone. One may well wonder how the work would have fared with critics if it had been presented a few years later, after the freedom of form championed by playwrights of the Theatre of the Absurd, such as Ionesco and Beckett, became acceptable to the theater establishment. Anna was proud of her association with this extraordinary production and inspired by the willingness of both Williams and Kazan to take artistic chances at a time when they were both in the prime of their careers.

Perhaps the most memorable performance of the opening night was given at the cast party by Sarah Sokolow, who had become quite a character in her later years. After receiving numerous compliments on her daughter's talents, the portly, egocentric, seventy-three-year-old mother could stand it no longer. In her thick Russian-Jewish accent she said, "If you think she is talented, you should have seen me when *I* was young. *I* was a dancer!" Whereupon she proceeded with a brief but lively demonstration.

In the final months of 1953, Anna was involved in a first-rate off-Broadway production that starred Jessica Tandy (who had created the role of Blanche in *A Streetcar Named Desire*) and her esteemed husband, actor Hume Cronyn. *Madam, Will You Walk,* was a second attempt to get Sidney Howard's charming play before an audience. The first, produced years earlier with George M. Cohan as the star, closed before it reached Broadway. This time it worked.

Madam was the first production in a refurbished theater on Second Avenue. (Built to house Yiddish-language productions, it had been closed for some time and was now reopening as an off-Broadway house, the Phoenix.) Anna was the choreographer for the show. The staging was done by Cronyn and the composer Norman Lloyd, an old friend of Anna's from the Bennington College days. Robert Emmett portrayed the taxi-driving object of the heroine's affection, who yearns to be a dancer. The charming, seemingly impromptu dance Anna created for him received special praise from the critics. The play was well reviewed and the first of many successful ventures for the new Phoenix Theater. It could have and should have moved to Broadway, but never did.

On December 18, 1954, the Stravinsky theater-dance piece, *L'Histoire du Soldat*, was presented at the "Y" with Fritz Weaver as the Reader; John Harkins, the Soldier; Frederick Warriner, the Devil; and Annabelle Gamson as the Princess. The story, which makes only occasional sense, is told through acting, dancing, pantomine, and rhymed narration, with a chamber orchestra adding biting musical commentary. Stravinsky spoke of this unique little work as "une espèce de petit théâtre ambulant...," making it clear that he wanted those who produced and watched it to see it as fun — delightful foolishness, geared to make some not so foolish points about the soldier mentality. Both the director Muriel Sharon and Anna, who staged the work, took the opportunity to explore their crafts playfully, using the device of a stage within a stage to tell the tale of a soldier fallen prey to the devil. The only actual dance was a brash and brassy solo for the princess in Part Two. Louis Horst commented in the February 1955 *Dance Observer* that the princess' dance "was choreographed with great wit and jazzy seductiveness by Anna Sokolow and was brilliantly performed by Annabelle Gamson." The production received a good deal of favorable attention and turned out to be the first of many *Histoires* for Anna. Once again, it was the mixture of theater and dance that had fascinated her. Her overall goal was to examine a broad range of human emotion through every means the theater had to offer.

12

ANNA IN THE PROMISED LAND: ISRAEL

We hope that because of this 'more' of Anna's, although we work like little donkeys, we will bloom like a bouquet of flowers. (Sara Levi-Tanai, newspaper interview, 1954)

It was a hot July afternoon in 1983. Anna was back on familiar turf. As her taxi headed toward the Yemenite quarter of Tel Aviv, Neveh Tsadek, she gazed out the window and took it all in: the dusty, narrow roads; the low, modest, white stucco houses placed every which way, with their tile roofs and solid walls edged up to the street. This section of the city, some of it on desirable beachfront property, was undergoing extensive redevelopment. Even the Arman Hotel — where on past visits she had stayed for months at a time — had succumbed to the wrecking ball.

The taxi wended its way through the quaint old district, finally reaching Inbal House, home of the renowned dance ensemble whose coming-of-age had been aided by Anna's devotion and advice. Why, she mused, had they sent for her today? Once inside the studio offices, she was greeted by the office staff. Ignoring her questioning glances, they ushered her into the main building of the Inbal facility. There, to her complete surprise, stood some two hundred people — dancers, actors, writers, designers, sponsors, musicians, photographers, friends — each one a figure in her longstanding relationship with the cultural life of Israel. They had arrived bearing testimonials, gifts, and most fitting of all, dances to offer their friend and co-worker of the past thirty years. It was a thirtieth anniversary surprise party!

Sara Levi-Tanai, founder and director of Inbal, stood beaming her affection toward Anna throughout the afternoon. Nathan Mishori, the puckish musician and critic, played master of ceremonies, introducing those who offered tributes of words and dance. He read congratulatory telegrams from luminaries such as Isaac Stern and Jerome Robbins. Perhaps the most fitting words came from Judith Gottlieb of the America-Israel Cultural Foundation (A.-I.C.F.). She had played an instrumental role in bringing Anna to Israel in 1953 and had, on countless occasions, opened her home and heart to the choreographer:

> Your love affair with Israel has been a constant one, which has reflected not only on Inbal, but on so many in the dance community in Israel. It was you who laid the initial foundations that led to the creation of the professional companies that eventually emerged.

> You have never forgotten your Jewish roots and continuously gain spir-
> itual nourishment from all that concerns our people. I know you are happiest
> when you touch home base here.
>   The calendar tells us that thirty years have passed since our first en-
> counter, but your enthusiasm has been unabating and 1953 was only yesterday.

Anna's association with Israel had begun with a phone call from Jerome Robbins in December 1953. Robbins had been invited to Israel two years earlier by the American Fund for Israel Institutions (later the A.-I.C.F.) and given a mission: to seek out for their support an Israeli dance ensemble that could best represent the art form in Europe and America. After an exhaustive search, he chose Inbal (the Hebrew word for tongue of the bell) Dance Theater, the creation of the gifted choreographer and composer Sara Levi-Tanai.

In the late 1940s, this small, intense, and energetic woman had organized a group of young Jewish newcomers from Yemen. These singers, dancers, and musicians belonged to an extraordinary people who had managed to preserve Jewish traditions that dated back nearly two thousand years, despite centuries of exile. In her dances Levi-Tanai forged both ancient and contemporary images into a magical, dynamic vision. Although Inbal's gifts were immediately apparent, Robbins could also see that a great deal of work had to be done. The company needed to achieve international performing and production standards if the extraordinary beauty of their work was to be shared with an audience outside of the country.

Levi-Tanai was undeniably a creative genius when working with the music and dance of the Yemenites; her background had not, however, provided her with technical theatrical experience to shape her creative work into a polished theater-dance form. Her company members knew little about the demands of professional theater. Most of them came from the ranks of the refugees who had been flown to Israel from the southern tip of Saudi Arabia (in the famous "Operation Magic Carpet") soon after the creation of the Jewish state in 1948. Certainly, they carried with them a rich cultural tradition, but concepts of dance as a profession — with its requisite study of disciplined technique, rigid rehearsal schedules, and proper backstage decorum — were odd notions indeed. Dance, for them, was part of life, ritual, and celebration. Clearly, help was essential if the group was to become a professional dance organization touring on international theater circuits.

Heavy choreographic and directorial commitments prevented Robbins from taking on the job himself. Instead, he recommended Anna and in turn was authorized by the foundation to attempt to recruit her. He felt that her credentials were splendid: she had done similar work in Mexico, she certainly understood discipline, and she had frequently used Jewish themes in her dances. So it was that in mid-December 1953, Robbins told Anna about the extraordinary group of artists and then invited her to join him in Israel to see if the job interested her.

Anna was strongly tempted to see Israel; the possibility of working there made it especially appealing. It did not take long for her to agree to Robbins' offer. The next week she was on a plane with him heading toward the Promised Land. After a grueling twenty-seven-hour flight, she touched down for the first time on Israeli soil. It was a cold, rainy, winter day, and she was exhausted from the flight. But she had more important things on her mind that day than her personal comfort; she wanted to get to work. Years later she recalled that she "didn't know what to expect. I certainly didn't expect to be affected so deeply, but the minute the plane landed I was overwhelmed with an indescribable feeling about being there. I didn't have any kind of strong Zionist background, but going there changed my point of view. It is now one of the deepest things in my life — Israel."

Karl Gabriel Glaser, a veteran administrator of the A.-I.C.F., remembered Anna's arrival vividly:

> I drove out to the airport to pick up Anna and Jerry Robbins. She insisted on going directly to the Inbal studio, though she was clearly exhausted. She sat there for perhaps three hours without saying a word. We had introduced her to Sara Levi-Tanai and the dancers. All she said was "Go ahead with your work." And she watched. When it was over, she said: "So far, no comments. I need some time to digest it."

The next day, she sat next to Sara and commented quietly on the individual dances. They liked each other from the first meeting. It was decided that Anna would give the company some classes in modern movement, which was quite new to them. And she would sit in on all rehearsals. To everyone's surprise, the fiercely independent Levi-Tanai gave Anna more and more of a free hand to work on things *her way* during rehearsals.

Beneath Anna's air of confidence, a sincere self-questioning had begun:

> At the start of my work with them, I was frankly not quite sure how to go about it. Having seen them perform, I realized that their dancing represented a cultural expression I had never seen before and it presented a strange kind of problem to me. On the one hand, I felt that I must not trample certain ground; I must not touch the flower, but rather try to find out how the flower could be nourished and made to grow larger. . . .
> Actually, they were, and are, extremely innocent. I felt the enormous responsibility on my part not to touch this innocence, but at the same time to give them a kind of strength and an understanding of what they were and to help them project this more effectively.

What Anna observed during that initial journey was a troupe of performers steeped in the impulses and beguiling rhythms and movements of Jewish Yemen. From the beginning, Sara Levi-Tanai brought to life the time of the Jewish prophets and biblical kings and the many influences that feed into the dance of the

Jewish people. The music, which combines singing with sounds of drums, tambourines, finger cymbals, and ankle bells, harks back to the Bible as well. Inbal's work today is broader and reflects many influences of other Jewish communities and cultures.

The dancers themselves offer a startling contrast of sensitivity and strength. The women, most of them fragile-looking beauties with dark, smooth complexions, stand absolutely upright, their regal bearing a result of centuries spent carrying heavy burdens on their heads. The men are dark, lithe, and handsome and carry themselves beautifully. Their physical prowess is formidable. Rehearsals in the early years would sometimes turn into competitions, each man vying with his fellow dancer in the execution of difficult steps.

The Inbal dancers' strength was not only physical. To get to Israel they had survived nearly impossible odds, trekking enormous distances through the desert. Then, they had flown into the twentieth century by plane. Their joy in the new life was boundless, but to support themselves as performers they had to lead double lives, working also in factories or as domestics, zoo keepers, mechanics. They traveled to their performances by truck, carrying their scenery, lights, and musical instruments with them. Performance conditions once they arrived were often crude. Communal dining halls frequently doubled as theaters when the dancers visited farm settlements, or *kibbutzim*, and military camps. The stages were improvised affairs — sometimes little more than dining tables tied together. The dancers doubled as carpenters, stage managers, and musicians as needed.

These limitations, however, would not quench the spirit of a group for whom struggle and pioneering were a way of life. Inbal proved an inspirational force wherever they performed. They were the strength of Israel made incarnate through dance.

Anna found her new friends to be unique in their temperament, as she reflected in a 1960 essay:

> The nearest I have ever seen were the Mexicans, who were also very innocent. But the Yemenites were extremely sensitive and highly refined, with a delicacy the extent of which completely overwhelmed me. At the same time, they possessed the oriental [i.e., Middle Eastern] quality of boundless talkativeness, yelling, and screaming. I used to think they were constantly angry with each other, until I realized it was just their manner of speaking.

She was also profoundly impressed by the dancers' dedication to their work, which they treated with an almost religious fervor. It was this dedication, moreover, that enabled Anna, the intense disciplinarian, to progress as rapidly as she did in rehearsals. Working long hours, she immersed the group in modern and ballet techniques. "The prime object of my work," she wrote, "was to get them to know what their bodies could do. There was no need to tamper with their creative work; it was exquisite."

Just as important as a trained body, Anna told the company, is a professional attitude. She taught them how to use their time to best advantage, how to marshall their energy, how to apply makeup and care for costumes, and how to approach rehearsals and performance. The essay continued:

> This meant, in rehearsals, "Sheket," or "Keep quiet." Regarding the performances, though I hated the task, I had to convince them that it was not professional to bring their families backstage. This practice included tea and refreshments for everyone, at times making it difficult to get the dancers on stage at their cues. On one occasion, they were ready to go on strike if their families were not allowed backstage. "Factory workers work in the factory," I told them. "You work in the theater. It is the same thing." They finally understood.

The educational process took some time to resolve itself. "I must admit," Anna wrote, "that I did some screaming and yelling myself because the more I loved them the more I wanted to make them good, to make other people proud of them." Inbal received the full treatment of Anna's intensity and aggressive methods. Coming from a culture light-years removed from her high-pressure New York dance world, the performers had to find ways of adapting to her insistent tactics. Sometimes it became a little too much, even for the Inbal dancers. One later commented, "We really didn't need her to teach us how to eat hot red peppers. Being Israelis we already knew enough about that." For the most part, however, familiarity bred mutual respect and abiding affection.

Anna's arrival had caused quite a stir among segments of the Israeli artistic community of choreographers and dancers. Why had an outsider been called in to work with Inbal? There was no lack of talent in existing professional circles. What would intensive training in American modern dance techniques do to Inbal's dancing? Sara Levi-Tanai responded poetically to some of these questions in a 1954 interview: "We brought the raw materials from our authentic origins, but we have to build the buildings according to modern techniques. Anna uses one word over and over again, 'more, more, more.' We hope that because of the 'more' of Anna's, although we work like donkeys, we will bloom like a bouquet of flowers." (The homophone *mor* is the Hebrew name for a pungent spice.)

Three years later, on the evening of their triumphant European debut in The Hague under the aegis of Sol Hurok, Anna was unable to be with Inbal, but she was there to share in the pleasure of their success in London and again when they opened in New York on the first stop of a highly successful 1957 American tour. Her part in their success was then, and remains to this day, a matter of great pride for her.

As Inbal blossomed, Anna began to sow other creative seeds in Israel. In addition to her concentrated work with them, she had for some time taught free open classes in modern technique and choreography. All the classes were held in the gymnasium of the Levinsky Seminar, a centrally located high school in Tel

Aviv, blessed with a wooden floor (a rarity at that time). The students flocked from around the country, some of them trained in modern or ballet techniques, some of them folk dancers, all of them curious about Anna's American methods and style. Three times a week, as many as one hundred people worked in the stifling heat of this gymnasium, which had been laughingly described as "hermetically sealed."

Out of this horde, Anna chose thirteen of the most gifted participants — six of them members of the Israel Opera corps de ballet — to perform on a program of music, theater, and dance to celebrate the tenth anniversary of the birth of the state of Israel. These performances, given in Tel Aviv's new opera house, took place on two consecutive weekends in August 1958. This was Anna's first opportunity to exhibit her own choreography in Israel, and she wisely chose a varied program. After a musical curtain-raiser, performed by a chamber music ensemble, the audience was catapulted into the rhythms and tensions of *Opus Jazz* (a variation of Opus '58), set to Teo Macero's music. Then came her new version of *L'Histoire du Soldat*. The contrast of hot jazz followed by quirky neoclassicism made for an intriguing stylistic mixture. Both performances were sold out, and the evening proved a great critical and popular success.

Israeli audiences were very much taken with the vital new approach Anna had introduced. Her presence had, from the first visit, attracted attention. Until her arrival, modern dance choreography in Israel had been heavily influenced by German expressionism. The pioneer dancer/choreographer Gertrud Kraus' last public performance had taken place in 1951. Kraus had emigrated to Israel in 1935, after achieving considerable success in Vienna. Like her, the Ornstein sisters and most of the other well-known modern performance groups were still working in the old expressionist vein.

However, there were younger dancers who were ready for change and were already working in a more contemporary style. Three young women who attended the opera house performances were to play an important part in the next phase of Anna's work in Israel: Naomi Aleskovsky, Rena Gluck, and Rina Shaham were the guiding lights of Bamat Machol (Stage for Dancers), a ten-member modern dance ensemble — the only one of its kind in Israel at the time. Aleskovsky had been a leading dancer in the company of the formidably talented Kraus. Gluck and Shaham, both American-trained performers and choreographers, had been raised in the gritty independent tradition of American modern dance. In 1957, this trio had joined forces to form a dance collective. Over the course of two years, they had developed a modest but sound production unit as well as a responsive audience.

The Bamat Machol trio invited Anna to see their group. She was impressed with the framework that they had fashioned for their talents and offered to set a work on them. In August of 1959, the company performed her Scriabin

Poem. It was well danced and warmly received, although there were some in the audience who were scandalized by the eroticism of the piece, which had already raised some eyebrows in New York and Mexico City. A lively flow of letters to Tel Aviv's newspapers came on the heels of the performance. One outraged writer felt that "Miss Sokolow should not show on stage what people do in their bedroom or bathroom." The work was considerably ahead of its time in its frank sensuality, and a notable segment of the Israeli population still clung to a fairly conservative outlook as to what should and should not be shown in the theater.

After her initial contact with Bamat Machol Anna became excited about the idea of working with Israeli modern dancers. She began to envision a permanent repertory dance group under her direction. But for a long time it remained just that — a vision.

13

BUILDING A REPERTOIRE
LYRIC SUITE • ROOMS • POEM

*After the performance, Louis Horst came backstage and said, "Now, Anna, you are a
choreographer!" It was the most important compliment I have ever received because it
came from Louis. But I already knew that I had reached a turning point in my career.
(Lucille Rhodes and Margaret Murphy, outtakes from a film interview of Anna Sokolow,
December 27, 1975)*

In Mexico City in the late 1940s, the popular painter Miguel Covarrubias, then
head of the government's Dance Department, set out to recreate the brief but shin-
ing experiment of La Paloma Azul, in which musicians, painters, and dancers
worked closely together to produce memorable results. For a time, his efforts
were quite successful and, through a fine public relations campaign, the new era
was touted everywhere in Mexico City. There were notices of coming events in
newspapers, on billboards, and on flyers that were posted everywhere from train
stations to barber shops.

Among the gifted young people to gain recognition during this period
was the dancer/choreographer Guillermo Keys. As a young man, Keys, like many
dancers of his generation, had been inspired by Anna and her work. When he had
an opportunity in August 1953 to produce a three-day-long modern dance season
in the new Teatro de los Insurgentes, he invited her to stage a new work.

For music Anna selected Alban Berg's exquisite *Lyric Suite*, an atonal,
rhythmically complex work that is nonlinear yet emotionally evocative. Anna, in
her innovative use of the music, does not respond to the individual sounds or
tones Berg created, but to the music's cumulative effect. It is the dramatic merging
of the dance with the music that makes them seem inseparable in their expression.
Anna was among the first of her generation to free choreography from a close cor-
relation with either meter or melodic line.

First-rate sponsorship, achieved through the Covarrubias program, assured a first-rate production. Costumes, scenery, and programs were all of the
high caliber Anna remembered from the Paloma Azul era. The music was played
live by some of Mexico's finest concert musicians. The dancers, selected from the
Ballet Bellas Artes, were also among Mexico's finest, including Keys, an American expatriate named Xavier Francis, and several "Sokolovas." Anna even

received a fee, six thousand pesos (about five hundred dollars) for her choreography. It was a large sum of money for one who usually worked in Mexico for travel expenses and a small honorarium.

The new work, *Lyric Suite,* was a stunning success with both audiences and critics in Mexico City. The choreography, like the music, is designed in suite form. There is no narrative line. The parts are related by the underlying emotional pull of the work. The sections — "Allegreto jioviale," "Andante amoroso," "Allegro misterioso," "Largo desolato," "Presto delirando" (added later), and "Adagio apassionato" — are essentially vignettes tied together by the music and by what appears to have been Anna's overall goal: to examine a broad range of human emotion.

Each emotionally intense vignette is followed by some relief in a section that soars lyrically or is thoughtfully serene. In the intense sections, the gestures are wound tightly; when they are released, it is not to relieve tension, but to rewind again, someplace else in the body. The recognizably lyrical sections of *Lyric Suite* are fluid and crystal clear in their simplicity: the duet, "Largo desolato," an exquisite love idyll; the quartet, "Adagio apassionato," an evocation of harmony.

Although she had sometimes employed the suite form in her years as a soloist, here the expressive range is immensely broadened by journeys into the individual worlds of a variety of characters, male and female. The dancers neither personify characters from literature or mythology, as was usual in longer modern dances at the time, nor are they universal symbols of any kind. They do not, in fact, represent anything other than what is immediately apparent at the moment they are seen. They, themselves, are the subject of the dance.

In rehearsals then and now performers are coached, as actors are coached, detail by detail, to deliver a thoroughly honest statement, finely tuned to the ideas and images Anna has set forth. Each dancer is expected to take an active part in the realization of those images during the rehearsal process so that on stage the character comes alive as a human being living his or her part in Anna's vision of life.

Anna brought the experience of over twenty years of solo dancing to the development of each of these individual characterizations, creating a climate — a landscape — that belongs uniquely to that performer and through that performer to the audience. Unlike Martha Graham, who relinquished her performing career with great emotional pain and anguish, Anna made neither an effort to recreate herself on stage after she stopped performing nor works in which the dancers are the background or a chorus for an Anna.

The opening male soloist portrays a virile figure, a hunter perhaps. Alert and cautious, his sharp, controlled runs are punctuated by a slow lowering toward the earth. The "Andante amoroso" introduces a solo female figure who tosses her head and clasps her hands. She turns her head sharply, her hair whips around, she reaches her arms outward. The solo is marked by a controlled exhilaration. In the

"Allegro misterioso" another woman enters, agitated. She flutters her fingers as she bends forward and back. She runs about the stage as if in a frenzy, arms pulled behind her, her face thrusting forward. She finally sinks into a pool of light in the upstage right corner and bends backward. Has she given up? Has she died?

A beautiful young couple enter for the "Largo desolato." Their sensuous duet is contained and yet joyous: at one point, after a stylized ballroom dance sequence, they sit on the floor and the man places his head on the woman's lap. Suddenly, ecstatically, his body arches as he thrusts his leg upward and at the same instant her upper body responds by arching as her head falls back. They rise and leap softly together in a circular pattern which carries them into the wings.

The man in "Presto delirando" is a victim, but of what agony? He moves robotlike around the stage, barely on balance. One hand covers his mouth while the other vibrates forward. He is perhaps the dehumanized one in Kafka's stories, or a soldier, or a prisoner. Whoever he is, it is clear that there is no escape for him.

In the "Adagio apassionato" four women wearing full-cut red dresses weave about one another like fingers interlacing. Their movement is harmonious, the group pattern is one of nearly perfect formal design. Toward the end, their legs circle in sequence, creating an undulating red wave that peaks and breaks with their skirts. It is almost as if Anna wants to console us after the mood we have been coaxed into, and perhaps to leave us with a bit of cautious hope.

In recent years, Anna has referred to the opening solo as her tribute to Nijinsky. The second solo, she says, is for Isadora, and the "Presto delirando" is for Kafka. Not all of these thoughts were made known to the first performers of the piece; some may have been revealed to her after years of working on it.

Lyric Suite was given its American premiere on a concert series at the "Y" in late March 1954, sponsored by the New Dance Group. Anna was invited by the Group to be part of the series and to audition the outstanding young professionals who had been selected for the concert season. She accepted the invitation and from the audition chose Donald McKayle, Jeff Duncan, Lenore Landau, Sandra Pine, and Laura Sheleen, several of whom would later become the nucleus of her Theatre Dance Company. In addition, Anna invited three more seasoned dancers, Beatrice Seckler, Mary Anthony, and Ethel Winter to join the cast. Jeff Duncan remembered the audition:

> Anna was no longer dancing at this time, but she never gave up performing and this audition was one of her best performances. It was powerful and intense and we never forgot it. At one point, when she was dissatisfied with the sedate way the women were going through one of the combinations, she cried out, "No! You must give more. You must be willing to show your whole self." Then to illustrate her point, she tore her blouse open and flew through the movement.
> Eve Beck and I were cast in the duet and the next day Anna brought Carmen Gutiérrez and Xavier Francis in to show what they had done a few months earlier in Mexico. The top of my head nearly went off. This was exactly the kind of

dancing I wanted to do. I especially remember one of her remarks during rehearsals: "True lyricism has to have passion and steel underneath it. For an arm to
come up beautifully and with meaning, it has to have great power and energy."

Of the eighteen works performed on the New Dance Group Concert Series,
Lyric Suite was the most highly praised in the press. The work was acknowledged to
be a major contribution to the modern dance repertoire. For Anna, the most important recognition came from the teacher for whom she had the greatest respect, Louis
Horst. With an atypical surge of unbridled enthusiasm, he wrote in the May 1954
issue of his magazine *Dance Observer*, "It is one of the finest examples of lyric theater
dance seen in many a season . . . it speaks in abstract and stark simplicity, translating the qualitative moods of the music into penetrating and evocative movement
designs. Superbly choreographed and thoroughly integrated, its lyric beauty has a
direct appeal to kinesthetic response."

After the performance, Horst had gone backstage to find Anna and ex-
claimed, "Now, Anna, you are a choreographer!" "I hung my head like a kid who
just received a medal," she remembers. "I never received another compliment in
my entire career that meant more to me." If Louis Horst thought she had made the
grade, then she had made the grade. Forever afterward Anna regarded *Lyric Suite*
as an artistic turning point. She had found a language of movement of her own
and a focus for the expression of her deepest feelings as an artist. She also found
herself directing a company of her own for the first time in over ten years.

According to an article John Martin wrote a few years later, the first Theatre Dance Company was born at the suggestion of some of the dancers who had
taken part in the New York premiere of *Lyric Suite*:

> Apparently they were happy in the association, for they constituted themselves
> as a performing unit and asked her to direct them. It is they who take responsibil-
> ity for most of the grubby details, leaving her free for creative work. Having been
> through the ordeal in earlier years of trying to form a group of her own, Miss
> Sokolow says that she would never have made the attempt to organize another
> one. This time the group organized her, so to speak.

Just how well that unique company structure worked out is open to question because, as much as Anna hated attending to the niggling details associated
with the running of a company, she was not comfortable delegating authority.
When group members began to assume responsibilities and make decisions, she
tended to snatch the reins away from them and do the job her own way, a way that
did not always prove effective or successful. This often rendered the dancers' efforts
useless, in addition to making them look and feel foolish for having tried.

To her credit, Anna did commit herself to taking on any choreographic
assignments that would help the members of her company support themselves as
dancers. As often as possible she insisted that she be allowed to use her own

company members in any professional assignment she was given. This willingness to put herself on the line to keep the group together led to a wide range of
work in television, opera, and on Broadway. Some of those experiences she could
well have done without; some were quite rewarding; all would eventually prove
to be worth the effort. It was with this group of young dancers that the *Rooms*
project, begun a few years earlier at the Actors Studio, became the basis for a major choreographic work.

Betty Walberg, who played for Anna's classes at the Actors Studio and
was rehearsal pianist when the dance version of *Rooms* was created, recounted:

> My first memory of *Rooms* was a showing of a work in progress at the [Actors]
> Studio. Offstage was jazz music — what you would call "classics of jazz," sig-
> nature works of the top artists. It depicted isolation in the city. The actors were
> responsible for some dialogue. After a run-through Anna told me she felt some
> dissatisfaction with it; the combination of movement and dialogue wasn't
> working for her. Out of that dissatisfaction came her decision to do it as a dance
> work.
>
> At the time I was studying orchestration with Kenyon Hopkins, who
> was the orchestrator for Radio City Music Hall. He was a very astute musician
> and a quiet man. When Anna asked if I had any suggestions for someone to do the
> job I mentioned Kenyon, who I knew was a composer as well. I brought him to a
> rehearsal and in his quiet but intense way he nodded in a 'yes-yes' manner while
> Anna told him of her ideas, her movement, and her structural plans. He would
> watch rehearsal, do some composing, and then send the music over with me. The
> writing of the score went through different processes at different times. Some-
> times he would initiate a section with the music, sometimes she would just work
> with a tempo and then he would compose. . . .
>
> I believe that she was the first choreographer in contemporary modern
> dance to commission a jazz score for a concert piece and to treat it as a classical
> score. The idea of using jazz for a concert work was quite startling at that time and
> it caused much talk and excitement, along with suspicion and doubts. Anna was
> not concerned. The use of chairs was new then too. Now how many dances do we
> see using chairs?
>
> When we were working on it, we knew instinctively that something
> very special was happening. It was the same feeling I had when I worked with
> Jerry a few years later on *West Side Story*; you know something is happening that
> is going to change the face of things.

Rooms deals with the devastating aloneness that can grip people who cannot make contact with others except on the most superficial level. There are no
heroes, no central characters. The work portrays not so much how these people
act in their isolated worlds, but how they feel being there. The central character
could by any one of us. By touching on the universality of human isolation in so
direct and visceral a way, Anna created one of the enduring masterpieces of twentieth-century art.

Anna does not like to speak about her works in detail, but for an oral history project in the mid-1970s she made a rare exception and talked about the dominant images in some of the sections of *Rooms*.

> "Alone"
> Each person in a chair is alone in a room, and they are looking out of the window. The room is very small and they don't know who lives next door. They don't know who they pass on the stairs going up and down. In the first section you see all eight of them projected. It is called "Alone" so it's like saying alone, alone, alone, eight times.

After the overture, the curtain opens to reveal eight dimly lit dancers seated in simple wooden chairs. The backdrop is the brick wall at the rear of the stage. A mournful trumpet sets a bittersweet tone for what is to follow.

The dancers lean, twist, vibrate in their chairs. Their arms and legs are lifted and dropped as if lifeless. They get up, run in circles, and then fall into splits next to their chairs. They sit once more before leaving. The chairs are their rooms; the rooms set the boundaries of their lives. They can see and be seen through their windows, but only the occupants of the rooms go through the doors.

Sections of the work are linked by rearrangements of the chairs. What follows are glimpses into the little hells of aloneness people make for themselves and each other.

> "Dream"
> After "Alone" you see a boy by himself and it is called "Dream." He dreams contrary to what he is in life; he may be a post-office clerk. He dreams he is an explorer. On his little room walls he has pictures of mountains; he is climbing and discovering things that are way beyond his comprehension, but this is his dream.

The figure rises, then falls to the floor and writhes. He launches into a circle of slow cartwheels punctuated by even slower falls onto his back, then begins a slow, treading run in place. He seems sometimes grandiose, sometimes pathetic.

> "Escape"
> The next room is called "Escape." You see a girl with an evening dress on and she has the greatest romantic image of herself. She thinks she is Greta Garbo waiting for a lover to come in.

A woman moves randomly among the chairs to a slow blues melody. The chairs become fantasy people and she attempts to relive her past. She picks up an imaginary mirror, checks her makeup, her fingers shiver across her face and down to her breast in nervous, expectant ecstasy. She dances wildly in nervous anticipation. She pulls the chairs together, sits in one, and then makes love with an imaginary lover. (At the premiere, Tennessee Williams turned to Anna and said, "That's Blanche!" — the protagonist in one of his great plays, *A Streetcar Named Desire*.)

"Going"

Another room — "Going" — the boy in this room dashes in and he's the greatest champ that ever walked the streets of the neighborhood. He's the best boxer, the best football player. He's the best of everything, but in reality he's nothing. Only in his room, he's the champ.

A man in a satin jersey team jacket is carried away by an insistent jazz rhythm. His movement is compulsive and frenzied, filled with spasmodic starts and stops and much wrenching, tossing, and shaking of the head. He slides away from the chair and then returns to lean on it. His shoulders pulse and his fingers snap to the music. He masks his terror of being a nobody with frenzied, desperate action. As the section ends, he looks vacantly into space.

"Desire"

These young men and women see each other at a distance by looking out the window. They have a great desire to meet, to be intimate, but they never will be. The possibility is never fulfilled. They can never even get as far as having a friendship. They may see each other through those windows, but nothing else will ever happen.

Five people sit and face each other but there is no physical or visual contact. A sixth stares out in the direction of the audience. They slide their feet rhythmically as their arms extend forward, reaching. They rise and then sink to the floor. The sexual tension is unmistakable as their arms and legs open out yearningly. Except for a brief moment of touching, the possibility of physical contact is always missed by a beat or two. They don't even seem to know how to try.

"Panic"

This boy is frightened by the sounds that he hears all the time. To him they are sounds of destruction and he fears that they are going to destroy him. He looks for comfort but there is none. He hides where he thinks he may be safe.

A man sits motionless with light pouring over him. He reaches out and collapses forward. Suddenly there is a sound; perhaps it is some explosion in the street below. It triggers a run forward. Nothing is there now. He runs again, this time toward four other people seated on stage, but he is invisible to them. He sits down, covers his face. Then he falls to the floor and beats his head against the floor. As the others leave the stage one by one, he turns to crouch behind the barricade of his chair.

"Daydream"

It is a very special time. You see a beautiful sky outside the window. The light is exquisite. It's like a dream. The first movement of the arm and wrist is brushing back the curtain and peering outside.

"Daydream" is meant to provide lyrical release, but the images leave many in the audience uneasy. Three standing female dancers move in slow counterpoint as if in a reverie. They hold on to their chairs and their dreams are masked by the dance exercises they appear to be going through. They smile occasionally, but for no apparent reason. Is it narcissism that keeps them forever isolated? At the end they hook their legs suggestively over the backs of the chairs, but even this touch of sensuality is forced and lifeless.

"The End?"

The fingers on her outstretched arms are like voices of other people talking, screaming at you. You're trying to get away from them, but you can't. The voices may be inside you. You swing your head from side to side but you can't get rid of them.

A dejected woman endlessly repeats arm and hand gestures which suggest self-inflicted pain. She puts her hands over her eyes; her body sags and then her arms flutter hopelessly. At the end of the solo she climbs on the chair and moves her arms as if they were wings. Will she jump? Will this be the end, or will she go through her ritual of despair over and over? We will never know.

The work closes with a return of the group to their opening positions — "Alone." They repeat bits and pieces of their solo material as they stare numbly out of their windows. The dreams, angers, and fears that they have revealed throughout the dance have been replaced by resignation.

In her beautifully detailed description of *Rooms* in *The Shapes of Change*, critic Marcia B. Siegel describes her reaction to the closing section of the work:

Seeing them all together again, seeing how much of their behavior has the same movement origin, I somehow feel compassionate toward them. I see them as forming much more of a community than they have ever imagined, and I find them all the more pitiable for their lack of recognition. Since they have only themes, no development — only rooms, no corridors or common shelter — they will go on doing the same things indefinitely. With five crashing chords, the music ends and the curtain falls.

With the creation of *Rooms*, Anna had taken a hard look at the life around her as well as into her own life and come up with a searing statement, without offering solutions to the problems addressed. "I'm not asking you to do something," she seemed to be saying, "I'm only asking you to look." She wanted her audience to feel the compassion she felt and to become angry as she was angry. Twenty years earlier, in *Waiting for Lefty*, a group of angry men had sat around on chairs in an open circle, talking about the need to act. Anna's people sat on chairs, too, but now the issue was no longer political but personal.

It has been said that with her great works Martha Graham shifted the emphasis of modern dance choreography from sociology to psychology. Unlike Graham, who spent many years in therapy exploring her own psyche in order to better understand herself and thereby enrich the characterizations of the people she wished to portray on stage, Anna has never taken a serious interest in such introspection. The truth she seeks on stage has nothing to do with a narrative — with why her characters behave as they do or the consequences of that behavior — but rather about how it feels to live in their inner worlds. To perform such great Sokolow works as *Lyric Suite* and *Rooms* effectively, dancers have to allow Anna to lead them into the essence of the character they are portraying, and then project their own gut-level understanding of how that character experiences life.

Betty Walberg spoke about how Anna coaxed an explosive performance out of mild-mannered, soft-spoken Jack Moore:

> Anna is uncanny in her use of dancers. She seems to be able to pinpoint those secret places in a person that have never been revealed in performance. For example, she saw beyond Jack Moore's calm exterior to someone who could reveal the essence of the fidgety, jazzy figure in the "Going" section of *Rooms*. If she had a process at all, it was her version of Stanislavsky applied to dancers.

Anna's use of acting and dancing in combination and her reliance not on virtuoso technique, but on depth of emotional projection, was a further development of her pioneering work in *Lyric Suite*. Through her example, this simple yet profound search for truth in movement became part of the artistic consciousness of the dance world in 1955, and it remains so to the present day.

When *Rooms* was first presented at the "Y" in late February 1955, the audience was bowled over by its emotional impact. Reviews were almost unanimous in their praise: something important had happened in American modern dance.

The premiere performance featured Jeff Duncan ("Dream"), Jack Moore ("Going"), Donald McKayle ("Panic"), Eve Beck ("The End?"), and Beatrice Seckler ("Escape"). In a brilliant cast, which also included Sandra Pine, Judith Coy, and Paul Sanasardo, Seckler was particularly moving. The fragility and poignancy of her interpretation prompted Doris Hering to equate her performance with those of Nora Kaye, one of the great dramatic ballerinas of the twentieth century.

All the musicians were well known in the world of jazz. Teo Macero, Clem Da Rosa, Charlie Mingus, Hall Overton, and Bart Wallace, conducted by the composer, Kenyon Hopkins, won cheers from the audience and special praise from Walter Terry, John Martin, and Louis Horst in their reviews.

The following May the work was given an official Broadway premiere as part of the Festival of American Dance, sponsored by Bethsabee de Rothschild at the ANTA Theatre. For three weeks Martha Graham, Doris Humphrey, José Limón, Pearl Lang, and other noted American choreographers filled the stage with a brilliance never seen before in a series of this kind. *Rooms* was the second work, first presented in a matinee performance that opened with Pearl Lang's *And Joy Is My Witness* (Paul Taylor and Bruce Marks were in the cast) and closed with *Appalachian Spring*, featuring the fifty-nine-year-old Martha Graham as the young bride.

The performance of *Rooms* was exceptionally powerful. For fifty minutes the audience seemed to be transported by the intensity of the new work and the startling freshness of the jazz score. After the intermission the audience came back, still in a state of high excitement from the electrifying experience. A few noisy minutes into *Appalachian Spring*, Martha Graham shot a fiery glance at the restless audience. It was a warning that everyone understood. Thereafter, one heard only the glorious Copland music and the sounds of the dancers breathing.

Walter Terry was most eloquent in his review in the *Herald-Tribune* the next day:

> Anna Sokolow's *Rooms*, which has had a few off-Broadway showings, was presented yesterday afternoon at the ANTA Theater on the American Dance series. Those who had attended the earlier performances had circulated enthusiastic reports about Miss Sokolow's new group creation, a procedure which sometimes invites too great expectations. However, the prophets were right. *Rooms* is a powerful, deeply penetrating exploration of man's aloneness. . . .
>
> Miss Sokolow has given her subject stunning theatrical treatment through movements which are striking as pure dance action but also revelatory of the individual dreams of each of the participants or groups of participants. Indeed, she makes you care about her characters to the degree that their problems replace your own. And what more effective magic can a choreographer work?

The year 1956 turned out to be remarkable in Anna's career. She choreographed a full season for the New York City Opera Company and premiered another important and highly original work, *Poem* (Scriabin). In addition, she taught with Mary Wigman, Victor Gzovsky, and others in Zurich and made appearances with her newly formed Theatre Dance Company at the American Dance Festival, Jacob's Pillow, the White Barn Theater, and the Brooklyn Academy of Music. She also shared a program with Sophie Maslow at the "Y," spent several weeks in Israel working with Inbal, and managed to provoke a controversy during a teaching stint in Mexico City.

That summer, Anna and Merce Cunningham were among the guest artists brought in to teach the Ballet Bellas Artes in Mexico City. They were also invited to participate in two conferences. At the second, Anna suggested that the presentation be followed by an open discussion. It is remembered to this day by many of those who attended.

Her topic was "The Art of Choreography." She managed to stick to that subject at first, emphasizing that a choreographer must have intellectual breadth, a passionate love of dance, and a willingness to put creative concerns before concerns of audience response. Then, imperceptibly, the ad-libbed talk began to shift to a thinly veiled expression of the annoyance and frustration she had felt through the years at having to do her work in Mexico in an atmosphere of constant questioning about nationalistic content or lack of it from some quarters.

From her standpoint, she had ample reason to be upset. Years earlier she had had to compete for resources and dancers with Waldeen, who was hell-bent on expressing nationalism in her work and had declared, unabashedly, "Yo soy Mexicana!" More recently, José Limón had come to be regarded with near reverence because of his Mexican heritage and because of his major success with *Tonantzintla*, a dance based on the famous plaster decorations in a church built during the colonial period. Added to this was that Anna always enjoyed being at the center of a controversy. So the stage was set.

When she sensed that hackles were beginning to rise, she pressed on. Her strongest point was that pressure to make nationalistic or picturesque statements in art compromises the larger potential of that art. However, in the presentation of her ideas, it was not quite clear whether she was attacking nationalism or the nationals themselves. Questions and challenges began to fly during the discussion period. Finally, Anna said:

> I know it is a problem to avoid being influenced by things that are so dramatic and so brilliant as they are here in Mexico. But it seems to me that in Mexico as in any other place in the world, the picturesque point of view is death to any art. That is especially true here because things are so vivid. My general impression of the dance here now is that it is too small, too *pintoresco* and too concerned with being nationalistic and patriotic.

"I know what you mean, Anna," one of the artists in the audience called out. "I am a painter and a Mexican, but not a professional Mexican." There were cheers. Others were less taken with her statement. Had she seen enough to judge? Had she seen Guillermo Ariaga's *Zapata*? She should stick to the subject of choreography. Miguel Covarrubias and David Siqueiros, both admirers of Anna's work, tried to mediate. As the discussion continued to heat up, Siqueiros found himself in accord with some of Anna's ideas and seriously opposed to others. He finally proposed a round table discussion a few days later: "I don't mean to scream only, but to work!"

Not much more was accomplished at the later discussion. Everyone came knowing exactly what they thought and left in about the same condition. However, some important questions had been held up to scrutiny. Within a few days, lengthy articles appeared in several newspapers. In an open letter to *Excelsior*, Waldeen not only expressed her general indignation, but also attacked Anna's points one by one and managed as well to get in a few digs at the blatant sensuality of *Poem*, which had just been premiered by the Ballet Bellas Artes. She called the work pornographic.

At worst, the controversy was nothing more than harmless bickering; at best, it was stimulating to those who had some room in their minds to reconsider their attitudes. No new issues had been raised, but because of the attention the conference and round table discussions received, they left deep impressions and were discussed and written about for years afterward.

Poem, which Waldeen complained about, had first been shown at the Brooklyn Academy of Music in early 1956 by Anna's Theatre Dance Company, as attractive and gifted a group as a modern dance choreographer could dream of. The company now included Alvin Ailey, Eve Beck, Judith Coy, Jeff Duncan, David Gold, Jack Moore, Sandra Pine, Paul Sanasardo, Beatrice Seckler, and Anneliese Widman. Although it was an abstract lyrical piece, *Poem* had moments of frank sensuality that were startling for the time. In the mid-1950s on the American stage, both in theater and dance, portents of sexual intimacy were usually a cue for a slow fadeout of the lights. Anything beyond that might easily precipitate a scandal, and those were not daring times. Most choreographers leaned toward symbolic gesture and stylization was the order of the day. If the audience did not get the symbol, they went on without it.

In *Poem*, Anna nudged the taboos. Her dancers did not indicate contact with a gesture (a convention in modern dance at the time), they touched. They did not look near or above each other's eyes (another convention), but squarely into those eyes. In one passage a male dancer opens his legs and welcomes his female counterpart into an intimate embrace. At the moment he encircles her, she tosses her head back. There were several other equally provocative sections.

In an all-male passage, there were enough suggestions of homosexual love to cause comment for some time afterward. What prompted Anna to touch on such a forbidden subject can only be a source of conjecture. Several of her male company members were openly gay. She may simply have looked at those beautiful young men dancing together one day and said to herself, "Why not?"

Although *Poem* was not one of her more acclaimed works (there was considerable criticism about its length), it anticipated by several years a freedom and openness in the theater that would later make the work seem suitable entertainment for a church picnic. *Poem* broke another kind of ground as well. It was the first dance in which Anna explored her now famous and much imitated tight grouping of figures on stage, in which hands reach, arms extend, and limbs intertwine. The image was made all the more memorable by the lighting concept of designer Doris Einstein, whose dramatic pools of light heightened the Rodin-like sculptural effect of the groupings. Within a few years many choreographers, including Jerome Robbins in *New York Export: Opus Jazz* and Alvin Ailey in *Revelations*, were molding the idea to their own artistic needs.

14

WORKING THE MEDIA

If we are ever to have a theatrical theater in this country, it might be well to start off with choreographers to direct it. Apparently they are able to see under the literary surface of the script . . . to the bones and marrow of its basic form in terms of action. (John Martin, Review of "Metamorphosis", New York Times, March 17, 1957)

In the fall of 1956, Anna took on a project that was to reinforce her reputation as a maverick. John Martin interviewed her just before she and the Theatre Dance Company (with some additional dancers) were to start work in the New York City Center Opera's fall season. In his article, written a few weeks before the season was to open, Martin anticipated some of the difficulties that lay ahead.

He noted that the stage at the City Center was small for opera and that the administration of the company was not known for its generous consideration of the needs of choreographers. Citing the unusually varied and interesting upcoming repertory, which ran the gamut from *La Traviata* and *Carmen* to Carlisle Floyd's *Susannah* and Carl Orff's *The Moon*, he predicted that the artistic outcome of Anna's work would be largely dependent not on her talent, but on how much her position would be respected in the total theatrical collaboration.

He had good reason to express concern about the financially troubled City Center Opera that year. To cut production costs, a double concentric turntable, designed by Leo Kerz, was the basic set of each production. It turned out to be not very functional for anyone but singers. Only small and irregular spaces were left for dance, but no one, it seems, took the time to tell Anna just how much space she and her dancers would have to work with in each production. Jeff Duncan remembered that it seemed that she was always the last to know just what the configuration would be. Anna felt that it was clearly the responsibility of the management to inform her properly, but they appeared to have neither the time nor the inclination to do so and this led to some heated exchanges. Rehearsal space was practically nonexistent and the schedule was a tight one — there just was not enough time allowed for the work that needed to be done. There were other problems as well.

The soprano Gloria Lane was given dance movement for the tavern scene in which Carmen leads a gypsy song. Anna also gave the male dancers flamenco clapping and finger snapping to go along with the music and dancing. Lane was delighted with the innovation, but Jean Paul Morel, the conductor, flew into a rage. The sounds were not in the score. Morel was adamant; the clapping had to be taken out. Anna, equally adamant, insisted that they stay in. Morel suggested that she did not have a musical bone in her body; she countered with some thoughts about what he knew and did not know. Arbitration was clearly necessary and the director of the season, Erich Leinsdorf, was called in to mediate. Finally, the scene was performed as Anna had choreographed it and she received an apology. There were no complaints about the tavern scene, and *Carmen* was, in fact, one of the most highly praised works of the season.

But the famous Sokolow ire had been raised several times and she became as intransigent as she knew how to be after the *Carmen* affair. She passionately believed that in opera, as in any aspect of the theater, all of the contributing arts should be regarded as equal and was incensed that responsible professionals would think otherwise. She would not and could not negotiate for the respect to which she believed she was entitled.

As the situation worsened, *The Moon* was the only relief in the tense situation the dancers could look forward to. For this production Anna was to direct as well as choreograph. It was programmed to follow Stravinsky's *L'Histoire du Soldat*, staged by Marcella Cisney with choreography by Anna. The fine cast included Christopher Plummer, the narrator; James Mitchell, the soldier; Hurd Hatfield, the devil; and Judith Coy, the princess.

The first part of the evening was fine, but the Orff work, a stodgy and heavy-handed allegory, went badly. The problem was primarily the lack of basic substance in the work. (At one point St. Peter, a character in the opera, remarks, "You are sleepy. Well, then go to sleep." According to the *Daily News* critic, Douglas Watt, "If it hadn't been almost time to go home anyway, the entire audience would have adopted his suggestion en masse.")

But there is more to the story. The audience was sprinkled with hecklers who had come that night to protest the presentation of the work of a composer who had allegedly been a Nazi sympathizer. They did so noisily and, apparently unaware of the real reasons for the disturbance, some of the critics reported the catcalling and booing as a response to the opera. All told, it was a bizarre evening. Watt could easily see that the problem was not with Anna's work; he wrote that "the staging and the choreography (both by Miss Sokolow) were superb." According to Jeff Duncan, problems notwithstanding, Anna enjoyed the fracas.

Her contributions to the entire season were generally well received by audiences and critics alike, but she was exhausted by the whole affair and so were her dancers. By refusing to make some compromises when it might have been judicious to do so, Anna forfeited the possibility of negotiating a stronger position for herself and for her dancers. It was not an easy time for any of them. Anna comes from the school of thought that says you fight like hell for what you believe in, you do not beg for it. If you lose, you at least have the satisfaction of having put up a good fight and your dignity is intact. Throughout her career she has paid dearly for this approach, but it has won her an enviable reputation in the profession as a woman of unswerving integrity. At no point could Louis Horst, her early mentor, have said to her, "You gave in, Anna. You didn't have to, but you gave in."

Exhausted but undaunted, Anna returned to Broadway theater in late 1956 to do *Candide*. In September 1950, Lillian Hellman had first suggested to Leonard Bernstein the possibility of collaborating on a musical production of Voltaire's *Candide*. She was motivated by a desire to make a personal statement of her feelings about the political climate of the McCarthy era. In 1951, her lover, the mystery writer Dashiell Hammett, had refused to answer the questions of the House Committee on Un-American Activities and had challenged its authority. He was given a jail sentence and a popular radio serial based on his detective character, "Sam Spade, Private Investigator," was taken off the air. Hellman agreed to tell investigators about her own past involvements, but refused to name others. In a now-famous letter to the Committee she wrote: "Gentlemen, I cannot and will not cut my conscience to fit this year's fashions." They finally left her alone.

Hellman's politically flavored version of *Candide*, with a score by Bernstein and lyrics by Dorothy Parker, finally opened five years later on December 1, 1956. It ran fewer than eighty performances. In the opinion of many, the light and irreverent wit of Voltaire's writing worked against Hellman's attempts at serious social and political commentary. The music fared better with the critics than the overall production. Somehow, the score seemed more attuned than the text to the uniquely energetic quality of Voltaire's famed satire.

The work of the choreographer listed on the program, Wallace Siebert, did not please the producers and Anna was brought in as a consultant to improve the situation. Her work replaced most of Siebert's. It is not clear how successful she was because the major critical attention focused on the seemingly infallible Leonard Bernstein's connection with a Broadway musical that had not worked well. The most frequent explanation in the press of the weakness of the musical was that the brilliance of his score outshone the rest of the production — particularly the book.

The frank assessment of Tyrone Guthrie, the distinguished director, is revealing:

> From the start, the great risk was that the thing would seem wildly pretentious. And that is just what it did seem. Only Bernstein's mercurial, allusive score emerged with credit. I do not at all regret the skirmish. It was fun to be closely associated with a group so brilliantly and variously talented . . . [but] this was no medium for hard-hitting argument, shrewd, humorous characterization, the slow revelation of true values and the exposure of false ones.

My direction skipped along with the effortless grace of a freight train
heavy-laden on a steep gradient. As a result even the score was thrown out of key.
Rossini and Cole Porter seemed to have been rearranging *Götterdämmerung.*

Because of the boldness of its vision and the striking score, *Candide*, like
Camino Real earlier, was regarded as a *succês d'estime* by some eminent critics and
a significant number of theatergoers. (The extreme popularity of the original cast
recording over the next several years came as a considerable surprise to all concerned. Guthrie appears to have been wrong about the score.) Anna valued this
kind of success as others valued box-office hits and was proud of her association
with the production.

Her next venture was off Broadway. As part of its experimental theater
series, the American National Theatre and Academy (ANTA) invited two choreographers, Mary O'Donnell and Anna Sokolow, to direct plays of their own choosing, to be presented at the Theatre de Lys in Greenwich Village in February 1957.
According to an ANTA bulletin, the experimental program was inspired by the celebrated French actor/director Jean Louis Barrault's work in the field of total theater.

Anna chose to do a dramatization of Franz Kafka's short story, *Metamorphosis*, adapted for the theater by the Broadway actor Douglas Watson. Watson,
who had once danced for Martha Graham, played Gregor, a desperately over-
worked salesman whose life is dehumanized by his dreary occupation and by a
family that accepts his financial support as their due. He awakens one day to find
himself metamorphosed into a huge insect — a dung beetle. The impatient and
embarrassed reactions of his family, devoid of understanding or compassion, create a chilling indictment of a society in which a man's life can be rendered mean-
ingless when he follows all of its rules, but receives little or nothing in exchange to
sustain his humanity.

Anna had set as her objective the creation of Kafka's special kind of
world, in which reality and dreams become hopelessly entwined. It was a world
she had been delving into as an artist since the start of work on *Rooms* a few years
earlier. In *Metamorphosis* she used actors and dancers interchangeably, once again
exploring the combination of dialogue, mime, and dance. Her efforts brought
first-rate performances from Watson and the entire cast, which included Jeff
Duncan, David Gold, and Judith Coy, members of the Theatre Dance Company.

Both John Martin and Walter Terry praised the work. Martin, comparing
the production to Barrault's recent New York showing of his version of Kafka's
The Trial, found Anna's to have greater substance:

> If we are ever to have a theatrical theater in this country, it might be well to start
> off with choreographers to direct it. Apparently they are able to see under the lit-
> erary surface of the script . . . to the bones and marrow of its basic form in terms
> of action. Miss Sokolow kept her over-all directorial concept firm and spare; her

lines straight, fine, minimal, but formally unwavering and potent in function. . . . For Miss Sokolow's authoritative attack on a tough experiment there is nothing but admiration.

Although Walter Terry found the production terrifying, exhausting, and disturbing and lacking what he called resultant therapeutic effect, he wrote: "Miss Sokolow has done a masterful piece of creation. It is possible to hate her *Metamorphosis*, but it is impossible not to respect her theatrical mastery of an exceptionally difficult problem."

Metamorphosis was given only two performances, but in the process of working on it, Anna had clearly recognized her affinity for Kafka. During the next few years she produced the work for several of her own concerts, sometimes using dancers, sometimes actors in the major roles. Years later she would once again do several works based on both Kafka's work and his life. She has been sometimes called "The Kafka of the Dance" for, like his, her work has dealt with the bewildering demands of modern life and how our inability to deal with those demands leaves us detached and alienated. Anna's Eastern European Jewish ancestors believed that they had an intimate relationship with God. He could be complained to and pleaded with. They knew he would respond. The despair in so much of Anna's work indicates how she turned away from this belief. Her viewpoint is more akin to that of Kafka, who, as Irving Howe has suggested, knocks on the door of the Lord but never expects the door to be opened.

In the spring, after *Metamorphosis*, Anna was among several modern dance and ballet choreographers invited by Ballet Theatre to create new works for a workshop series at the downtown Phoenix Theatre. For the unique event Herbert Ross (later a successful film director) created a controversial all-male version of Jean Genet's *The Maids*. Anna's contribution, a turn of the corner for her, was *Le Grand Spectacle*, a hilarious circuslike spoof of dance and dancers, with music by the formidably talented composer and saxophonist, Teo Macero, who had performed in the original jazz group of *Rooms* (their professional relationship was to last for over thirty years).

The intriguing section titles of *Spectacle* give a hint of the humor: "Dance Poetique" (a shaky dance sur les pointes), "¿Como le Va?" (Tango Argentine), "L'amour de l'Apache" (the love of the Parisian gangster), "The Toppers" (four chugging tap dancers), and "Tzigane-Finale" (gypsy finale). Teo Macero later remembered another section, "La Nudes" [sic], which was removed at Lucia Chase's insistence because she saw implications of lesbianism in it (it was to be on the same program as *The Maids*; and she thought enough was enough).

Rather than using Ballet Theater dancers, Anna chose to work with the Theatre Dance Company, which for the season included a young choreographer/dancer named Paul Taylor. The light piece was a welcome one for her dancers and her followers as well. It remained in her repertory for some time.

In the summer of 1957, an opportunity to earn a much needed thousand dollars for a few weeks of work led Anna, against her better judgment, to San Diego to choreograph "The California Story" for the Fiesta del Pacifico. The Hollywood-style pageant was staged each summer for several years in the city's eighteen-thousand-seat Balboa Stadium.

The star attractions that season were the enormously popular radio and television star Arthur Godfrey, his almost equally famous horse, Goldie, and the opera singer Lucille Norman. Fortunately, the dancers were not scheduled to follow in Goldie's path — she did her routine in the playing field and they danced on the specially erected stage at one end of the stadium. They did, however, find out that in the Gold Rush section they had to come storming onto the stage just after the donkeys left, and that caused problems. It was *that* kind of production and Anna hated it.

From the beginning, nothing seemed to go right. Val Rosing, the director, had fallen asleep during Anna's initial interview with him as she was responding to his questions about her qualifications for the job (in retrospect she found that amusing, but not at the time). A few weeks later in San Diego she took another look at the lineup of twenty-two dancers she had auditioned in Los Angeles and decided that they were all Hollywood gypsies who knew nothing about her or about dance. They certainly would have difficulty understanding her particular way of working. She made that evaluation very plain to them from the beginning.

In actuality, few show-business dancers had come to the audition: the Actors' Equity minimum contract for the San Diego job paid very little and there was a good deal of film work available. After their expenses, the dancers were practically paying for the privilege of working with Anna. She later found out that many of them were serious ballet and modern dancers who did know her work. All but two or three of them had seen her choreography in New York at one time or another. Some clearly idolized her at the outset, if not when the job was finished, but during the grim and grueling rehearsal period there was little inclination on anyone's part to be chatty with Anna.

Rehearsals were held in a cavernous and steamy building in Balboa Park, with no air conditioning of any sort. An intense heat wave was gripping the city and the temperature seldom fell below one hundred degrees during the seven-hour rehearsals. Within a few days most of the dancers had agonizing shinsplints from dancing on the cement floor; two of the folk-type dances required stamping movement, making matters infinitely worse. Anna barely noticed their discomfort, but somehow found the kindness to limit her comments about the limping to one or two a day. She had other things to say.

One day, for example, in a moment of impatience she gathered the sweaty, red-faced dancers, some of them close to hallucinating from their leg pains and the heat, to tell them that their dancing was, by any professional standards, nothing. "What you are doing," she told them, "doesn't amount to a pile of beans." She stared at each of them in turn and none dared look away.

Not all of the dancers were fully accomplished, but among them was Francisco (Frank) Varcasia, who had been summoned to Hollywood to dance the role of Nijinsky in a film biography (never produced, this version was still under discussion twenty years later). Joan Lawrence could have had her pick of any ballet company in America, but she felt she was not yet ready. Willard Nagle was a strong enough dancer to be cast by Anna in *Copper and Brass*, a musical she choreographed for Broadway a few months later. And there were several others equally gifted.

But for those grueling rehearsal weeks Anna saw the group as a total disaster and never let them forget it. With whatever strength the dancers could muster, they worked to full capacity, and in three weeks they looked like a polished company. If her harshness was a tactic to make them work as hard for her as they did, it was as costly for her as for them. She looked utterly exhausted toward the end of the rehearsal period.

The ice was finally broken between the dancers and the choreographer at a dress rehearsal, when the imperious director, a leftover from Max Reinhardt's last production company, fell off the stage backwards while herding his large cast around as if they were cattle. Unhurt, he resurfaced drenched with black stage paint, looking as if he was covered with blood and miming like a character in a Mack Sennett silent-film comedy. Anna did not laugh aloud, but the dancers close to her could see her body rocking suspiciously and finally there were smiles and shared but stifled laughter.

After opening night the dancers had a surprise waiting for them when they limped and staggered wearily up to the door of their shabby hotel. Anna was sitting on the steps. "It was good," she said to each as they passed her. They were too exhausted to respond.

When the time came for her to leave, the dancers presented her with an enormous Mexican basket that she had admired on a trip to nearby Tijuana. "Why did you do this," she asked, "when I have been so awful to you?" Nobody answered, but there were tears visible on many faces. She spoke to each dancer individually.

"You are ready for New York *now*. Call me when you come and I'll help you if I can."

"Work on those feet!"

"Whoever you are studying with now is not helping you. Merce will know what you need. Go to New York."

"You have to learn not to be so serious all the time. Smile once in a while."

"But Anna . . ."

"Don't 'But Anna' me. Learn to smile!"

Just for a moment the dancers heard a tone of voice that they recognized all too well, but her face gave her away. *She* was smiling.

The failure of *Copper and Brass* in October must have been a bitter pill for Anna to swallow, especially coming at a time when *West Side Story* was enjoying a startling success on Broadway. Nancy Wilson, one of the funniest women in show business at the time, was the star of *Copper and Brass*. The very mention of her name was enough to bring a smile or laughter to anyone who had seen her perform in one of the delightful skits that were her specialty. Yet somehow she did not fit the part as it was structured for her. Jeff Duncan, who was in the cast, explained that Wilson's husband, the lyricist David Blair, appeared to want his wife to be seen as another Rosalind Russell and pushed her role in that direction. If that was indeed the case, it was an ill-advised idea. Wilson had a talent equal to Russell's, but one of a very different kind — more wacky than urbane. Moreover, Wilson was riding a crest of popularity at the time.

There were other difficulties as well. Both the book and the score of *Copper and Brass* had serious shortcomings that became painfully obvious during out-of-town tryouts. Anna struggled valiantly with the materials, but for every successful number she created, she appears to have had one that did not quite work. The fact that she was stuck with a poor property became clear when the successful Broadway choreographer Bob Fosse was brought in to doctor the dances and the results were no better. Leo Lerman wrote stingingly about the production in the December 1957 issue of *Dance Magazine* :

> Now about Anna Sokolow's choreography: it wasn't new either. Miss Sokolow is, and has been for quite a time, one of our most distinguished choreographers. Her dance works for the concert and theatre stage have, heretofore, been highly individual, her signature in dance being as unmistakable as Aaron Copland's in music . . . .
>
> Miss Sokolow, usually a master satirist, was, in "Copper and Brass," almost always cliche. It must be admitted that the dances in this show also suffered because it is impossible to view them without comparing them to Jerome Robbins' in "The West Side Story." Unfortunately, Miss Sokolow was working in Mr. Robbins' own milieu, but she was hemmed in by a piece of theatrical claptrap.

The irony of the reference to "Robbins' own milieu" could not have been lost on either him or Anna. It was a milieu that they both had been exploring since the 1940s.

Over the years Anna had been developing a movement vocabulary that emanated from the street life of the city — the life that was the pulse and energy of New York-style jazz. Part of the genius of *Rooms* is that the movement that evolves from a combination of dramatic projection and both modern and expressive jazz vocabularies is a nearly perfect metaphoric language for the subject matter. By 1957, Jerome Robbins appears to have melded the influence of Anna Sokolow's theater work and his own perception of the time to fashion a bold approach to musical theater in *West Side Story*.

This talent for appealing to popular taste is not one of Anna's particular gifts. She spoke about it candidly in later years, when she came to understand and accept the fact that her contributions to dance and theater were not necessarily the kind that were widely recognized or handsomely rewarded. For Anna, the most important thread in her life has been her work and that has always meant more to her than any popular or material success.

During the best years of their relationship, Anna and Johnny White traveled abroad together, went to the theater and concerts, and enjoyed a small but warm circle of friends. They gave each other moral support and sometimes practical help in their undertakings. When Anna's studio apartment on 73rd Street began to seem like cramped quarters, they found a fine two-level apartment on West 55th Street in a building whose tenants were primarily connected with the performing arts. It was a good location, just a few short blocks from Carnegie Hall, and for a hardy walker like Anna, close to practically everything that interested her.

By his own description, in those days Johnny was a frustrated writer, but he was one with considerable talent. His 1959 script for the short film *Skyscraper* won him an Academy Award nomination. Anna strongly encouraged him to keep writing and in later years directed some of his plays.

When reviews of Anna's works were less than favorable, Johnny was always there with a consoling "Screw those bastards! What do they know?" or some such sympathetic sentiment, flavored by what Anna referred to as his Irish temperament. When she was looking for a musical concept for *Rooms* it was Johnny and a friend who took her to Birdland to hear Dizzy Gillespie; she was, in Johnny's words, "blown away" by the latest sounds in jazz.

They encouraged and helped each other when things did not go right in one career or the other, and during many of their years together, that was quite a bit of the time.

In the late 1950s they scraped together enough money to rent an attractive four-room penthouse apartment on West 86th Street. The best view was out toward the Hudson and the New Jersey Palisades beyond. On a clear day, from their tiny balcony, they could see for miles in three directions. This was to be their home until they separated in 1961, after which Anna moved to an apartment on Central Park West.

Cracks began to appear in the relationship in the late 1950s, when Anna's career began to accelerate at a time when Johnny had difficulty finding work in the theater. Although he did some lucrative radio acting and, for a while, had a featured part on a television soap opera, this was far below his potential. To make ends meet he worked as a proofreader for a printing company, work that he abhorred. Handsome, short, and thickset, with a wry sense of humor that he could project on stage, Johnny was an ideal character type, but still too young to be cast in the best of those roles. Anna, on the other hand, was moving from one project to another at a speed that would have exhausted most people, and as always her absorption in work was total. There seemed to be less and less time for them to be together.

With the responsibilities of a busy company in New York added to frequent visits to Israel, Mexico, and Europe, it seemed that she was away more than she was with him. One time, when they had barely settled into a European vacation, Johnny received a cable from his agent concerning a lucrative job and he had no choice but to fly home immediately.

From the start of their life together, Johnny had been a steady drinker. As time went on, largely due to career frustrations, he began to drink more heavily. He later said that although he never lost any work over his drinking, there were long periods when he was only half sober. This put strain on the relationship, but Anna was confident that he would pull himself together when he was ready to and did not badger him. "I was the negative one in our relationship. She never was," he later said. One friend who knew them well in those years commented that Johnny "seemed to see himself as a kind of Dylan Thomas figure without Thomas' confidence in his own work." Eventually, he gave up drinking entirely and his drinking was not an issue in their later separation. Her long absences and his decision to seek comfort elsewhere during those intervals finally caused them to part. Her infatuation with the Israeli actor/mime Juki Arkin had not helped, either. After their separation, Anna and Johnny remained good friends and worked together on several projects.

15

THE JUILLIARD CONNECTION

Once you are taught by Anna, you stay taught. (Tony Azito, interview by Robert Berkvist, New York Times, September 27, 1981)

Everyone agrees the dance office is too small.[*] It has been too small since the Juilliard Dance Division first moved into the Lincoln Center complex in 1969. In an area scarcely larger than a tract-house living room, there are work spaces for a secretary, a receptionist, and an office for the director of the Dance Division, Martha Hill. Walls may as well not exist for all the privacy they afford.

Good-natured and hard-working Mary Chudick, for twenty-three years the division secretary, ignores the din of activity as she cheerfully taps away at her aging IBM Selectric typewriter. ("You wouldn't catch me dead with a computer. Never!") As a steady stream of dance majors wends its way through this tiny labyrinth of offices, the den mother/guardian angel shouts out greetings, reminders, and instructions, sometimes without looking up from her work.

Around the corner Martha Hill, mentor to generations of dancers during nearly sixty years of distinguished service to the dance world, is being interviewed. She interrupts a reminiscence about her work with Martha Graham in the early 1930s to answer a call from an out-of-work graduate of the department. "I'll ask around, dear, I'll try." A student barges in with an urgent question, gets his answer, and dashes off. "Sometimes," she sighs softly as she lowers the phone receiver, "I feel like the old woman who lived in a shoe." Then, without skipping a beat, she resumes the reminiscence precisely where she left off. She is forthright, unpretentious, and exceedingly modest.

In answer to a request for old Juilliard Dance Theater programs, she bounds into Mary Chudick's office, climbs onto a chair, and retrieves an armful dating back three decades, all the while fielding questions from Mary. Then, lightly and easily, she jumps down with her burden. Mary peers apprehensively over the rim of her eyeglasses, gasps, and mutters a prayer in Russian. Then, softly in English: "How does that woman do it?" She resumes typing, expecting no reply.

---

[*] This and the following observations were made in November 1985 at the Juilliard School of Music, Lincoln Center, New York. Martha Hill founded the dance program at Juilliard in 1951 and was the director until 1985. As Director Emerita, she continues to teach and advise Juilliard dance students.

More students pass through. Miss Hill knows each of them by name and will remember them, as she has the many hundreds of young dancers whose lives and careers she has touched. The astounding thing is not that Martha Hill can handle so much at one time, but that she appears to give each person or situation her complete concentration, managing to stay calm and poised all the while. Evidently she is enjoying every minute of it.

She speaks to the interviewer about Anna Sokolow's long association with Juilliard, which began in the spring of 1955, a few months after the resounding success of *Rooms*. At the suggestion of Doris Humphrey, director of the Juilliard Dance Ensemble, Hill invited Anna to create a work for the newly formed group. Anna responded with the sweetly lyrical *Primavera*. It was a lovely, small work with the dancers in *Primavera*-like costumes (Anna's design), exhilarant in the springtime of their youth. People who came to the performance expecting Anna's contribution to the program to be another *Lyric Suite* or *Rooms* were startled to learn that she enjoyed making lyrical pieces and was good at it.

It was not until 1958 that Anna was invited by Martha Hill to join the Juilliard faculty; she is still there over thirty years later. The relationship has been extremely valuable to the artist and to the school. Juilliard has provided a home base for Anna, the only one she has had for any great length of time throughout her career. It has afforded Juilliard students, hundreds of them, an opportunity to work with one of the most influential and one of the most demanding personalities in the modern dance world.

Many of these students, especially those from outside New York, have never seen anyone like her before. This beautiful little woman with the piercing blue-gray eyes seems at first so kindly and benign, so like a mother or a favorite aunt, but when they begin to work with her, impressions change rapidly. The urgency she projects in rehearsal sessions, combined with her mercurial temperament, instantly command the students' attention. She is not like any of the others on the faculty.

In the late 1950s, most of the important modern dance teachers were connected with a system of training techniques — techniques that, in some cases, they themselves had created. Graham, Limón, and Humphrey were then teaching at Juilliard, along with some of their principal disciples. Classes usually involved a body of knowledge to be studied, absorbed, and perfected. Two of those teachers at Juilliard, Graham and Limón, had major dance companies to which the dancers could aspire.

More so than now, it was an era in which serious young modern dance students set their hearts on the work of a particular choreographer and did their best to excel in that person's style of training. Hopefully, they would be noticed in class or at an audition and invited to join the company. But Anna was not teaching technique. If she taught technique classes at all in those years, it was usually at the

New Dance Group Studio on West 47th Street. As far as the students at Juilliard were concerned, it might as well have been on another planet.

Not only was there no Sokolow technique per se, but there was no major company either, only a small concert group. Moreover, Anna worked in such diverse media and in so many different places that she sometimes seemed like a guest stopping by on her way to another assignment. If you wanted to dance for her after graduation, you put everything you had into the intense rehearsal sessions she held for the pieces she staged — sometimes new works — for Juilliard performances. She either took special notice of you there or your chances were very slim. (Eliot Feld, who had not studied with her, recalled approaching Anna after a performance at the "Y" and telling her how much he would like to work with her. "That's very sweet," she told him, and kept walking.)

How is it that this sometimes cantankerous, sometimes angelic woman could exert such a profound effect on her students? She seems so full of contradictions. At Juilliard auditions she would often bypass the better-trained dancers and focus instead on the raw talent. There were instances in which she chose dancers who had a Graham or Limón look to their dancing and at other times she appeared to avoid any distinct style.

In fact neither style nor technique particularly interest Anna. In the studio she is looking for what she recognizes as truthful movement. Technique is of only secondary importance. "Motion comes from emotion," she has said repeatedly. "The technique will be there when you need it." In auditions she is drawn to dancers with passion, intensity, vulnerability, and a heightened aliveness in their projection, or if she sees sufficient potential she will take on the job of drawing out those traits. As they labor with her to bring her choreography to its fullest realization, student dancers learn from Anna's demand to explore their full expressive range. There is no other way to respond to her sometimes demonic intensity.

Anna has an uncanny ability to spot insincerity in a performer, and insincere dramatic projection is a sin far worse than blandness, which is also anathema to her. She trains dancers to give full physical form to their personal pain and anger as well as to more positive emotions. Precisely because she employs no systematic techniques or exercises to achieve these goals, the dancers must find their own way in. She does not teach them how to plumb their own depths, she simply demands that they do. It becomes *their* search, *their* quest for performance integrity, and when they find it, the results are long-lasting.

The dancers are directed through a unique process that demands patience, forbearance, deep concentration, and a willingness on their part to search internally for meanings and motivations in a way they are not likely to have searched before. In exchange for working through this sometimes harsh approach they learn things about performance and choreography in a few months of rehearsals that might otherwise take them years to discover on their own.

When Anna asks the dancers to look out into the distance, they must see beyond the horizon. She explains this with few words, but with an urgency that suggests that if they do not learn how to project that kind of focus *now*, they may never learn. Some find it quickly. It is not only the eyes, but the whole body that must see, so that the eyes can communicate a larger truth. If two dancers are asked to project anger toward each other, she expects to see two tigers preparing to fight it out — not simply the appearance of anger, but its essence. She demands a purity of intent that involves the whole body. If you run, you must run as if a strong wind is hurling you through space. If you throw your head back, the movement must stretch to your absolute physical limits. If you hold your body limply, it must look as if life has gone out of you completely. The dancer must be willing to be the raw material ready to be molded. One does not hold back or ask questions. Certainly one does not remind her that yesterday they were asked to do the movement differently.

Some understand right away and silently acknowledge: "Of course I can do that, I have just been waiting for someone to ask me for it." Others take longer and may try to mask their apprehension with exaggerated politeness. "Yes, Miss Sokolow," and "No, Miss Sokolow," are precisely what she does not want from them. "Look," she might say, "first of all, my name is Anna, and second of all, don't be polite! I don't want politeness from you, I want the *truth* of the movement, and *I* can't give that to you. You have to pull that out of yourself!"

She may have fits of anger if she is not getting results or, even worse for some of the dancers, she may shrug hopelessly in their direction. Sometimes there are tears. If it is a large group, one or two may edge toward the door, hoping to escape unnoticed. Anna spots them with her eagle eye and they are herded back. Martha Hill observed:

> Her intensity as a director keeps people excited about working for her. The others drop out. It is a self-selective process. Some students don't want to see life that way. She will take one of the dancers by the shirt and say, "Do you like what we're doing?" God help them if they are lukewarm about it. Anna will say, "Out! Get Out!"

Anna does not treat these students any differently from dancers in professional companies. She expects the same level of commitment from anyone who works with her. When she was working with the Boston Ballet in 1978, she was interviewed by Christine Temin for the *Boston Evening Globe*. "I like all dancers, except those who don't cooperate. Those I throw out," she commented. When was the last time she had to do that? "Today," she responded simply.

Sometimes they are back the next day, ready to work her way. By the time the work is performed for an audience, the hardy ones, the ones who have decided to see it through to the end (and they are always the majority), have found their individual versions of what Anna is looking for. The clarity and passion in their dancing is a wonder to behold in such young dancers. Martha Hill described another aspect of that intensity:

> When she fights for rehearsal time, sometimes unreasonably, she is like an evangelist. She is fighting for the outcome of the idea. Because the interest in the work is so intense it looks like ego. But it is a strange kind of ego. Her Sokolow is her work. That is what she is.

Martha Hill always knew precisely what she was doing when it came to choosing faculty, and she believed emphatically in what the experience of working with Anna would bring to her students.

Some of Anna's most important dances in the past thirty years were first created for Juilliard students. Other works have been honed, reworked, and revived there. There have been some fine choreographic successes among the new pieces as well as some less distinguished works, but one thing remains constant: students who work in a piece of Anna's are never quite the same afterward.

Among the dancers who worked with her there over the years were Libby Nye, Ray Cook, Cliff Keuter, Daniel Lewis, Martha Clarke, Paula Kelly, Michael Uthoff, Dennis Nahat, Linda Kent, Carla Maxwell, Lynne Wimmer, and Gary Masters.

Dennis Nahat, choreographer and director of the Cleveland and San Jose Ballet Companies, is one of the Juilliard graduates who openly acknowledges his indebtedness to Anna. As a choreographer, he learned from her "how to direct people and move them but not get bogged down in steps." As a dancer, he gives her credit for helping him to discover how to scale his acting and comedy performances into the movement quality of a work, an ability that would influence — almost define — his dance career at American Ballet Theatre.

Reviewers of Juilliard Dance Theater concerts have often noted that while the dancers looked proficient in other works, they seemed professional — even inspired — in Anna's pieces. In a long and well-researched article about Juilliard for *Dance Magazine* in July 1968, Robert Sabin wrote, "If it had produced nothing but the nine works of Anna Sokolow between 1955 and 1967, the Juilliard Dance Department would have amply justified itself. For Miss Sokolow, who is at home in Webern and Berio as well as Cimarosa, has added a whole new dimension to the modern theatre."[*]

16

A NEW ERA

The world is changing and artists who reflect this consciously or unconsciously are changing also. (Anna Sokolow, interview. Unidentified Mexico City newspaper clipping, Sokolow scrapbook)

On April 11, 1958, Juilliard Dance Theater premiered Anna's *Session '58*, which explored a theme that would fascinate her for over a decade. *Session* and the versions that followed are not merely about lost individuals, but about a lost society. The withdrawn sufferers she introduced to the American stage in *Rooms* no longer endure their pain in isolation; now they stand as an angry group, tired of feeling isolated and disconnected. Teo Macero's frenetic jazz score matched the new aggressive statement just as the darkly introspective Kenyon Hopkins music had set the mood for the brooding *Rooms*. Jazz continued to be the ideal accompaniment for such themes in Anna's work, and with Macero, a first-rate composer, she continued to explore the potential of combining jazz and serious dance themes.

In a one-year period *Session '58* appeared under several other titles: *Opus '58* (New York and Amsterdam), *Session For Eight* (New York), and *Opus Jazz 1958* (Israel). The work kept changing and growing. In the next few years it developed into *Opus '60* and then *Opus '63*. The exploration reached its fullest maturity in *Opus '65*, which was destined to become a classic in the Joffrey Ballet Company's repertory.

In the fall of 1960, Ana Mérida, then general director of Mexico City's Ballet de Bellas Artes, invited Anna to be a guest artist for the company's official fall season at the Palace of Fine Arts. Mérida, one of the original Sokolovas, had joined Waldeen's group in the early 1940s, but had never lost her deep respect for Anna and her work. In 1939, her father, Carlos, had introduced Anna to Mexican audiences. Twenty-one years later, his daughter wished to honor Anna in the way she would appreciate most — giving her an opportunity to do her work with the best dancers and resources Mexico had to offer.

During this landmark season Anna became involved in a complex and fascinating production — *Homenaje a Hidalgo* (Homage to Hidalgo), a cantata for actors, singers, and dancers — and, as happened so often in her professional life, she found herself embroiled in controversy. The homage to the Mexican priest and revolutionary Miguel Hidalgo was originally intended for the sesquicentennial celebration of the beginning of Mexico's war for independence from colonial rule in 1810, but it had never been presented. The librettist Emilio Carballido and the composer Rafael Elizondo had planned to use a full orchestra in addition to the chorus, actors, and dancers in their ambitious work. Initially, the project had generated a good deal of enthusiasm, but it was abandoned when the high cost of the production became clear.

In much the same way that Rodolfo Halffter and José Bergamin had brought their unproduced *Don Lindo de Almería* to Anna twenty years earlier, the creators told her about their Hidalgo homage. She was immediately enthusiastic about the project and helped to set the wheels in motion to make it a reality. Her offer was simple and direct: she would make a gift of her direction and choreography, in her words, "to express the profound love I feel for the people of Mexico." Pleased by the offer, Bellas Artes officials decided to go ahead with the production.

What they did not take into consideration was that although Anna planned to develop only the first half of the Carballido/Elizondo spectacle, the major costs of the undertaking would still be extraordinary — not much different from the earlier estimates for producing the whole work. Wishing to fill the stage with the excitement and energy the script called for, Anna chose to use all of the dancers and actors who came to the audition from the various Bellas Artes performance academies. Those groups plus the chorus brought the total cast to over eighty, not including the orchestra. Costume costs alone were staggering.

Besieged with budgetary and personnel problems associated with this and other productions in this ambitious 1960 season, Ana Mérida fought courageously so that Anna's vision of the *Homenaje* could be realized. There were some strong objections to having an outsider, even Anna Sokolow, do a major choreographic work on the subject of a revered Mexican historical figure. Mérida had to do battle behind closed doors as well as in the open forum provided by Mexico City's press, which has always given substantial coverage to artistic controversies.

As usual, Anna was too busy working to get into the fracas. She had boldly cast a young and relatively untried actor, Angel Pineda, in the only speaking role, that of the Hidalgo figure. It was an audacious choice when so much critical attention was being focused on this particular production. Newspaper accounts agree with Carballido's later assessment that the production far exceeded everyone's expectations. Pineda vindicated Anna's faith in him, and the overall effect of the work was compelling.

José Coronado recalls that Anna used images from an Orozco mural in Guadalajara as an inspiration for some of her choreography: "The gestures she used from everyday life, like hands turning quickly to make tortillas, were something we never saw before. A Mexican choreographer would not have thought of doing that in those days." He remembered a particularly touching scene in which an important message had to be sent to the rebel forces hiding in the hills. While a harpist played and sang *Vuela, vuela, palomita* (Fly, fly, little dove), a very little girl, dressed entirely in white, ran in a circular pattern around the stage with the message in her outstretched arm. Many in her audience were moved to tears by the image. At one climactic point, when everyone on stage linked arms and marched directly toward the footlights, the audience exploded with enthusiasm.

Anna was not there to enjoy the opening-night cheers. Her schedule had demanded an early return to New York. By leaving, she was spared the unsavory details of several apparently not-so-accidental mishaps during the season, including one in which the theater was temporarily plunged into total darkness. Some people had not reconciled themselves to the idea of a "Norte Americana" celebrating their beloved hero, and there may also have been leftover animosity from the fireworks of the Conferencia a few years earlier. For whatever reasons, a few relatively harmless acts of sabotage were carried out. For a while there was enough silliness going on to provide a libretto for a comic opera.

In one section of the work there was a fiesta scene in which the seven deadly sins were depicted in mime and dance. Anna's depiction of Lust, danced by Elena Noriega and Rosalio Ortega, was singled out by some viewers as obscene. (A drunken prostitute sprawls on a bench, legs apart. A man approaches her and kneels between her legs. She tosses her full head of hair over him.) Bellas Artes director Celestino Gorostiza told Ana Mérida to see that the troublesome section was changed or removed. Phone calls to Anna in New York met with a predictable response: her work was not to be tampered with. She later wrote to Mérida:

> When I did that part for Elena and Rosalio, I was searching for the truth, and I would *never* do an obscene thing on the stage in my whole life. . . . I do not understand how Maestro Gorostiza who has talked with me — and seen my face — can imagine that I would do anything obscene? Ana dear, I rely on you to use your artistic judgement and try to defend it.

Ana Mérida was somehow able to keep the work intact during the entire season.

Long before the days of the Conferencia, and especially after it, Anna was clearly a controversial as well as a revered figure in the Mexican dance world. The squabble about the Hidalgo work helped to solidify that position. In an art world so vulnerable to political meddling, negotiations were often made difficult for those who wanted to have Anna work creatively in the country as frequently as possible. Certainly most of the major critics and dance personalities supported her. Even the ones with whom she had professional differences welcomed her warmly when she visited. She was, after all, something of a matriarch among them. Having a cloud over her reputation was nothing new to Anna. Knowing full well the high price of her sometimes difficult personality, she was guided by rules of her own making. She seemed to say, "I am what I am. People can choose to take it or leave it." In the 1970s a laudatory article titled "Anna Sokolow: rebeldía con disciplina" appeared in a Mexico City magazine. For years afterward Anna would say, quite proudly, "In Mexico they call me the rebel with discipline."

As it turned out it was not the Hidalgo work that finally won Anna the lion's share of favorable reviews for that six-week season, which had included the work of many of Mexico's major choreographers. It was, rather, *Opus '60*, a further development of her *Session '58* exploration of alienation and rebellion. Mexican audiences and critics seemed able to identify with the themes, for there were murmurs of a coming rebellion of young people in Mexico City similar to the ones being heard in the United States and Europe. *Opus '60* was Anna's first work since her 1939 *Ballad in a Popular Style* to use jazz in Mexico, and a whole new audience was introduced to the idea that this kind of music could be used in dances that express deep human experience. To emphasize the universality of the theme, dancers were costumed in red, yellow, black, and white leotards, each representing a skin color of the world's races. The work was performed entirely in front of the bare walls at the rear of the stage — by this time a Sokolow staging signature.

The opening section of *Opus '60* mirrors a world without love or hope. The dancers encounter one another frequently, but the encounters are cold, impersonal, and sometimes hostile. In the second section, the hostility grows, the music becomes more hectic, and the message of youthful rebelliousness becomes clearer. The third section sets forth terrifying images of war, but also carries a message of hope and a challenge. There is an affirmative coming together, a spiritual linking of arms. Then, the whole cast progresses downstage. They sit at the edge of the stage. They accuse and challenge. At the same time they are pleading for understanding. It is a plea made especially effective by contrast with the aggressive earlier sections. Rich with dramatic images, yet with no recognizable narrative line, it was clearly a new kind of dance — certainly new to Mexican audiences. In discussing the work, Anna told an interviewer, "The world is changing and artists who reflect this consciously or unconsciously are changing also."

In summing up the season, José Alcaraz, a critic for the newspaper *Excelsior*, expressed the enthusiasm of many of Mexico City's critics: "Nineteen-sixty is the year of Anna Sokolow, the searcher of the human spirit." John Fealy, the Mexico City dance correspondent for *Dance Magazine*, sent in the minority report:

> The highly touted *Opus '60* failed to live up to advance reports. In her depiction of lost people and their ultimate reunion, Sokolow neglected to show us who they were and what and why they were trying to forget. Her concept of jazz, her idea of what constitutes brotherhood and her use of music seem elementary.

Whether or not *Opus '60* was a work of the highest artistic merit, it set the tone for a substantial number of works that in the next decade clearly identified Anna as a leader in the expression through dance of the alienation and anger of contemporary youth. At the same time, other world-shaking events were slowly surfacing from her subconscious memories.

When *Dreams* was first conceived in the spring of 1961, Anna had no conscious thought of concentration camps or Anne Frank. That came much later. She was having troubled dreams and decided to use them as the basis for a new work, not quite sure what the dreams meant or what would develop in her choreography. "I have always had bad dreams," Anna once told an interviewer in an unguarded moment. Although at other times she had candidly admitted that much of the material in her dances came from her own life experience, she usually did so in a rather detached and impersonal way, as if to say "Don't all artists express their inner life in their artistic works?"

The first draft of the work was shown, along with a revision of *Metamorphosis*, in the informal setting of the Herbert Berghof (HB) Studio, where she conducted Sunday-morning classes for actors. The cast included Jack Moore, Juki Arkin, Julie Arenal, Nancy Lewis, and Buck Heller. Still a work-in-progress, *Dreams* was developed a bit further and shown at the "Y" in May at the Freda Miller Memorial Concert, then again in August on a Sunday-afternoon concert at the American Dance Festival in Connecticut. By this time Juki Arkin had left and been replaced by James Payton. Significantly, *Dreams* was not presented as a premiere at any of those performances; in fact it was never actually given a formal premiere in the United States. Anna just kept showing it as it developed.

When she decided a few months later to present the work in Mexico City with a much larger group, there still was no suggestion of the Holocaust in the choreography — but the dance was changing. In Mexico she substituted the music of Webern for the original Macero score. (Eventually she used both and added Bach.) The lighting designer, Tom Skelton, later told Jack Anderson that he had seen the work at Connecticut College and in Mexico City and barely recognized it the second time.

Although *Dreams* went through many stages of development, including a return to the small-group version shown at the "Y" in the spring of 1962, it was not until much later that Anna began to tie those images to her earlier reading of André Schwarz-Bart's *The Last of the Just*, one of the most powerful books ever written about the Nazi death camps. She later came to the conclusion that Schwarz-Bart's writing had set her dream process in motion and kept her grappling with the work until she understood the meaning it held for her. Jack Moore, who was there at the beginning and knew Anna very well, felt that her troubled personal life — the recently ended relationship with John White — had also fed the nightmare visions. Whatever the sources of the imagery, this distinguished work went through an incubation period of about three years before Anna knew precisely what she wanted to do with it.

She later remembered that one summer, just before leaving Israel, she found herself staring at concentration-camp numbers on a man's arm and suddenly it was clear to her. In subsequent versions changes were made, but mostly in the way the work was described when being taught; at first, very little, if anything, was changed in the choreography. *Dreams* seemed to take its final form in much the same way that a photograph increases sharpness as it soaks in developing fluid.

Doris Hering described her reaction to *Dreams* as performed at the American Dance Festival in August 1966. At that time the work was not yet well known as a dance focusing on the Holocaust.

> *Dreams* gave one the sensation of being in the presence of a special kind of brav-
> ery. Because of it the spectator feels a little braver, too. Part of this comes from the
> subject matter with its relentless confrontation of life, not as the choreographer
> would like it to be, but as it is. Part also comes from the choice of movement. It is
> never naturalistic because it does not derive from social gesture. Rather it is abso-
> lutely natural because it derives from the secret domain of the emotions. . . . It has
> the effect of Käthe Kollwitz's "Old Woman Greeting Death"; of all of Kokoschka;
> of Auschwitz, Dachau; of the faces of soldiers in the grip of battle fatigue.

It is interesting to compare these observations to those made a decade later when the Holocaust interpretation of the work was well established. So universal are Anna's nightmare images that *Dreams* still allows for an open interpretation. It is still possible to see it as a timeless allegory of terror and hopelessness. Deborah Jowitt's moving description of the opening section of the dance in the July 28, 1976, *Village Voice* is a case in point:

> *Dreams*, typically, radiates pain. . . . In the first of this suite of agonized dances, a
> woman races past motionless, unseeing men in black; they clump around her,
> hoist her up, and she walks forward, groping for their hands, on an unending car-
> pet of shoulders. Since the men keep moving to replace each other, she can never
> get down.

If we, the audience, do not see that pitiful figure in the opening scene as Anne Frank (suggested by Anna's later dedication), we may perhaps see her as ourselves in our own nightmares.

Clive Barnes called the piece "a deeply psychological and gripping work — a despairing theatrical experience. *Dreams* reveals that unseen realm where feelings give birth to strange visions." These strange visions exist in the reality of nightmares, where one runs without escaping, reaches without touching, and acts without feeling. Feelings are there but cannot be associated with any reality, and screams are silent. The characters in *Dreams* crush us with their helplessness, desperation, remembered nobility, irretrievable relationships, and lost selves.

Anna's terrible anger, that sense of shocked outrage at the Holocaust, is no less evident because of the universality of the images. The dancers know precisely what they are doing when they work with her. In one rehearsal she told them, "When we see your face, we know your name. *They* may have given you a number, but *we* know your name."

On July 9, 1966, the day after the Netherlands Dance Theater gave the work its European premier, a review in the Dutch press made it amply clear that many in the Dutch audience understood the work through their experiences in World War II. From the *Haagsche Courant* (The Hague):

> The applause did not commence immediately after Anna Sokolov's [sic] *Dreams*, which the Netherlands Dance Theater premiered last night at the Royal Theater in a Holland Festival program. Personally I would have preferred leaving in silence. Not because the program was lacking in any way but because these nine scenes inspired by the concentration camps were not "theater" but oppressive nightmares. It is all so recent, so near, and still so alive. Dreams like this are still being dreamed by victims who were freed from the camps but not from their camp neurosis.

From *Het Vaterland* (Amsterdam) the same day:

> In total this choreo-drama moved the large public in the same way that *The Green Table* did before the Second World War. At the first performance last night, this was made apparent; there was a tense silence and a long applause for the interpreters who performed it with such conviction, and for Anna Sokolov [sic] who was brought on stage to share the ovation.

Anna Sokolow at the airport,
circa 1961. Photographer unknown.
Courtesy of Stephen Bank.

Beatrice Seckler, Sandra Pine, Jeff Duncan, and
Alvin Ailey, Anna Sokolow Dance Company,
Poem, 1956. Photograph by W. H. Stephen.
Anna Sokolow collection.

Jürgen Otte, Netherlands Dance Theater, *Dreams*,
Amsterdam, 1966. Photograph by Anthony
Crickmay.

Ofra Ben Zvi, Avraham Montzour, Gideon Avrahami, Yinon Ne'eman, Liora Hachmi, Rina Shaham, Johanna Peled, and Avraham Tzuri, Lyric Theatre, Tel Aviv, *Odes*, 1964. Photograph by Yakov Agor. Courtesy of the photographer.

Rex Bickmore, The Joffrey Ballet, *Opus '65*, 1966. Photograph by Herbert Migdoll. Courtesy of the photographer.

Ballet Rambert, *Opus '65*, Photograph by Rosemary Winkley, 1970. Courtesy of the photographer.

Chester Wolenski, Julie Arenal, Jack Moore, Linda Tarnay, and Jac Venza on *Far Rockaway* set [television], 1965. Photograph by Matthias Tarnay. Courtesy of Linda Tarnay.

Clyde Morgan, David Krohn, Trina Parks, John Parks, Ze'eva Cohen, and Martha Clarke (on the floor), Anna Sokolow Dance Company, *And the Disciples Departed* [televison], 1967. Photographer unknown. Anna Sokolow collection.

Anna Sokolow conducting rehearsal at Clark Center, New York City, circa 1967. Photograph by Herbert Migdoll. Courtesy of the photographer.

Raúl Flores Canelo,
Ballet Independiente,
Deserts, 1968. Copyright
© J. Contreras Chacel.
Courtesy of the
photographer.

David Krohn, Kathy
Posin, Ray Cook, and
Ze'eva Cohen, Anna
Sokolow Dance Company,
Deserts, 1967. Photograph
by Edward Effron.
Courtesy of the
photographer.

Rex Bickmore, Lyric
Theatre, *Act Without
Words*, 1970. Photograph
by Van Williams.
Courtesy of the
photographer.

Cynthia Morales and Michael
Simon, Juilliard Dance
Ensemble, "Two Lovers" from
Magritte, Magritte, 1980.
Photograph by Jane Rady.
Courtesy of the photographer.

Randall Faxon, (center high),
Laura Glenn (center low), Victor
Vargas (right high), Ko Yukihiro
(right low), Contemporary Dance
System, *Moods*, 1975.
Photograph by M. B. Honnewell.

Ze'eva Cohen, "Escape" section from *Rooms*, 1980. Photograph by David Fullard. Courtesy of the photographer.

Juilliard Dance Ensemble, *Ellis Island*, 1976. Photograph by Milton Oleaga.

Gregory DeJean and Rodney McGuire, Juilliard Dance Ensemble, "La Noche de los Mayas," from *Así es la Vida en México*, 1979. Copyright © 1979 Peter Schaaf.

Lorry May, Jim May, *The Evolution of Tiger Rag*, Players' Project. Photographer unknown. Courtesy of Lorry May.

Jim May in *Ballade,* circa 1986. Photograph by David Fullard. Courtesy of the photographer.

John Passafiume, Stuart Smith, Lorry May, Jim May, and Susan Thomasson, Players' Project, *Steps of Silence*, 1986. Photograph by Tom Brazil. Courtesy of the photographer.

Anna conducts rehearsal of Limón Company at Clark Center, New York City, 1974. Photographs by Rad Bascome. Anna Sokolow collection.

Anna Sokolow, 1986. Photograph by David Fullard. Courtesy of the photographer.

17

LYRIC THEATRE (ISRAEL)

Her demand, as always, was that the performers find within themselves the passion in-dispensable to the realization of her images. (Rina Shaham, personal interview, June 17, 1983, Tel Aviv)

With each of Anna's visits to Israel she increasingly felt at home. When Eliezer Peri, then chairman of the Board of the America-Israel Cultural Foundation, approa-ched her with the idea of creating a new dance company in Israel, the time and place seemed right and a formal plan was set in motion.

In early spring of 1962, Anna, no stranger to the challenge of building groups from the ground up, presented a proposal to the A.-I.C.F. board.

> My plan is to form a company of no more than ten dancers, train them and create a repertory for three months, and then perform for three months. This group of dancers should be paid a monthly salary for six months. I suggest a very nominal sum of £150 a month. . . . The company would perform four times a week, once a week in Tel Aviv, once a week in Haifa, once a week in Jerusalem and once a week for the kibbutzim. I am convinced that there is public interest and that there will be audiences for it. No scenery; the simplest stage production; music taped.

The important stipulation, that some salary be paid to the dancers, "was a revolution," explains Judith Gottlieb. "No one thought about dancers at the time, but only about creators. The major support went to choreographers. Although Inbal was already in existence, no one really understood that dancers would have to be paid if a permanent group was to be set up."

Anna's proposal troubled some members of the board. Concern was ex-pressed that by encouraging a non-Israeli to embark on such a venture, other out-side choreographers might follow suit, bringing in their own performers as well. In retrospect, it seems an odd concern, since Anna had been deeply involved in the cultural development of the country for nearly a decade and had made it clear that she planned to use Israeli artists exclusively. The sceptics, fortunately, were in the minority and support for the project was solicited by the A.-I.C.F. and by Anna herself. Help came from the Lena Robbins Foundation, the Rebekah Harkness Foundation, and Rabbi Arthur Lilyveld's Cleveland, Ohio, congregation, but the funding level could best be described as limited. The time seemed right for such a venture, and the Lyric Theatre was born.

Anna, with typical intensity, moved quickly to implement her ideas. Knowing that commitments in the United States and elsewhere would be summoning her in the early fall, she held auditions in mid-April, immediately after the board's approval of her plan. She had described to them a theatrical enterprise in which acting and dancing would merge into an artistic whole.

By April 29, an excited Anna wrote to Martha Hill at Juilliard: "I have formed a company of thirteen young actor-dancers that I call Lyric Theatre. . . . I am preparing two programs, and expect to be ready for performances the first week in July. We expect to perform about 4 times a week, touring Israel for about 4 months — so you see, I am happy working!"

There was cause for happiness among the dancers as well. Although their salaries were minimal, even by the standards of the day, this was the first time that working dancers in Israel had been given professional standing. Among the members of the new company were Bamat Machol dancers Rina Shaham, Avraham Zouri, and Ze'eva Cohen. Others were Rina Schenfeld (who had trained at the Juilliard School), Galia Gat, Ehud Ben-David, Yigal Paz, Leora Hachmi, Dalia Harlap, Shimon Siani, Yitzhak Ben-Nissim, and Dalia Kimchi.

And then, there was Yossi Kipnis.

Anna had met Yossi on a shopping trip in downtown Tel Aviv, soon after her arrival that spring. The jocular young actor recognized her — she was a celebrity in the world of the arts — and introduced himself. His boundless energy and raucous humor won her over immediately; a romantic involvement followed quickly on the heels of a warm friendship. She was fifty-two, Kipnis was in his middle twenties. As Juki Arkin, another of her former young lovers, later said, "We never thought of Anna in terms of age. She was ageless. There was such a lot to be learned from her and we had a wonderful time together." The age difference seemed to matter even less to Yossi, for there was a nearly perfect balance between them. Anna was characteristically high-strung and easily upset. Yossi — bright, brash and a little vulgar, and an inveterate tease — was larger than life in many ways. He ribbed her mercilessly about anything and everything and she loved it. He was able to dissolve her dark, brooding moods with an irreverent silliness. Yossi was her lover, her sabra-harlequin, and for a time the ideal companion for Anna.

A typical scene in those years: A performance of Anna's work is over. Crowds of friends and admirers, old and new, inundate her with praise. Although such moments make her uncomfortable, she is warm and gracious; if she is tired, she hides it well. More praise, more gracious smiles, and then suddenly a look of exhaustion and near-panic crosses her face. "Where is Yossi?" She excuses herself and goes in search of the jester. He says something outrageous, hugs her warmly, and starts talking a blue streak, while the color and composure come back to her face. Her body softens visibly; she can now go another round with her public.

The new company rehearsed in whatever space was available — a rented hall, a synagogue. The ballet teacher Mia Arbatova graciously allowed them use of her studio whenever possible. From all accounts, rehearsals proved intense and unforgettable. Rina Shaham remembered, her demand, as always, was that the performers find within themselves the passion indispensable to the realization of her images. Within a few weeks they began to look like a company.

Two decades later, Shaham spoke glowingly about her experience in Lyric Theatre rehearsals:

> Anna taught us how to listen to the music and extend it through our bodies. It wasn't just a matter of staying with the music, but of attempting to find a way to connect the musical phrase with the movement phrase. She emphasized the importance of understanding legato quality in movement. And we learned not to be afraid of moving against the music.
>
> She spoke of lengthening the body line, of opening, of giving the feeling of hope, of optimism in our dancing. Eventually, it helped me to find a way of moving that has made a big difference in how I have danced and taught. After these rehearsals, performances almost seemed to be an anticlimax.

The program, designed to emphasize the relationship between theater, music, and dance, included *L'Histoire du Soldat, The Treasure* (score by Nathan Mishori, from a fairy tale by the Yiddish writer, Isaac Loeb Peretz), and *Dreams*. Each of the works, whether primarily theater or dance, required of the dancers a strong dramatic sensibility.

The new venture aroused controversy. A carelessly written and uncredited article in the June 7, 1962, issue of the *Jerusalem Post* set off friction between the choreographer and her dance-affiliated colleagues in Israel. After a brief summary of her past work there, the article stated:

> The main problem in organizing the company [Lyric Theatre] was, of course, the lack of trained dancing talent in a country which has no ballet tradition, no ballet, and no school to speak of. The company Miss Sokolow assembled consists of 12 [sic] young men and women, some of them trained abroad, some who have benefited from her own teaching during her many prolonged visits in the past 9 years.

The article unfairly and unnecessarily insulted those artists who had labored long and well to train dancers in that country. Israeli teachers and choreographers had never quite grown used to seeing foreign artists treated as messiahs by the press, while they themselves were largely taken for granted. Gertrud Kraus, universally respected as a teacher and a choreographer, was the sole artist who had most consistently escaped this cavalier treatment. It was she who responded to this journalistic heavy-handedness in a letter to the editor that appeared in the same newspaper on the day of the Lyric Theatre's premiere performance, July 4, 1962:

We refer to the portion of your feature of June 7 dealing with Miss Sokolow's proposed dance theatre. We, the dancers, teachers, and choreographers welcome any advancement in the field of art or theater in this country. It was in this spirit that large and small dance schools gave their moral, collegial support to her venture, allowing and encouraging their best and most veteran pupils to join her group, despite obvious interruptions of routine, work and study. Miss Sokolow's group is composed of the product of those schools and institutes which your writer stated are nonexistent. Her venture will, therefore, benefit from many years of hard work invested by the local artists who also prepared and educated her potential public. She has also obtained financial support, an advantage never enjoyed by local choreographers who nevertheless staged many fine and valuable works despite the difficulties arising from the lack of such support.

Yours for the Dancers Association of Israel,

Gertrud Kraus

If Anna was aware of the controversy her activities had engendered it must have been only peripherally. The task she had set for herself and her fledgling troupe was a prodigious one and took all her concentration. On July 1, she wrote to Martha Hill, "The work goes well, it's just the technical stuff which is careless and exasperating — and I have to fight for what I need — constantly."

Three days later, the Lyric Theatre gave its first performance in Tel Aviv's Nachmani Hall. The audience response was highly enthusiastic, some of the critical reaction less so. Years later, Karl Glaser of the A.-I.C.F. suggested that, at the time, Israeli critics lacked the professional background to review dance, and this may well have been true. Nevertheless, the program Anna had put together had been overly ambitious for the amount of work time, and weaknesses had surfaced. Anna's and the dancers' total expectations could not possibly have been fulfilled on the first try. Yet, if the result had not been quite up to her exacting standards, the pioneering effort had been made and eventually won Anna some close allies in and out of the dance community. Gertrud Kraus soon became a particularly staunch supporter and a good friend.

Following the performances in Tel Aviv, the company embarked on a grueling tour of the country: forty concerts in a variety of settings. Like Inbal before them, they danced not only in urban centers such as Jerusalem, Natanya, and Haifa, but also in *kibbutzim* and other settlements throughout the country. They danced on improvised stages, in sometimes unbearable heat. Their only luxury was a portable wooden floor they had been able to borrow from Inbal. In the first months Anna was always there, encouraging, chastening, and helping the company to adjust to the conditions as they encountered them. In her youth she, too, had performed under far from ideal conditions when she toured workers' clubs and union halls. She knew how hard it was and she knew it could be done.

It was not only physical hardships that the Lyric Theatre faced. Some audiences in the outlying areas were disturbed, as the critics in Tel Aviv had been, with Anna's stark, uncompromising theatrical ways. At the time the younger members of the Israeli audience in particular were unused to such unmitigated emotional rawness on the stage. Their response was sometimes tinged with impatience and irritation. To aggravate matters further, many Israelis resented an outsider bringing Jewish themes to Israel. Detractors notwithstanding, the majority of dancegoers were impressed and wanted to see more. The response was for the most part heartening.

Anna's young dance artists watched her and learned. They were developing criteria that would guide them throughout their own careers (and several of those careers were to be quite distinguished). Sometimes they felt that her volatility and tactlessness got in the way of what she was trying to achieve, but as many had before them they accepted this all too human side of the choreographer in exchange for her brilliance as an artist, her rapier-sharp eye as a movement coach, her willpower, and her indefatigable efforts on their behalf.

In the fall, knowing of Anna's impending departure the dancers and her older friends urged her to consider making Israel her home base. Eliezer Peri in particular wanted her to stay. He offered to help her acquire one of the marvelous old houses in Jaffa, which were being converted into artists' quarters. It could be hers practically for the cost of fixing it up, but she felt she knew too little of such things to do a proper job and, much to her regret in later years, she declined the offer.

She knew that she needed New York to refuel her energy, that giving it up would mean giving up an essential ingredient of her artistic life. Unlike others who escaped from New York to renew themselves, Anna continued to thrive on the city's bustle and intensity. There were choreographic assignments, teaching engagements, and the stimulation of the Juilliard School. Just as she had flown away from the offer to settle down and make a new home in Mexico over twenty years earlier, once again the falcon flew.

After Anna left Israel in the fall of 1962, the Lyric Theatre continued to accept and fulfill engagements for a time, but they themselves were now responsible for finding these engagements. The monthly stipend from the A.-I.C.F. was discontinued upon Anna's departure because the board assumed that the venture would be able to continue on its own momentum until Anna returned the following year.

The dancers were ill-prepared to handle the Lyric Theatre alone. Anna had done her utmost to impart to them all she knew of professionalism, but she had never developed strong management skills in her own career and had little knowledge of that area to pass on. The phantom hope was that such things would take care of themselves, and of course they never did. Without Anna in Israel to generate excitement through personal appearances and to continue to build the repertoire, the troupe lost momentum. The dancers taught, performed in musicals, and did whatever other work they could find in order to support themselves until her return.

Some of the dancers had suggested to Anna that they could create new works for the company in her absence, but she did not care for the idea. The Lyric Theatre was her creation and she wanted to keep artistic control in her own hands. Some company members agreed with her and were willing to wait for her return, others felt stymied. Rina Shaham, in need of an outlet for her choreographic interests, decided to leave the group after its first season. Rina Schenfeld defected for another reason: she knew she possessed star quality, and felt entitled to that sort of recognition. Anna's avowed dislike of any version of a star system made for considerable tension between them and Schenfeld left shortly after the beginning of rehearsals for the second season. Yossi Kipnis left because he was anxious to establish himself in New York. He spent a good deal of time with Anna there and was a frequent visitor at her Central Park West apartment.[*]

Changes notwithstanding, when Anna returned to Israel in late spring of 1963, many of her original company members were waiting for her. Newcomers, among them Moshe Romano, Yanon Ne'eman, and Miriam Farber, were recruited from her open classes. The rich 1963 season included the dancey *Suite No. 5* (Bach) and *Opus '62*, along with *Rooms* and *Lyric Suite*. She was giving them her best. For the season she also developed a lecture-demonstration. As in the previous year, there were two separate programs, with *Rooms* the featured work on one and *Lyric Suite* on the other.

What had been a cooperative venture in the first year, with administrative duties shared between members, was formalized in the second year. This stronger organizational structure included Avraham Zouri as assistant director. The company's 1963 programs show a succession of different individuals in the positions of business manager, public relations representative, and administrator. The frequent changes in personnel during the short season suggest that all did not go smoothly in this area. And although naysayers still made themselves heard, the Lyric Theatre fared considerably better with the critics than it had during the first season.

It was during the course of this artistically productive year that the Baroness Bethsabee de Rothschild announced the formation of a new modern dance repertory company, Batsheva, to be based in Tel Aviv. The Baroness, daughter of the financier-philanthropist Edmond de Rothschild, had for some time served on the board of A.-I.C.F. She was also, at the time, the principal benefactress for Martha Graham's dance company. After years of helping to support the artistic endeavors of others, she had decided to launch her own enterprise.

In announcing her auditions, Rothschild offered potential company members advantages that up until this time had been unavailable to them in Israel: a full-time salary, far greater than the tiny stipend paid to Lyric Theatre dancers, and

---

[*] Cf. Notes

handsomely equipped facilities. Plans for Batsheva included commissioned chore-ography and scores and professionally designed costumes, sets, and lighting. Martha Graham had agreed to give not only her artistic support, but also works from her repertoire. Most enticing of all was the opportunity to tour internationally.

This dealt a serious blow to Anna's young company. Avraham Zouri re-membered that "when they announced that auditions were going to be held for the Batsheva Company, the Lyric Theatre was still at work. We were all tense and kept quiet. We didn't talk to one another about it and did not know who would go to the audition." Though stunned, Anna knew she was in no position to compete with the stability and glamor that the new company offered.

Some of the group's strongest dancers, people Anna had nurtured during her yearly visits, had been unable to resist all that Batsheva offered and had audi-tioned successfully. They made their peace with her, each in his or her own way, and were gone. After recovering from the initial shock, Anna vowed to continue the work of the Lyric Theatre no matter who had left. If necessary, she would start again from scratch. But it was not going to be easy. Her dream, the establishment of a permanent full-time repertory company in Israel, was about to be realized, but not by her — it was a harsh reality she had to face. She had risked this when she chose to return to New York after the first season. Had she stayed on, the story might have had a very different ending.

Owing to Anna's persistence, there was to be one more season for the Lyric Theatre. In 1964 a small group was assembled. Of the prior years' company, only Avraham Zouri, Yanon Ne'eman, and Leora Hachmi remained. (In the fall of 1963, Anna had encouraged and helped Ze'eva Cohen to come to the United States, where she was to continue her career dancing with distinction for Anna for the next several years.) Ofra Ben Zvi, Gideon Abrahami, Joanna Peled, and Avraham Manzur were the new performers, and Rina Shaham returned as a guest artist. The dancers received no pay, and some of the rehearsals had to be held on a stone floor in the foyer of the Cameri Theatre, where the performances were to take place.

Although the Lyric Theatre had little or no chance of survival, while they were preparing the concert they were honored with an invitation to appear at the American embassy, to represent dance in Israel. Five sections of *Rooms* were per-formed for an audience that included Acting Prime Minister Abba Eban and the United States Ambassador to Israel, Warworth Barbour.

The 1964 season, under the auspices of the Cameri Theatre and with some assistance from A.-I.C.F., received excellent notices. The program included a new work, *Odes*, with a score by the Israeli composer A.U. Boskovich (later restaged to music of Edgard Varèse), and two works, *Forms* (Macero) and *The Question* (Webern), that had been well received in the United States. It was a notable pro-gram for their farewell season.

Anna continued to work in Israel. Assignments changed from year to year. She taught several sessions at the Nissan Nativ Studio of Acting in Tel Aviv and worked for many summers with dance students at the Jerusalem Academy of Music. And there were always work sessions with the Inbal dancers. She and Sara Levi-Tanai had become close friends, a friendship that endures to this day.

This early phase of Anna's work in Israel coincided with the first period in her professional life in which many dance groups — large and small, inside and outside the United States — were actively seeking her out for choreographic commissions. It was work that she loved and did masterfully well. But when summers approached, no matter how attractive the offer, her reply was always, "I work in Israel during the summer." If other summer assignments could be fitted into the schedule that was fine, but the work in Israel came first.

For eleven years, Anna had come to Israel and given liberally of her time and talents. The A.-I.C.F. had provided transportation from the United States and housing in Israel. Sponsoring organizations had paid her a small stipend for her expenses while there, but seldom, if ever, had there been anything resembling a fee for her work. It was a most generous gift she chose to give to the people of this young country that she had come to love. She knew the Israelis could ill afford her professional fees; her way of helping was to give of herself. Israel had become her second home.

18

OTHER VENTURES
LINCOLN CENTER REPERTORY THEATER
AMERICAN DANCE THEATER
DANCE THEATER WORKSHOP

My first aim is to free the actor from his self-consciousness . . . It may seem to the actor that he is learning how to move and how to use his body, but what he really learns is to be simple, honest and human. (Anna Sokolow, quoted by Walter Sorell, Dance Magazine, January 1964)

In Anna's life, as in the making of a complicated tapestry, many threads are being worked at once. In the spring of 1962, when she was presenting her proposal for a new dance group to the A.-I.C.F. in Israel, plans were in progress for the physical plant of the Repertory Theater at Lincoln Center. Even before the blueprints were completed, Robert Whitehead and Elia Kazan, co-producers for the Repertory Theater, had outlined plans for a thirty-member company of performers who would participate in a specialized program to prepare them for performance in any style and any period. They would work in temporary downtown headquarters until the new building was completed. Robert Lewis was appointed head of their actor's training program and, at the suggestion of Kazan, Anna Sokolow was recruited to work with Lewis as instructor in body movement.

Anna was the ideal co-worker for Robert Lewis. Neither believed that the intense soul-searching demanded by "the method" was fully necessary to the development of a stage character. They favored instead a direct and simple expression of honest emotion. They had enjoyed working together at the Actors Studio and on the Broadway production of *Regina* in the late 1940s.

The Lincoln Center Repertory Theater's actors training program was planned as a detailed process. Initial work was on "etudes" designed, in Lewis' words, "to force the actor into patterns of behavior which extend his expressive range to many periods of history and to characters not usually encountered in contemporary plays including work on songs and dances of various nations, periods, and social classes." Anna's emphasis was supposed to be on dance of various periods and styles, but she was soon doing what she did best with actors — daring them to move boldly and without preconceptions.

Faye Dunaway, John Philip Law, Jean Stapleton, Barry Primus, Frank Langella, and Barbara Loden were among the gifted artists selected to participate in the process. In his autobiography, *Slings and Arrows,* Lewis wrote of the young actors working "under Anna Sokolow's benevolent whip." Anna cracked that whip for the Lincoln Center Repertory Theater School until, unexpectedly, the teaching program was terminated, just when the first full production, scheduled for the fall of 1963, got under way. It was Arthur Miller's *After the Fall,* inspired by the emotionally devastating final months of his marriage to Marilyn Monroe.

Barry Primus felt that the results of Anna's training were clearly discernable in the memorable, gut-wrenching performances of the *After the Fall cast.* Remembering the studio work, he said, "I can't think of anybody who didn't find Anna's classes exceptional. Even the most cynical of the actors felt there was great value in the wildness, the fierceness, of her training."

Just before the announcement that the school was to be discontinued, Walter Sorell interviewed Anna for a *Dance Magazine* article in which she talked about her classes for actors. It was appropriately titled "We Work Toward Freedom."

> My first aim is to free the actor from his self-consciousness. I help him to stop worrying about what he is to do with his hands. I make him forget about the cliches about having to smoke, to touch or handle something. It is amazing to see how this freedom from artificial contrivances conditions the quality of his face, how it colors his acting. It may seem to the actor that he is learning how to move and how to use his body, but what he really learns is to be simple, honest and human.

Anna's association with Lincoln Center did not die with the Repertory Theater school. In October 1964, the American Dance Theater, designed to be a repertory company for modern dance, was organized with the assistance of the New York State Council on the Arts. José Limón was named artistic director, and Roger Englander, producer. The goal of the pilot project was to create a permanent company of dancers versatile enough to perform the works of all modern dance choreographers. Classics of contemporary dance were to be revived and new works by composers and choreographers commissioned. Dancers were to be guaranteed long-term employment and a wide variety of roles.

The American Dance Theater was the first modern dance company to perform at Lincoln Center's New York State Theater. The theater, built especially for dance, had opened the previous April with a New York City Ballet performance. The first modern programs, with works by Limón, Doris Humphrey, Donald McKayle, and Anna Sokolow, were presented on November 18 and 19, 1964, and played to two sold-out houses. Tickets were scaled at $1.05 to $4.95, the same prices charged for performances of Balanchine's company.

The season included a premier by McKayle, *Workout*; Doris Humphrey's *Lament for Ignacio Sánchez Mejías*; a reworking of Anna Sokolow's *The Question*, which she had recently presented at Juilliard; and the New York premiere of Limón's tribute to Doris Humphrey, A *Choreographic Offering.*

A few weeks later Walter Terry wrote a long piece about the brief American Dance Theater season, with some pointed thoughts about Anna's contribution to the program:

> Anna Sokolow's *The Question* is not an easy piece but it is a challenging and disturbing one. And one of the purposes of modern dance is to challenge and disturb, rather than to divert or simply amuse. Except for a very few pieces with a comic touch or a satiric comment, Miss Sokolow's works view humanity by a standard which makes Medea seem like Little Nell. Her *Dreams* is really a nightmare, her *Rooms* (a masterpiece of theater dance) is sinister and her *Metamorphosis* almost induces suicidal thoughts. *The Question* won't make you happy (indeed, it does go on too long) but it has power and purpose to it. Miss Sokolow is essential to the American Dance Theater.

For the article, Terry had interviewed John Hightower, the director of the New York State Council on the Arts, which had sponsored the program. Hightower expressed his delight at the size of the audience and his surprise that fifteen thousand dollars of the Council's initial thirty-five thousand dollar expenditure had been recovered at the box office, which had to turn away some customers because the house was sold out. Then, he voiced the hope that as a result of the performances an energetic and knowledgeable board of directors would be found to raise enough funds to support the venture. The Council would continue to offer only partial support.

The idea was basically unrealistic. In the mid-1960s, with few exceptions, modern dancers were unfamiliar with the notion of a working board of directors and knew even less about fund-raising. They were accustomed to struggling on their own and making sacrifices every inch of the way in order to present their work properly. What little foundation money was made available to dance went primarily to ballet companies. In the late 1950s, Doris Humphrey and Helen Tamiris had tried to get financial support for a venture similar to this one. They were turned down by every organization to which they had sent their carefully prepared repertory project description. A few well-publicized performances could not begin to attract the financial support needed for the present project.

Terry sensed the difficulties that lay ahead for the new venture:

> Where the American Dance Theater will go from here remains to be seen. The New York State Council on the Arts gave it a boost and will, undoubtedly, assist it in the future, but it must now find its own supports if it is to continue. . . . How it

should be organized, directed and managed, as well as supported, constitutes a problem. We are living in a ballet age.

A second set of performances was given under the same aegis and at the same theater from March 2 to 7, 1965. The program was put together rather hastily because of the last-minute availability of the theater. Lincoln Center had waived charges for use of the theater to help the cause. Many people, it seemed, were trying to make this second group of performances successful, so that the idea could continue to grow. "American Dance Theater and Invited Companies" was the title given to this second season, which featured the work of Valerie Bettis, Merce Cunningham, Paul Draper, Lucas Hoving, Pearl Lang, Sophie Maslow, Alwin Nikolais, and once again Doris Humphrey, José Limón, and Anna Sokolow.

Most of these artists used the new pool of American Dance Theater dancers; Merce and Anna chose instead to use their own. She presented *Ballade* with the same Juilliard Dance Ensemble group that had premiered the piece three weeks earlier. Her work was preceded on the exciting program by Humphrey's *Passacaglia and Fugue in C Minor* and followed by the New York premier of Cunningham's *Winterbranch*. Sophie Maslow's well-known 1950 work, *The Village I knew*, came last.

Ballade, which explores the restlessness and inconclusiveness of young love, was created at a time when Anna seemed to be firmly and irretrievably entrenched in painful probing into far darker sides of life. Yet *Ballade* was a lyrical dance. Ann Barzel described it simply and well in the March 1965 *Dance News*: "*Ballade* plays the age old game of youth and its discoveries, with a touching grace and understanding straight out of their own youngness".

Macy's department store paid for a full-page ad in the *New York Times* to help draw attention to the Lincoln Center series, but, as was feared, no major supporters were found for the continuation of the project. The Council had been impressed with the results of the pilot programs but felt that with obligations to the arts throughout the state, the expense of supporting such a company on a permanent basis was prohibitive. Hope lingered for some time after the second series that the project might be revived, but it never was.

The third major venture with which Anna was involved in the 1960s was Dance Theatre Workshop (DTW). In a 1987 interview, Jack Moore recalled that the founding of DTW was an outgrowth of his and Jeff Duncan's work with Anna. In the late 1950s she had recognized the need for some of her dancers to try their wings as choreographers. Although it was not easy at first for her to watch Duncan and Moore (whom she half-jokingly referred to as her sons) developing their own creative talents, she generously gave them opportunities to show their work, sharing several programs with them at the "Y" and elsewhere. If they wanted her help or advice on any aspect of the production, she was there for them. If they wanted to work on their own, that too was fine with her. It was a professional endeavor and she treated them like professionals.

The "Y," which had been so valuable to the growth and development of modern dance in the 1930s, was available to new talent, but within a limited structure. "Audition Winners Concerts" were adjudicated by a board that had its own strong artistic biases, based on the aesthetics of an older generation; new ideas were not particularly welcome. If choreographers made it through the audition process they could, at best, look forward to only one or perhaps two showings of their work there each season. The generation of the 1960s finally bypassed the "Y," looking instead for churches and free halls that offered an enthusiastic and open attitude toward experimentation.

In 1964, Duncan decided to outfit his studio/home on West 20th Street for weekend use as a theater space. He initiated there a program he called "Artists in Residence." The idea was to give young choreographers a chance to show their work in a series of weekend performances at virtually no cost to them. They were given a place to rehearse and perform along with briefings on the public relations work needed to bring in an audience and reviewers. The idea caught on.

Soon, he was joined in the venture by Jack Moore. Together they formed the new organization, Dance Theater Workshop, which they incorporated in 1965. In the fall of that year, they produced a series of Monday-evening concerts at the East 74th Street Theater. In a reversal of the 1950s exchange, Anna was invited to show one of her pieces on *their* concert. She chose to do *Dreams*, and from all accounts the work was given one of its most brilliant performances. The outstanding cast included Ze'eva Cohen, Martha Clarke, Lenore Latimer, Peggy Cicierska, and Laura Roth (in the child's role); the men were Jack Moore, Chester Wolenski, Jeff Duncan, Ray Cook, and Eddy Effron. Anna's participation was valuable in lending some credence to that first official DTW season.

By the next year she was too busy fulfilling choreographic assignments and working with her own company to assist DTW, but by this time the young organization was ready to stand on its own. The ambitious 1966 season included two series at Duncan's studio, "Saturdays at Nine" and "Sundays at Three."

On November 14, 1966, Clive Barnes wrote supportively in the *New York Times*: "The Dance Theater Workshop is one of our more dependable modern dance organizations, maintaining a steady standard of achievement and aspiration. It is poor but honest, and not only tries harder than most. . . but often succeeds." This "steady standard of achievement and aspiration" was reached without grants or subsidies of any kind. Most of the work was done by Duncan and Moore, who were later joined by the gifted choreographer and all-around theater man, Art Bauman.

Anna was asked to teach choreography at DTW and thus, for the first time, there was a place where people who danced for her could develop their choreographic ideas under her direct guidance. Sokolow dancers Kathryn Posin, Linda Tarnay, Ze'eva Cohen, and Martha Clarke were enrolled in these choreography classes and profited from her shrewd criticisms, which allowed for and respected individual differences. Each of these dancers would one day create her own important works that were quite different from Anna's, both in style and content. Up until then, unless her dancers had studied composition with her at Juilliard, they learned largely through osmosis and unconsciously tried to emulate her in some way. It was a situation not unlike the one experienced by many of those who worked closely with Martha Graham, and later, with Merce Cunningham.

Art Bauman remembered that in her role as a member of the DTW Board of Directors Anna was *very* supportive when she was being supportive and *very* critical when she was being critical. Although she was frequently traveling to one job assignment or another, whenever she was in New York she spent time at DTW teaching, advising, helping. In 1966, Duncan and Moore, who had by now withdrawn from Anna's company to devote themselves fully to DTW, invited her to serve as artistic director of the organization, but she had recently received a grant from the National Endowment for the Arts and chose instead to put her primary energy into the creation of a new work, *Deserts*, for her company.

Another reason for her polite refusal of the position was her suspicion of DTW's involvement in that popular 1960s notion of the co-op, an organization in which everybody involved usually had an equal voice. In Art Bauman's words, "For a time DTW became so open, so nonjudgmental that it began to fall apart." Anna could not fit into such a scheme, nor did she care to. By the time the organization got around to instituting a panel selection process for works to be shown, she was too focused on her new group to be involved at all.

Deborah Jowitt wrote about DTW's eleventh anniversary retrospective season in the June 28, 1976, *Village Voice*:

> DTW has a family tree of sorts. Jack Moore, Jeff Duncan, and Ze'eva Cohen were members of Anna Sokolow's company; Wendy Summit, Linda Tarnay, Kathryn Posin were students of Jack Moore's at Bennington. I see a lot of variegated foliage right there branching from Sokolow's passionate and vividly gestural approach to dance.

It would seem that just as the Judson Church was the center for the most radical experimentation stemming from the work of Merce Cunningham, John Cage, and Robert Dunn, so, a few years later, DTW filled that need for a new generation of young expressionists. Many of them were directly or indirectly influenced by Anna's teaching and choreography. Interestingly, as Art Bauman points out, when Judson Church began to phase out programs of experimental dance, it was to DTW that many of the artists came to show their work. A number of them, he notes, such as Kenneth King, Meredith Monk, and Elaine Sommers, had been associated with DTW in some way nearly from its beginnings.

In the 1950s and before, dancers had tended to follow the lead of the earlier generations and to distance themselves from other modern dancers working differently from themselves. If you danced for Martha Graham, you were not likely to be chummy with a Limón dancer. DTW helped to change all of that. It became one of the most significant common meeting grounds for a new generation of choreographers and dancers who followed radically diverse aesthetic paths. They could share the same space, sometimes dance for one another, and most important, watch and learn from one another.

The organization now flourishes in its home on West 19th Street, in the theater first developed by Jerome Robbins for his American Theatre Lab. It is just around the corner from DTW's first home. As one of the most important low-budget dance producing units in America, DTW provides a performance outlet for a whole new generation of choreographers. It also serves as a prototype for similar organizations elsewhere in the country. It all started twenty-five years ago with some of Anna Sokolow's dancers who were ready to share the stage with others, as she had shared it with them.

19

THE SPIRIT OF REBELLION

Miss Sokolow's lighthearted yet horrifying description of the shook-up, switched-on psychedelic teen-ager, dancing to jazz with grins not so much insolent as totally unaligned, frankly scares me to hell. (Clive Barnes, New York Times, March 20, 1967)

In the spring of 1961, Anna Sokolow, Melissa Hayden, and Gwen Verdon received *Dance Magazine's* annual awards. Anna's citation, read by Robert Lewis, said in part:

> To Anna Sokolow, whose career as concert dancer, choreographer, and teacher in this country and on the international scene has been distinguished by integrity [and] creative boldness, and whose recent concert works have opened the road to a penetratingly human approach to the jazz idiom.

The climax of that work was yet to come. The increasing potency and timeliness of her choreography in the jazz idiom would be experienced by audiences in *Opus '63* and later in *Opus '65*, the powerful work she created for the Joffrey Ballet.

Working with Juilliard students in the spring of 1963, Anna continued to explore the themes that had begun with *Session '58* and continued with *Opus '60* in Mexico and *Opus '62* in Israel. Until 1963 these works had seemed to many viewers to be ahead of their time. After that, some people were ready to see that Anna's insights powerfully expressed what they were experiencing in the world around them. With a kind of raw theatrical energy, she was capturing the essence of a bewildering and painful time.

In *Opus '63* Anna's ability to evoke the times through dance was becoming ever more apparent. Marcia Marks wrote in *Dance Magazine* in July 1963:

> The Sokolow work was indeed 1963 — to the hilt. It was explosive, violent, laughing, alive, matched by Teo Macero's music, alternately blaring, melodic, silenced.
>
> The pulse was jazz; the mass movements were keyed to excitement. But, as in all Miss Sokolow's works, it was not excitement for its own sake, and it was not the mass movement of nonentities. These were individuals, separately aware though caught up in the general contagion.*

The contrasts of the times are evident throughout the work. The music is angry and cacophanous at the outset. Couples hug and roll over one another on the floor, then slide on their stomachs. They stand and intermingle. There are sudden lifts. Women are carried upside down. Changes are abrupt. Despite the physical interactions, the dancers seem curiously detached. At one point one woman appears to be servicing four men. When they do a social dance, the Twist, practically on top of her she pays little attention to their activities. Even as they lift her and carry her through space she seems uninvolved. In parts of the dance the dancers touch and interact, but do not appear to recognize each other. The work is characterized by this coolness, yet there are sections that intensify suddenly into near- violence. There are also sequences of wry humor — an almost desperate version of fun. And there are suggestions of hope. The choreographer was leaving it to the audience, as she so often does, to make their own final sense of it.

Anna came close to having her work seen in Russia again when, in 1963, Rebekah Harkness asked her to create a work for the Robert Joffrey Ballet, which was scheduled to tour the U.S.S.R. later that year. Anna was invited to stay at Harkness' seaside estate in Watch Hill, Rhode Island, where the company was in residence while she worked on the choreography. Teo Macero did the score. *Time + 6*, one of their most powerfully expressive collaborations, was the result. Joffrey liked the work, but, according to Anna, Harkness took one look at it when it was nearing completion and decided that it was a dirty piece. "She hated it, and threw it out." There was too much blatant sexuality, too much rough play for Harkness' taste. Was that the way we wanted the Russians to see us? According to dancer/musician John Wilson, who was dancing for Joffrey at the time, the work (which was called *Perspectives* in its early stages) did not make a big hit with State Department representatives, either. He remembered that it was the State Department, along with some people from the Russian embassy, who were primarily responsible for the cancellation.

For several years afterward, Anna and Teo jokingly referred to the piece as their "Harkness reject," even when the Boston Ballet produced it in 1966 (with the title *Time + 6*) and it was a major success. The general perception of just how troubled the times were had at last caught up with Anna's own.

By 1965 the spirit of rebellion was riding high among young people throughout the United States. Robert Joffrey, now on his own, thought that Anna would be a good person to express this spirit in a work for his apprentice group. Joffrey was in the process of rebuilding his company after a rupture in relations with Harkness, and there was very little money. Anna, remembering her own lean years, created *Opus '65* as a gift.

The young ballet dancers in the cast were quite taken with Anna. For one thing, her eye did not go only to those who were the most technically accomplished. Some were given attention and recognition because of a special look or quality she saw in them. The dancers were also impressed with the fact that, from the earliest rehearsals, Anna made it clear that she not only understood the spirit of the times, but that she was in perfect sympathy with it.

Rex Bickmore, an apprentice dancer with Joffrey who later became a significant figure in Anna's life, remembered:

> To have someone of Anna's stature, a rebellious person herself, working with us, made quite an impression. She had just written her big article, "I Hate Academies . . ." [later reprinted as "The Rebel and the Bourgeois"], for *Dance Magazine*, celebrating those ideas. In it she said that the artist has to be a bastard. We thought, that was great stuff. In rehearsals the things she said made it clear to us that she had always gone her own way and done her own thing. There was something very pure about that.

For most of the young Joffrey dancers she was like a breath of fresh air in their highly structured and competitive professional world. Many of them had never encountered anyone like her in their polite, formal, ballet-school training. They were awed by the power of her personality, by the intensity of rehearsals, and by the sometimes shocking directness of her imagery. It was her way of getting the best she could out of them.

The premiere of *Opus '65* in Central Park's outdoor Delacorte Theater was a resounding success and Joffrey decided to take the work into the repertoire of the senior company. It was an important decision, which helped to reestablish him as someone who was open to new ideas. To the ballet world this kind of dance was certainly a new idea. Jacqueline Maskey described *Opus '65* in the May 1966 issue of *Dance Magazine*[*]:

> The stage is peeled right back to its brick backwall. The kids rush on at breakneck speed. They grab. . . desperately, fling one another about. A bored girl (Margo Sappington) and four boys shimmy and twist frenetically, crowded together as though packed into a telephone booth. The bunch assembles into what looks, in its first amiability, like a high school lunch period dance. But they turn ugly. They turn their sunglasses and vinyl jackets, their crazy footgear and headgear toward us in a spasm of hostility. They look directly at us and they gibber. The words are not distinguishable, but the tone is: they accuse. And in a final defiant gesture, they wash their hands of us and the whole mess they find their lives to be by dropping, one by one, over the lip of the stage, out of sight.

Clive Barnes wrote, when it was revived by Joffrey in 1967:

> Miss Sokolow's lighthearted yet horrifying description of the shook-up, switched-on psychedelic teen-ager, dancing to jazz with grins not so much insolent as totally unaligned, frankly scares me to hell.

---

[*] Copyright © 1997 *Dance Magazine*.

In the past, I have always rationalized that by suggesting that it wasn't a particularly good ballet. Now I'm not sure that the ballet is not too good . . . too disturbing, too uncomfortable. These kids, swinging in a world I can't understand, make a sense I don't wish to notice.

Opus '65, Anna's most famous work for a ballet company, was seen by a much larger audience than any of her previous variations of this genre, which had been created for modern dance groups. The work was later staged for other companies and became the prototype for a plethora of rock ballets by other choreographers. It had a potent influence on Broadway as well. In one of those ironies one often finds in the world of art, with so many like works being shown the innovator's own began to seem cliché. That did not happen until later. For a few years Anna was recognized as the creator of the first rock ballet, but by 1967, when the Public Theater produced *Hair*, the musical that would challenge the accepted conventions of the musical theater, there seemed to be a lapse of memory on the part of critics as to where and when the movement had started. After a still later restaging of *Opus '65*, some critics accused Anna of having borrowed ideas from *Hair*!

Anna's achievement was clearly recognized in a *New York Times* review by Anna Kisselgoff of the Joffrey Ballet's 1976 revival of *Opus '65*:

> *Opus '65* . . . is typical of a social protest ballet that Miss Sokolow virtually invented. This is a genre that has been widely copied throughout the world — it is called the "alienated youth" ballet — but there is still no one who can come up with the conviction of the genuine article better than Miss Sokolow herself.

The mid-1960s was an extraordinarily busy period for Anna. Between the summer of 1965, when she set *Opus* on the Joffrey company, and the period of her involvement with the production of *Hair* two years later, she found time and energy to choreograph two major works, *Night* (Berio) and *Memories* (Macero), at Juilliard; teach at HB Studio, Clark Center for the Performing Arts, Dance Theater Workshop, and the American Theater Lab in New York; direct John White's two one-act plays, *Bugs* and *Veronica*, off-Broadway; stage *Time + 6* on the Boston Ballet and *Untitled* (Walden) for the Manhattan Festival Ballet; stage *Dreams* and *Seven Deadly Sins* for the Netherlands Dance Theater and *Deserts* for the Ballet Rambert in London; create three works for television — *Far Rockaway* (Rochberg, celebrating the second anniversary of Lincoln Center), *The Celebrations* (Summerlin), and *And the Disciples Departed* (Macero); revise *Rooms* for television (twenty-nine-minute version); do a residency at Ohio State University; direct a synagogue service that combined poetry and dance for a Jewish Music Festival (narrated by Leonard Bernstein's wife, Felicia Montealegre); go to Japan on a Fulbright-Hays Fellowship for three months; set *Night* on the National Ballet of Washington; teach in Israel and in Sweden; and stage *Rooms* for the Joffrey Ballet.

With all of this going on, Anna somehow found time to accompany her group on several college and university tours.

Such an intensive work period, with its constant uprooting, made it harder for her to deal with certain transitions in her personal life. Although still a close personal friend, Yossi was now married and no longer a frequent visitor at the Central Park West apartment. She was beginning to feel that this post-World War II modern building no longer served her needs. It was too far uptown for her. She wanted to be back in the heart of things, and to her that meant Greenwich Village.

By a stroke of good luck she found an attractive, large, and airy three-room apartment on the fifth floor at a much sought-after Christopher Street address in the West Village. Anna loved it from the day she moved in. There were at last enough clear white walls for her magnificent collection of books, paintings, and folk art. The apartment on Christopher Street became her first real home. She was delighted that it was only a short walk to the tenement building where she had lived as a child on St. Mark's Place, and took people over to point out the top-floor windows she and Rose had perched in to watch the crowds below.

Unfortunately, the new apartment looked directly into the ugly women's prison building across the street, and in warm weather one could hear the inmates at the windows carrying on colorful conversations with passersby in the street. Several years later, however, the building was torn down and replaced by a beautiful community-tended garden. With the prison gone, Anna now had one of the finest views that that part of the city affords.

There was another major transition going on in the mid-1960s, a time when Anna was increasingly in demand to stage works on professional modern dance and ballet companies and university groups in the United States and abroad. With so many exciting and challenging choreographic offers coming her way, she decided to disband her group. For the first time in over a decade, there would be no Anna Sokolow Company, in New York or anywhere else. There was a small, devoted group who worked closely with her whenever special opportunities arose, but no company.

A closer look at some of the activities during that astonishingly active two-year period helps to paint a clearer picture of the diverse roles she had to fill and suggests the degree of stress she must have been under to meet all of those obligations.

In the fall of 1965, when Johnny White was given the opportunity to present two of his one-act plays, *Bugs* and *Veronica*, at New York's Pocket Theatre, he asked Anna to serve as director.

Bugs was a mysterious and gloom-ridden story about a mentally ill young man who escapes from an asylum to spend a bizarre afternoon with his girlfriend and his demonic father. It appears to have been only a fair play, but one that was very well acted and directed.

Veronica (lyrics by White, music by Macero) was startlingly different. A couple of Broadway song writers are trying to work their way out of a creative slump. They warm themselves over the fire of past successes, consoled by a blonde showgirl in leotard and black lace. A robber enters the scene and he proceeds, unwittingly, to serve as the inspiration for the long-awaited creative breakthrough.

Critics were not overly impressed with *Bugs*, but reviews for *Veronica* were quite favorable. Anna's direction was clearly important to the success of the evening, although Johnny remembered vividly his unsuccessful pleading with her to pay more attention to the text in rehearsals. "The lines, Anna! The lines!" he would entreat. She ignored his pleas. It appears that although she loved directing, coaching dialogue was neither her great interest nor strength. "Don't worry, Johnny," she would reassure him. "If they can get to the truth, the lines will take care of themselves." The headlines of the reviews speak for themselves: AUTHOR SHOWS TALENT (Thompson, *New York Journal American*); JOHN WHITE IS A WRITER OF FACILITY AND VERVE (Pasolli, *Village Voice*); TWO SPLENDID PLAYS (Harris, *New York World Telegram*). In this case Anna appears to have been right about the lines.

For many artists the culture-shock of working in Israel, The Netherlands, Stockholm, and Tokyo in quick succession would have been disorienting enough, but Anna did not even have time in her schedule to allow for adaptation to each new environment. She always was, from the moment of arrival, the central focus. Her first trip, January 18 to February 14, 1966, was to Columbus, Ohio.

There was an air of apprehension in the studio as the group of Ohio State University dance students warmed up. Anna Sokolow, their world-famous artist-in-residence, was due to arrive any moment for her first rehearsal of *Odes*, a work she had shown at Juilliard a year earlier. Anna had already startled everybody there the day before by casting some relatively inexperienced dancers in the work, bypassing some who were far more technically proficient.

When she arrived for the rehearsal, one student timidly asked, "What would you like us to call you?" "You'll call her Miss Sokolow," Helen Alkire, the head of the Dance Division answered before Anna had a chance to speak. "They will call me Anna," the guest artist announced, as if no one else had spoken. The tone was clearly set. Anna was not aligning herself with the departmental hierarchy. She was the artist who would be at the center of their lives as long as she was among them, but she was *not* part of the establishment. In fact, she would make it clear to everyone during her stay that she did not really believe in dance in the universities, an opinion that softened years later.

A documentary film designed to capture Anna's rehearsal process was scheduled to be made by cinematographer David Parker, film director at the university. Later, a full performance of the completed dance would be filmed as well and included in the documentary. Anna recognized Parker's artistic sensitivity at the outset; she decided to trust him completely and never waivered in that trust during the entire time she was at Ohio State. She almost, but not quite, forgot that his cameras were at work. (One of the dancers, Dianne Brown, later told Parker that Anna was hard and fair when his cameras were rolling, but only hard when they were not.) The filming proceeded almost from the moment Anna entered the studio for that first rehearsal.

Most of the dancers were well-scrubbed and eager young people with a respectful demeanor and sedate manners carried over from the 1950s. The wilder 1960s glimmered in a few pairs of eyes here and there, but only softly in Anna's presence. Among the dancers were Senta Driver (graduate student), Fred Strickler, and Larry Clark. These, and several others in the film, would go on to rich careers as performers, teachers, and choreographers.

Faculty members James Payton (who had danced professionally for Anna) and Vera Blaine (today chairperson of the department) were in the cast as well. Payton had given the dancers some hints about how to behave in Anna's rehearsals the night before she arrived, doubtless saving them a considerable amount of grief. Senta Driver recalled his sage advice in a September 16, 1966, article for *Dance Scope*:

> She doesn't like jewelry in the studio, particularly earrings. Don't ask questions or discuss what she is asking you to do — just do it. It is very important not to break her train of thought, because she works with a terrific intensity — so if she is not using you, stay out of her line of sight or sit down and watch. And whatever you do, don't laugh in rehearsals, just not at all. And you must not take anything she says to you personally.

Payton told the dancers that in his short association with Anna he had learned more than from any other professional experience in his career. As the younger dancers labored through the physical and emotional demands of the next few weeks, many were to discover, as he had, technical strengths, dramatic depth, and a capacity for forbearance they were unaware they possessed. Again from Senta Driver:

> She was always urging us to be passionate. "You are all afraid to suffer, you're afraid to show deep feeling. You must *tear* at your head, *grab* your faces as if you could rip them off. It's the effort of doing the movement that makes it beautiful, that makes it real. Don't try to conceal your effort. It should be *difficult* to pull your head down." And again, "Drop down as if you are never going to move again, as if you would stay there forever." And again, "Now that you know the dance you must work to take away the strangeness of it. You must get used to it, until it is the only thing you can do at that moment."

Feet were torn, egos bruised, backs ached, and work in other classes suffered, but as this hurricane intensity tore through their lives, their dancing became fuller, richer, and more potently expressive. Technique was the means to the end. The end was to deliver *Odes* as the powerful statement about humanity it was designed to be. At one point, as the dancers were noticeably wincing under the pain and pressure of her demands, she said: "I don't dislike you, that's not why I'm hard on you. But I love dance *more* than I love you."

In three weeks Anna had taken a group of eager and frightened university students and molded them into dancers who could deliver a professional-looking and deeply moving performance. David Parker's excellent documentary film, *Anna Sokolow Directs Odes*, has been shown in United States embassies throughout the world by the United States Information Agency.

However trying it must have been for Helen Alkire (once, like Anna, a protégé of Louis Horst) and her colleagues to reconcile themselves to Anna's demands and her way of working, they invited her back to stage another piece of choreography, *Moods* (Ligeti), in the 1970s and in 1978 sponsored her successful candidacy for an honorary doctorate from Ohio State University.

London's Ballet Rambert beckoned next. Since 1930, the company has nurtured some of the great creative dance talents of the century. Both Frederick Ashton and Antony Tudor were among those given their first choreographic opportunities in the troupe's modest Mercury Theater. It was the company's visionary director, Marie Rambert, who encouraged and helped Agnes de Mille to develop her talents at a time when the American dance establishment had all but dismissed her. At the Mercury, de Mille did the choreography that she later developed into *Rodeo* and Antony Tudor first staged *Lilac Garden*. Some of the most distinguished dancers of the London Festival Ballet and the Royal Ballet received their earliest training at Rambert's school and then, when they began to show professional promise, moved on to one of the larger companies.

In the mid-1960s, the Ballet Rambert was in an artistic slump from years of touring tired classics in the provinces to make ends meet financially. Change was clearly needed. Part of the company's plan to restore its legendary vitality and to reestablish its reputation as a leader of the avant-garde was an exploration of current developments in dance, and that, of course, meant opening the door to the modern idiom.

Anna was highly regarded in London at the time because of the splendid version of *Rooms* that Alvin Ailey had shown the year before, with a fine cast that included Dudley Williams, Hope Clark, William Louther, James Truitte, and Loretta Abbot. Anna was invited to do a work for Ballet Rambert's 1966 season and chose *Time + 6*. It went well enough with London audiences to warrant a return invitation the following summer. This time she staged *Deserts*, which her own company had recently premiered in New York. The work won mostly glowing responses from some of London's best-known critics: Alexander Bland (*The Observer*), Richard Buckle (*The Sunday Times*), John Percival (*The Times*).

As usual, there was griping. Certain complaints in the press concerned the length, intensity, and in one case the similarity of this work to European expressionism of the mid-1930s. One reviewer wrote grumpily that he was reminded of a World War II bombing raid in which everyone panicked; another referred to *Deserts* as "So far the non-ballet of 1967." But high praise predominated, such as these poetic words from Andrew Porter: "[*Deserts*] is exhausting in its sustained intensity; a crushing burden of inarticulate agony made eloquent by art: the wordless scream of a 20th century Laocoön and his sons given plastic form."

The point was made in several reviews that with this work and Tetley's *Ricercare* the company was off to a good start toward its new goals. Perhaps the most significant outcome of Anna's participation may be gleaned from a remark made by Norman Morrice, then associate director of the company. Anna's effect on him was, he said, "like an explosion. . . . My next ballet will be much affected by her concern for the truth."

Anna's impact on Japan was considerably less clearcut. AMERICAN CULTURAL CENTER IMPORTS AN 'IMPOLITE' BUT ENORMOUSLY STIMULATING TASKMASTER headed an article by Ernestine Stodelle, in the January 1967 *Dance Magazine*.

The visit did not start well. After a long and fatiguing flight from Stockholm, Anna was detained at the mammoth Tokyo airport. She had not been informed that she needed a special visitor's permit and found herself being treated to one version of Japanese red tape — the one in which one is detained interminably while people behind the counter smile, seemingly unconcerned about expediting matters. Why were the dancers who had come to greet her, their arms full of flowers, not doing something to get her out of there? And why were *they* smiling? What was there to smile about? She was hungry and tired and suffering from considerable back pain. It took two hours to receive her clearance to enter the country.

Anna did not care for Japanese food. Her valuables were stolen from her hotel room within a few days of her arrival — the first time in her life that that had ever happened to her. She found the Japanese custom of smiling to mask embarrassment and discomfort especially irritating; she did not see it as politeness. Jack Moore, who was in Tokyo at the same time, did his best to keep her in good spirits. During their frequent dinners together she enumerated all the reasons she did not like the country. She also confided in him about more personal matters. Something was going on that did not have anything directly to do with Japan; she was beginning to experience periods of depression.

She spoke openly with Jack:

"I wish I had a home," she said to me, and I don't think she meant a place to live; she liked her new apartment in New York. There was no special person in her life at that time, and Anna needed someone — not just a lover — she needed to feel more grounded. That was the problem.

Anna was at a low ebb and her Japanese students felt it. Kei Takei, who was enrolled in the course, remembered:

> We never had anyone teaching modern dance in such a demanding way. There were twenty-five people in the composition class at the beginning. At the end there were maybe five people left. In Japan I think we have loose time. When somebody says ten o'clock we think maybe ten past ten is all right. She screamed if we got there late. Once she closed the door at ten.
>
> When she said "Fall!" in technique class, she meant right away, this second. When she did not like our homework, she would say, "No! It's not honest enough," and we would smile and she would scream, "What are you smiling about?"
>
> So I fell when she said fall and I did not smile. Somehow I knew Anna had marked me. She was sort of watching. I never got a "no" from her. She sometimes said "yes."

At the end of the session Kei Takei was one of three Japanese dance students invited to apply for Fulbright fellowships for study in the United States.

Anna's two-year duress culminated in the *Hair* fiasco. The program distributed on the opening night of the famous rock musical contains no mention of Anna Sokolow. She had, however, spent as much time working with the cast as the director of record, Gerald Freedman.

Hair was launched when James Rado and Gerome Ragni approached Joseph Papp with the book, lyrics, and music for a rock musical about hippies, love children, the Vietnam war, and racism. After convincing them to drop their own score and work with composer Galt McDermot, Papp decided to take a chance on it. The gifted Gerald Freedman, then artistic director of the Public Theatre, was given the assignment of directing the show. He recalls that what Rado and Ragni first presented him with was a collection of looseleaf scraps that outlined a unique concept. Although haphazardly put together, it was nonetheless full of energy and fresh vision. Working with the authors, Freedman created a viable script without losing the spontaneous quality of the original concept. (After *Hair* opened on Broadway, Rado and Ragni were irreverently described as authors of the "non-book and lyrics.") Ragni had studied with Anna at Jerome Robbins' American Theatre Lab, and it was at Ragni's suggestion that she was asked to choreograph the show.

The whole undertaking was a complex one for all concerned. A non-narrative tribal love rock musical had never been attempted before. It started out as a collage, something like vaudeville, but in this case there were no traditions to call on, no accepted conventions to replace the narrative form. There was not even a complete book with which to work.

From the first rehearsals, Freedman had difficulty dealing with Rado and Ragni, who were upset with him about his casting. Both of them had expected to play leading parts even though they were considerably older than the draft-eligible young men the script called for. Freedman was willing to work with Ragni, a first-rate actor, but was adamant in his refusal to cast the energetic but older-looking Rado in a leading role. Another actor was brought in to play the part Rado wanted.

The anger the playwrights felt toward Freedman over the casting was carried into rehearsals, and Anna seemed to be the only one who could keep the peace. She also began to work faster than Freedman (who was still trying to find his way) and was soon doing a good deal of the staging which would, under normal circumstances, have been the director's province. When she brought to Papp's attention how much of the staging was hers, Papp agreed to change her title from "Choreographer" to "Assistant Director."

After about ten days of rehearsal, Anna required emergency abdominal surgery. According to Lynda Gudde, her assistant on the production, during the time Anna was away rehearsals were limited almost entirely to improvisation sessions. Freedman was struggling with the scripted materials he had been given to work with and at the same time trying to deal with the creators of the show, who seemed spitefully to be doing everything they could to make his job harder.

Joseph Papp seemed disinclined to intervene, although he was quite attentive. Perhaps more than anyone else connected with the production, he was under enormous pressure; time was short and the stakes were very high. *Hair* was slated to open the new New York Shakespeare Festival Public Theater. His credibility, and that of his whole organization, was on the line.

The mounting tension between the director and the writers over casting led to a nearly complete breakdown of the work within a few weeks. Not long after Anna returned to this troubled situation, she found herself in the middle of it. Rather than maintaining neutrality, she sided with Rado and Ragni. She also made it quite clear that she thought she could save the production and as usual pushed hard for her own point of view. Anna knew how to work with these fellows and with this kind of thematic material. She was in familiar territory — a territory she had staked out two years earlier in *Opus '65* and before that. Still shaky from her surgery, she braced herself and got to work.

In the midst of all the turmoil Freedman decided that whatever potential *Hair* had had at the outset was now diminished beyond his helping. Feeling that his authority as a director was being continually undermined, he withdrew from the production. Papp decided to take his chances with Anna as director, but during the next few weeks things did not get appreciably better. Now, there were problems of a different kind. In Anna's version, dance was heavily emphasized; the results seemed over-choreographed and lacking in the spontaneity and abandon essential to its commercial success. Anna also had carried her antiwar anger into the production, and while that had been effective on the concert stage, there was valid concern that it would not necessarily work for audiences that come to see musicals.

With previews only a day or two away, Papp knew that *Hair* was in seri-ous trouble. In desperation, he emplored Freedman to return. Freedman said he would come back only if he got carte blanche and if Anna was out. He was prom-ised that his conditions would be met. The next day Papp marched into the re-hearsal and asked Anna to get her coat and come into his office. There, he told her that her services were no longer required.

According to Anna, he did so without kindness and without tact. She had never pressed for an amended contract, describing her position as director, and even if she had it would have offered little protection. In those days it was not considered unusual for directors both on and off Broadway to be replaced at the last minute. This was especially true in the case of musicals that were not going well. But Anna had never been dismissed from a production of any kind and she was livid.

There seem to be as many versions of what happened during the re-hearsal period of *Hair* as there were people involved. There are also many ver-sions of the details of Anna's dismissal. The one most frequently told is that Papp wrote a small check to Anna, which she tore up in his presence, and did her best to forget the whole affair. A more probable version is that later, as a matter of prin-ciple, she filed a grievance with the Society of Choreographers and Stage Direc-tors and was awarded a small settlement. Both may well be true. She chooses not to speak about it.

In one of those rare miracles that takes place from time to time in the the-ater, Freedman, now seeing the production with fresh and rested eyes, and with-out opposition from Rado and Ragni, reworked the first act in one day. The play was previewed with Freedman's first act and Anna's second. Anna's name was omitted on the program and covered over on the poster. A day later, both acts were completely Freedman's, or so the story goes.

Reviews were ecstatic. It was called "a spontaneous, controlled celebra-tion," and "The representative musical of the youth generation." *Hair* was to the 1960s what *West Side Story* had been to the decade before: a theatrical expression of the energy and force of the times, readily recognized by audiences as their own. The tremendous vitality of the concept and the exuberant music and lyrics more than compensated for the unevenness of the book. Like *West Side Story, Hair* broke new ground on Broadway.

The question remains: What, if anything, survived of Anna's work after she left the production? Doris Hering, who came to watch and write about re-hearsals for *Dance Magazine* while Anna was still directing, described "the sinewy toughness of Miss Sokolow's approach . . . the eerie beauty of the actors reaching upward, curling fetally, crossing the stage on their knees."

On opening night one could discern Sokolow-style moments throughout the performance, and they were there in subsequent versions as well. Dancers Mary Anthony and José Coronado, choreographer Art Bauman, and theater/

dance entrepreneur Gideon Paz were among the knowledgeable theater people who recognized Anna's stamp — even some of her trademarks — in the Public Theater and Cheetah productions, and later in the Broadway version of *Hair*.

Anna also made less tangible contributions to the success of *Hair*. According to Rado, she had instilled her enormous personal intensity into the overall production and had helped the cast to a better understanding of theater discipline during the rugged rehearsal period. She kept the process going when it looked like the whole enterprise would collapse. One must question Gerald Freedman's later assertion that he cleared the stage of Anna's ideas in a few days.

After a sold-out six-week run, the production was moved to a disco, Cheetah, where it did not do well. The work was then taken over by the producer Michael Butler, and with a new director, set designer, and lighting designer as well as several cast changes, a much slicker version (with some nudity that might be seen if one did not blink) opened on Broadway, where it enjoyed a long and successful run. Rado was, at last, cast in the role he wanted to play. *Hair* became the representative musical of the youth generation and made great fortunes from that point forward. Neither Sokolow nor Freedman were ever to benefit financially from the famous production they helped bring to life.

At one point, Anna was invited to rejoin *Hair* as choreographer for the Broadway production. Had she done so she might very well be a wealthy woman today, but when she heard that the new director, Tom O'Horgan, was going to use nudity, she said, "No, thank you." She regarded the nudity as a cheap ploy to attract audiences.

Her pride had been deeply hurt by the sudden and crudely handled dismissal and the invitation did not relieve the pain. She later said, "they picked my brains for months, and then when they didn't need me any more . . .," then she extended her thumb and tossed it over her shoulder. The fact that last-minute dismissals continue to be commonplace in the New York theater world is of no interest to Anna.

The Broadway version of *Hair* was choreographed by Julie Arenal, who had worked closely with Anna for several years, often as her assistant. Arenal was one of the people who recognized the Sokolow stamp when she first saw the production at Cheetah. Later, when she was asked how much Anna influenced her own choreography, she replied that Anna's focus had been much angrier than her own, but otherwise the influence was clearly there: "After all of those years I spent with her, how could it not be?"

Perhaps theater and dance historians should one day ponder whether or not there would have been a *Hair* without an *Opus '65*. The answer would probably be no. In his disarmingly candid chronicle about Broadway in the late 1960s, *The Season*, William Goldman asked an astute Broadway businessman what he thought the effect of *Hair* would be on the future of musicals on Broadway. He responded, "There will now be a spate of shitty rock musicals."

20

THEATER DANCED AND DANCED THEATER

It was a great relief and joy to see something on a stage that is visually exciting and intellectually stimulating. I am grateful that Anna Sokolow continues to experiment with theatre danced and danced theatre. (Walter Sorell, Dance News, April 1972)

Almost a year before Anna began working on *Hair*, she had begun to rebuild her company, holding rehearsals at the Clark Center on Eighth Avenue. Ze'eva Cohen, Chester Wolenski, Jeff Duncan, and Jack Moore (all fine performers from her previous company) were part of the new group, although Duncan and Moore were soon focusing their energies on DTW. By 1967, they danced for Anna only on special projects.

The new and exceptionally fine group also included, at one time or another, Martha Clarke, Margaret Cicierska, Irene Feigenheimer, Lenore Latimer, Kathryn Posin, Ray Cook, Edward Effron, David Krohn, Clyde Morgan, John Parks, Trina Parks, Jim May, and Lorry May. Several of them had worked with Anna at Juilliard. All had learned one way or another to weather the storms of her difficult periods because they appreciated and respected her powers as an artist and as a mentor. They loved and were fiercely loyal to Anna, her stormy disposition notwithstanding.

In the spring of 1967, Anna was one of six major American choreographers to receive a ten-thousand-dollar grant from the National Council on the Arts (soon to be known as the National Endowment). She decided to make a major new piece with the money and to have a New York season in which it would be premiered.

The dance she created, *Deserts* (Varèse), is one of her most powerful, and was for a time one of her most widely performed works. Although mildly flawed by its length, it is nevertheless a formidable artistic accomplishment. For her program notes, Anna quoted words Varèse affixed to his score:

> . . . deserts suggests not only all physical deserts (of sand, sea, snow, of outer space, of empty city streets) but also the deserts in the mind of man; not only those stripped aspects of nature that suggest bareness, aloofness, timelessness, but also that remote inner space no telescope can reach, where man is alone, a world of mystery and essential loneliness.

As Jacqueline Maskey suggested in her March 1967 *Dance Magazine* review of the premiere, Varèse's statement could be used to sum up Anna's direction as choreographer at the time:

> *Deserts* begins and ends with the same image: a dozen individuals are seated on the floor, heads bowed, their peculiarly defenseless postures suggesting exhaustion. When they move, it is with the frantic quality of people under attack by invisible assailants: they writhe; they spin feverishly; their eyeballs bulge with the pressure of panic. They jump straight into the air, then fall, their arms flailing against bodies which burn with a thousand itches. It is as if each is experiencing a personal Inferno, unreachable and unrelievable.*

In his *New York Times* review on March 11, 1967, Clive Barnes expressed sentiments that would later appear in reviews of the work in Mexico, Israel, and England as well as in the United States:

> Who needs her sad-faced visions and tautly shaking bodies? Well, certainly I do. Her madness of the psyche is neither pretty nor pleasant, yet her recognition of pain, the force and value she gives to pain, to me seems valuable in a callous world. Miss Sokolow cares — if only to the extent of pointing out that the world is bleeding. I find hope in such pessimism.

For about two-and-a-half years the Anna Sokolow Dance Company performed in and around New York City and on the East Coast college dance circuit. There were also appearances in California and Canada. Most of these performances were grouped in relatively short blocks of time because of Anna's many other professional commitments.

The touring repertory was overall a stark one. *Time + 7* was a sometimes amusing but mostly grim exploration of the hippie generation. *Lyric Suite* had as many searing moments as lyrical ones, and the somberly beautiful *Deserts* offered no relief. Lynda Gudde remembered that her sister had to leave a Chicago performance during the intermission because she was so emotionally drained. One respectful but troubled reviewer commented, "Each individual dance displays such a firm sense of theater that one wonders why this astuteness does not extend to gauging the program's overall effect." It was a complaint that was voiced over and over on the tour: the dancers were outstanding, the choreography memorable, but there was just too much emotional intensity to bear in one evening.

The program was especially difficult for people who were unfamiliar with the modern dance idiom. For many who first saw modern dance during those early dance-boom years, the only frame of reference was what they had seen on television — some variation or other of a toe-dancing sugarplum fairy or perhaps a dance featuring feather-bedecked swan ladies in tutus. It was an even

---

* Copyright © 1997 *Dance Magazine*.

more difficult program for the sensitive souls who were fully able to empathize with the painful subject matter: there were no reassuring endings and there was no catharsis. Critics began to label Anna with titles such as "prophet of doom" and "an apostle of darkness." Many of those writers also admitted to finding her work deeply inspiring, the gloom and doom notwithstanding. They appreciated Anna's unornamented humanism and could find strength and courage in her vision.

She could easily have lightened the program, as she was often advised to do. There were works such as *Ballade* and the Jelly Roll Morton piece that would have balanced the evening considerably, but she would not give an inch. "The dance is my particular way of seeing life through art," Anna said in a lecture at the Lincoln Center library auditorium in February 1968. "I don't care if the public likes me or not. But I do care if people care about what they see."

Al Pischl — the founder/publisher of Dance Horizons, co-worker at Juilliard, and old friend — was the careful and sensitive manager of the Anna Sokolow Dance Company. But in spite of all his efforts he could not keep them from encountering some of the difficulties small touring companies are sometimes subjected to in this country. The main concern was the performing space. On a good day they would arrive at an auditorium to find the lights properly hung, the stage freshly mopped, and an eager stage crew ready to work with them. Other times, they arrived from a previous engagement with just enough time to set light cues, do a warmup, and run the dances, only to find a class tying up the stage space. Yet somehow, through the intense efforts of the stage technicians and the dancers, the stage was transformed into a workable performance area by the time the audience arrived.

The Anna Sokolow Dance Company sometimes received standing ovations. More often the audience reaction was one of appreciation mixed with emotional exhaustion. Ray Cook remembered Anna during his years with the ensemble:

> Even after performing that repertory for a whole year she would say, "Don't think I can't get any more out of it," and then do a four hour rehearsal. She had such high expectations — such high ideals. She was, at times, very warm, very generous. Then something would trigger her — maybe an injustice that she saw or felt, and she would be very difficult.

Difficult times notwithstanding, most of the dancers stayed with Anna a minimum of two or three years and were proud to be part of her company. It was the poor salary of low-budget touring that took the greatest toll in personnel. When the dancers were in New York they could supplement their tiny incomes with other jobs. On tour, they had to rely solely on their salaries as dancers. Before the National Endowment for the Arts touring program was instituted, most modern dance choreographers could not pay their dancers anything approaching a living wage. As Cook put it, "We knew that Anna was putting everything she earned right back into the company, but some of us got tired of *never* having any money."

In addition to the stress of having continually to train new dancers to do her work her way, year after year Anna had to apply for grants to help underwrite the cost of the tours. Through the help of various state arts councils and the National Endowment for the Arts, her group was able, however spartanly, to travel up and down the Eastern seaboard and across the entire country. But the very thought of writing grant applications was as appalling to Anna as asking for financial help of any kind had ever been. If people worked as hard as she and her dancers did and they were good, why, she questioned, should they have to beg to survive?

Near the end of the 1969 tour Anna began to think about the Lyric Theatre concept again and announced to her company that she wanted to focus completely on works that would combine acting, mime, and dance. She suggested to a few of her dancers that it was time for them to try their own wings; some left for their own reasons. Jim and Lorry May, both trained as actors, were intrigued by the idea and stayed on. Anna invited Rex Bickmore to join the new group (which would encore the name Lyric Theatre). He, in turn, convinced Marjorie Mussman, then a dancer with the City Center Joffrey Ballet, to join the venture. There were to be two dancers, Rex and Marjorie; two actors (at early engagements, Jack Davidson and Janet Copée); and two skilled in both disciplines, the Mays. Rex was named assistant director.

Rex Bickmore had become a senior company member of the Joffrey Ballet at the same time that *Opus '65* was taken into the regular repertoire, but even before that he and Anna had become attracted to each other. A warm personal relationship had developed between them after the *Opus '65* premiere and he had become a regular visitor at her Christopher Street apartment, a few blocks away from the Joffrey studio.

Rex began performing as a guest artist in Anna's works whenever he was not tied to commitments with Joffrey. His first performance for her was on Christmas Eve 1967 in a production of *L'Histoire du Soldat* in Carnegie Hall (he played the part of the Devil, Moses Gunn was the Narrator, and Ze'eva Cohen was the Princess). He assisted her in the staging of *Opus '65* which, because of its originality and timeliness, was very much in demand by other companies. They set the work for the Royal Winnipeg Ballet, the Houston Ballet, and Ballet Rambert in England. Rex eventually left Joffrey for the New York City Ballet, but he continued to work with Anna whenever his schedule allowed.

In planning her new Lyric Theatre, Anna had established a close working relationship with the composer/conductor Joel Thome and the group he was then working with, the Philadelphia Composers Forum. In shared programs, the Forum played for her works and presented nonmainstream musical selections as well. (The composer George Crumb was associated with the group at the time, and on one of these programs he premiered his well-known work, *Night of the Four Moons*.) In some programs the names of the musicians, actors, and dancers appeared in one listing as artists of the Lyric Theatre.

After Rex joined Anna in the new venture they collaborated on a mime / dance for him, based on Samuel Beckett's mime / drama *Act Without Words*, with an electronic score created by Thome. The results were quintessential Sokolow — tortured and unsparing, and difficult for many in the audience to sit through. Every nuance, every detail, was built on Rex's unique combination of boyishness and dramatic intensity. The work was filmed for Maryland Public Television and his fine performance is preserved on videotape. The dance and theater photographer Max Waldman later captured another version of the work, with Henry Smith in the soloist's role, and four of those photos were included in a memorable published collection of his photographs called *Waldman on Dance*.

Anna's most extraordinary work for the Lyric Theatre was *Magritte, Magritte* (Scriabin, Lizst, Ravel, Satie, Thome), which was inspired by the paintings of the Belgian surrealist artist. It was with *Magritte* that Anna most clearly achieved the balance between theater, music, and dance that she had been pursuing with varying degrees of success for many years. In developing her choreography she made full use of the painter's familiar images, such as a pipe, a candle, a derby hat, an apple, and boots that mysteriously have lower legs growing out of them. With these pictorial ideas and the evocative and haunting poetry of Edgar Allan Poe, John White, and Paul Éluard, she created a surrealistic dance / theater piece that carried Magritte's images into action.

The first vignette, "The Lovers," was inspired by a painting in which Magritte depicted a couple isolated by their passionate involvement with each other. Their faces are covered by cloth bags tied at the neck. The sexual energy that carries them through a ballroom dance-like duet is breathtaking. According to Lorry May, the dance was clearly influenced by Anna's personal relationship with Rex. The duet, as preserved in the 1971 television filming in Holland, is surely one of the most sensuous Anna ever created.

The work goes in many directions, as do the paintings of Magritte. There is, for example, one delightfully droll section, "The Threatened Assassin," in the style of a French farce, in which a man who has murdered his mistress cavorts zanily with two inept detectives who are investigating the crime.

In other sections a nightmarish dream world alternates with a sometimes macabre, sometimes wry humor. When the work was shown in New York in 1972, Don McDonagh commented in his February 25 *New York Times* review: "The rules of logic are twisted to draw sense from contradiction and conviction from poetic allusion." The most outstanding dramatic section is "The Troubled Sleeper," tailored to Jim May's acting skill and boyish good looks. Writing in the April 1972 *Dance News*, Walter Sorell described "Sleeper" as "a harrowing somnambulistic scene with many sexual overtones, magnificently perceived by Miss Sokolow. . . . It was a great relief and joy to see something on a stage that is visually exciting and intellectually stimulating. I am grateful that Anna Sokolow continue to experiment with theatre danced and danced theatre."

In the course of their often interrupted three-year relationship, Anna allowed herself to become fully invested emotionally in Rex, without stopping to think clearly about how long that relationship could continue. She lost control of the situation — something that had seldom happened to her in her personal life. Rex, raised in ultraconservative Salt Lake City, was far more serious, quieter, and more vulnerable than her previous young lovers. He was awed by Anna from the start and too young and inexperienced to consider where the relationship could go. An intense love developed between them and Rex adapted easily to her needs. She had become his mentor. It was she who took over the management of their relationship and his development as an artist. He soon took over the responsibilities of the Lyric Theatre:

> I was only about twenty-six years old when I joined Anna in the Lyric Theatre, but I took the whole thing on. We worked with a professional producer, but we were primarily on our own. Anna has no interest in handling administrative details. That became my job.

He went after that job with an extraordinary intensity, fascinated by the challenge and very much in love. When they traveled together it was Anna, the experienced one, who made the arrangements. She took him to Canada, Mexico, Israel, England, and Turkey. She was sharing her world with him. They spoke sometimes about the French writer, Colette, who immortalized her own relationships with younger men in her novels *Cheri* and *The Last of Cheri*.

Anna was increasingly plagued by dark moods in the late 1960s, and it took Rex's constant attention and the warm support of her young friend and protégée, Lynda Gudde, to help ease the bouts of emotional pain she was experiencing. She had become fixated on the horrors of the Vietnam war and was anguished by the waste of lives there. At the same time she was experiencing the anxieties associated with the passage through middle age, a time when one often loses close family members and the shape of one's own lifetime becomes clearer.

Sarah had died in 1965, Isadore six years earlier, and Gertie many years before that. Anna and Rose were the only ones left of the immediate family, and Rose, Arnold, and their son Stephen were now living in England. Even with the company of Rex and Lynda and other close friends, such as Martha Hill and Mary Anthony, she somehow felt alone. She was either unwilling or unable to recognize the need for greater balance in her life and pursued her hectic work schedule with full and often angry intensity.

There is little question, too, that a contributing factor to her deepening depression was the medication she was taking for the old back injury, medication that acted as a depressant. The cumulative effect of all of this made her increasingly dependent on Rex and Lynda for comfort and companionship. For a while after the *Hair* fiasco, she could not stand to be alone for more than a few hours at a time.

The final straw had been Robert Joffrey's decision to drop his fine production of *Rooms* after only one performance because some members of the audience had walked out on it. With *Hair* and the staging of *Rooms* for Joffrey, Anna had risked high professional and public visibility and the extremes of success and failure that accompany it. Her awareness that her contribution to *Hair* had been invaluable and that the critics, if not everyone in the ballet audience, had been enthusiastic about this version of *Rooms* did not change the fact that her work had been rejected.

Notwithstanding her denials through the years, Anna had no more ability to tolerate failure — either real or perceived — than she had had as a young woman. It was partially the fear of failure that kept her angry and agitated a good deal of the time. Mary Anthony commented that during the mid-1960s Anna veered dangerously between enormous self-confidence and a painful lack of it. Remarkably, even while enduring so much physical and emotional pain, Anna was able to carry on a full schedule and her rehearsals and classes lacked none of the famous Sokolow intensity and energy. It was in the hours afterward, when she had to face her personal demons, that she needed someone with her.

By the last months of 1969 and into 1970, Rex was devoting himself full time to the new Lyric Theatre venture. He wrote grant proposals, drove the car when they toured, stood by to see that all the details of production were executed properly, and then, somehow, found the energy to perform as a featured soloist. It was in the midst of all of this that he began to feel the need to strike out on his own, to find out more about himself as a man and as an artist than he could in Anna's shadow. His position as assistant director of the company, which should have helped him build a professional name of his own, had only served to bind him more closely to Anna's name and reputation. He later said: "Everywhere we went, it was Anna's personality that absorbed everyone. Finally, I knew I had to establish something that was me." Anna was devastated by the news.

A few weeks after Rex told her about his plans to leave the company, Bill Bales became concerned because he could not reach her by phone after three days of trying. Martha Hill had assured him that Anna was in the city. He went to her apartment, managed to get in, and found her sitting quietly in her kitchen, not so much unwilling as unable to move.

For the next few months Anna was in and out of the hospital for treatment of severe depression. Attempts at counseling proved ineffective. She needed help from someone who understood the special world in which an artist works and lives — someone who could understand the psyche of a genius in her art who had never learned to be properly attentive to her own emotional needs. Such help was not found, or if it was, she was too ill by that time to accept it. Some of the heavy medications that were tried produced adverse effects. It took several months to arrive at a balanced treatment plan.

Jim May, Joel Thome, and Rex were among those who went to visit her during hospital stays, but all three found it very difficult. "There was so little energy. It just wasn't Anna," May recalled. Other friends concur, describing it as a nightmare period. She herself barely remembers it. "I just didn't know what was happening to me," is all that Anna can bring herself to say about that time of her life.

Finally, as the medication began to alleviate the worst of her symptoms, Anna reasoned that work would be the best medicine for her. More than anything else she needed the vitality of the studio and the release of choreographing and rehearsing again. Her good friend Mary Anthony, looking back at that period, said, "I think some deep inner part of Anna knew she was at a precipice, a point from which she might not return, and so she fought very hard. When she got back to work I could see that she was grateful. I think that choreography is as necessary to Anna as breathing."

During her periods of intense illness she had periodically called rehearsals and then failed to attend them herself. Sometimes she forgot because of the heavy medication she was taking; other times she was simply too ill to walk out the door. Some people in her company stopped taking the calls seriously, knowing how ill she was. Jim May remembers a day when he received such a call and decided to ignore it. Later that evening Anna called again, wanting to know why he had not been at rehearsal. "We needed you," she said, with some of the old urgency back in her voice. She was back at work again.

According to May, she came back to the studio a somewhat different Anna, one who was gentler with her dancers and more willing to accept help and advice from them. Mary Anthony remembers that she clearly was more patient and accepting in the choreography classes that she taught weekly at the Anthony studio. It took some time, however, before the symptoms eased off significantly, and it was well over a year before she felt fully recovered. But she was working again, nearly at full steam, within a few months of her breakdown.

The first major project that Anna took on was a play that dealt with the Vietnam war, a subject that had always been an emotionally charged one for her. She simply could not at this time distance herself enough from it as an artist to do her best work. *Pinkville* was an angry, Brechtian play by George Tabori that protested the My Lai massacre in Vietnam. It divided critics sharply. To begin with, it was not a good play. Although it came at a time when antiwar activism was making itself felt in almost any available arena, this one hit too hard. The fiercely anti-militaristic plot centers around a quartet of young Army recruits in training by a crude and aggressive sergeant to be murderers. Michael Douglas played the part of Jerry the Naz, initially the most naive of the group ("I wasn't born a killer and nobody's gonna make me one"). By the time they assault a small village and brutally slay terrified women and children, the Naz is as bad as the worst of them. Raul Julia was also featured in the cast.

Pinkville was conceived as a play with music and stylized movement (Stanley Walden, music; Anna Sokolow, movement). According to critics, the music was passable and the staging inventive, but somewhat overwrought. It is clear from the majority of reviews that the playwright, by turning the play into what *Newsweek* writer Jack Kroll called a "bellow of rage," had aborted the possibility of eliciting a truly empathetic response from the audience. Anna and the director had simply followed his lead.

Arthur Sainer wrote about Anna's contribution in the March 18, 1971, *Village Voice* :

> Formalized movement is certainly an interesting approach to a war play, but unfortunately it's a two-edged sword. Its vivid depiction of automaton qualities reinforces a sense of helplessness. It aggravates that sense in us that makes us believe we can have no determination over the important acts of our lives.

Without knowing it, Sainer was, in a sense, writing something about how the choreographer had been feeling about herself a few months earlier.

The following fall this courageous woman, still under heavy sedation, was creating an important new work, *Scenes from the Music of Charles Ives*, for the Juilliard Dance Ensemble and by late 1971, though still not back to herself, Anna was ready to think about new directions for her own company.

21

THE SEVENTIES
FIRST PLAYERS PROJECT
BALLET INDEPENDIENTE • BATSHEVA
CONTEMPORARY DANCE SYSTEM

Perhaps the greatest tribute anyone can pay to Anna Sokolow is to perform her work with strength and sincerity. (Katy Duncan, Dance News, January 1976)

Rex Bickmore had stayed by Anna's side during the worst period of her illness and danced a few more times to fulfill the last engagements of the Lyric Theatre. When she was able to get back to work again in the spring of 1971, he moved on to a new life, settling for a time on a commune in New Mexico and eventually returning to a career in the ballet world. With Rex gone and the professional relationship with the Philadelphia Composers Forum now a thing of the past, Anna organized a new group, The Players Project.

The emphasis, again, was to be on the integration of theater, music, and dance, as it had been in the Lyric Theatre. Jim and Lorry May, still both firmly committed to working with Anna whenever and wherever possible, were ready. By this time they had a daughter, Jessica, whose earliest years were spent playing in the corner of the studio during rehearsals. She watched her parents dance all around the room for hours at a time, looking quite serious, while the lady in front seemed to be telling them when to stop and when to go. (At a very early age she decided she would *never* be a dancer when she grew up!)

Others in the new group were dancers Tonia Shimin, Margaret Fargnoli, Charles Sumner Hayward, and actors Tony Azito and Henry Smith who both acted and danced. Smith took over the demanding solo role in *Act Without Words*; Jim May continued to grow in the important "Troubled Sleeper" solo in *Magritte*. Both won high praise in the press for their work.

The first major undertaking of the group was a six-day season in February 1972 in Lincoln Center's Forum Theater, as part of the Explorations in the Forum series. It was the same theater in which Johnny White's *Bananas* (conceived and directed by Anna) had played four years earlier. In addition to *Act* and *Magritte*, the repertoire included the twenty-year-old but still captivating *Jelly Roll*. In advance publicity, Jules Irving, director of the Repertory Theater, announced that

Players Project had been chosen to be the first dance company ever to perform in the Vivian Beaumont complex.

In the spring, Judith Hankins, general manager for Players Project, arranged for a central European tour with the same repertoire. They were scheduled to appear in Bonn, Frankfurt, Paris, Vienna, Brussels, and, as part of the Holland Festival, in Amsterdam, Rotterdam, and Groningen. Tony Azito was gone by this time. William Otterson was now part of the touring group.

It was an odd experience for the dancers: sometimes exhilarating, sometimes exasperating, and curiously without the sense of drama usually associated with Anna's ventures. Tired and not fully recovered, she was quiet and composed most of the time — even when the theater in Brussels where they were to be presented suddenly and unaccountably became unavailable; the State Department came to the company's rescue and another theater was found. It was clear from the reception Players Project received in each city they visited that Anna was well known in the European dance world. She had taught for two summers in Zurich in the 1950s and had chaired the modern dance program at the Summer Academy of Dance at Cologne in 1962. In Holland they knew her for her numerous works for Netherlands Dance Theater and in several of the other countries they visited, audiences had been exposed to Alvin Ailey's fine production of *Rooms*.

Audience response on the tour was generally quite favorable, but only in Paris was there any kind of reception for the performers after the concert. Pierre Cardin was a particularly gracious host following the performance of Players Project at his new theater, *L'Espace Cardin*, on the Champs-Élysées. Most often after the audience left, the Mays went home to be with Jessica, some of the other dancers joined Anna for a quiet late-night dinner and then a good night's sleep, and a few went out exploring. "We were a group primarily unto ourselves," Tonia Shimin remembered.

The audiences were neither titillated nor outraged by the program, but sometimes they were just a little puzzled: it was so unlike what European theatergoers expected at a modern dance concert in 1972. The enormously popular German Tanztheater was not to come into vogue for several years. This early encounter with highly stylized dance combined with theater (particularly in the surrealistic *Magritte*) needed time to be absorbed.

In Brussels there was a flurry of negative responses from some of the critics. The complaint, voiced also at times in Mexico and Israel, was that an American had no business making a dance about a subject that was close to them — in this case *their* painter, Magritte. The Dutch, on the other hand, were completely taken with the work and it was filmed for their public television with great artistry and care. The results won acclaim and some special awards. (Unfortunately, rights to show the film in the United States have not been released.)

There were problems with music rights on the tour, but the group was undaunted. Lorry's mother, a composer, who was along to help look after the new baby, created a simple but effective score to replace the Satie, and Charles Hayward improvised on the saxophone in place of the Ravel.

About midway through the tour, Anna began to feel too exhausted to continue and returned to the United States. That she was able to stay with the discomforts and stresses of touring as long as she did at a time when she was still in the process of recovering is a tribute to her unique ability to put her work before anything else in her life.

Soon after the group returned to the United States there was a tour to the West Coast. *Magritte*, at the center of the repertoire, was particularly well liked and understood at the University of California's Berkeley campus. Anna's ability to evoke Magritte's style of fashioning elaborate fantasies around common situations appealed to the temper of the times in the San Francisco/Berkeley area, but left some other audiences more puzzled than entertained.

When Players Project was invited to perform in the three-week-long Dance Marathon at the ANTA Theater in New York, as part of a festival featuring some of America's most lively dance companies, Anna decided to substitute *L'Histoire du Soldat* for *Magritte*, her original choice for the event. It was an unfortunate decision because this particular version of *L'Histoire* was not a strong one, and in terms of style and content it clashed with the other works on the series. It was a disaster in terms of audience response. Doris Hering, comparing it to the successful 1954 version, wrote:

> This time the whole thing sagged. The tale of the soldier bargaining his innocence with the devil seems passé. The script creaked with faded moralisms. And Miss Sokolow staged the little theater piece as though it were a sermon. The audience on the night I attended was most vociferous in its disapproval. I'm afraid my sympathies were with [the audience].

Lorry May remembers that after the initial audience reaction, it was a nightmare having to go back there night after night. Anna's response to the humiliation was to disband the company. "I don't have to be doing this," she told her dancers. "I'm a choreographer and people want my works."

Anna was right. People did want her works. Within a few months, offers to do full-evening programs came from the two countries to which she felt most closely connected spiritually: Mexico and Israel.

Raúl Flores was a promising young dancer in the group of Waldeen-trained Guillermina Bravo when, in 1959, an important new dance company, Official Ballet of the Bellas Artes, was created in Mexico City. Flores (later nicknamed Canelo because of his hair color) was among the dancers drafted from every corner of the city's dance community. Flores had his first contact with Anna Sokolow in the 1960 season of the Ballet de Bellas Artes, when she staged the Hidalgo homage and *Opus '60*. He had heard that she was difficult and temperamental and a few "Waldeenas" had suggested to him that her choreography was not that great, either. He wanted to see for himself. At the first rehearsal he found himself full of apprehension:

> It was the time of the beehive hairstyle and two of the girls showed up at the first rehearsal with their hair in beehives and wearing bright nail polish. Anna walked over to them, undid their hair, and explained that only prostitutes wore their hair and painted their nails that way.
>   I decided to keep my distance, but somehow there was a current between us and we became friendly. You know how sweet she can be sometimes and how difficult she can be. It was good for me to let the friendship grow between us. I am shy and had to get over that to be around her.

Several years after his first meeting with Anna, Flores formed a company (with Gladiola Orozco) called Ballet Independiente. He very much wanted to have a work of Anna's in the repertoire and the opportunity came when she was in Mexico City working with the students of the National Academy of Dance in the summer of 1968. She agreed to set her new work, *Deserts*, on his group. The well-publicized venture was so popular that people had to be turned away from the theater, E1 Teatro Antonio, on the night of the performance. Anna still had many friends in Mexico City who wanted to see her choreography again, and the younger generation was curious about this controversial and much-revered dance personality. *Deserts* was the only work shown on the program, followed by a speech by the choreographer about her experiences in Mexico through the years. Both the young company and the speaker got excellent reviews.

Anna's extremely busy schedule, then her illness, kept her from returning to Mexico for several years. By the time she did return in 1973 to create a full-evening program for Ballet Independiente, the group had become one of the most distinguished dance companies in Mexico. Flores tried to prepare his dancers for their rehearsals with Anna, basing his advice on what he had witnessed in the early 1960s and again in 1968: "You will learn a great deal from her, but she will yell at you. She is going to hit you in the stomach." When Anna first arrived in Mexico that summer, it appeared that Flores' concerns were justified:

> I don't know if you have seen how Anna's eyes will change suddenly. It happened when I picked her up at the airport and I knew something was going to happen. When I took her to the hotel where she would be staying, she took one look at the red and orange carpet and said it looked like a cheap French whorehouse. She ended up staying at my house. I was a little worried because she isn't used to children, and I have two, but it all worked out. She had changed quite a bit.

Once rehearsals began he realized that he had over prepared his dancers and, in his words, "they were like frightened mice when she first arrived." Because of the time it took for her to get used to speaking Spanish again and the dancers' initial fears, it was a while before the communication became comfortable. Then things started to pull together quickly. According to Anadel Lynton, an American who performed with Ballet Independiente for several years, Anna got along splendidly with the company and they became extremely fond of her. She was clearly becoming gentler in rehearsals. The program she chose to do was an odd collection of fine bits of older works combined with *Night* and an only moderately successful premiere, *Homage to García Lorca*.

Night, which Anna had created at Juilliard when its composer, Luciano Berio, was her colleague there in 1966, is one of her most terrifying works. Her description of the piece gives some suggestion of the images that had come to her when she first listened to the searing Berio score:

> The night is beautiful in a big city if you go down the streets and nobody is there. But it can also have an ominous quality when you don't know who is coming around the corner. Those forms on a dark street could be people turned by the night into strange animals.

In *Night*, dancers quiver, then tear around the stage in agitation; some appear to be hanging, heads thrown back, knees bent; the movement is sometimes convulsive. The dance begins and ends with people crouching with their hands on their chins, and at the very end they move toward the audience with inaudible screams and silent sighs. The Mexico City audience was mesmerized.

Less successful was the homage to Lorca, with music by Silvestre Revueltas, a collaborator from her early years in Mexico. Poetry of both Lorca and Pablo Neruda was read during the dance, as Anna blended images from the two great writers (neither one a Mexican) with her own images of the life of the Mexican people. It worked, but not well. Some critics commented that it seemed more like a tribute to Revueltas than to Lorca.

The highest compliments were saved for the duet from *Odes* (danced by Herminia Grootenboer and Mario Rodriguez) and for the solo, "The Pond and the Cage," performed by the Jamaican guest artist, Namron. Namron had appeared in the dance, an excerpt from *Scenes from the Music of Charles Ives*, when Anna did it for the London Contemporary Dance Theatre the year before. The audience cheered his work as they had the *Odes* duet.

The dance community treated the program as a celebration of Anna's return to Mexico. The final bows brought a standing ovation from the audience and there were many bouquets for Anna and the performers. It was a major event for Mexico City's cultural community and was featured in many of the city's important newspapers both before and after the performance. In Anna's scrapbook there is a photo that shows her shaking hands with Carlos Chavez, her friend and admirer for over thirty years. One writer, naming eighteen famous male and female dancers whose careers were profoundly affected by Anna, refers to her earlier years in Mexico as "una epoca de oro" (a golden epoch). He goes on to say that another generation of Mexican dancers and audience members was being exposed to and influenced by "La Fundadora."

In 1972, American-trained dancer, choreographer, and teacher William Louther took on the notoriously difficult job of directing Israel's Batsheva Dance Company. For many years this group was known not only for its splendid performers and rich repertoire, but also for the dancers' propensity for driving directors to distraction with their volatile personalities and profoundly exaggerated notions of democratic organization — notions which sometimes bordered on anarchy. Louther managed to survive in the position until 1974.

It was during his tenure that Anna finally was given the opportunity to work with the company she had indirectly helped to found ten years earlier. Louther was a great admirer of Anna, having first danced for her as a student at Juilliard, later in Ailey's production of *Rooms*, and finally as a leading member of the London Contemporary Dance Theatre. He was pleased when, in the fall of 1973, she accepted his invitation to do a full evening of her work for Batsheva. At that time she was the only choreographer other than Martha Graham who had ever been invited to do a full concert.

She decided to do *Deserts* and three new works: *Poem* (Ives), a solo for Louther; *In Memory of No. 52436* (Baird), a study of a concentration camp victim; and a group work, *Friendship* (Avni). *In Memory* was created for Rina Schenfeld, one of Israel's foremost dancers. The work was designed to be performed on a stage strewn with debris, old possessions, dolls — fragments of a childhood cut short by Nazi terror. Some members of the company felt that a piece dealing with the Holocaust poured too much salt into old wounds, a sentiment echoed by critics of *Dreams* when Batsheva did that work a few years later. Others found it quite touching. Typical of Batsheva, everyone had strong opinions and let them be known. Anna was at home in that kind of atmosphere.

Her rehearsal process was, as always, controversial. Many of the Batsheva dancers found it difficult to adjust to her way of wringing out her dancers emotionally and there was some tension over which dancers were to be featured. Some of them who had danced for Anna before expected better roles. But with the exception of *Friendship*, work on which was progressing slowly, things were going reasonably well. Then, on October 6, the Yom Kippur War exploded.

Anna was spending the holiday with Avraham Zouri at his home on the outskirts of Tel Aviv when they heard the news. They returned to the city, where she was advised by Judith Gottlieb and others at the A.-I.C.F. to leave the country as quickly as possible. It was clear in the emergency situation that the best thing she could do to help her friends was to relieve their fears for her welfare. Her hasty departure came just two weeks before the all-Sokolow evening was to be presented.

By December, the Israelis were cleaning up after their victory over their surprise attackers. Batsheva was functioning normally again, and the three completed works were all premiered within the next six weeks. *Deserts* was particularly well received and was an important work in the touring repertoire that season. *Poem* was successfully performed by the director and by Ehud Ben-David who, like Schenfeld, had been in the Lyric Theatre.

In Memory was not done again after its premiere performances, possibly because of its intensely painful subject matter or perhaps, as Joan Cass suggested in the *Jerusalem Post*, because "literal, emotional dances were out of fashion at the time, while plotless works in emulation of Balanchine and Cunningham were 'in.'" But when *In Memory* was first performed, the same writer noted the appropriateness of the theme; the country was still in shock from the recent war. "Rina Schenfeld," she wrote, "interpreted in bare, powerful movements, the numbing shock, the anguish, the search for the 'Why?'"

One of the job obligations Anna had to fulfill after leaving Israel was a residency at State University of New York Purchase campus. She was reluctant to accept work that would keep her in the suburbs three days and nights each week, but her old friend Bill Bales, an original member of the New Dance Trio who was dean of the dance program at Purchase, had convinced her on the grounds that getting away from the city had aided in her recuperation when she did the residency the year before. The young dancers were hard workers and would once again give her the kind of attention and respect she was used to receiving at Juilliard.

In 1973, student dissent and the aftereffects of the antiwar riots were still felt on university campuses around the country. At Purchase, which had many students from the volatile New York City area, this was especially true. Not surprisingly, the dancers enrolled there liked the unconventional Anna Sokolow and her fiery choreography. When the Purchase Dance Company presented her ten-year-old piece *The Question* (Webern) in January 1974, the choreography retained its original impact. An impassioned student writer, Susan Solomon, described the effect of the work on the largely student audience in the university newspaper, *The Load*, on January 22:

> Anna Sokolow is a genius. Her choreography plunged into me. I felt my insides shattering with the impact. The dance was aptly and simply called *The Question*. It is a long series of questions that have no happy replies — I was sometimes terrified watching. *The Question* reverberated inside like the primal screams I heard in the library last year. And people laughed then the way they did Wednesday during the first few sections of the dance — nervously, uncomfortably, unwilling to acknowledge the pain they were seeing. The dance charted the tortures of living; the laughter stopped.

Successful though she was at Purchase — Bill Bales admitted quite candidly that she had been instrumental in focusing the energy of the majors in his young department — she finally wrote him, apologetically, that she would not be coming back the following semester. She liked the students there and adored him, but she was not happy in the countrylike atmosphere. The weekly rides from the city through the beautiful rural areas made her uncomfortable; the peace and serenity, the sounds of nature at night, were disquieting. It was a reprise of her feelings about summer camp when she was a little girl. She needed the city and the stimulation of her work abroad.

By 1975 she was closely aligned with a New York group, largely composed of Juilliard graduates. Here she would find an ongoing outlet for her creativity until she was ready once again to establish her own group.

After José Limón's death in 1972, longtime Limón Company member Daniel Lewis, who had acted as assistant artistic director of the company during Limón's last years and as temporary director after his death, decided to devote his energy to a new enterprise, Contemporary Dance System (CDS). Lewis' vision was to develop a repertory company for the performance of choreography by important artists whose works were seldom seen in New York, principally those of Doris Humphrey and Anna Sokolow. In addition to this, he planned to continue to stage Limón's works and the works of young choreographers, including his own. He explained in an interview that there would be no trendy pure-movement dances that shun communication with the audience. The company would not be ruled by current fashion.

Lewis organized a group of attractive and versatile young performers that included Teri Weksler, Hannah Kahn, Matthew Diamond, Laura Glenn, Peter Sparling, and Miguel Godreau, and later, Peter Heeley, Randall Faxon, Victor Vargas, and Clifford Schulman. Many of the company members had worked with both Anna and José at Juilliard. Within a few years CDS blossomed into a first-rate showcase for modern dance classics, such as *Rooms, Lyric Suite*, and *Ballade* (Sokolow); *Night Spell* and *Day on Earth* (Humphrey), and a large variety of Limón works.

In December 1975, the company presented a week-long gala season of Anna's choreography, called "A Tribute To Anna Sokolow," at the American Place Theatre. At the intermission on opening night, the "Y," so much a part of Anna's life as an artist through the early years, arranged to present her with a special award for her contributions to the world of dance and to the Jewish people.

Reviews of the season were mixed but encouraging. It seemed clear that if CDS dancers were to perform Anna's choreography well they would have to have more frequent contact with her. One of the most consistent complaints in the press about the young company centered on a shortage of deep emotional intensity in the performers, the kind of committed risk especially essential to Anna's work. It was a time when cool behavior was fashionable and the arts reflected that trend.

In such a climate young artists had difficulty committing themselves to the depth of feeling needed to bring Anna's choreography fully to life.

In her *Village Voice* review Deborah Jowitt quoted a dancer in the audience who commented to her that it sometimes seemed that his generation performed Anna's work under gauze. Diana Theodore, writing in *eddy about dance, mostly* the previous spring, had acknowledged that the company had the talent, resources, and potential to become an extremely exciting dance experience, but, she wrote, "as technically proficient as each member of the company was that evening, I came away feeling a little hungry."

Realizing that Anna's touch was needed, Lewis had just invited her to be resident choreographer when the gala was presented. It turned out to be a long and productive relationship. She applied her intense rehearsal techniques to the group and got some fine results. Sometimes though, she was simply not in New York long enough to give the dancers more than a rough idea of the emotional depth the choreography required to be fully realized.

In those years of association with Daniel Lewis, Anna created several new works, including *Moods*, to the music of the contemporary Hungarian composer, Gyorgy Ligeti, and *Homage to Scriabin* (acting and dancing combined), which was later revised and presented at the Spoleto Festival in South Carolina. At Lewis' suggestion she also restaged three of her most famous solos, *Kaddish, Ballad in a Popular Style*, and *Lament for the Death of a Bullfighter*. The suite of solos was aptly called *As I Remember*. Because Anna had not thought of some of that material for well over thirty-five years, the memory was less than perfect. For example, *Ballad* (with Chick Corea's music replacing Alex North's memorable whistled accompaniment), if compared with the descriptions of that dance in the late 1930s, seems to be more of a danced reminiscence than a reconstruction. For restaging *Lament* there was the Shirley Clarke film to study and the results were fuller. How close *Kaddish* was to the original is anybody's guess, but the version was a warm reminder of why audiences were so moved by modern dance performances in the early years. Regardless of what may have been lost through time, many who saw these restaged works were delighted to have even the slightest glimpse of the kinds of solos that had helped Anna to win her fine reputation as a dancer and choreographer in the 1930s and 1940s. It is only in the Shirley Clarke film, however, that we can get any idea of the kind of impassioned performance she was capable of.

The most significant single achievement during those years of collaboration with Lewis was an adaptation of *Dreams* for television, filmed under the excellent direction of Roger Englander, with whom she had worked in the American Dance Theater project at Lincoln Center. Outstanding performances by the entire cast and the inspired choice of an abandoned warehouse for the setting made *Dreams*, like *Rooms*, a classic of dance filmmaking.

CDS (later the Daniel Lewis Dance Repertory Company) provided Anna with an ongoing relationship with a group of fine New York dancers who were willing to go through her uniquely demanding rehearsal process. She could see her work performed by professionals, as she wished it to be performed. It was a good exchange. CDS profited from the association with Anna both artistically and in terms of funding: her name on a grant application almost always assured a second look from funding agencies.

22

RESURGENCE

From childhood's hour I have not been / As others were — I have not seen / As others saw — I could not bring / My passions from a common spring. (From Edgar Allan Poe's Alone)

By the mid-1970s, Anna was able to put the breakdown and the difficult years of adjustment that followed it completely behind her and return to the intensely busy professional life of a decade earlier — the pace at which she was the happiest. She had at last begun to recognize that her own emotional fragility was as much a part of her as her courage and her unique capacity for hard work. Mary Anthony remembered that around this time Anna spoke about how moved she was by Vincent van Gogh's capacity to keep working in spite of the mental agonies he was experiencing, finally seeing, perhaps, how courageously she had faced her own darkest hours.

She became fascinated by Edgar Allan Poe and hung a copy of his poem, *Alone*, in her bedroom. Once, when someone wryly wrote of her as "The Poe of the dance," she responded that she could not be prouder. Within the next few years she worked on several Poe-inspired works, including *Untitled* (Druckman) for the Utah-based Repertory Dance Company, *Visions of the Dark Night* (Baird) for the Boston Ballet, and a production with the actors at Juilliard (like *Visions*, on the subject of Poe). More and more frequently Anna was comfortable admitting how much of her own life she had allowed into her works — that each of the people in *Rooms* was her at one stage or another of her own life. Now, for the first time in many years, she was able to admit that nothing of importance was missing in her life. She had her health again; she was very much in demand professionally; there was a wealth of new works.

In *Ellis Island* (Ives), which she dedicated to her parents, she created memorable vignettes depicting immigrants aboard a ship who relive memories of the Old World and project their fears, their hopes, and their yearnings as they look toward the new. These were not abstract characters but people who, like Sarah and Samuel, had staked everything on a dream when they came to America.

In *Ecuatorial* (Varèse), *The Holy Place* (Bloch), and *La Noche de los Mayas* (Revueltas), she rediscovered the potential of exploring themes inspired by Mexico and Israel. Freed from the compulsion to concentrate solely on darker thematic material, Anna seemed to be saying in each new work, "I can go any way I want to now." Although *Come, Come Travel With Dreams* (Scriabin) and *Ride the Culture Loop* (Macero) dealt with those dark trademark themes, even they contained, as did her earlier great pieces, an affirmation — the suggestion of the potential for resurgence.

It is a brisk Sunday morning in late autumn 1978. A rehearsal is scheduled for Juilliard dancers in the Dance Notation Bureau's studios on Union Square West. Anna walks there from her apartment, roughly a mile away, at so lively a pace that her two companions, twenty-two and thirty-three years younger than she, respectively, are having trouble keeping up. One stops to tie a flapping shoe lace; Anna keeps walking. If she arrives one minute late, she will give the student dancers the license to do the same.

Most of the sleepy-eyed young people who are there waiting for her show the signs of their Saturday-night debauches. The three or four who wander in a few minutes late mumble something to Anna about slow trains and buses. Her response is a warning glance. They toss on the tattered leotards and tights and bulky leg-warmers currently in vogue and warm up, looking bland and disinterested. "Hey, it's Sunday morning. Give me a break," is implied but not stated. She will do no such thing, and they know it.

They stretch and bend, occasionally flinging a leg into the air, while she works with an older dancer who is planning to use Anna's choreography in her solo repertoire and has come by for some coaching. The sleepyheads barely notice the touchingly beautiful dancing at the other end of the room.

Then, it is their turn and they snap to something like attention. Slowly, carefully, Anna begins to mold the material. She is working on *La Noche de los Mayas*, inspired by a painting of Mayan warriors, a work she created for Sophie Maslow's company the year before. The movement is gorgeous. The dancers are frightful. Even as she reviews movement phrases they already know and adds new ones, Anna insists that they perform full out regardless of their awkwardness. How can she see where work is needed if they mark through the material? One of the guests is drafted into the job of sound engineer, responsible for cuing the music on the rickety tape recorder. He is expected to do his job right the first time.

The rehearsal is over. Anna shakes her head and sighs, leaning her forehead into her hand. "They just don't understand how to work yet; they just don't understand." Regardless of the words, her tone does not imply discouragement, but determination. The subject is closed and the crusty sixty-eight-year-old choreographer links arms with her friends and leads them off to the bus. A new exhibit has just opened at the Museum of Modern Art and she wants to have a look before the crowds pour in. "We can have lunch later."

Two months later, in concert at the Juilliard Concert Hall, the Mayan piece has become the opening section of a panoramic work that includes scenes of

Mexican life at different points in history. It is now called *Así es la Vida en México*. As the curtain opens on the "La Noche" section, it is immediately clear that Anna has worked a minor miracle. The dancers look polished and their performances are a model of conviction and maturity. The women look alluring, the men virile. Anna studies the stage wondering what she can tell them after the performance that will make it better the next night.

At home on Christopher Street, the elevator operators plainly adore her. She exchanges pleasantries with them in Spanish and, at her request they call her by her first name. Some of them remember, even a year after your last visit, that you come to the building as her guest. When she comes home late in the evening they wait until she is safely in her apartment before closing the elevator door. They probably know she is a famous lady, but more importantly, she is their "Anna."

The deep blue carpeting and white walls in the living room and halls were her idea, and they work wonderfully well as a background for the dazzling collection of books, paintings, posters, and folk and religious art that adorn the walls and shelves. Generous windows flood the room with light. There are pieces in brass, wood, terra cotta, and tin, all displayed with equal importance. There is a feeling of harmony. These are the choices of a tasteful soul who has always been hungry for learning — who has seen with the keen eye of the lifelong observer how much one can learn from a painting of a gnarled tree or from a Pre-Columbian clay figure of a mother and child.

Jewish religious items sit side by side with Catholic icons. Her *hamsas* (metal hands, many with an eye in the center — an eye that wards off evil) from Israel must be one of the best private collections anywhere. Against one wall sits a delightful desk decorated for her by Nacho during his visit to New York in the 1940s. There are paintings inscribed to her by famous artists hung alongside works that have caught her eye, done by others far less well known. They clearly are of equal importance to her. Everything in the room is beautifully displayed. It is no wonder that friends have often asked her for decorating advice.

But it is the books that are most extraordinary. Several shelves about fourteen feet long are loaded with them. One glance at the art books reveals an enormous volume on the painter Marc Chagall near a slim French book on African sculpture, with Reginald Marsh and Charles Munch wedged in between. There are biographies of composers, writers, political revolutionaries, reference books on the Aztecs and the Incas. If you look closely you can see that in each decade from the 1930s onward she has chosen to study some of the most compelling writings to better understand her time. (Anna does not buy newspapers and does not listen to the radio for the news. The cheap hype, the exaggeration, the propensity to glorify disaster are anathema to her.)

There are more, many more books on the shelves in the bedroom. The collection has been trimmed down by a generous recent gift to the Dance Library of Israel; and still there is barely enough room. How can a woman who has had to live frugally for most of her life possess such a rich library? An incident that took place in the early 1980s sheds some light. Anna was in the bookstore of the Jewish Museum on upper Fifth Avenue when she noticed a few books on the Marranos. They were Jews who lived in Spain and Portugal and converted to Christianity under pressure, at first to live as equals in the society, later, during the Inquisition, to avoid torture and death. They spoke their own language (Ladino) and many continued to practice Judaism in secret. Anna was planning to do a work based on the Marrano way of life and was delighted to see the references. She opened her purse, counted out the money she needed for carfare to get home, and spent the rest on books, all the while gleaming with pleasure. On the bus she met Jim May, exchanged hugs with him and dumped the books on his lap for his perusal.

Jim May's first impression of Anna Sokolow in 1967 had been that of an intense little woman darting in and out of the rehearsal spaces she shared with Antony Tudor and José Limón at Juilliard. When he asked the students about her, some responded with adulation, some with complaints, and some with both. Nobody was neutral.

A few years earlier Jim had seen *Opus '65* at Delacorte Park. As he recalls, "I hated it . . . it wasn't dance. I had no interest in doing anything like it." It happened, however, that Anna needed a male dancer around the same time that Jim was between concert assignments, and so their paths crossed:

> When we were introduced it was clear that she had already checked me out. She knew that I had danced for Limón, Ruth Currier, and several others. I told her I wasn't sure I liked her work. She said I was a company-jumper and an egomaniac. Once we got that out of the way, we agreed to try it for a year.
>
> I joined her on a tour in 1969 to Chicago, Minneapolis, and Ames, Iowa. It was a dark program which included *Odes* and *Rooms*. She was very troubled about the war in Vietnam and didn't think it was a time to be showing any of her lighter pieces. She even refused to do *Ballade* which we wanted to dance and which would have helped to balance the program. But she felt it was too light a work to perform at a time when young people were dying senselessly in Southeast Asia.

Jim and his wife, Lorry, became devoted to Anna in the next few years. They believed in her work and liked the way their own artistic talents were developing as they learned to perform her repertoire in the distinctive way she wanted it performed. They stayed with her through the often difficult and challenging late 1960s and early 1970s. Both were an integral part of the second Lyric Theatre and both were there when the disastrous 1972 performances at the ANTA Theater led to Anna's decision to disband the company.

In an effort to stay professionally connected with Anna during the mid-1970s, Jim made himself available whenever he heard that she was about to show a work that needed an extra male dancer. This eventually led to his affiliation with the Daniel Lewis Dance Repertory Company. During this time Anna's group choreography was seen in New York only if a work of hers was included on a program at Juilliard, or if either Lewis or Mary Anthony had a piece of hers in their repertoire.

Jim and Lorry appeared in several duet performances in and around the city that featured excerpts from Anna's work, often dedicating the evening to her. They wanted, in whatever way they could, to keep attention focused on her works. Both Mays appeared in Roger Englander's film version of *Dreams*, with six-year-old Jessica performing the child's role. Whenever Jim appears professionally, he refers to himself in program notes with unabashed pride as "a disciple of Anna Sokolow."

Even when the three were not working together, their friendship continued to grow. Anna, who had no children, was herself adopted by these two. If she mentioned a book that interested her, it showed up on her doorstep in a day or two with a scribbled note from Jim. When she said something to him about how the sun's glare in Israel was beginning to bother her eyes, she found a visor on her doorknob just before her next trip there. Other friends and visitors brought flowers to Anna; Lorry came with pencils and pads and helped her to keep her accounts straight.

In the spring of 1980, Anna created *From the Diaries of Franz Kafka*, based on the life and work of the writer, for the theater repertory season at Juilliard. The piece, performed by the advanced acting students, was quite successful, and Jim and Lorry, who were both teaching the less experienced actors at the school (essentially to get them ready for Anna) convinced her that the Kafka work was important enough to warrant staging again. This time, they all agreed, it should be staged primarily with dancers who could act.

Anna was teaching choreography at the Hebrew Arts School at the same time, and they had asked her to present an evening of her work in their upcoming Heritage Concert Series. The timing seemed right. She assembled a group of dancer/actors who had worked with her before, including the Mays (now separated), Yossi Kipnis, Lynda Gudde, Dian Dong, Leah Dreutzer, Michael Lengsfield, Tom d'Mastri, Andrew and Kathleen Quinlan-Krichels, and Stuart Smith. They were to be known as the New Players' Project.

The program notes for the Hebrew Arts concert described the new group:

> The company . . . New Players' Project . . . is working with Miss Sokolow to recreate her older works, act as a vehicle for her new works, and provide a fertile and supportive ground for performers and choreographers who share her artistic convictions. . . . The religious, the social and the ethnic converge in Sokolow's

art, and emerge as a single voice. Subtle, inflected by a hundred accents, the voice is nonetheless finally as simple and pure as Sokolow's vision of dance itself . . . "movement impelled by truth."

To round out the program on Jewish thematic materials Anna created a tender new version of *Song of Songs* and a solo recitation of Bible excerpts, read in Hebrew (by Judith Gottlieb's daughter, Aviva Davidson) to the accompaniment of Bach's music. The all-Sokolow evening was such a rarity at the time and attracted so much interest that a considerable number of people had to be turned away from the 457-seat theater. Anna was clearly pleased. For the first time in five years an entire evening of her work was being presented in New York.

Jim May was brilliant as the central Kafka figure, delivering his lines with the same level of authority and maturity that he brought to his dancing. The younger members of the cast came through admirably and Edward Effron's effective lighting turned a rather untheatrical concert hall into the eerie, sunless world that Franz Kafka envisioned in *Metamorphosis*.

Jennifer Dunning, in her *New York Times* review, noted "the grain of optimism that lurks beneath her [Anna's] darkest compositions. . . . At its best," she wrote, "'Kafka' is one of Miss Sokolow's most handsome — though not fully realized — weavings in theater-dance of works of art and literature."

The enthusiasm of the audiences and warm reactions in the press were enough to convince Anna that the group (later simply The Players' Project) should go on for a little while at least. But she was very clear in her statements to the dancers and the press about the kind of company she was interested in. If there was to be an ongoing group at all, it would have to be a noncommercial one.

This notion, while strange to many younger dancers, seemed only right to Anna and many choreographer/dancers of her generation. Modern dance was, after all, rooted in the spirit of revolution, and one does not go into a revolution looking for money. For those of Anna's era and before, the goal of the dance was art. The motivation did not lie in a weekly paycheck; rather, their hard work and loyalty to their artistic leader stemmed from a desire to be a part of the creative process with an artist of their choice. Money was a matter of secondary importance. The new company members would have to be interested in acting and have some talent for it. There would be selective presentations for special occasions only. There would be no applying for grants and no honoraria. Any money the company earned would be used to support its activities and pay expenses.

"The dancers who are working with me," she later told an interviewer, "did not come to me for jobs. The Players' Project came to be because ten performers believed in what I am doing in the art." The group of dancers who were willing and able to meet these conditions that Anna assembled was described in the *New York Times* as featuring "some of the best performers on the modern dance circuit." By placing restrictions on the commercial development of the group, she had to content herself with eight to ten hours of rehearsal weekly; the dancers needed time to earn a living. Anna was willing to work around that.

Company members had been selected not only for their talent, but also for their willingness to rehearse at odd hours and at ever-changing locations. They might find themselves in Lorry May's loft studio one evening and in the heart of Chinatown the next. Wherever the rehearsal was held, they could not arrive two minutes late or leave five minutes early and they certainly could not miss a rehearsal unless the situation was desperate.

Meanwhile, the dancers earned their living in a variety of ways: one was a wine-taster, another, a window dresser, and a third, a department-store clerk; a few were teachers. For a long time, bookings were sparse because, in accordance with Anna's wishes, little was being done to promote the group. Recalling that period, Jim May related that after a couple of years, it was no longer satisfying. The dancers began to want more performance opportunities and finally some of them left the group. For a while the size of Players' Project fell from ten performers to eight, and then to six. Jim May said:

> We finally convinced Anna to let us start fundraising as the next step towards building a more permanent company. Our first grant, in 1983, came from The Jerome Robbins Foundation to appear at the Riverside Church. It was clear that people were willing to help us — so was the New York State Council on the Arts — but we weren't incorporated as a nonprofit organization. We finally did that in 1987. When some grants started coming in, we were able to plan ahead for the next season instead of just responding to calls that came in from potential sponsors.

In the fall of 1986 an event took place that may have helped to convince Anna to go ahead to that next phase of the development of Players' Project, which has since performed at the Bellas Artes Theatre in Mexico City, the Kennedy Center in Washington, and the National Theater in Taipai, Taiwan. It was a gala evening in her honor.

New York's Joyce Theater was filled on the evening of September 20 with people who had come to honor Anna Sokolow. It was the opening event of a three-day conference entitled "Jews and Judaism in Dance: Reflections and Celebrations." The seats for the benefit concert had been sold out for weeks and a festival-like excitement filled the theater lobby as the audience waited for the lights to signal the beginning of the performance. There seemed to be no doubt that the evening was going to be a special one, with solo performances by Ze'eva Cohen and Margalit Oved, along with works by Anna, Sophie Maslow, Ohad Naharin, and Meredith Monk. A group of Inbal dancers had flown all the way from Israel to perform a special dance made for the occasion by Sara Levi-Tanai. People who came to participate in the conference from all over the United States, Canada, and Israel were at the theater. Before the performance, some remarks from Anna's old students were overheard in the bustling lobby.

"She taught us at Camp Sharon in the early 1940s ... "

"I studied with her in Boston ... "

"I wonder if she remembers teaching in Great Neck in the fifties? We didn't really know who she was or why she was so mean sometimes, but none of us would miss a class with her for anything ... "

A few ladies from Montreal mused about the way she had influenced their lives. "She told us we were too provincial — that we had to get *out* of there and learn something about how the rest of the world lived if we were ever going to amount to anything. We had a hard time with our families, but a group of us went to live in New York for a while. None of us was the same after that, even after we moved back home ... "

Others were there who had seen Anna as a fiery young agitprop dancer and recalled titles of dances that had not been performed for nearly fifty years.

"Do you remember her in *Slaughter of the Innocents?*"

"There was one about a juvenile delinquent called *A History of Cases* or something like that ... "

And, of course, there were those who knew her as a choreographer, past and present.

"I bumped into Clifford Odets in Mexico City in 1939. He told me the Sokolow Troupe was performing at the Bellas Artes and I went ... "

"I was there at the premiere of *Rooms*. You could have heard a pin drop when the curtain came down. We were stunned, and when I see it today it has the same effect on me ... "

And there were the professional dancers who had worked for her or studied with her at Juilliard. "No one has ever filled me with terror the way that woman could. But I knew what I was getting from her, and in the process I learned how to dance."

When the audience was seated and the house lights finally dimmed, Anna's seat was still empty. The lights went out and suddenly the stage was lit. A joyous sound of drums and flutes burst from the rear of the theater. Down the steps, as if in a holiday procession, came the richly costumed Inbal Dance Theatre, twelve dancers and musicians who had arrived only a few hours earlier from Israel to honor Anna. At the center of the procession, a diminutive figure walked with head held high while the dancers reached their arms tenderly and protectively around her. When they reached the stage, she moved with small, delicate steps as the group performed rich serpentine and circular patterns about her. Was Anna, for the moment, a Yemenite bride or a desert chieftain about to be honored?

The choreography by Sara Levi-Tanai expressed a warmth and affection rarely seen on stage today. The dancers, themselves dressed in traditional Yemenite costumes evoking the splendor of biblical festive times, encircled Anna with a movement motif that built into a symbolic placing of a crown on her head.

Suddenly, this coronation gesture was transformed into the placement on Anna's shoulders of a real mantle, shimmering with golden threads. Levi-Tanai was later to tell the audience that her daughter had woven it especially for Anna.

After the presentation, Anna quietly relinquished center stage as a performer, but remained a delighted observer until she was welcomed back for the stirring climax of the dance, a memorable "Chain of Hands" which, according to the program, symbolically unifies Israel with the Diaspora. In those last moments her spine lengthened, a serene beauty illuminated her face, and Anna revealed something to the audience of her old majesty as a stage performer.

After the intermission, a formal presentation once again found Anna on stage. Congratulatory letters and telegrams were read from Mayor Ed Koch of New York; Shimon Peres, prime minister of Israel; and such luminaries of the arts as Isaac Stern, Leonard Bernstein, Agnes de Mille, James Mitchell, and Jerome Robbins. De Mille's telegram was simple and direct:

> *I SALUTE ANNA SOKOLOW, A TRUE PIONEER AND A STAUNCH ARTIST WHO NEVER IN HER LIFE HAS COMPROMISED. SHE HAS CARRIED A BANNER FOR ALL OF US. I ALSO SEND LOVE.*

Anna listened attentively and when asked to speak she said simply, "When I hear these things, it makes me feel that the most important thing I can do is continue my work and do more and more and more."

23

PS
ANNA TODAY

Ten years have gone by, and the phenomenon that is Anna Sokolow has known no real interruption. She is still teaching, choreographing, making public appearances, and winning awards. (Some of the most recent awards have been the Samuel H. Scripps American Dance Festival Award, presented in 1991, and The American Academy of Arts and Letters Award and the The Tiffany Award, both presented in 1993). In September 1996 a bronze plaque, with Anna's likeness, was permanently placed in Mexico City's Teatro De La Danza in honor of her contributions to the growth of modern dance in Mexico.

In addition to choreographing some new works, Anna has been rethinking some of her older ones. Sometimes she chooses to change the title / or the music, and at times, when restaging one of her older works, she will alter the contents considerably. Why not, they are *her* dances, aren't they? At the most basic level of creativity, she never seems to run out of ideas. Among her newest works, *September Sonnet* (1995) has won high praise for its evocation of a middle-age love that stands the test of time. *Sonnet* was created for and is stunningly performed by Jim and Lorry May, who continue to be lead dancers in Anna's performance group, Players' Project. In his *New York Times* column, Jack Anderson commented:

> There was great dignity in the way this man and woman touched each other. In their moments alone, he rose from the floor with what appeared to be both pain and hope, as if recalling old troubles while retaining faith in the future. She, in turn, let her eyes search the space around her, as if beholding ghosts of the past visible only to her. At last, the lovers huddled together to experience an emotional warmth each appeared to realize only the other could provide.

A later article also by Anderson in the *Sunday Times* celebrated the continuous achievements of three elders of modern dance: the late Erick Hawkins; Merce Cunningham; and Anna. Tom Brazil's striking photo of Jim and Lorry in *September Sonnet* accompanied the article.

Some young dancers and some who have known her for many years come to Anna for help and advice with their choreography. Seldom, if ever, does she turn away from a reaching hand. Anna loves to work and manages to always stay busy, because she is happiest that way.

*   *   *

The evening of Feburary 15, 1995, was one of those cold, rainy February nights when no amount of bundling up seems to keep the body warm enough. Umbrellas were blown in the wrong direction, and if the wind didn't get you, the rain did. In New York City on a night like this cabs are not easy to find; but that did not deter the crowd at the Cosmopolitan Club on E. 66th St. from coming to pay tribute to Anna Sokolow in celebration of her eighty-fifth birthday a few days before. The crowd included people Anna had known (some she had danced with) for over sixty years, as well as dancers and musicians who were relatively new in her life. Anna, dressed very simply in black, her hair pulled back, stood quietly greeting friends near the piano. One of her closest friends, Chaim Freiberg, a gifted piano player and teacher, came over and began to play some Chopin in her honor. For a few magical moments it seemed as if the music had been written for her.

The reception was a prelude to a Gala evening in honor of Anna at the Sylvia and Danny Kaye Playhouse at Hunter College, several blocks away. The evening included speeches by celebrities in both dance and theater. Film clips and performances of Anna's work, opened with an excerpt from Shirley Clarke's 1957 experimental film of an astonishly intense Anna performing an excerpt from her *Bullfight*. Next, an old friend and colleague, Sophie Maslow, recalled with warmth and spirit how she and Anna met as children in dance classes at the Neighborhood Playhouse, graduated into Martha Graham's company and, in their politically active days, gave joint performances of their choreography in union halls.

Uta Hagen, at whose HB (Herbert Berghof) Studio Anna was still teaching every Sunday morning, spoke as both an actress and a teacher: "Anna's work with actors is set apart by her awareness of the physical being. Movement is used by her as a human experience, not formally, not mechanistically." Jim and Lorry May then performed the "Tiger Rag" section from the long-time favorite spoof on lecture-demonstrations, *The Evolution of Ragtime*, to the music of Jelly Roll Morton and with Uta Hagan as Narrator.

Manuel Hiram, Artistic Director of Mexico's Ballet Independiente, spoke glowingly of Anna's contributions to the growth of modern dance in his country since her first appearance there in 1939 and introduced one of his dancers, Joaquin Hernandez, who performed "The Pond and the Cage" section from *Scenes from Music of Charles Ives*. David Manion, from the Dance Library of Israel, noted Anna's profound influence on the growth of modern dance in that country and introduced Hassia Levy-Agron and the Springboard Dance Company of Jerusalem.

Gerald Arpino, the director of the Joffrey Ballet of Chicago, then presented his own tribute to Anna:

Anna Sokolow is one of my heroines. She is one of the most powerful and creative forces in dance in the 20th century. I became a dancer because of the pure joy and spirit of dance. I have remained in the field ever since because pioneers as Anna Sokolow showed the deep commitment and intense humanism that dance is capable of expressing. Her indomitable spirit, her courage, her uncompromising truths are beacons for not only the dance world, but for all humankind. And these formidable virtues are leavened by her kindness and generosity. (I wish we could bottle these Sokolow traits and present them to our city, state, and federal legislators).

When Robert Joffrey invited Anna to choreograph for our newly re-formed company in 1965, she gave us OPUS '65. The occasion highlighted all of Anna's outstanding qualities. Not only did she create an important work of social protest (which was then a rare form for ballet), but she literally presented the ballet to us as a gift. She would not charge us for it because she knew how little money we had as we struggled to start over. And the Joffrey dancers were also given a gift: the gift of working with this remarkable innovator of dance, who always gives and demands the best.

Anna's Players' Project followed with a performance of "Quintet" from *Opus '65*, with music written for the work by Teo Macero.

After intermission, Jac Venza, executive producer of public television's "Great Performances" series, spoke with reverence of Anna's 1955 *Rooms*. In 1966 he produced a version of the masterpiece which he claimed was the precursor to his "Dance in America" series on PBS. The Anna Sokolow Dance Company followed with "Desire," an excerpt from the piece. The internationally-known Paul Taylor then introduced the last performance, Anna's 1961 *Dreams* — her indictment of Nazi Germany — which was danced by an ensemble from her Player's Project. Before the dance actually began, Jerome Robbins, referring to Anna's social conscience, added: "She has influenced us all."

After *Dreams*, two graduates from Juilliard, Linda Kent and Laura Glenn, recited an open letter to Anna from Benjamin Harkarvy, artistic director of the Dance Division of The Juilliard School, which praised Anna's "immense contributions to the dance art and to the American theatre as a whole." The finale came when the president of the borough of Manhattan, Ruth W. Messinger, cajoled Anna onto the stage (with help from Jerome Robbins) and read the following proclamation:

Whereas   As a dancer, choreographer and teacher and as the founder and director of the Players' Project, Anna Sokolow has been a leading figure in the growth and development of modern dance in the United States and internationally; and

Whereas   Critics have characterized her work as lyrical, penetrating, startling, engaging, and charged with a power "derived from the secret domain of the emotions"; and

Whereas   Since her professional premiere in New York as a dancer with Martha Graham in 1928, Anna Sokolow has been a powerful artistic presence in our city, influencing the course of dance in America through her performances and her instruction of dancers at the 92nd Street "Y" and the Juilliard School; and

Whereas   Friends, pupils, colleagues and admirers of Anna Sokolow are gathered today to salute her achievements and to celebrate her 85th birthday;

Now Therefore: I, Ruth W. Messinger, President of the Borough of Manhattan, in recognition of a woman who is one the great artistic treasures of this city, do hereby proclaim Wednesday, February 15, 1995 in the Borough of Manhattan as:

"Anna Sokolow Day"

*   *   *

Walking through the West Village with Anna continues to be a delightful lesson in seeing and hearing. "Look at those children playing." "Did you see the dog chase that big gray bird? For a minute I thought the dog was flying." A passing car blasts extremely loud music. "Can you hear that music? AWFUL!" She pauses to look into a few darkened hallways. During the walk we pass some people who have known her over the past five or six decades. The warmth and the love tossed her way are intense and sincere.

More observations. "Why don't they do that privately?" "Those shoes. . . . That hair!" "Did I show you where I lived on St. Mark's when I was a kid?" Many of the vendors close to her apartment building seem to know her as a neighborhood symbol. A Villager, talking to a friends, points. That is where Millay lived; in that direction on Waverly Place. This is the bar where the gay revolution started. Anna Sokolow lives up the street.

A few words in Spanish to some of the shopkeepers: "They all know me around here." Her tone of voice is a mixture of pride and modesty — both sincere. She checks her appointment book, looks at her watch and quickens her pace. "I'm meeting Linda at 5:00 for an hour rehearsal. . . . I'll be back by 6:30. Want to come and watch?" She tears down the subway stairs. It is not easy to keep up with her.

APPENDIXES

A.C.

(An Acrostical Sonnet, on Aaron Copland's Eightieth Birthday.)

Anna Sokolow, bless her golden soul,
At her dance debut, provided purest leaven,
Raising my lowly loaf to heights of heaven,
Overfilling my already brimming bowl —
November Fourteenth, in Nineteen-Thirty-Seven.

Copland, you were seated on my right —
Old Patriarch, as I'd dreamed of you, beard and all.
Patriarch? Beard? No, quite another sight.
Lean, young, charming, Lincolnesquely tall.
At your birthday party, later, we Amen'd.
Now, decades later, you remain my Friend,
Daedalus, Master, Guide, til time shall end.

Let us thank God for our meeting, for He was so kind as to plan it.
But also thank Anna Sokolow, who actually began it.

— Leonard Bernstein
November 8, 1980

FOUR MEMORIES, A POEM, AND A CRITICAL ANALYSIS

Some Special Memories of the Early Years

I remember the great contribution that Anna made to Louis Horst's work in teaching pre-classic and modern dance forms. I think a lot of credit should be given to her because I don't think those forms could have been completed without her. For every problem Louis assigned, Anna had a solution. For many years he used her dances as a criterion for study in pre-classic forms.

Anna and I used to go to the library on [East] 58th Street and look for dance forms in the Music Department, where we found music especially written for the ones we were studying. Some of them were described in Old English or Old French. We were not always able to translate but we did our best to reconstruct the dances as we understood them. They would not let us take the music out so there we were, dancing in the stacks, music in hand, whispering to each other as we tried to do the reconstructions. Anna was always able to find the dance movements and patterns that fit each form that Louis assigned to the class.

I remember vividly when Anna first came to the Graham studio. She looked like an angel with an exquisite long and oval face that reminded me of a Modigliani figure. It was wonderful to watch her. She had great intensity and terrific concentration. We used to say that she was like a mountain goat. A jumper. She turned fast and she moved fast. After she was with Graham for a few years, the younger company members circled around her. She told them how to make up, how to take care of their costumes, and how to behave backstage. She was a tremendous influence on the younger dancers.

When Anna became a teacher she was very demanding and had high standards. Sometimes there were students in tears but she got the truth out of the movement from them. When you worked with Anna you really had something to hang onto.

—Gertrude Shurr
Letter, June 24, 1988

Gertrude Shurr's first performing experience was with Denishawn. She later danced in the first Humphrey-Weidman group and then, for eight years, with Martha Graham. She was a consultant and teacher for many years at the High School of Performing Arts and was dance director of the Utah State University's annual summer dance workshop.

Anna and Inbal

For the members of INBAL, this is a great evening. There is the feeling that comes with the realization of dreams. There is no more pleasant emotion than that which is felt when dreams nurtured in sorrow and in pain for years and years begin to take on flesh. Next month will mark the fifth anniversary of the founding of INBAL. This evening seems to me to be a significant summary — not only of Miss Anna Sokolow's work — but also of all that has happened during these years.

The four months of work with Anna Sokolow epitomizes all of INBAL's achievements up to the present. It is strange how different the history of INBAL has been from that of all other companies. Others study first then perform. Only now, after five years, have we reached the point which should have been the beginning of our work — an opportunity to study.

It is difficult for you to imagine the soul-stirring effect upon me while watching the members of the Company during the demonstration of technique taught by Miss Sokolow. Boys and girls who were not privileged to study much, whose discipline and sense of organization were not what they should have been, have finally reached the stage of concentration, discipline and of responsibility toward their art. Their bodies are disciplined, their efforts are focused on a definite goal. An atmosphere of serious work has been created. All this has been achieved only after we have performed for several years.

INBAL's performances had an amateur look. The critics emphasized that we should not appear before we were prepared. But we had no other way, and our study became possible only after we proved that our existence was justified — and only after great artists like Jerome Robbins confirmed that there was artistic merit to INBAL — only then were we entitled to that toward which we had worked for years on end — a spacious studio and an extended intensive course by Miss Sokolow, an outstanding teacher.

Since the time the American Fund adopted INBAL, the organization has functioned on our behalf energetically and with great concern. Within the past ten months we have leaped years ahead. When speaking of Miss Sokolow, I should like first of all to stress her personality. Outside of her vast knowledge, experience and pedagogical gifts, it was important for us to meet with this kind of personality. Serving as an example to us in her approach to art, with one bold stroke, she was able to raise the level of our standards. Classes, conversations and consultations with her took on a very clearcut pattern — direct and on a high level. I would describe Anna with but one word — "more." Anna has a hatred for complacency with "half as good." In the material world you can be satisfied with less, but not so in the realm of art.

Anna has the reputation of being a strict teacher, and whoever has been burnt by this fire within her has felt the cleansing flame. She believes in what she preaches — however, not blindly. In her choreography classes, we could see the clarity of her opinions, her judgment and discerning quality.

It is not the quality of the movement or the style which is important but its structure, logic, sincerity and honesty. She always knew how to direct her counsel and remarks to the core of the matter. It was she who would point out to her student the seeming contradictions that are revealed to the artist — on the one hand, ironclad rules, a clear frame within which to work, and on the other hand, no enslavement to conventionality nor excess of dry and cold logic. She works with divine purpose and roots out disturbing elements. The temple of art is her home.

With all this, she is pliant to reality. She does not indulge in visions and does not ask for the inhuman. She brings with her a great respect for those who work sincerely and modestly, and she encourages the slightest achievement. Anna scorns boastfulness and audacity, and, like a true teacher, does not extol only those who are outstandingly talented. She has a good word also for those less gifted who show sincere effort to learn and to progress.

Without a common tongue, she was a true friend to all of us. There was always mutual understanding.

And here I must make a very important point. Many have expressed the concern that perhaps Miss Sokolow, as a stranger, might alter the special quality of INBAL. I should like to point out that the very suspicion expressed seems to stem from the lack of artists who know what art is and what style is and cannot for a moment allow themselves to indulge in the thought of spoiling that unique quality which attracted them and which induces them to come from afar and give of their time and their hearts to INBAL.

And one thing more, which I say with a degree of sadness. The warmth, courage and respect for the creations of INBAL with which these Americans like Robbins, Chujoy, Sokolow and Hurok surrounded us have not come from our own artists. Our spokesmen did not hasten to give us recognition, and these "strangers," each of whom is outstanding in his field — these not only encouraged us but gave us wings. Anna, in her day-to-day work, has harnessed our wild talent and has compelled us to march boldly in the path of art. And she has done this with insistence and, at the same time, with modesty.

— Sara Levi-Tanai
Israel Life and Letters
September–October 1954

Sara Levi-Tanai, a close friend of Anna Sokolow, is the founding director-choreographer of Inbal, a company of primarily Yemenite Jews who lived in the southwestern part of the Arabian peninsula until 1948 when Israel became a state, after which most resettled in Tel Aviv. Under Levi-Tanai's careful guidance Inbal has become a fine dance company that not only preserves the cultural history of the Yemenites but has extended the range of the culture of Israel.

Posdata Mexicana: Mexican Post Script

Anna assembled us in the towering wings of Mexico City's Bellas Artes Theatre. It was her tradition to imbue us with some inspiration or focus before each performance. This preperformance ritual felt different — she was lost in her own memories of an earlier time.

"The stage was so big," she said. Her eyes remembered the emotions, while her face remained composed. "I felt so lost, so lonely. Again and again I had asked the Mexicans, 'But will anyone come?' They came. They came."

She smiled a small smile. Anna was describing her own debut at the Bellas Artes in 1939. The mixture of awe and fear she felt at stepping onto that magnificent stage for an unknown audience was still palpable.

Now, forty-nine years later, Anna's words exactly described our own feelings. We were about to transfer the dances we had rehearsed in a cramped space in New York's Chinatown to the huge expanse of stage in Mexico City's renowned opera house. Our previous performances in this Mexican tour had confirmed that Anna was revered as an artist, and beloved as a teacher, but we could not imagine who would fill the 2,800 seats.

Even as experienced performers, we were struck by the seeming impossibility of projecting emotional nuance across the enormous orchestra pit and connecting with the audience. I felt particularly panicked at the thought of beginning my solo at the end of *Rooms* — in a harsh circle of light I was to lower my head and very slowly raise my arms to shoulder height. This simple movement in complete silence would have to hold the audience, and draw them into the intense, but contained, frenzy of the solo. I had no elaborate costume, no romantic light, no virtuoso movement to help me command the attention of the audience. Using Anna's single-word rehearsal directive I would have to bring a new concentration to the solo. As she had said so many times — "More!"

From the first lighting cue, *vayan* (the Spanish word for go), the performance would stay in our memories like no other. The stage crew was everywhere in staggering numbers. Nurses stood by backstage. We gasped for breath as we raced across the huge backstage crossover from one side of the stage to the other. Large tanks of oxygen were stationed in the wings to help us with the altitude and the pollution.

In response to the scale of the theater, the company naturally projected a fuller, more spacious presence. We felt a warm energy come back from the audience, almost embracing the dances. Just as the audience had come for Anna's 1939 performance, so they arrived in huge numbers for this 1988 performance.

An edge of nervousness still hung over us — we Americans were about to tango (*Kurt Weill*) for a Latin American audience. Could we convince them that the soul of that dance could be projected by North Americans?

We need not have worried. Our bodies sank deeper into the diagonals of the tango as we relaxed into the work. Anna's themes spoke on their own — jealousy, regret, passion, separation. Transcending language and style, the audience could understand and feel our common humanity. In fact, they had come to the theater to *feel*, and were willing to go where the emotions of the dance took them. Experienced, but not jaded, enthusiastic, but not naive, they sought not to be entertained, but to be moved.

This was a triumphant moment for the company. Quite apart from the reaction of the audience, we had been able to bring the work to a new level. The sense of unity and completeness was almost overwhelming.

The applause rained down on us, and it seemed as if the whole theater pressed forward to touch Anna. From the orchestra seats audience members rushed toward the stage, and from backstage people streamed in our direction. We stood, a bit stunned, as an impromptu receiving line, while a parade of people offered flowers, gifts, and expressions of congratulations. The processional was a combination of dignitaries and "Las Sokolovas," the Mexican dancers who had formed Anna's first group in that country. Still beautiful, with regal bearing, the Sokolovas seemed filled with emotion, both at seeing Anna and the work. Anna stood in the center of the company looking even tinier than usual. Her eyes were dark pools of feelings — joy, embarrassment, nostalgia, surprise.

Gradually, the formal arrangement of the stage was broken as the space filled with United States Embassy officials, audience members, and representatives of Mexico's Cultural Ministry. Anna remained in the center of a throng of artists and students, clustered about her like living pages of a scrapbook of her life. Standing proudly and wordlessly to the side was painter and graphic artist Ignacio Aguirre (Nacho), Anna's friend for fifty years.

We returned to our dressing rooms for the mundane tasks of packing costumes and removing makeup. Later the company celebrated at Plaza Garibaldi amid mariachi bands and a colorful floorshow, while Anna went quietly back to our hotel, maintaining a deeply spiritual mood.

— Susan Thomasson
August 1989

A graduate of the University of Utah, Susan Thomasson has performed with Kathryn Posin, Bill T. Jones, and Raymond Johnson and, for several seasons, in Anna Sokolow's Players' Project. She prepared the preceding reminiscence to describe the company's experience in Mexico City in October 1988.

Nichtav Batsad: Israeli Post Script

The gathering in honor of Anna Sokolow's eightieth birthday began in the courtyard garden of the Rubin Academy of Music in Jerusalem. A host of distinguished
guests — among them the mayor of Jerusalem, Teddy Kollek, and Dan Ronen of
the Ministry of Education and Culture — assembled at the reception with dancers
who had performed with Anna, along with fans, and many old friends. Eventually they all wandered into the large adjacent studio.

Five dancers from Inbal began the ceremonies with a special greeting
dance. A decorative copper tray laden with candles and Yemenite incense was
carried in by one while the other four ushered Anna into the studio with a huge
colorful silk scarf billowing over her like a *khupe* (a wedding canopy). After seat-
ing her, they continued with an expressive dance filled with the special crouching
stance that gives these dancers an accessibility to the earth — a kind of grounded
joy that is riveting to watch. It had first captured Anna on her original trip to Israel
to work with Inbal. The syncopated rhythm of the Yemenite drumming, the glee-
ful look on the dancers' faces, the occasional throaty yodel of the women dancers
set a magical atmosphere — a festive beginning for Anna's celebration.

Sara Levi-Tanai was invited to speak. She remembered that when Jerome
Robbins came to her from America he told her that the Inbal dancers were wonderful
but they didn't have any technical quality. "I didn't know what he meant, so I started
to cry, but he said never mind, he would help and the help would be Anna Sokolow."

Tributes followed from Giora Manor, Hassia Levy-Agron, Ze'eva Cohen,
and the founder of the Rubin Academy, Yochoved Yushtrovsky, who presented
Anna with an olive-wood plaque. Hassia Levy-Agron announced that Anna had
been made an honorary member of the Academy. Giora Manor wove all the
speakers' words together with a slide presentation about Anna's life. He also
called on the cultural attaché of Mexico, who brought official greetings from his
government. His speech in Spanish illuminated the geographical and cultural triangle between America, Israel, and Mexico that has been Anna's life map.

Danced tributes followed. Among them was a performance by Indian dancer
Astad Deboo whom Anna had met at the Academy; a version of Jules Perrot's *Pas de
Quatre*, prepared by Nina Timofeyeva, a fellow teacher at the Academy, who had recently arrived from Moscow; and most moving, a demonstration of Anna's own work
— an open rehearsal with students from her summer workshop at the Academy.

She stood before the audience in her trademark outfit: a simple black dress. As
always, her hair was pulled back and neatly knotted at the nape of her neck. It seemed as
though no time had passed since she had first come to Israel. Standing next to a camera-
man, she seemed diminutive; he offered her a protective arm as she searched for the
proper place to stand to oversee her dance. The dancers took their places and she nod-
ded toward her accompanist, who began to play Beethoven's *Moonlight Sonata*.

The students came from the corners and met in the center with lifted heads, their arms rising majestically. They executed simple but elegant movements which Anna directed eloquently with her voice and a slight indication of her hand. One dancer lifted a knee and hugged it, another put a hand to her shoulder. One did a slow pivot turn and then, on cue, everyone dropped to the floor. "It is important to introduce Beethoven to this very young group of dancers," Anna told the audience. "You can see that I never feel finished, but they did very well."

Anna was greeted with thunderous applause, and people rushed up to her with flowers and hugs and kisses. Then they began to drift out back into the darkened courtyard, speaking in small clusters about old times.

— Judith Brin Ingber
August 1990

Judith Brin Ingber has taught at the Bat Dor school in Israel and assisted Sara Levi-Tenai at Inbal. She has written extensively about dance in Israel and Jewish dance and is the author of *Victory Dances*, the life of Fred Berk. She is resident choreographer and dancer for Voices of Sepharad, a music and dance performing quartet, and teaches dance at the University of Minnesota.

A Strange Funeral in Braddock

Listen! Listen to the drums of a strange American funeral
Listen to the story of a strange American funeral
In the town of Braddock, Pennsylvania
Where the steel mills live like foul dragons,
Burning, devouring man and earth and sky
It is spring. . . . . . .

Now the spring has wandered in
A frightened child in the land of the steel ogres
And Jan Clepak, the great grinning Bohemian
On his way to work at six in the morning
Sees buttons of bright grass on the hills above the river,
Plum trees hung with wild white blossoms.

And as he sweats half naked at his puddling trough
A fiend by the lake of brimstone,
The plum trees soften his heart,
and he forgets to be hard as steel
and he remembers only his wife's breasts, his baby's little laughter,
and he remembers cows and sheep and grinning peasants
and the villages and fields of sunny Bohemia.

Listen to the mournful drums of a strange funeral.

Listen to the story of a strange American funeral!

Wake up! Wake up! Jan Clepak!
The furnaces are roaring like tigers
The flames are flinging themselves at the high roof.
Wake up — it is ten o'clock and the next batch of flowing metal
is to be poured in your puddling trough. Wake up!
Wake up! For a flawed lever is cracking
in one of the fiendish cauldrons and now the lever has cracked,
and the steel is raging and running like a madman,
Wake up!
Oh, the dream is ended and the steel has swallowed you forever,
Jan Clepak!

Listen to the mournful drum of a strange funeral. . . .

Now three tons of hard steel
Hold at their heart the bones, flesh, nerves,
the muscles, brains and heart of Jan Clepak.
They hold memories of green grass and sheep,
the plum trees, the baby laughter and the sunny Bohemian villages.
And the directors of the steel mill
present the great coffin of steel and man memories
to the widow of Jan Clepak,
with many mournful speeches on a great truck it is borne now
to a great trench in the graveyard
and Jan Clepak's widow and two friends ride in a carriage
behind the block of steel
and mourn the soft man who was killed by hard steel.

Listen to the drums of a strange funeral
Listen to the story of a strange American funeral.

And Jan Clepak's widow is thinking —
I'll wash clothes, I'll scrub floors
But my children never will work in a steel mill.
And the three mourners were sitting in a grave yard and thinking
strange thoughts.

I'll make myself hard as steel, harder!
I'll come some day and make bullets out of Jan's body
and shoot them into a tyrant's heart.
Listen to the drums, to the mournful drums
Listen to the drums, to the drums, Listen . . . !

— Michael Gold

A Critical Analysis

All the Sokolow dance works I know seem to have an inner connection with one another, as if they were all parts of some greater whole, aspects of one still unfolding confession. Not that they look so much alike, though the Sokolow movement vocabulary has an idiosyncratic stamp that is unmistakable; in other words a vividly personal style. Nor is it the case that their mood or import is the same; in fact, these range from sheer sportiveness or wit to dreamlike lyricism to bitter desperation. But they all share a certain muscular intensity of purpose, even the "lighter" works. Miss Sokolow's career began in an atmosphere of social protest generated by war and depression. As an artist she seems to have been stung into her most incisive utterances by the specters of human misery and injustice. But in her dances, the engagement with life experience at its most elemental levels is combined with a startling talent for abstract design. It is this fusion which makes her work appear both timely and timeless. In this sense, for all her expressionism, Miss Sokolow had one foot firmly implanted within classical tradition; she belongs among those who cling to the notion that form is the sine qua non of durable art. The undercurrent of polemic fervor in her choreography only seldom erupts into concrete statement. As keenly as she feels about the fate of her fellow men, she is no propagandist. The goal of her art is illumination of the human condition, not socio-political analysis.

On the plane of pure movement, Sokolow dances tend toward the extremes of the kinesthetic spectrum. At one end, dancers hang so loose that they veer around a stage in what looks like aimless dysphoria. Limbs droop, heads loll in listless arcs, bodies fold up like collapsing balloons, and bundles of dancers flop to the floor like laundry from a chute. At the other end, everything becomes instantaneously uptight. Movements are acute, convulsive and anguished, as if induced by the impact of electric shock, bullets or whips. Measured, smooth or temporate motion is the exception, and is often used to throw the disjunct extremes into relief. Yet another fundamental ingredient is motionlessness — not just rest, for Miss Sokolow's suspensions of movement may imply a tension more violent than explosions. She uses stasis as the contemporary composer has learned to use silence (forcefully illustrated in the music of Varèse and Vieru) — not just as a dead interval between phases of action, but as a highly charged metaphor for mystery, ennervation or terror.

> — Alan M. Kriegsman
> Excerpts from "Sokolow Steps up Philadelphia"
> *Washington Post*
> November 3, 1968

Alan Kriegsman, who received a Pulitzer Prize for his dance criticism in the *Washington Post*, once commented that his only real claim to fame is that he introduced Anna to the Anatol Vieru score, *Steps of Silence*, that she used for one of her most stirring works of the same title.

TESTIMONIALS

Statements from actors, dancers, musicians, and others connected with the theater; some well known, some less so. All have had close professional contact with Anna. Most of the statements were solicited for the biography; others were gleaned from the record.

Juki Arkin

An outstanding pantomime artist, Arkin teaches both mime and jazz in Tel Aviv. He is best known in the United States for his portrayal of the role of Adi in the Broadway production of *Milk and Honey*, with Robert Weede, Mimi Benzell, and Molly Picon.

She opened a window for me to see things in a creative way, to take a piece of the cycle of your life and be willing and able to project that on stage. She has the talent, the force, to leave marks — wrinkles on you. If she doesn't leave those marks, you didn't really work with Anna. Sometimes I watch Anna teach and I see a beautiful girl resisting what Anna is doing. I know this girl is going to stay pretty — no wrinkles, no scars, no understanding. (Interview: March 19, 1989, New York City)

William Bales

From 1942 to 1954 Bales was a member of the Dudley-Maslow-Bales Trio as a dancer and choreographer. He was associated with the New Dance Group Studio in New York for many years and the first Dean of the Division of Dance at the State University of New York at Purchase.

So many people meet Anna while they are in a transitional state in their own lives. There are certain things they will absorb from her one way or another. She teaches them that dance is not merely a self-expressive medium but a language in which you communicate your deep nonverbal experiences to your audience. She teaches dance as an art that enables you to communicate in very personal terms your experience of living. She has absolute honesty in trying to communicate experiences as she has lived them.

Anna developed a sense of values which she holds on to. There is a very positive sense of life. There is nothing trivial in any of Anna's work. Life has been a battle for her. She can't suffer fools and she can't suffer anyone who is a fake. She sees it immediately. Whether you like her works or not, they have a profound sense of her own persona, her own qualities that she lives by. (Interview: February 5, 1979, New York City)

Art Bauman

Art Bauman has danced in the companies of Charles Weidman, Lucas Hoving and Paul Sanasardo. A noted choreographer, he also served for several years as one of the directors of Dance Theater Workshop.

I always liked dance with a lot of guts. In the mid-sixties Anna was at the cutting edge of expressionism. By then Graham was old hat. It was Anna who captured my imagination — Anna and Jack Moore, whose work, very much influenced by Anna, could be called minimalist expressionism. Almost anyone who came to see Anna's work could not help but be very influenced by it. Only the "cool" choreographers missed it. They found it too emotional and therefore old-fashioned. They missed the point that it came screaming out of the *zeitgeist* of the sixties. (Interview: March 18, 1989, New York City)

Charles Bennett

Charles Bennett was a soloist with American Ballet Theatre and later danced with New York City Ballet. He was one of the founders of the First Chamber Dance Quartet. Bennett currently resides in Mexico but frequently works in the United States as a guest teacher and choreographer.

Anna. How to start? Well how about with what she is not? Her costumes are not by Halston, her themes are not "chic" or Greek, she is not a darling of the "demi-monde," she cannot be compromised, she will not succumb to a barren human heart, she will not forget her background, will not abandon her vision, is not interested in the surface — is not imitatable. She is unquestionably one of the most significant choreographers of the 20th century. (Letter: May 5, 1989)

Herbert Berghof

Mr. Berghof has taught acting at the New School, the Theater Wing, the Neighborhood Playhouse, Columbia University, and at his own school. He has been an actor-director on Broadway since 1939.

In my long years in the theater, Anna is the only teacher of movement I have found who fully understands that movement carries us, just as words propel us, to the destination — the object of attention we wish to lead the audience to. She knows, just as my teacher, Max Reinhardt knew, that the verbal and physical lives of the actor must be combined. I was very excited when I first studied with her at the Actors Studio to see how simply and practically she communicates this in her teaching. (Phone interview: April 15, 1989, New York City)

Raúl Flores Canelo

Raúl Flores Canelo, a Mexican dancer, choreographer, and scenic designer, has worked with the Ballet Nacional and with the Ballet de Bellas Artes. He currently directs the Ballet Independiente, which he founded in 1966.

Working with Anna was like having the world turned over for me as an artist. My choreography has become more intense, more emotional. Not only because of what I have learned from dancing for her and watching her rehearse, but watching her as she deals with whether her work is accepted or not. She claims not to care about audience reaction, but I think she cares very much. The important thing is that no matter how audiences and critics respond, she still goes ahead and takes chances. That is an important lesson. (Interview: May 21, 1981, Mexico City)

Martha Clarke

Fifteen years after leaving Anna's company, years in which she did pioneer work with the famed Pilobolus group, Martha Clarke started her own company, Crow's Nest. She then went on to create the widely acclaimed *Garden of Earthly Delights* and *Vienna Lusthaus*.

When I was fifteen, Shirley Clarke, who is my aunt, took me to see a performance of Anna's work and I decided on the spot that I wanted to be in her company. Two years later, I was. It was my first contact with theater and dance. Every day that I worked with Anna I went to rehearsals with clammy hands and shaky knees. At night I had nightmares. Still, I wouldn't trade what I learned from her for anything.
        Today in rehearsals for my new work, *Endangered Species*, I told the dancers that the purity of emotional statement that I was looking for on stage had more to do with Anna's influence than anything else. She showed me the way on that. (Phone interview: December 14, 1989)

Ze'eva Cohen

Ze'eva Cohen has danced as a soloist with the companies of Anna Sokolow, The American Dance Theater at Lincoln Center, Dance Theatre Workshop, and as a guest artist with Pearl Lang. She has presented her solo program throughout the United States and Europe and has choreographed for companies here and abroad. She is currently teaching at Princeton University in the modern dance program, which she initiated in 1969.

Anna gave me permission to open myself as an artist to the full power of my passion and fantasy with no fear. She taught me that there was no other way to dance but to invest myself totally, physically and mentally, in the work. She could not tolerate an apologetic approach to dancing — standing tall, strong, being direct, honest, and simple, are qualities she encouraged and demanded. I remember Anna in class, easily pushing down the outstretched arms of strong men, then challenging them to do the same to her. They almost never succeeded. This demonstrated that gesture should always be weighted and physically committed. Anna taught me to take the time to listen to what was truly personal and unique in my way of moving and feeling. (Letter: August 12, 1989)

Eddy Effron

After graduation from Juilliard, Eddy performed for Anna for a few years and then began to follow his interest in lighting for dance. He has designed for many famous companies, including Players' Project, and has written a successful book on the subject of lighting.

I have the proud and unusual distinction of having danced in and lit most of Anna's major works. Probably because I have always enjoyed her trust and confidence, she very rarely gives me lighting instructions. I do lots of homework to make things go fast and because she is impatient, I don't let her in the theater until I have the cues set up on the light board. She is usually very happy with what she sees.

In all my years of working with Anna, each time I am constantly refreshed and amazed at her infallible sense of timing and the relationship of that timing to her belief in the "truth." This applies to movement of the body as well as to light. For helping me to see and understand this, I shall always be indebted to her. (Letter: October 12, 1989)

Annabelle Gamson

As Annabelle Gold, Gamson performed with Anna in the 1950s. In the 1970s, after a period in which she devoted herself to raising a family, she came back to the stage and a brilliant career in which she performs the solos of Isadora Duncan and Mary Wigman.

Anna, the Anna that I worked with when I was a young dancer, was an inspiration to me; an inspiration for her encouragement, her direction of me in her works, and for my good fortune in being a witness to her unswerving energy in her pursuit of her artistic goals. (Letter: June 13, 1989)

Benjamin Harkarvy

Benjamin Harkarvy, founding artistic director of the Netherlands Dance Theatre, has served as artistic director of the Royal Winnipeg, Harkness, Pennsylvania, and Dutch National Ballets. Currently, he is a freelance choreographer/teacher in the United States, Canada, and Europe, and is a faculty member of the Juilliard School of Music.

One of my first acts upon founding the Netherlands Dance Theatre in 1959 was to invite Anna Sokolow to set her work *Rooms* on us. I had a vision of a company trained in modern as well as classical techniques devoted to creating new work with occasional restagings of already created contemporary masterpieces by their choreographers. These would help develop the dancers' art, stimulate the "home" choreographers and stretch the public's view of what dance was. *Rooms*, which I had seen at its New York premiere, would be the perfect vehicle for that vision.

We were very poor. Subsidy was not to come until the third year. But all concerned were highly idealistic, open-eyed and dedicated. Perfect soil for Anna.

We had no permanent studio but were working that fall/winter in an abandoned small church in the Hague, heated unfortunately by only one tiny coal stove at the end of a long high-ceilinged space defined by old scenery pieces lent by the Hague Theatre Company. This rehearsal period was imprinted in my mind forever by the intensity of the cold, the heat of Anna's coaching and the responsive "give her everything" attitude of the dancers. (Letter: August 20, 1989)

Page Johnson

Johnson has worked as both an actor and dancer on and off Broadway. On Broadway he appeared in *You Can't Take It With You, Equus,* and worked with Anna in both *Red Roses For Me* and *Camino Real.*

I think I connected easily with Anna in that I am an actor, but in a dancer's body with a dancer's responses. Anna strips all the fat off you as a performer or even a student — all the posings, the "look Ma I'm dancin" syndrome. I remember most: "NEVER move unless you have to." I didn't understand that at first, but when Anna said "A rest is part of the music, too," it became clear to me. She taught me that the most interesting part of a movement or spoken scene is the time between the movement — a sudden turn — and hold, a spoken word — and pause. In that pause to let the beholder ponder "What can he be thinking — what will he do next?" Not just us demonstrating. Anna said, "It's most glorious, that brief moment before the bird takes flight — the wings all taut and ready to unfold."

Most choreographers I've worked with use you as a tool for their movement. Anna, both in *Camino Real* and *Red Roses for Me*, had the ability to look deep in our hearts — find our secrets and bring them to nurture. Every actor-dancer was unique and had a life of his own — a life Anna helped him discover.

Even though the dancers in *Red Roses for Me* had small parts, she developed in each one of us a full-blown character who could answer any question about the scene, about Dublin, or about what's behind the provocative smile. In *Metamorphosis* she created a private hell for all of us — through Gregor Samsa (the bug), and when rehearsals or performances were over, you felt as if you'd been through God's wringer — or Anna's. (Letter: May 16, 1989)

Elia Kazan

One of the most distinguished Broadway and Hollywood film directors of his time, Kazan was involved with the Group Theater in the 1930s and was one of the founders of the Actors Studio in 1947. His most famous Hollywood films include *A Streetcar Named Desire, On the Waterfront,* and *East of Eden.*

Anna is a very intense person. Her work is personal, not imitative. You can't mistake her work for anyone else's. Anna is a true and devoted artist. A damned fine and honest woman. (Phone interview: summer of 1981)

Teo Macero

A Juilliard graduate, for twenty years Teo Macero was a producer for Columbia Records and the winner of fourteen Gold Record awards. He has also been a conductor, composer, and performer (saxophone). His works have been performed by the New York Philharmonic and other U.S. symphonies and he has written music for fifty ballets. Twenty-two of Anna's works bear his name as composer.

Those of you who have been fortunate enough to work with Anna know that she is not an ordinary lady. She is high-spirited, imaginative, and creative to the point of awesomeness. She possesses great vitality. To be in one of her many productions, one knows that it is not a day on the beach. She accepts nothing less than perfection and gets it. She is lovable, charming, and TOUGH!

We all love you, Anna.

Donald McKayle

Donald McKayle has danced with many of the leading modern dance choreographers. He is the director and choreographer for his own modern dance company and for Broadway musicals and television. He has received Tony nominations for best choreography for

Golden Boy, Raisin, Dr. Jazz and *Sophisticated Ladies*. Choreographer of the modern dance classics *Games* and *Rainbow 'Round My Shoulder*.

[Remembering working on the solo "Panic" for the premiere of *Rooms*] I was a man in terror. The movement was extremely violent. There was one section where I had to bang my head repeatedly, just a hair short of striking the floor surface, and then roll my body upward, balancing on the crown of my head. Anna would work on this particular passage for three quarters of an hour without letup. It was draining, exhausting, and terribly exciting. The rehearsal process was so filled with Anna's intention and so completely focused that the performances flowed from it without that transition into limbo that so often precedes a premiere.

I will always feel close to Anna. When you work with an artist of her calibre there is something that remains with you forever.

Alex North

After his work as a composer for Anna Sokolow, Hanya Holm, and Martha Graham, Alex North went on to a distinguished career as a composer for Hollywood films. His work includes the scores for *Cleopatra*, *A Streetcar Named Desire*, and *Spartacus*. He received a Lifetime Accomplishment Academy Award in 1986 and the first annual Golden Sound Track award (from ASCAP) for lifetime achievement in film composition.

She was very instrumental in my putting notes down on paper. I really have to give her a lot of credit for where I am today. I had the opportunity — the privilege — of working with her, and it was invaluable to me later when I was writing film scores. The dancer does the dance first. The film is shot first. You have to tailor the music to the dance as music is tailored to a film. This skill I first learned working with Anna. Through her I met people connected with the theater; this eventually led to my work in films. (Interview: January 7, 1982, Pacific Palisades, California)

Kathryn Posin

Kathryn Posin has danced with the companies of Anna Sokolow, Valerie Bettis, and Lotte Goslar and with Dance Theater Workshop and the American Dance Theatre at Lincoln Center. Her works have appeared in the repertory of several companies, including the Ohio Ballet, the Alvin Ailey American Dance Theatre, and the Netherlands Dance Theatre. She has her own company, which bears her name.

I was with Anna when she created *Deserts*, a piece to Varèse's composition of that title. The music sounded like outer space objects screeching to earth and millions of people applauding in the distance. We laid on our backs and waited for instructions:

You hear an unknown sound!!
You look up!!
How fast can you turn!!
How quick can you stop!!
How far can you twist!!

We were splitting our guts responding to the hurled directions that Anna cried to us. We whirled like desert winds in our Army blanket ponchos, we mated like animals, we beseeched the heavens and flung ourselves relentlessly around the Clark Center studios. I had nightmares about the unknown spirits that wafted across the desert. I woke up in character — with the same lurches and starts the dance contained, angry with Anna for taking over even my dreams. Was there no evading that piercing, falcon-like stare? At one rehearsal the twelve of us lay on our stomachs in our existential desert, trying not to catch each other's eye. "Jump!" she cried. We told the story for years.

Today it's all right to be an expressionist if you are from Germany and it's all right to be a romantic in the ballet, but we still seem to have a hard time acknowledging the validity and timeliness of Anna's kind of choreography. But now is the time we need it most. Technology is not the problem — humanity is. Anna has always been the lone individual dealing honestly with their pain, their joy and their very aloneness. In our faceless anesthetized times her truths are all the more needed — unfashionable and frumpy as they may appear. They are timeless and necessary. (Letter: May 10, 1989)

Barry Primus

The actor Barry Primus was featured in the films *The River, Absence of Malice, Heartland,* and *The Rose.* He has appeared on television in *Cagney and Lacey* and *Murder She Wrote.* Mr. Primus currently teaches at UCLA and the Lee Strasberg Acting Institute.

I started working with Anna around 1960. My first classes with her were at the Herbert Berghof Studio. A few years later I studied with her at Lincoln Center and after that at Jerome Robbins Theatre Lab. Anna was very much against the slickness which was prevalent in theater in the late fifties and early sixties. She loved working with actors and believed that anyone could move beautifully as long as they were genuinely expressing something that was going on inside of them. It had nothing to do with being a dancer.

The real sin for Anna was dullness. When anyone would really go for something with energy she would get excited and she was not above doing something to get what she wanted. My earliest memory of her was when she walked over to an actor who towered above her — he was about 6'3", and slugged him in the stomach. "Stand up! Do you always want to play street people? Don't you ever want to play a king?" Then, when he responded, she stopped the class and said, "Look at him. Doesn't he look beautiful?"

Anna could bring you into the sense of immediacy you needed if you couldn't find it yourself. When I was playing Gregor in her *Metamorphosis* in 1961, I was having trouble with the opening scene. I had just awakened to find that I am a cockroach. She came over to me and hit me in the head with her shoe. I got the feeling of shock she wanted and didn't forget it. (Tape: Los Angeles, August 1989)

Naomi Sorkin

Naomi Sorkin has appeared with American Ballet Theatre and the Eliot Feld Ballet and as a guest artist with other dance companies, both ballet and modern. She currently resides in London, where she recently performed the role of Zobeide in *Scheherazade* for a Nijinsky gala at the London Palladium.

Working with Anna Sokolow was a source of great inspiration. The knowledge that you are in the hands of a great master . . . her vision always so clear, the gestures so simple, honest, and direct. She demands the deepest self-scrutiny and the challenge of eliminating any extraneous thoughts or feelings.

I feel her genius is the ability to touch universal emotions, understanding the dark side of our natures better than most and yet she surprises one with her humor, tenderness and joy. (Letter: July 7, 1989)

Ernestine Stodelle

Former member of the Humphrey-Weidman Company, writer, dance critic, and teacher Ernestine Stodelle has seen the work of Anna Sokolow since they both presented solos on the same program in 1935. Stodelle has authored *The Dance Technique of Doris Humphrey and Its Creative Potential* (Second Edition, Princeton Book Company) and *Deep Song, The Dance Story of Martha Graham* (Schmirmer Books).

In gratitude for her role in cultivating modern dance awareness in Israel, over three hundred and seventy-five trees have been planted in the name of Anna Sokolow on the slopes of Jerusalem. And in those countries where Anna has personally directed her works or taught technique and composition, new growth — as sturdy and fruitful as trees — has made significant changes in the dance consciousness of whole nations.

What is it that this small, intensely charged yet soft-spoken woman brings to the dancers who perform her choreography and to the audiences that attend her programs? A powerful personal vision? That is only part of it. If sparks fly when Anna Sokolow's dances are on stage, there are undeniable reasons why no one leaves the theater untouched. In her hands, life itself is invaded. There are head-on clashes between fundamental issues rising from the depths of human feeling. Even humor emerges, sometimes ironically, sometimes fantastically.

We all honor Anna Sokolow. She is the spokesman for the realities of our times . . . the Solzhenitsyn of twentieth-century dance.

Kei Takei

Kei Takei received her first dance training in her native city, Tokyo. A Fulbright Scholarship brought her to the U.S. in 1968. After making her choreographic debut, she received choreographic grants from the National Endowment and in 1978 was named Guggenheim Fellow in Choreography. Miss Takei's efforts have been directed toward a continuing opus, *Light*, presently twenty-one sections. Her work has been commissioned by several major dance companies around the world.

When I first met her when I was a student in Japan, I felt that she was a beautiful and strong person. She loves creation and when she sees something good or bad, she shoots out. My own "I" was better recognized when I first met her. I was not a very happy child. Something was missing in the world for me. I had to have creativity to live in this world. Anna, too, and I think we recognized each other. I liked her strong screaming although it scared me at first. Later, when I was in New York (you know she helped me to get there) I passed her in Greenwich Village. She had been watching me at Juilliard and she said, "Keep up the good work." Anna was very important to me. I learned so much from her.

Linda Tarnay

Linda Tarnay has performed with Anna Sokolow, James Cunningham, Jack Moore, and others, and has directed her own company, Linda Tarnay and Dancers. She has taught at Bennington College, Princeton University, Connecticut College, and at the American Dance Festival. She is currently on the faculty at New York University Tisch School of the Arts.

Anna taught me, both by her example and exhortation, that a dramatic idea or feeling calls up its own specific movement. The imagination must be allowed to enter the flesh and move the body. Since working with her, I have had to dig deeper for a new movement vocabulary for each piece. When, out of fatigue or desperation, I resort to a generalized vocabulary, I am painfully, guiltily aware of it. (Letter: March 7, 1989)

Joel Thome

Joel Thome, composer and conductor, is an accomplished interpreter of classical as well as contemporary music. His career as a composer has been filled with numerous interarts collaborations and works for theater performances. He has composed five scores for dance theater commissioned by Anna Sokolow, including tributes to Janos Korczak and Golda Meir. They are currently planning a new work together.

Anna's path is her search for truth. Her courage, devotion, and commitment illuminate The Way. She is the total embodiment of the meaning of the word artist. She has been one of the most inspiring people [in my life] and one of the closest of friends.

Silvia Unzueta

Silvia Unzueta was trained in the Academy of Mexican Dance, where she performed with the Ballet Contemporaneo. Then, for several years, she both danced and choreographed for Ballet Independiente. In 1987, she founded the contemporary dance company Purpura.

The first time I worked with Anna was when she was choreographing some works for the advanced students of the Mexican Dance Academy. I also worked with her when she was choreographing for Ballet Independiente, but it wasn't until she created *The Diary of Kafka* [for that company] that I understood the way she worked. I was very influenced by her style and the importance she placed on the interior rather than the exterior form.

Anna wants to portray in the choreography what she feels at that moment. Many choreographers look at themselves in a mirror to see how a movement looks; Anna doesn't work this way. She gives you images and your body responds naturally with movement.

She does not give too much explanation but she makes you look and find the movement from within you. This was one of the most important things I learned from her. Her works are very theatrical. You have to concentrate; you have to act — this is a different way to dance. (Excerpted from *Anna Sokolow, Cuadernos, Cenida-Danza, José Limón* by Anadel Lynton, Mexico City, October 1988. Translated by Anna Soler)

Eli Wallach

Eli Wallach has had a long and distinguished career both on Broadway and in Hollywood films. Some of his most important work has included leading roles in *Camino Real, Rose*

Tattoo, and *Luv* on Broadway and, in films, *The Misfits*, *Baby Doll*, and *How the West Was Won*. He has won an Emmy, a Tony, and a British Academy Award.

Anna is a creative dynamo . . . an innovative worker, especially with actors who are not trained dancers. I worked with her on *Rooms* in the Actors Studio and in Kazan's production of Tennessee Williams' *Camino Real*. *Rooms* had a roaming-camera's-eye look at life in a tenement — it was choreographed superbly . . . each window of the house being a window of life . . . giving us an exciting peek into each apartment. . . .

In *Camino* Anna recreated the slow, steamy life of a south of the border country. As Kilroy I was called on to dance in a contest, the prize being a free-go with Esmeralda, the little prostitute. Anna incorporated wonderful character elements into the dance. I played an ex-boxer . . . but with a heart condition . . . she taught me shuffling steps and incorporated a great leap into the dance from a high flight of stairs, heart-condition or no. One had to be in shape to carry out Anna's brilliant choreographic plan.

I also sat and watched her teach classes at Juilliard. In Israel, on Broadway, in the theatre or at the studio, Anna was, and still is, the consummate choreographer — a dedicated and serious dance-teacher. (Letter: January 14, 1988)

HONORS, AWARDS, AND GRANTS

Partial List

Bennington College Choreographic Fellowship. With Esther Junger and José Limón, Summer, 1937.

American Dancer [Dance Magazine], Dance Award for the Best Solo in Modern Dance, 1938.

Dance Magazine Award, 1961. Honored with Gwen Verdon and Melissa Hayden.

Senior Fulbright to Japan, 1966.

Brandeis University, Creative Arts Medal. Whitney Museum, New York, April 28, 1974.

America-Israel Cultural Foundation, Tarbut Medal. Juilliard Theater, Lincoln Center, New York, June 5, 1974. Honored with Lee Strasberg, Nadia Reisenberg, Jennie Tourel (posthumously).

Senior Fulbright to England, 1975.

92nd Street YM-YWHA, "To Anna Sokolow — Choreographer, Dancer, For her great and prolonged record of service to the world of Dance," December 2, 1975.

Ohio State University, Honorary Doctor of Humanities (Honoris Causa), December 8, 1978.

Maryland Dance Theater Performance, "A Tribute to Anna Sokolow." Terrace Theater, Kennedy Center, Washington, D.C., January 27, 1982.

Ballet Independiente Performance, "Homenaje a Anna Sokolow." Teatro de la Ciudad, Mexico City, October 6, 1982.

30th Anniversary Celebration of Anna Sokolow's Work in Israel. Inbal House, Tel Aviv, July 21, 1983.

"A Gala Benefit Performance Honoring Anna Sokolow," Joyce Theater, New York, September 20, 1986.

Boston Conservatory, Honorary Doctor of Fine Arts (Honoris Causa), May 7, 1988.

Encomienda, Aztec Eagle Honor (the highest civilian honor awarded in Mexico to a foreigner). Mexico City, October 25, 1988.

80th Birthday Tribute at the Rubin Academy of Music, Jerusalem, Israel, August 1990.

80th Birthday Tribute at the 92nd Street Y.M.H.A., New York, January 17, 1991. With introductory remarks by Agnes de Mille.

Samuel H. Scripps American Dance Festival Award, July 14, 1991.

American Academy of Arts and Letters Award, New York City, 1993.

Tiffany Award, New York City, 1993.

85th Birthday Gala, February 15, 1995, at The Sylvia and Danny Kaye Playhouse. The President of the Borough of Manhattan, Ruth W. Messinger, proclaimed that date to be "Anna Sokolow Day" in Manhattan.

Guest of Honor at Northeast American College Dance Festival, County College of Morris, Randolph, New Jersey. April 10–14, 1995.

First to be inaugurated into The Dance Library of Israel Hall of Fame along with Pauline Koner and Sophie Maslow on April 22, 1996 in New York City.

On September 18, 1996, Mexico's National Institute of Bellas Artes honored Anna for her contributions to the growth of modern dance in Mexico by the permanent installation of a bronze plaque, with her likeness, in the Teatro De La Danza in Mexico City.

PROFESSIONAL ASSOCIATIONS

Professional Companies Having Performed Anna's Work

Partial List

Companies based in New York, except as noted.

Alvin Ailey American Dance Theater

Mary Anthony Dance Theatre

American Dance Theater

American Youth Theater

Anna Sokolow and Group

Anna Sokolow Dance Company

Ballet Bellas Artes (Mexico)

Ballet Concerto (Miami)

Ballet Contemporaneo de Camara (Venezuela)

Ballet Hispanico

Ballet Independiente (Mexico)

Ballet Internacional de Caracas (Venezuela)

Ballet Rambert (England)

Ballet San Marcos (Peru)

Ballet Theatre

Bamat Machol (Israel)

Batsheva (Israel)

Berlin Opera Ballet

Berlin Opera Company

Beyondance Company (New Jersey)

Boston Ballet

Chen and Dancers

Chicago Dance Center

Chicago Moving Company

Compania de Danza (Mexico)

Concert Dance Company of Boston

Contemporary Dance System

Contemporary Ballet Theatre (Williamsburg, Virginia)

Dance Company of New South Wales

Dance Detroit

Dance Kaleidoscope (Indianapolis)

Dance Unit of New Dance League

Dans Kern (Netherlands)

Daniel Lewis Dance Company

Linda Diamond and Company

Dublin City Ballet

Eleo Pomare Dance Company

First Chamber Dance Company

Gloria Newman Dance Company (California)

Grupo Mexicano de Danzas Clasicas y Modernas

Houston Ballet

Inbal (Israel)

Israel Opera

Diane Jacobwitz Dance Theater

Jerusalem Dance Workshop
Juilliard Dance Ensemble
Kibbutz Dance Company (Israel)
Kol Demama (Israel)
La Paloma Azul (Mexico)
José Limón Dance Company
London Contemporary Dance
  Theatre
Lyric Theatre (Israel)
Lyric Theatre
Manhattan Festival Ballet
Maryland Dance Theater
Momentum Dance Company
  (Miami)
National Ballet (Washington,
  D.C.)
Netherlands Dance Theatre
New Dance Group [company]
New York City Opera Ballet
  (1956 season)
Oakland Ballet
Pennsylvania Ballet
Perspectives in Motion
Players Project (early 1970s)

Players' Project (early 1980s to
  present)
Polish Dance Theater
Quinlan-Krichels Ensemble
Repertory Dance Theatre
  (Utah)
Robert Joffrey Ballet Company
Rod Rodgers Dance Company
Rondo Dance Theater
  (Westchester County, New
  York)
Roumanian State Opera Ballet
Royal Winnepeg Ballet
San Francisco Moving Company
Sanasardo Dance Company
Sophie Maslow Dance Company
South Street Dance Company
  (Philadelphia)
Springboard Dance Camp (Israel)
Stage for Dancers
Syracuse Ballet Theatre
Anna Sokolow's Theatre Dance
  Company
Theater Dance Trio

Professional Schools Where Anna Sokolow Has Taught

Partial List

In New York, except as noted.

Actors Studio
Actor's Movement Studio (Lloyd
  Williamson)
Alvin Ailey American Dance
  Center
American Cultural Centers,
  Japan (Fukuoka, Nara,
  Osaka, Tokyo)
American National Theater and
  Academy

American Theater Lab
American Theatre Wing
Ballet Concerto, Miami
Cameri Theatre, Tel Aviv
Clark Center, West Side Branch
  YWCA
Contemporary Dance Studio, Boston
  New Dance Group
Dance Theater Workshop
Group Theatre School

Habima Theatre, Tel Aviv
Haifa Theatre, Haifa
Hebrew Arts School
Herbert Berghof (HB) Studio
The Juilliard School (Dance
  Division and Theatre
  Division)
Lia Schubert's School, Stockholm
Lincoln Center Repertory
  Theatre
Mary Anthony Studio
Negro Dance Company (Wilson
  Williams)
Neighborhood Playhouse

New Dance Group
Nissan Nativ Theatre School,
  Tel Aviv
Ohel Theatre, Tel Aviv
Rubin Academy of Music (Dance
  Department), Jerusalem
School of American Ballet
Summer Academy of Dance at
  Cologne
Swiss Association for Dancers
  and Gymnasts, Zurich
Walker Art Center,
  Minneapolis
YM/YWHA (92nd Street "Y")

Anna Sokolow College and University Residencies

Partial List

Bennington College (Vermont)
Boston Conservatory of Music
Brooklyn College
City College of New York
Danza Experimental de la
  Universidad del Zulia
  (Venezuela)
Indiana University
The Juilliard School (New
  York)
La Compania de Danza
  Contemporaria de la
  Universidad Veracruzana
  (Mexico)
Long Beach State University
  (California)
Marygrove College (Michigan)
Ohio State University
Radcliffe College (Massachusetts)
Rutgers University (New Jersey)

Smith College (Massachusetts)
State University of New York at
  Purchase
Sarah Lawrence College
  (Bronxville, New York)
Universidad del Julia (Mexico)
University of California at Los
  Angeles
University of Georgia
University of Illinois
University of Hawaii
University of Maryland at
  College Park
University of Utah
University of Wisconsin
  (Madison)
Wolfson Campus of Miami-Dade
  Community College
York University (Toronto,
  Ontario)

CHRONOLOGY OF PREMIERES OF SOKOLOW CHOREOGRAPHY

Partial List

For dance works, choreographic credit for Anna Sokolow is assumed. Juilliard student Marc Stevens did a research project called "The Choreographic Works of Anna Sokolow" in 1972 that served as a useful foundation upon which to build this chronology.

1931–1939

- May 20, 1931
  Neighborhood Playhouse, New York
  Student Program

  City Rhythms, Part 2 [Part 1, *The Immigrant and the City Street*, was composed and directed by Georgia Graham, Martha's sister]

  Music: Frederick Daly
  Composed and Directed by Anna Sokolow
  Costumes: No credit listed
  Cast: Student Group

- August 29, 1933
  St. Nicholas Arena, New York
  American League Against War and Fascism
  Anti-War Congress
  Theatre Union Dance Group

  Anti-War Trilogy [later retitled *Anti-War Cycle*]
    I. "Depression, Starvation"
   II. "Diplomacy — War"
  III. "Protest" [later retitled "Defiance"]

  Music: Alexis Soifer (Alex North)
  Costumes: No credit listed

Dancers: Anita Alvarez, Ethel Butler, Ronya Chernin, Celia Dembroe, Ruth Freedman, Eleanor Lapides, Marie Marchowsky, Florence Schneider, Ethel Solitar

- October 28, 1933
  Grand Street Playhouse, New York
  Solo Concert by Anna Sokolow

Derision

Music: Serge Prokofiev
Costume: Anna Sokolow and Rose Bank

Folk Motifs
  I. Song
  II. Dance
  III. Legend

Music: Béla Bartók, Nicholas Miaskovsky
Costumes: No credit listed

Histrionics

Music: Paul Hindemith
Costume: Anna Sokolow and Rose Bank

Homage to Lenin

Music: Nicholas Miaskovsky
Costume: Anna Sokolow and Rose Bank

Jazz Waltz

Music: Louis Gruenberg
Costume: Anna Sokolow and Rose Bank

Pre-Classic Suite

Music: Alexis Soifer (Alex North)
Costume: Anna Sokolow and Rose Bank

Prelude and Chorale

Music: César Franck
Costume: Anna Sokolow and Rose Bank

Romantic Dances
  I. "Illusion"
  II. "Desire"

Music: Alexander Scriabin
Costumes: Anna Sokolow and Rose Bank

Salutation to the Morning

Music: Alexis Soifer (Alex North)
Costume: Anna Sokolow and Rose Bank

• January 7, 1934 [earliest known performance]
City College, New York
Theatre Union Dance Group

Two Pioneer Marches

Music: Serge Prokofiev
Costumes: No credit listed
Dancers: Anita Alvarez, Ethel Butler, Ronya Chernin, Celia Dembroe, Ruth Freedman, Eleanor Lapidus, Marie Marchowsky, Florence Schneider, Ethel Solitar

• November 25, 1934
Civic Repertory Theatre, New York
Workers' Dance League Concert

Death of a Tradition

Music: Lopatnikoff
Costumes: No credit listed
Dancers: Sophie Maslow, Lily Mehlman, Anna Sokolow

Challenge

Music: Lopatnikoff
Costumes: No credit listed
Choreography: Anna Sokolow, Sophie Maslow, Lily Mehlman
Dancers: Anna Sokolow, Sophie Maslow, Lily Mehlman

• December 23, 1934
Town Hall, New York
Workers' Dance League Group Recital
Theatre Union Dance Group

Forces in Opposition

Music: Swift
Poem: Sergei Essenin
Costumes: Rose Bank

Dancers: Anita Alvarez, Aza Cefkin, Ronya Chernin, Celia Dembroe, Ruth Freedman, Eleanor Lapidus, Marie Marchowsky, Florence Schneider, Ethel Solitar

- February 13, 1935
  Longacre Theatre, New York

  Noah [stage play]

  Writer: André Obey
  Director: Jacques Copeau
  Music: Louis Horst
  Sets: Cleon Throckmorton
  Masks and Animal Costumes: Remo Bufano Visual Effects Under the Supervision of Ludwig Bemelmans Dances Directed by Louis Horst and Anna Sokolow
  Cast:
  Noah   Pierre Fresnay
  Dancers: Charles Holden, Richard Spater, Milton Feher, Joseph Willis, Igene Stuart, Richard Fleming, Jane Churchill, Georgia Graham

- June 9, 1935
  Park Circle Theatre, New York
  New Dance League June Dance Festival
  Anna Sokolow and the Dance Unit of the New Dance League

  Strange American Funeral

  Music: Elie Siegmeister
  Poem: Michael Gold ("A Strange Funeral in Braddock")
  Costumes: No credit listed
  Dancers: Aza Cefkin, Ronya Chernin, Rose Cohen, Celia Dembroe, Ruth Freedman, Eleanor Lapidus, Rose Levy, Marie Marchowsky, Ruth Nissenson, Florence Schneider

- December 22, 1935
  Adelphi Theatre, New York
  New Dance League Recital of Soloists

  American Dance Hall [may be *Jazz Waltz*, 1933, retitled; later retitled *Impressions of a Dance Hall*]

  Music: Louis Gruenberg
  Costume: Anna Sokolow and Rose Bank
  Dancer: Anna Sokolow

  Speaker [first known performance]

Music: Alex North
Costume: Anna Sokolow and Rose Bank
Dancer: Anna Sokolow

- 1936

  Valley Forge [stage play]
  Other information unknown

- April 5, 1936
  Theresa L. Kaufmann Auditorium, YMHA, New York
  Anna Sokolow and Dance Unit

  Opening Dance

  Music: Vissarion Shebalin
  Costume: Rose Bank
  Dancer: Anna Sokolow

  Ballad (in a Popular Style) [first known performance; later entitled without parentheses *Ballad in a Popular Style*]

  Music: Alex North
  Costume: Rose Bank
  Dancer: Anna Sokolow

  Four Little Salon Pieces

  Music: Dimitri Shostakovitch
  Costume: Rose Bank
  Dancer: Anna Sokolow

  Inquisition '36
     I. "Provocateur"
    II. "Vigilante"

  Music: Alex North
  Costume: Rose Bank
  Dancer: Anna Sokolow

  Suite of Soviet Songs [later retitled *Four Soviet Songs*]
     I. "Sailors' Holiday"
    II. "Defend Our Land"
   III. "Lullaby" [A song about the Soviet stratospheric flight]
    IV. "Sailors' Chorus"

  Music: Lan Adomain

Costumes: Rose Bank

Dancers: Ronya Chernin, Aza Cefkin, Celia Dembroe, Ruth Freedman, Eleanor Lapidus, Rose Levy, Marie Marchowsky, Ruth Nissenson, Florence Schneider, Louise Stodolsky

- January 11, 1937 [first known performance]
  Detroit Art Institute, Detroit
  Soloists from the New Dance League

War-Monger

Music: Alex North
Dancer: Anna Sokolow

- February 28, 1937
  Theresa L. Kaufmann Auditorium, YMHA, New York
  Anna Sokolow and Dance Unit

Case History No. — [later retitled *Crime Pays — Until*, see *The Street*, 1939; also later performed in *En las Calles de la Ciudad*, 1945]

Music: Wallingford Riegger
Costume: No credit listed
Dancer: Anna Sokolow

Excerpts from a War Poem

  I. "War is Beautiful"
 II. "War is Beautiful because it fuses Strength, Harmony, and Kindness"
III. "War is Beautiful because it realizes the long dreamed of metalization of the human body"
 IV. "War is Beautiful because it symphonizes pauses choked by silence, the perfume and odors of putrification, and creates the spiral smoke of burning villages."
  V. "War is Beautiful because it serves the greatness of our great Fascist Italy."

Music: Alex North
Poem: F. T. Marinetti
Costumes: Anton Refregier
Dancers: Anna Sokolow with Alex Berg, Aza Cefkin, Ronya Chernin, Milton Feher, Ruth Freedman, Rose Levy, Grusha Mark, Mary Monroe, Ruth Nissenson, Florence Schneider

- August 12, 1937
  Palmer Auditorium, Bennington College, Bennington, Vermont Bennington Dance Festival
  Anna Sokolow and Bennington Dance Festival Students

Facade — Esposizione Italiana

   I. "Spectacle"
  II. "Belle Arti"
 III. "Giovanezza"
 IV. "Phantasmagoria"

Music: Alex North
Costumes: No credit listed
Dancers: Anna Sokolow with students of the Bennington Dance Festival

- November 14, 1937
  Guild Theatre, New York
  Anna Sokolow and Dance Unit

Opening Dance [revised for soloist and group]

Music: Alex North
Costumes: No credit listed
Dancers: Anna Sokolow with Aza Cefkin, Ronya Chernin, Frances Hellman, Ruth Freedman, Rose Levy, Grusha Mark, Mary Monroe, Ruth Nissenson, Florence Schneider, June Sokolow, Sasha Spector, Alex Berg, Lew Rosen, Allen Wayne, Michael Gray

Slaughter of the Innocents [later retitled *Madrid, 1937*, revised 1943]

Music: Alex North
Costume: Anna Sokolow and Rose Bank
Dancer: Anna Sokolow

- January 19, 1938
  Madison Square Garden, New York [first site]

Dance of All Nations [pageant for the fourteenth anniversary of the death of Lenin]

Music: Unknown
Costumes: Unknown
Dancers: Group

- May 1938
  New York
  Negro Cultural Committee

The Bourbons Got the Blues [musical revue]

Writers: Carlton Moss and Dorothy Hailparn

Music: Excerpts from speeches by Senators Ellender and Bilbo (filibustering against the Anti-Lynching Bill)
Costumes: No credit listed
Cast: Included Duke Ellington, Rex Ingram, and Frank Wilson

- February 26, 1939
  Alvin Theatre, New York
  Anna Sokolow and Dance Unit

The Exile

    I. "I had a garden . . ."
    II. "The beast is in the garden . . ."

Music: Traditional Palestinian folk music, arranged by Alex North. Excerpts from Sol Funaroff's poem *The Exiles*, written for this dance, were spoken aloud sometimes by a singer, sometimes by Anna
Costume: Rose Bank.
Dancer: Anna Sokolow

The Street

    I. "The Street"
    II. "Crime Pays — Until" [*Case History No. —* , 1937 retitled]

Music: Alex North, Wallingford Riegger
Costumes: Rose Bank
Dancers: Anna Sokolow with Aza Cefkin, Ruth Freedman, Rose Levy, Grusha Mark, Kathleen O'Brien, Rebecca Rowen, Florence Schneider, Sasha Spector, Martin Michel, Daniel Nagrin, Lou Rosen, Maurice Silvers, Allan Wayne

- April 24, 1939
  Adelphi Theatre, New York
  Federal Theater (A Division of the Works Progress Administration)

Sing for Your Supper [musical revue; includes *The Last Waltz*, choreography by Anna Sokolow and music by Alex North]

Revue Compiled and Directed by Harold Hecht
Music: Lee Wainer and Ned Lehac
Ensembles: Anna Sokolow
Costumes: Mary Merrill
Dancers: Modern Dance Ensemble: Joseph Belsky, Naomi Bodine, Mann Brown, Marjorie Church, John Connolly, William Elliott, Lily Verne, William Garrett, Julia Lane, Israel Lansky, Ray Lieb, Eve Lord, Virginia Mansfield, Anne Marcus, Martin Michel, Lou Rosen, Attilio Salzano, Georgette Schneer, Maurice Silvers, Sidney Stark

1940–1949

- February 18, 1940
  Theresa L. Kaufmann Auditorium, YMHA, New York
  Anna Sokolow and Alex North in a Joint Recital of Dance and Music

  Songs for Children

  I."The little horse"
  II."At one o'clock the moon comes out"
  III."Song of the foolish child" (Mama, I want to be of silver)
  IV."The alligator's lament" (The alligator is crying because he lost his wedding ring)
  V."Cradle song" (Go to sleep, my carnation)
  VI."Serenade"
  VII."The Truth" (Ay; it is very hard to love you in the way I love you)

  Music: Silvestre Revueltas
  Lyrics: Excerpts from the poetry of Federico García Lorca
  Costumes: No credit listed
  Dancer: Anna Sokolow

- March 23, 1940
  Palace of Fine Arts, Mexico City
  Grupo de Danzas Clasicas y Modernas

  Don Lindo de Almería [Don Lindo of Almería]

  Music: Rodolfo Halffter
  Libretto: JoséBergamin
  Costumes: Antonio Ruiz
  Dancers: Alicia Reyna, Alba Estela Garfias, Alicia Ceballos Vences, Marta Bracho, Raquel Gutiérrez Lejarza, Ana Maria Mérida, Luis Rostan, Mario Fernandez, Floriza Ruiz Velazquez, Josefina Luna Montalvo, Delia Ruiz Velazquez, Carmen Gutiérrez Lejarza, Alejandro Martinez, Juan Ruiz, Mario Camberos, Ramon Rivero
  Note: Described in program as a *Mojiganga* (a masquerade or mummery)

  Entre Sombras Anda el Fuego [The Fire Walks Between Shadows]

  Music: Blas Galindo
  Costumes: Antonio Ruiz
  Dancers: Marta Bracho, Alicia Ceballos, Alba Estela Garfias, Raquel Gutiérrez Lejarza, Carmen Gutiérrez Lejarza, Josefina Luna Montalvo, Ana Maria Mérida, Alicia Reyna, Emma Ruiz, Delia Ruiz, Luis Rostand, Juan Ruiz

Los Pies de Pluma [*The Feathered Feet*, Suite Classica]

   I. "Sarabande"
  II. "Gagliarda"
 III. "Allemande"
 IV. "Gigue et Rondeau"

Music: François Couperin, Girolamo Frescobaldi, Johann Mattheson, Jean-Philippe Rameau
Costumes: Ignacio Aguirre
Dancers: Marta Bracho, Alicia Ceballos, Alba Estela Garfias, Raquel Gutiérrez Lejarza, Josefina Luna Montalvo, Ana Maria Mérida, Alicia Reyna, Emma Ruiz, Delia Ruiz

• April 5, 1940 [earliest known performance]
The Theatre, Bennington College, Bennington, Vermont Anna Sokolow and Group

Three Jazz Preludes

Music: Norman Lloyd
Costumes: No credit listed
Dancers: Aza Cefkin, Ruth Freedman, Judith Martin, Rose Levy, Rebecca Rowen, Katherine Russell, Florence Schneider, Hilda Sheldon, Sasha Spector

• September 20, 1940
Palace of Fine Arts, Mexico City
La Paloma Azul

Balcon de España o Enterrar y Callar y Lluvia de Toros [*Spanish Balcony* or *To Bury and To Keep Silence and Rain of Bulls*] Excerpts later retitled *Lluvia de Toros, Caprichosas* [*Whimsies*], *Goyescas,* and *Vision Fantastica* [*Fantastic Vision*]

Libretto: José Bergamin, based on Goya's etchings
Music: Antonio Soler, arranged by Rodolfo Halffter
Costumes: No credit listed
Dancers: Raquel Gutiérrez, Carmen Gutiérrez, Ana Maria Mérida, Isabel Gutiérrez, Alicia Ceballos, Delia Ruiz, Josephina Luna, Alicia Reyna, Rosa Reyna, Alba Estela Garfias, Marta Bracho, Emma Ruiz, Aurora Aristi, Delia Gonzalez, Antonio Cordova, Alejandro Martinez, Mario Camberos, Ramon Riviero, Augusto Fernandez, Gustavo Salas

La Madrugada del Panadero [*The Dawn of the Baker*]

Libretto: José Bergamin
Music: Rodolfo Halffter
Sets and Costumes: Manuel Rodriguez Lozano

Dancers: Rosa Reyna, Marta Bracho, Raquel Gutiérrez, Alicia Reyna, Josefina Luna, Delia Ruiz, Carmen Gutiérrez, Ana Maria Mérida, Alejandro Martinez

Sinfonia de Antigona [*Antigone Symphony*]

Music: Carlos Chavez
Costumes and Decoration: Carlos Obregón Santacilia
Dancers:
Antigone   Anna Sokolow
The Two Brothers of Antigone   Josefina Luna and Delia Ruiz
The Chorus: Marta Bracho, Aurora Aristi, Delia Gonzalez, Antonio Cordova, Alejandro Martinez, Mario Camberos, Ramon Rivero, Augusto Fernandez, Gustavo Salas, Raquel Gutiérrez, Carmen Gutiérrez, Ana Maria Mérida, Isabel Gutiérrez, Alicia Ceballos, Josefina Luna, Alicia Reyna, Rosa Reyna, Alba Estela Garfias

- October 8, 1940
  Palace of Fine Arts, Mexico City
  La Paloma Azul

El Renacuajo Paseador [*The Wandering Tadpole*]

Libretto: Based on a popular children's story

Music: Silvestre Revueltas
Sets and Costumes: Carlos Mérida
Dancers: Alba Estella Garfias, Isabel Gutiérrez Lejarza, Alicia Reyna, Ana Maria Mérida, Raquel Gutiérrez Lejarza, Marta Bracho, Rosa Reyna, Carmen Gutiérrez Lejarza, Alicia Ceballos, Josefina Luna, Delia Ruiz

- March 3, 1941
  Mansfield Theatre, New York
  Anna Sokolow and Dance Group

Homage to García Lorca [includes the solo *Lament for the Death of a Bullfighter*]

Music: Silvestre Revueltas
Costumes: No credit listed
Dancer: Anna Sokolow

- December 13, 1941
  Theresa L. Kaufmann Auditorium, YMHA, New York
  Anna Sokolow and Group

Caprichiosas [kaleidoscope impressions from a series of etchings; "Caprices" by Goya]

    I. "El Torito" (The little bull fighter)
   II. "Gallina Ceiga" (Blind man's buff)
  III. "Reina del Circa" (Queen of the circus)
  IV. "El Manteo del Pelele" (Hazing of the effigy)
   V. "Coqueteria" (The flirtation)
  VI. "Carnival"

Music: Padre Antonio Soler
Costumes: No credit listed
Dancers: Anna Sokolow with Nina Caiserman, Aza Cefkin, Lillian Chasnoff, Sylvia Gellman, Phyllis Kahn, Natalie Krigstein, Clara Nezin, Rhoda Rich, Rose Levy

Mill Doors

Music: Max Helfman
Poem: Carl Sandburg
Costumes: Rose Bank
Dancers: Aza Cefkin, Clara Nezin, Rose Levy

Mama Beautiful [later performed in *En los Calles de la Ciudad*, 1945]

Music: Alex North
Poem: Michael Quinn
Costume: Rose Bank
Dancer: Anna Sokolow

Prelude

Music: Dimitri Shostakovitch
Costumes: No credit listed
Dancers: Anna Sokolow with Nina Caiserman, Aza Cefkin, Lillian Chasnoff, Sylvia Gellman, Phyllis Kahn, Natalie Krigstein, Clara Nezin, Rhoda Rich, Rose Levy

- November 19, 1942
  Harkaway Theatre, Bennett Junior College, Millbrook, New York

  Three Dances to Russian Songs
      I. "Cossack Song"
    II. "Lullaby"
   III. "Ukrainian Song"

  Music: Djerjinsky, Alexander Gretchaninoff, Dunayevsky
  Costumes: No credit listed
  Dancers: Group

- May 15, 1943
  Monument National Theatre, Montreal, Canada
  Montreal Jewish Choir Program

  Revelations [a suite of dances]
     I. "The Exile"
    II. "Visions"
       a. "Ruth and Naomi"
       b. "Miriam"
       c. "At the Well"
       d. "Fantasy — Confusion of Dreams"
   III. "The Exile"
       a. "I had a garden..."
       b. "The Beast is in the garden..."
   IV. "Vision of Deborah"

  Text: Passages from the Old Testament
  Music: Richard Neuman and Alex North
  Narrator: Harry Ostrovsky
  Costumes: No credit listed
  Dancers: Anna Sokolow, Clara Nezin, Frances Sunstein, Rose Levy

  The Land Calls

  Scene One: "The Peaceful Village"
  Scene Two: "The Attack"
  Scene Three: "The Land Calls to Arms"
  Music: Polanski, Ludwig van Beethoven, Franz Liszt
  Text: L. Miller
  Narration: Sholem Stern
  Director: Anna Sokolow
  Costumes: Moe Kashtan
  Dancers: The Modern Dance Unit [Montreal group]

- December 5, 1943
  Theresa L. Kaufmann Auditorium, YMHA, New York
  Anna Sokolow with Aza Bard, Clara Nezin, Frances Sunstein

  Madrid, 1937 [revision of *Slaughter of the Innocents*, 1937]

  Music: Alex North
  Costume: Rose Bank
  Dancer: Anna Sokolow

  Prelude [revision]

Music: Dimitri Shostakovich
Costumes: No credit listed
Dancers: Aza Bard, Clara Nezin, Frances Sunstein

Songs of a Semite [Title from a book of poems by Emma Lazarus. Excerpts from this work sometimes performed as *Three Biblical Characters*]
  1. "The Exile"
  2. "Visions"
     a. "Ruth and Naomi"
     b. "Miriam"
     c. "At The Well"
     d. "Fantasy — Confusion of Dreams"
  3. "The Exile"
     a. "I had a garden..."
     b. "The Beast is in the garden..."
  4. "Vision of Deborah" [later retitled *Deborah*, 1948]
  5. "March of the Semite Women"

Music: Richard Neuman and Alex North
Poem III: Sol Funaroff
Text: Passages from the Old Testament
Costumes: Rose Bank
Narrator: Jay William
Dancers: Anna Sokolow, Clara Nezin, Aza Bard, Frances Sunstein

* January 20, 1944
  Sans Souci (Night Club), Mexico City

  Carmen

  Music: Georges Bizet
  Costumes: Ignacio Aguirre and Carlos Mérida
  Dancers:

Carmen	Raquel Rojas
José	Oscar Tarriba
Escamillo	José Valente
	and Group

* August 20, 1945
  Palace of Fine Arts, Mexico City
  Anna Sokolow and Dance Group

  Danzas sobre Temas Rusos [*Dances on Russian Themes*]

  Music: Tchaikovsky

Costumes: No credit listed
Dancers: Marta Bracho, Socorro Bastida, Carmen Gutiérrez, Alicia Reyna, Rosa Reyna

Dos Preludios [*Two Preludes*]

Music: J. S. Bach
Costumes: No credit listed
Dancer: Anna Sokolow

En las Calles de la Ciudad [*In the Streets of the City*]
   I. "Caso Num . . ." ["Case History No. — ," first performed in 1937]
  II. "Mi Mama cree in los cuentos" ["Mama Beautiful," first performed in 1942]

Music: Wallingford Riegger, Alex North
Costumes: No credit listed
Dancers: Marta Bracho, Socorro Bastida, Carmen Gutiérrez, Alicia Reyna, Rosa Reyna

Kaddish

Music: Maurice Ravel
Costumes: No credit listed
Dancer: Anna Sokolow

Preludio y Mazurkas [*Preludes and Mazurkas*]

Music: Frederic Chopin
Costumes: No credit listed
Dancers: Socorro Bastida, Marta Bracho, Carmen Gutiérrez, Alicia Reyna, Rosa Reyna

- May 4, 1946 [first known performance]
  Jordan Hall, Boston
  Solo Concert

The Bride

Music: Traditional Jewish folk music
Costume: Rose Bank

Danza

Music: Rodolfo Halffter
Costume: Rose Bank

- May 12, 1946
  Theresa L. Kaufmann Auditorium, YM/YWHA, New York Solo Concert

Images from the Old Testament
   I. "Rose of Sharon"
  II. "Miriam"
 III. "Pastoral"
Music: Hemsi, Engel, and folk music
Costumes: Rose Bank

Mexican Retablo
  I. "Our Lady"
 II. "Senora, save him and I will adore you on my knees until my last days"
Music: Traditional Mexican folk music
Costume: Rose Bank

- December 16, 1946
  Shubert Theatre, Philadelphia

Street Scene [musical]

Writer: Elmer Rice
Music, Arrangements, and Orchestration: Kurt Weill
Lyrics: Langston Hughes
Director: Charles Friedman
Scenery and Lighting: Jo Mielziner
Costumes: Lucinda Ballard
Cast:

Anna Maurrant	Polyna Stoska
Frank Maurrant	Norman Gordon
Sam Kaplan	Brian Sullivan
Rose Maurrant	Anne Jeffreys

Dancers: Sheila Bond, Danny Daniels, Aza Bard, Sasha Pressman, Larry Baker

- March 30, 1947
  Princess Theater, New York
  Sponsored by Experimental Theatre Inc. (ANTA)

The Great Campaign [musical]

Writer: Arnold Sundgaard
Director: Joseph Losey
Associate Director: Helen Tamiris
Sets: Robert Davison
Costumes: Rose Bogdanoff
Music: Alex North
Dancers: Clara Cordery, Margaret McCallion, Ruth Rowen, Solvei Wiberg, Richard Astor, John Eaton, Glen Tetley

- February 1, 1948
Theresa L. Kaufmann Auditorium, YM/YWHA, New York
Solo Concert

Ballad in a Popular Style, No. 2

Music: Alex North
Costume: Rose Bank
Dancer: Anna Sokolow

Deborah [revision of *Vision of Deborah*, 1943]

Music: Paul Hindemith
Costume: Rose Bank
Dancer: Anna Sokolow

Life is a Fandango

Music: Traditional Mexican folk music arranged by Robert Didomenica
Costume: Rose Bank
Hat designed and made by Bess Newman
Dancer: Anna Sokolow

- May 10, 1948
Shubert Theatre, Philadelphia

Sleepy Hollow [musical]

Writers: Russel Maloney and Miriam Battista
Director: John O'Shaughnessy
Music: George Lessner
Sets and Lighting: Jo Mielziner
Costumes: David Ffolkes
Dancers: Aza Bard, Clara Corderey, Ann Dunbar, Kate Friedlich, Saida Gerrard, Carmen Gutiérrez, Margaret McCallion, Kaja Sumdsten, Alex Dunaeff, Don Farnsworth, Jay Lloyd, Joseph Milan, Shaun O'Brien, George Tatar, Franklin Wagner, John Ward

- Summer 1948
Palace of Fine Arts, Mexico City
Academia de la Danza Mexicana

Orfeo [*Orpheus*, opera]

Music: Christoph Gluck
Costumes: No credit listed
Dancers: Ana Mérida, Jose Silva, Gloria Mestre, Ricardo Silva, Beatriz Flores,

Guillermo Keys, Marta Castro, Marta Bracho, Socorro Bastida, Carmen Sagedo, Raquel Gutiérrez, Rosa Reyna, Felipe Seguro, Antonio de la Torre, Ricardo Luna, Elena Noriega, Valentina Castro, Rocio Sagaon, Josefina Luna

Mephistopheles [opera]

Music: Arrigo Boito
Costumes: No credit listed
Dancers: Ana Mérida, José Silva, Gloria Mestre, Ricardo Silva, Beatriz Flores, Guillermo Keys, Marta Castro, Marta Bracho, Socorro Bastida, Carmen Sagedo, Raquel Gutiérrez, Rosa Reyna, Felipe Seguro, Antonio de la Torre, Ricardo Luna, Elena Noriega, Valentina Castro, Rocio Sagaon, Josefina Luna

- October 6, 1949
  Shubert Theatre, New Haven, Connecticut

  Regina [musical]

  Text: *The Little Foxes* adapted by Lillian Hellman
  Music and Lyrics: Marc Blitzstein
  Director: Robert Lewis
  Sets: Horace Armistead
  Costumes: Aline Bernstein
  Cast:

Regina Giddens	Jane Pickens
Birdie Hubbard	Brenda Lewis
Oscar Hubbard	David Thomas
Leo Hubbard	Russell Nype
Marshall	Donald Clarke
Ben Hubbard	George Lipton

  Dancers: Wana Allison, Joab Engel, Barbara Ferguson, Kate Friedlich, Gisella Weidner, Ohna White, Leo Guerand, Robert Hanlin, Regis Powers, Boris Runanin, Walter Stane, John Ward

1950–1959

- January 6, 1950
  Coronet Theatre, New York

  Happy as Larry [musical]

  Writer: Donagh MacDonagh
  Director: Burgess Meredith

Music: Misha and Wesley Portnoff
Sets and Costumes: Motley
Cast (Principals): Burgess Meredith, Marguerite Piazza, Ralph Hertz, Barbara Perry, Gene Barry, Irwin Corey
Dancers: Mara Kun, Diane Sinclair, Royce Wallace, et al.

- March 11, 1951
  Weidman Studio Theater, New York

The Dybbuk [A dance based on the play by S. Ansky]

Music: Siegfried Landau
Costumes: Rose Bank
Cast:

The Rabbi (speaking role)	Lou Gilbert
Leah	Anna Sokolow
Channon	Richard Malek
Gittel	Aza Bard
Frade	Vivian Nathan

with: Don Keefer, Zairo Curtis, Justin Smith, John Bowman, Elizabeth Riggs, Lucille Patton, Shirlee Clarke, John Mandia, Bob St. Clair, Maurice Edwards, Selma Stern, Alix Tairoff

- March 17, 1952
  Madison Square Garden, New York
  Purim Festival and Pageant

Purim Jubilee [pageant]

Writer: Norman Rosten
Staged by: John O'Shaughnessy
Music: Sholem Secunda
Costumes: No credit listed
Cast (Principals): Betty Field and Melvyn Douglas
Dancers: Dorothy Bird, with Louis Ampolo, Natya Vazques Fontaine, Vivian Joyce, George R. Lake, Jose LaPresti, Rudolph Mattiace, Jo Anne Melsher, Arthur Mitchell, Jr., Vivian Nathan, Lucille Patton, Conchita Figuera del Rivero, Justin Smith, Rachel Talitman

- December 21, 1952
  Theresa L. Kaufmann Auditorium, YM/YWHA, New York

A Short Lecture and Demonstration on the Tiger Rag [later retitled *A Short Lecture and Demonstration on the Evolution of Ragtime as Presented by Jelly Roll Morton*]

Music: Jelly Roll Morton
Narrator: Larry Blyden
Costumes: No credit listed
Dancers: Carmen Gutiérrez and Danny Daniels

- March 19, 1953
  National Theatre, New York

Camino Real [stage play]

Writer: Tennessee Williams
Director: Elia Kazan
Assistant to the Director: Anna Sokolow
Incidental Music: Bernardo Segall
Designer: Lemuel Ayers
Cast: Eli Wallach, Jo Van Fleet, Joseph Anthony, Jennie Goldstein, Frank Silvera, Barbara Baxley, Hurd Hatfield with Aza Bard, Vivian Nathan, Nehemiah Persoff, Fred Sadoff, Martin Balsam, Ronnie Aul, Gluck Sandor, Lucille Patton

- October 20, 1953
  Madison Square Garden, New York
  Fundraising: State of Israel Bonds
  3,000th Anniversary of Jerusalem

City of the Ages [pageant]

Writer: Maurice Samuel
Director: Brett Warren
Music: A. W. Binder
Costumes: No credit listed
Designer: Howard Bay
Cast:

The Voice	Edward G. Robinson
King David	Paul Sparer (on stage), Alfred Ruscio (voice)
Aravnah	John Bryan (on stage), Frank Borgman (voice)
Soloist	Vivian Nathan

Dancers: Tommy Abbott, Aza Bard, Thesley Beverly, Dina Blackmann, Nicholas di Sailly, Annabelle Gold, Mary Hinkson, Page Johnson, William Korf, Herb Kummel, William Lennard, Jack Moore, Lucille Patton, Bernice Sacks, Alix Tairoff, Joanna Vischer
Other Participants: José Ferrer, Cary Grant, Jan Peerce, Gregor Piatigorsky

- August 7, 1953
  Teatro de los Insurgentes, Mexico City

  Suite Lirica [Lyric Suite]
     I. "Allegretto joviale"
    II. "Andante amoroso"
   III. "Allegro misterioso"
   IV. "Largo desolato"
    V. "Adagio apassionato"

  Music: Alban Berg
  Costumes and Scenery: Julio Prieto
  Dancers: Guillermo Keys, Raquel Gutiérrez, Rosa Reyna, Nellie Happee, Valentina Castro, Bodyl Genkel, Beatriz Flores, Guillermina Penaloza, Elena Noriega, Edmundo Mendoza, Luis Fandino, Carlos Gaona, John Sakmari, Rosalio Ortega, Carmen Gutiérrez, Xavier Francis, Marta Bracho

- December 1, 1953
  Phoenix Theatre, New York

  "Madam, Will You Walk" [musical]

  Writer: Sidney Howard
  Directors: Hume Cronyn and Norman Lloyd
  Incidental Music: Max Marlin
  Sets: Donald Oenslager
  Costumes: Alvin Colt
  Cast: John Randolph, Edwin Jerome, Norman Lloyd, Jessica Tandy, Hume Cronyn, Robert Emmett, and Nora Dunfee, Jill Andre, Donald Draper, Dan Hogan, Elizabeth Johnstone, Mavis Mitchell, Fred Smith

- March 31, 1954
  Theresa L. Kaufmann Auditorium, YM/YWHA, New York
  New Dance Group Company

  Lyric Suite [revision, American premiere]
     I. "Allegretto"
    II. "Andante"
   III. "Allegro"
   IV. "Largo"
    V. "Adagio"
  Note: "Presto" [Delirando] was added a few years later
  Score: Alban Berg
  Costumes: Rose Bank

Dancers: Donald McKayle, Mary Anthony, Beatrice Seckler, Eve Beck, Jeff Duncan, Leonore Landau, Sandra Pine, Laura Sheleen, Ethel Winter

- December 18, 1954
  Theresa L. Kaufmann Auditorium, YM/YWHA, New York
  An Evening of Music, Drama and Dance

  Histoire de Soldat

  Director: Muriel Sharon
  Music: Igor Stravinsky
  Sets and Costumes: Paul Sherman
  Cast:
  Reader   Fritz Weaver
  Soldier   John Harkins
  Devil   Frederick Warriner
  Princess   Annabelle Gold

- December 23, 1954
  Madison Square Garden (Old Site), New York
  Chanukah Festival for Israel

  The Great Dreamer [pageant]

  Writer: Norman Rosten
  Director: Himan Brown
  Music: Johann Strauss, David Roitman, Felix Mendelssohn, Darius Milhaud, Anton Rubinstein, Georg Schumann, Arthur Honegger
  Costumes: Paul DuPont
  Set: Samuel Leve
  Cast:
  Narrator   Louis Calhern
  Captain Alfred Dreyfus   Joseph Schildkraut
  Dr. Theodor Herzl   Dana Andrews
  Mrs. Herzl   Kim Stanley
  Emile Zola   Ralph Bell
  Dancers: Aza Bard, Eve Beck, Judith Coy, Jeff Duncan, Michael George, Page Johnson, William Korff, Harvey Lichtenstein, Rudy Mattice, Donald McKayle, Esta McKayle, Jack Moore, Miriam Pandar, Sandra Pine, Laura Sheleen, Annaliese Widman

- February 24, 1955
  Theresa L. Kaufmann Auditorium, YM/YWHA, New York
  An Evening of Dance Works by Anna Sokolow

Rooms
- I. "Alone"
- II. "Dream"
- III. "Escape"
- IV. "Going"
- V. "Desire"
- VI. "Panic"
- VII. "Daydream"
- VIII. "The End?"
- IX. "Alone"

Music: Kenyon Hopkins
Costumes: Donald McKayle
Dancers: Eve Beck, Judith Coy, Sandra Pine, Beatrice Seckler, Jeff Duncan, Donald McKayle, Jack Moore, Paul Sanasardo

- April 19, 1955
  Juilliard Concert Hall, New York
  Juilliard Dance Theatre Company

Primavera
- I. "Introduzione"
- II. "Allegro"
- III. "Siciliana"
- IV. "Allegro Guisto"

Music: Arthur Benjamin (piano sonatas composed by Domenico Cimarosa)
Costumes: No credit listed
Dancers: Patricia Christopher, Anna Friedland, Lola Huth, Melisa Nicolaides, Joyce Trisler, Bruce Carlisle, Jeff Duncan, Richard Fitz-Gerald, Don Redlich, Jack Spencer

- December 13, 1955
  Wilbur Theatre, Boston

Red Roses for Me [musical]

Writer: Sean O'Casey
Music: Edwin Finckel
Staging: John O'Shaughnessy
Costumes: Ballou
Sets: Howard Bay
Cast (Principals): Kevin McCarthy, Eileen Crowe, Joyce Sullivan, Michael Clarke Laurence, Virginia Bosler, Shamus Locke, Ann Dere, Whitford Kane,

Casey Walters, Katherine Hynes, Eamon Flynn, Barry Macollum, E. G. Marshall
Dancers: Paul Sanasardo, Jeff Duncan, Beatrice Seckler, Judith Coy, David Gold, Sandra Pine, Eve Beck, Jack Moore

- February 12, 1956
  Brooklyn Academy of Music, Brooklyn
  Theater Dance Company

Poem

Music: Alexander Scriabin
Costumes: Helen Alexander
Dancers: Alvin Ailey, Eve Beck, Judith Coy, Jeff Duncan, David Gold, Jack Moore, Sandra Pine, Paul Sanasardo, Beatrice Seckler, Anneliese Widman

- September 20, 1956
  New York City Center of Music and Drama, New York
  New York City Opera
  New York City Opera Ballet

Orpheus in the Underworld [opera]

Music: Jacques Offenbach
English Libretto: Eric Bentley
Producers and Directors: Leo Kerz and Erich Leinsdorf
Costumes: Leo Van Witsen
Dancers: Eve Beck, Irving Burton, Judith Coy, Jeff Duncan, David Gold, Marvin Gordon, Leonore Landau, Rhoda Levine, Jack Moore, Paul Sanasardo, Beatrice Seckler, Annaliese Widman

- September 22, 1956
  New York City Center of Music and Drama, New York
  New York City Opera
  New York City Opera Ballet

La Traviata [opera]

Music: Giuseppe Verdi
Director: David Pressman
Dancers: Eve Beck, Irving Burton, Judith Coy, Jeff Duncan, David Gold, Marvin Gordon, Leonore Landau, Rhoda Levine, Jack Moore, Paul Sanasardo, Beatrice Seckler, Annaliese Widman

• October 2, 1956
New York City Center of Music and Drama, New York
New York City Opera
New York City Opera Ballet

Mignon [opera]

Music: Ambroise Thomas
Costumes: Leo Van Witsen
Gypsy Dancer: Raymonda Orselli
Dancers: Eve Beck, Irving Burton, Judith Coy, Jeff Duncan, David Gold, Marvin
Gordon, Leonore Landau, Rhoda Levine, Jack Moore, Paul Sanasardo, Beatrice
Seckler, Annaliese Widman

• October 16, 1956
New York City Center of Music and Drama, New York
New York City Opera
New York City Opera Ballet

L'Histoire du Soldat [opera/drama]

Director: Marcella Cisney
Music: Igor Stravinsky
Costumes: No credit listed
Cast:

The Narrator	Christopher Plummer
The Soldier	James Mitchell
The Devil	Hurd Hatfield
The Princess	Judith Coy

The Moon [opera]

Music: Carl Orff
English Translation: Maria Massey
Staging: Anna Sokolow
Costumes: Leo Van Witsen
Dancers: Eve Beck, Irving Burton, Judith Coy, Jeff Duncan, David Gold, Marvin
Gordon, Leonore Landau, Rhoda Levine, Jack Moore, Paul Sanasardo, Beatrice
Seckler, Annaliese Widman

• October 17, 1956
New York City Center of Music and Drama, New York
New York City Opera
New York City Opera Ballet

The Tempest [opera]

Writer: William Shakespeare
Producers and Directors: Leo Kerz and Erich Leinsdorf
Music: Frank Martin
Dances: Anna Sokolow
Costumes: Leo Van Witsen
Dancers: Eve Beck, Irving Burton, Judith Coy, Jeff Duncan, David Gold, Marvin Gordon, Leonore Landau, Rhoda Levine, Jack Moore, Paul Sanasardo, Beatrice Seckler, Annaliese Widman

- October 19, 1956
  New York City Center of Music and Drama, New York
  New York City Opera
  New York City Opera Ballet

Susannah [a musical drama in two acts, ten scenes]

Music and Text: Carlisle Floyd
Producers and Directors: Leo Kerz and Erich Leinsdorf
Women's Costumes: Courtesy of the School of Music, Florida State University
Dances: Anna Sokolow
Dancers: Eve Beck, Irving Burton, Judith Coy, Jeff Duncan, David Gold, Marvin Gordon, Leonore Landau, Rhoda Levine, Jack Moore, Paul Sanasardo, Beatrice Seckler, Annaliese Widman

- October 25, 1956
  New York City Center of Music and Drama, New York
  New York City Opera
  New York City Opera Ballet

Carmen [opera]

No other information found

- December 1, 1956
  Martin Beck Theater, New York

Candide [musical]

Book: Adapted by Lillian Hellman from the book by Voltaire
Director: Tyrone Guthrie
Music: Leonard Bernstein
Lyrics: Richard Wilbur

Other Lyrics: John Latouche and Dorothy Parker
Choreography: Wallace Siebert
Choreography Revision: Anna Sokolow
Costumes: Irene Sharaff
Cast:

Dr. Pangloss and Martin	Max Adrian
Candide	Robert Rounseville
Cunegonde	Barbara Cook
Old Lady	Irra Petina

Dancers: Alvin Beam, Charles Czarny, Marvin Gordon, Carmen Gutiérrez, Charles Morrell, Frances Noble, Liane Plane, Gloria Stevens

- February 19, 1957
  Theatre de Lys, New York
  American National Theatre and Academy (ANTA) Play series

Metamorphosis [stage play with mime and dance]

Writer: Adapted by Douglas Watson from the story by Franz Kafka
Director and Choreographer: Anna Sokolow
Music: Kenyon Hopkins, Betty Walberg
Costumes: Rose Bank
Cast:

Gregor (actor)	Douglas Watson
Mother	Katherine Calee
Father	Page Johnson
Chief Clerk	David Gold
Charwoman and Maria, a girl in his dream	Judith Coy
First Lodger	Nesbitt Blaisdell
Second Lodger	Jeff Duncan

- May 13, 1957
  Phoenix Theatre, New York
  Ballet Theatre Workshop

Le Grand Spectacle

Music: Teo Macero
Costumes: Manhattan Costumers
Dancers: Paul Taylor, Jeff Duncan, Eve Beck, Anita Dencks, Kate Friedlich, David Gold, Dorothy Krooks, Jack Moore

- July 25, 1957
Balboa Park Stadium, San Diego San Diego's Fiesta del Pacifico, 1957

The California Story [pageant]

Dancers: Fran Amitin, Julius Bengtsson, Fanchon Bennet, Eve Cassidy, Joan Chodorow, Ben Jonson, Gail Kaller, Marketa Kimbrell, Phillip Lanza, Joan Lawrence, Judy Lawrence, James Mehl, Willard Nagel, Jo Neal, Sherry Price, Mark Rose, Joe Rudon, Evonne Samajia, Joe Stember, Joan Tyson, Frank Varcasia, Jerry Wallace, Larry Warren

- October 17, 1957 [first New York performance]
Martin Beck Theater, New York

Copper and Brass [musical]

Book: Ellen Volett and David Craig
Music: David Baker
Lyrics: David Craig
Director: Marc Daniels
Sets: William and Jean Eckart
Costumes: Alvin Colt
Cast: Nancy Walker, Benay Venuta, Dick Williams, Alice Pearce, with Alan Bunce, Norma Douglas, Peter Conlow, Evelyn Russell, Michelle Burke, Doreen McLean, Byron Mitchell, Bruce McKay, Doug Rogers, Hank Jones, Frank Rehak, Ernie Furtado
Dancers: Shawneequa Baker, Eve Beck, Judith Coy, Anita Dencks, Kate Friedlich, Ellen Hubel, Coco Ramirez, Ella Thompson, Kevin Carlisle, Jeff Duncan, David Gold, Donald McKayle, Jack Moore, Stanley Papich, Harold Pierson, Willard Nagel

- February 19, 1958
Theresa L. Kaufmann Concert Hall, YM/YWHA, New York
Anna Sokolow Dance Company

Session for Six

Music: Teo Macero
Costumes: Jack Moore
Dancers: Eve Beck, Kate Friedlich, Dorothy Krooks, Jeff Duncan, David Gold, Jack Moore

- April 11, 1958
Juilliard Concert Hall, New York

Juilliard Dance Theatre Group

Session '58

Music: Teo Macero
Costumes: No credit listed
Dancers: Patricia Christopher, Yemima Ben-Gal, Baird Searles, Yvonne Brenner, Ronald Tassone, Maureen Gillick, John Wilson, Diane Quitzow, James Payton, Joyce Trisler, John Blanchard, Martha Wittman, David Wynne, Diane Adler, Florence Peters, Poligena Rogers
Note: Later that year retitled *Opus '58* when performed by the Netherlands Dance Theatre, *Opus Jazz 1958* in Israel and *Session for Eight* in New York; information on the performances in Israel and New York follows

- August 1958
The Israel National Opera
Opus Jazz 1958 [revision of *Session '58*]
Music: Teo Macero
Costumes: No credit listed
Dancers: Bruria Aviezer, Yaakov Arkin, Meir Avraham, Aaron Ben-Aroya, Moshe Romano, Nurit Ronnen, Bathsheba Rosenbaum, Naomi Wiener, Dominique Writer, Dahlia Yuval

- December 26, 1958
York Playhouse, New York
The Anna Sokolow Dance Company

Session for Eight [revision of *Session '58*]

Music: Teo Macero
Costumes: Rose Bank
Dancers: Anita Dencks, Kate Friedlich, Annabelle Gold, Dorothy Krooks, Jeff Duncan, Bill Frank, Jack Moore, Noel Schwartz

- Fall 1959
Israel Opera House, Tel Aviv
Theater Opening

Alexandra [*Alexander the Hashmonai*, opera]

Music: M. Avidom
Costumes: H. Dorf
Dancers: Ilana Aron, Agnes Blau, Josef Davidovitz, Dominic Rieter, Bila Locker, Nathan Lifshitz, Yakov Solomon, Mariana Solomon, Ofra Fuchs, Dalia Koshet, Robin Komisione, Moshe Romano, Alisa Sadeh, Eliahu Shedlash, Avram Shemesh

- April 12, 1959
  Beekman Tower Hotel Theater, New York
  New York Theatre Society

  Death of Cuchulain [stage play]

  On Baile's Strand [stage play]

  Writer: William Butler Yeats
  Director: Gloria Monty
  Incidental Music: Charles Paul
  Costumes: Eleanor Knowles
  Casts:
  The Death of Cuchulain: Burgess Meredith, Ellen Cobb Hill, John Colicos, Katherine Meskill, Kate Friedlich, Dorothy Patten, Neil Fitzgerald, Jack Betts, Shirley Carter, John Miller
  On Baile's Strand: Liam Clancy, Neil Fitzgerald, John Colicos, Basil Langton, Michael Higgins, Ford Rainey, Jack Betts, Dorothy Patten, Mary Seaman, Betty Hartmine

1960–1969

- September 20, 1960
  Palace of Fine Arts, Mexico City
  Ballet de Bellas Artes

  Opus '60

  Music: Teo Macero
  Costumes: No credit listed
  Dancers: Aurora Agüeria, Juan Casados, Farnesio de Bernal, Raúl Flores, Raquel Gutiérrez, Josefina Lavalle, Roseyra Marenco, Colombia Moya, Elena Noriega, Luz Maria Ordiales, Rosalío Ortega, Sara Pardo, Guillermo Palomares, Marcos Paredes, Rosa Reyna, John Sakmari, Adriana Siqueiros

- October 20, 1960
  Palace of Fine Arts, Mexico City
  Ballet de Bellas Artes with chorus and actors from National Institute of Fine Arts (INBA)

  Homenaje a Hidalgo [*Homage to Hidalgo*]

  Director: Anna Sokolow
  Music: Rafael Elizondo

Libretto: Emilio Carballido
Costumes: Lucille Donay
Cast:

Hidalgo	Angel Pineda
Niños del Corrido	Leonardo Flores Delgado, Guillermo Flores Delgado
Palomita	Azucena Aviles Estrado, Patricia Ladron de Guevara

Dancers: Juan Casados, Farnesio de Bernal, Raúl Flores, Rosalio Ortega, Guillermo Palomares, Marcos Paredes, John Sakmari, Aurora Agueria, Maria Fierro, Raquel Gutiérrez, Josefina Lavalle, Roseyra Marenco, Elena Noriega, Sara Pardo, Rosa Reyna, Adriana Siqueiros

Orfeo [suite from the opera *Orfeo*]

Music: Christoph Gluck
Scenery and Costumes: Antonio Lopez Mancera
Dancers: Aurora Agüeria, Juan Casados, Farnesio de Bernal, Raúl Flores, Raquel Gutiérrez, Josefina Lavalle, Roseyra Marenco, Colombia Moya, Elena Noriega, Luz Maria Ordiales, Rosalío Ortega, Sara Pardo, Guillermo Palomares, Marcos Paredes, Rosa Reyna, John Sakmari, Adriana Siqueiros

- May 8, 1961
  Theresa L. Kaufmann Concert Hall, YM/YWHA, New York
  Freda Miller Memorial Concert
  Anna Sokolow Dance Company

Dreams [first performed in the early spring of 1961 at the Herbert Berghof studio as an experimental piece with the same cast]

Music: Teo Macero
Costumes: No credit listed
Dancers: Julie Arenal, Juki Arkin, Buck Heller, Nancy Lewis, Jack Moore

- November 7, 1961
  Palace of Fine Arts, Mexico City
  Ballet de Bellas Artes

Ofrenda Musical [*Musical Offering*]

Music: J. S. Bach and Lan Adomian
Costumes: Farnesio De Bernal
Dancers: Aurora Agüeria, Miguel Araiza, Mireya Barbosa, Rafael Carapia, Juan Casados, Jay Fletcher, Beatriz Flores, Josefina Lavalle, Roseyra Marenco, Carlo

McNielli, Luz Maria Ordiales, Rosalío Ortega, Nieves Paniagua, Rosa Reyna, José Rosas, Rocio Sagaón, Adriana Siqueiros, Clara Villalobos, Sergio Lezama, Francisco Martinez

- November 13, 1961
  Palace of Fine Arts, Mexico City
  Ballet de Bellas Artes

  Sueños [revision of *Dreams*, 1961]

  Music: Anton Webern
  Scenery and Costumes: Antonio Lopez Mancera
  Dancers: Aurora Agüeria, Miguel Araiza, Amparo Bonett, Rafael Carapia, Juan Casados, Beatriz Flores, Josefina Lavalle, Sergio Lezama, Roseyra Marenco, Francisco Martinez, Carlo McNielli, Rosalío Ortega, Rosa Reyna, José Rosas, Rocio Sagaón, Adriana Siqueiros

- July 4, 1962
  Nachmani Hall, Tel Aviv
  Lyric Theatre

  The Treasure [stage play]

  Writer: Itzchak Peretz
  Director: Anna Sokolow
  Music: Nathan Mishori
  Costumes: No credit listed
  Cast: Yitzhak Ben-Nissim, Yossi Kipnis, Dalia Harlap

- July 1962 [exact date unknown]
  Nachmani Theatre, Tel Aviv
  Lyric Theatre

  4 Short Jazz Pieces

  Music: Teo Macero
  Costumes: No credit listed
  Dancers: Ze'eva Cohen, Galia Gat, Leora Hachmi, Dalia Harlap, Miriam Prever, Ehud Ben-David, Yitzhak Ben-Nissim, Yossi Kipnis, Shlomo Nadav, Yigal Paz, Avraham Tzuri

- October 1962 [exact date unknown]
  Nachmani Theatre, Tel Aviv
  Lyric Theatre

Opus '62

Music: Teo Macero
Costumes: No credit listed
Dancers: Ze'eva Cohen, Galia Gat, Leora Hachmi, Dalia Harlap, Miriam Prever, Ehud Ben-David, Yitzhak Ben-Nissim, Yossi Kipnis, Shlomo Nadav, Yigal Paz, Avraham Tzuri

- March 9, 1963
  Theresa L. Kaufmann Concert Hall, YM/YWHA, New York
  New Dance Group Studio (sponsor)

Suite No. 5 in C Minor

Music: J. S. Bach
Costumes: No credit listed
Dancers: Ahuva Anbary, Julie Arenal, Jeff Duncan, Dalia Harlap, Ronny Johnston, Jack Moore, Martha Wittman, Chester Wolenski

- April 21, 1963
  Herbert Berghof Studio, New York
  People Who Make Theater — Lecture and Demonstration Series

The Waiting Room

Solo for Alto

Twist

[three stage plays]

Writer: John White
Director: Anna Sokolow
Costumes: No credit listed
Cast: Sonny Chandler, Yossi Kipnis, Morrie Pierce, Larry Robinson, John Starkweather, Joan Tyson, Jack Waltzer

- May 10, 1963
  Juilliard Concert Hall, New York
  Juilliard Dance Ensemble

Opus '63

Music: Teo Macero
Costumes: No credit listed
Dancers: Julie Arenal, Lynne Fippinger, Marcia Kurtz, Margaretha Asberg, Margaret Goettelmann, Oshra Ronen, Martha Clarke, Dana Holby, Francia

Roxin, Ronald Ball, Cliff Keuter, Raymond Cook, Daniel Lewis, Morris Donaldson, John Parks, Robert Kappel, Michael Podwal

- April 17, 1964
  Juilliard Concert Hall, New York
  Juilliard Dance Ensemble

  The Question

  Music: Anton Webern
  Costumes: No credit listed
  Dancers: Margaret Cicierska, Martha Clarke, Ze'eva Cohen, Marcia Goff, Charlotte Mitzenmacher, Yigal Paz, Dennis Nahat, John Parks, Ramon Rivera, David Taylor, Michael Uthoff, Lance Westergard

- April 26, 1964
  Theresa L. Kaufmann Concert Hall, YM/YWHA, New York
  Anna Sokolow Dance Company

  Forms

  Music: Teo Macero
  Costumes: No credit listed
  Dancers: Julie Arenal, Margaretha Asberg, Jeff Duncan, Ronny Johnston, Jack Moore, Francia Roxin, Chester Wolenski

- September 18, 1964
  Cameri Theatre, Tel Aviv
  Lyric Theatre

  Odes

  Music: A. U. Boskovich
  Costumes: No credit listed
  Dancers: Rina Shaham (guest artist), Ofra Ben Zvi, Gideon Abrahami, Joanna Peled, Enon Ne'eman, Leora Hachmi-Zirlin, Avraham Manzur

- November 18, 1964
  New York State Theater, New York
  American Dance Theater

  The Question [revision]

  Music: Anton Webern
  Dancers: Julie Arenal, Patricia Christopher, Nancy Lewis, Nancy Stevens, Lenore Latimer, Alma Robinson, Joan Miller, Marcos Paredes, Larry Richardson, Joseph

Amaral, John Parks, Elbert Morris, Miguel Godreau, Michael Uthoff, Peter Randazzo

- February 12, 1965
  Juilliard Concert Hall, New York
  Juilliard Dance Ensemble

  Ballade

  Music: Alexander Scriabin
  Costumes: Charles Tomlinson
  Dancers: Ze'eva Cohen, Eric Hampton, Tamara Woshakiwsky, Dennis Nahat

  Odes [Section II later performed as *Density 21.5*]

  Music: Edgard Varèse
  Costumes: Charles Tomlinson
  Dancers: Lance Westergard, Charlotte Bailis, Mary Barnett, Margaret Cicierska, Ellen Cohen, Sarah Ford, Joann Friedman, Kaoru Ishii, Judith Kaplan, Linda Kent, Rimona Kuschnir, Sharon Miller, Diane Mohrmann, Lee Wagner, Ernestine Williams, Sheila Zatroch, Clifford Allen, Toney Brealond, Peter DeNicola, Edward De Soto, Edward Effron, John Giffin, Eric Hampton

- September 11, 1965
  Delacorte Theater, New York
  Apprentices and Scholarship Students of the Robert Joffrey Ballet

  Opus '65

  Music: Teo Macero
  Costumes: No credit listed
  Dancers: Ann Axtmann, Esther Jaenn, Yvonne McDowell, Ximena Quintana, Margo Sappington, Arlene Shuler, Donna Silva, Martha Vaala, Frank Bays, Rex Bickmore, Dermot Burke, Raymond Bussey, Jorge Fatauros, George Montalbano, Haynes Owens, Don Richard

- November 17, 1965
  Pocket Theatre, New York

  Bugs and *Veronica* [two one-act plays]

  Writer: John White
  Director: Anna Sokolow
  Original Music: Teo Macero
  Costumes: No credit listed

Design: Koski-Long
Cast:

Bugs Alice Scudder,
Dylan Green, Joan Tyson,
Jess Osuna,
Lorraine Serabian

Veronica Bernard Grant,
Ralph Bell, Dylan Green,
Lorraine Serabian,
Jess Osuna

- January 17, 1966
  Back Bay Theatre, Boston
  Boston Ballet Company

Time + 6

Music: Teo Macero
Costumes: Evelyn Rassias
Dancers: Shanna Bereska, Linda DiBona, Phyllis Heath, Carolyn La Fleur, Ellen O'Reilly, Denise Plouffe, Carol Ravich, Gloria Sotir, Valerie Windsor, Laura Young, Fred Alexson, Robert Harlow, Mark Hudson, Raymond King, Warren Lynch, Robert Pierce, Robert Steele, Tony Williams, Steven Wistrich, June Perry, Cynthia Heaton

- May 6, 1966
  Juilliard Concert Hall, New York
  Juilliard Dance Ensemble

Night

Music: Luciano Berio
Costumes: Ashley Bryan
Dancers: Sandra Brown, Ellen Cohen, Linda Kent, Carla Maxwell, Charlotte Mitzenmacher, Irine Nute, Linda Rabin, Janet Sumner, Lynne Wimmer, Sheila Zatroch, Thomas Baker, Edward DeSoto, Edward Effron, John Giffin, Robert Iscove, Anthony Salatino, Gene Stulgaitis

- May 13, 1966
  Jewish Community Center, White Plains, New York
  Jewish Music Festival

Love Songs for Sabbath [a new service with poetry and dance, celebrating the holiness of time]

Director: Anna Sokolow
Music: Jack Gottlieb
Reader: Felicia Montealegre

Costume: No credit listed
Dancer: Ora Pilch

- March 10, 1967
  Hunter College Playhouse, New York
  Anna Sokolow Dance Company

Deserts

Music: Edgard Varèse
Costumes: Ashley Bryan, Philip Grausman, Glenn Brooks
Dancers: Margaret Cicierska, Martha Clarke, Ze'eva Cohen, Lenore Latimer, Trina Parks, Kathryn Posin, Ray Cook, Edward Effron, David Krohn, Clyde Morgan, John Parks, Chester Wolenski

Time + 7

Music: Teo Macero
Costumes: Bernard Johnson
Dancers: Martha Clarke, Ze'eva Cohen, Lenore Latimer, Trina Parks, Edward Effron, Clyde Morgan, John Parks, Chester Wolenski, Margaret Cicierska, Kathryn Posin, Ray Cook, David Krohn

- March 27, 1967
  New York City Center
  The National Ballet (of Washington)

Night [revision]

Music: Luciano Berio
Costumes: No credit listed
Dancers: Hiller Huhn, Michele Lynn, Judy Rhodes, James Thompson, Fredric Strobel, Betty Risen, Sheryl McKechnie, James Capp, Susan Gore, Karen Brown, Katherine Laqueur, Patricia Sorrell, Michelle Lees, Judith Reece

- April 20, 1967
  Juilliard Concert Hall, New York
  Juilliard Dance Ensemble

Memories

Music: Teo Macero
Costumes: No credit listed
Dancers: Pamela Anderson, Sandra Brown, Robyn Cutler, Erroll Booker, John Giffin, Graciela Figueroa, Linda Kent, Sue Roberta Melworth, Irine Nute, Gary

Masters, James Murphy, Stephen Reinhardt, Linda Rabin, Lee Wagner, Lynne Wimmer, David Tisdale, Lance Westergard

- July 7, 1967
  Stadsschouwburg Theater, Tilburg, Holland
  Holland Festival in Amsterdam
  Netherlands Dance Theater

Seven Deadly Sins

Libretto: Bertolt Brecht
English Version: W. H. Auden and Chester Kallman
Director: Anna Sokolow
Music: Kurt Weill
Costumes: Jan Van Der Wal
Cast: Anna the dancer   Marian Sarstadt
Anna the singer   Ileana Melita

- September 1967 [exact date unknown]
  Lecture-Demonstration at American Cultural Center, Tokyo, Japan Students at American Cultural Center

Bird

Music: Alexander Scriabin
Dancers: Students at American Cultural Center

- October 17, 1967
  New York Shakespeare Festival Public Theater

Hair [musical]

Book and Lyrics: Gerome Ragni, James Rado
Director: Gerald Freedman
Music: Galt MacDermot
Costumes: Theoni V. Aldredge
Cast: Jonelle Allen, Ed Crowley, Walker Daniels, Steve Dean, Sally Eaton, Marijane Maricle, Jill O'Hara, Shelley Plimpton, Gerome Ragni, Arnold Wilkerson, with Susan Batson, Warren Burton, Thommie Bush, Linda Compton, Suzannah Evans, William Herter, Paul Jabara, Bob Johnson, Jane Levin, Edward Murphy, Jr., Alma Robinson

- October 23, 1967
  Theatre 80 St. Mark's, New York
  Manhattan Festival Ballet

Untitled

Music: Stanley Walden
Costumes: Mel Juan
Dancers: Esther Chaves, Kathleen Carlin, Maralia Reca, Donna Baldwin, Ron Sequoio, Thomas Enckell, Paul Keller, Gordon Peavy

- June 27, 1968
  Jacob's Pillow, Lee, Massachusetts
  Pennsylvania Ballet Company

Time Plus [revision of *Time + 7*]

Music: Teo Macero
Costumes: No credit listed
Dancers: Group of twelve

- June 29, 1968
  Academia de la Danza Mexicana, Mexico City
  Students of the Academia de la Danza Mexicana

Family of Man

Music: Unknown
Dancers: Students of the Academia de la Danza Mexicana

- September 23, 1968
  The Forum / Vivian Beaumont Theatre Building, New York
  The Repertory Theater of Lincoln Center

Bananas [stage play]

Writer: John White
Director and Original Concept: Anna Sokolow
Music and Songs: James Hodges
Costumes: Holly Haas
Sets: Karl Eigsti
Cast: Patricia Rowe, Ralph Bell, Arnold Soboloff, Larry Robinson, Ray Fry

- October 22, 1968
  Theater of the Living Arts, Philadelphia
  Anna Sokolow Dance Company

Memories [revision]

Music: Tadeusz Baird

Costumes: Ashley Bryan
Dancers: Sue Brown, Irene Feigenheimer, Lorry May, Kathryn Posin, Ana San Antonio, Tonia Shimin, Lisbeth Whaley, Michael Ebbin, Phillip Jonson, Jim May, Barry Moncrieffe, Ernest Royster

Tribute

Music: J. S. Bach
Costumes: Judi Dearing
Dancers: Sue Brown, Margaret Cicierska, Michael Ebbin, Edward Effron, Irene Feigenheimer, Lynda Gudde, Phillip Jonson, Jim May, Lorry May, Barry Moncrieffe, John Parks, Kathryn Posin, Ernest Royster, Ana San Antonio, Tonia Shimin, Lisbeth Whaley

• October 25, 1968
Kingsbury Hall, University of Utah, Salt Lake City
Repertory Dance Theatre

Steps of Silence

Music: Anatol Vieru
Costumes: No credit listed
Dancers: Joan Butler, Kay Clark, Bill Evans, Gregg Lizenbery, Kathleen McClintock, Richard Rowsell, Tim Wengerd, Lynne Wimmer

• November 13, 1968
Brooklyn Academy of Music, Brooklyn
Anna Sokolow Dance Company

Steps of Silence [revision]

Music: Anatol Vieru
Costumes: Judi Dearing
Dancers: Margaret Cicierska, Michael Ebbin, Edward Effron, Lynda Gudde, John Parks, Tonia Shimin, Ernest Royster, Lisbeth Whaley

• March 20, 1969
Juilliard Concert Hall, New York
Juilliard Dance Ensemble

Echoes

Music: John Weinzweig
Costumes: No credit listed
Dancers: Jean Anderson, Maria Barrios, Robyn Cutler, E. Irene Dowd, Andy Bew, Blake Brown, Mary Margaret Giannone, Micki Goodman, Pamela Knisel,

Raymond Clay, Larry Grenier, Gary Masters, Risa Steinberg, Etsuko Takahara, Yasuko Tokunaga, Sylvia Yamada, Francis Patrelle, Gene Stulgaitis

- May 12, 1969
  Fleisher Auditorium, YM/YWHA, Philadelphia
  Philadelphia Composers' Forum
  Anna Sokolow Dance Company

  Intégrales

  Music: Edgard Varèse
  Costumes: No credit listed
  Dancers: Lynne Taylor, Tonia Shimin, Irene Feigenheimer, Lorry May, Philip Jonson, Barry Moncrieffe, Daryll Stipek

- November 6, 1969
  For Washington and Jefferson College at Trinity High School
  Auditorium, Washington, Pennsylvania
  Lyric Theatre with the Philadelphia Composers' Forum

  Act Without Words, No. 1 [based on the play by Samuel Beckett]

  Music: Joel Thome
  Costumes and Scenery: As per Samuel Beckett's instructions in the play
  Dancer: Rex Bickmore

1970–1979

- February 2, 1970
  Kraushaar Auditorium, Goucher College, Towson, Maryland
  Lyric Theatre

  L'Histoire de Soldat [revision]

  Libretto: C. F. Ramuz
  English Version: Michael Flanders and Kitty Black
  Director: Anna Sokolow
  Music: Igor Stravinsky
  Costumes: Maria Contessa
  Cast:

The Narrator	Jack Davidson
The Soldier	Jim May
The Devil	Rex Bickmore
The Princess	Lorry May

- February 15, 1970
  Towson State College, Stephens Auditorium, Baltimore, Maryland
  Lyric Theatre

  Magritte, Magritte
     I. "The Lovers"
    II. "The Son of Man"
   III. "The Reckless Sleeper"
    IV. "Acrobatic Ideas"
     V. "The Time of the Harvest"
    VI. "The Threatened Assassin"
   VII. "The Red Model"
  Inspired by the paintings of René Magritte
  Music played by Renaldo Reyes
  Poems: Edgar Allen Poe and Paul Éluard
  Original text by John White
  Music: Liszt, Satie, Scriabin, Thome, and French songs arranged by Virginia Hutchings
  Costumes: Marie Countessa
  Dancers: Rex Bickmore, Anthony Favello, Lorry May, Jim May,
  Marjorie Mussman
  Actors: Janet Coppee, Jack Davidson

- March 1970
  Auditorium Theater, Chicago, Illinois
  Chamber Dance Company

  Where to . . . ?

  Music: Tadeusz Baird
  Costumes: Alan Madsen
  Dancers: Charles Bennett, Lisa Bradley, Janice Groman, Marjorie
  Mussman, Michael Uthoff

- May 26, 1970
  Juilliard Concert Hall, New York
  Juilliard Dance Ensemble

  The Dove

  Music: Cristóbal Halffter
  Costumes: No credit listed
  Dancers: Ann DeGange, Ilze Dreimanis, Margaret Fargnoli, Mary Margaret Giannone, Pamela Knisel, Gretchen Langstaff, Linda Levy, Jane Lowe, Dalienne Majors, Bonnie Oda, Eleana Plaskett, Whitney Rau, Socorro Santiago, Wendy Smith,

Risa Steinberg, Evelyn Thomas, Yasuko Tokunaga, Andy Bew, Blake Brown, Gary Masters, Peter Sparling, Marc Stevens, Gene Stulgaitis, Patrick Suzeau, Jerome Weiss

- October 8, 1970
  Cubiculo Theater, New York
  Clyde Morgan and Carla Maxwell with guest artists

Duets for Unaccompanied Cello

Music: J. S. Bach, Iannis Xenakis
Costumes: No credit listed
Dancers: Clyde Morgan, Carla Maxwell

- March 17, 1971
  The American Place Theater, St. Clement's Church, New York

Pinkville [stage play]

Writer: George Tabori
Director: Martin Fried
Music Composer and Director: Stanley Walden
Electronic Music: Jacob Druckman
Production/Lighting Design: Wolfgang Roth
Costumes: Ruth Morley
Cast: The Squad:

Jerry the Naz	Michael Douglas
The Honeychild	Milton Earl Forrest
Consequently Joe	Raul Julia
The Jock	Bob Lesser
Two Ton Tessie (The Sergeant)	James Tolkan
Suck Ass (Henchman)	Art Evans
Acting Jack (Henchman)	Constantine Katsanos
The Captain	Lane Smith
Papasan	Dimo Condos
The Girl	Barbara Tai Sing

- May 20, 1971
  The Juilliard American Opera Center, New York
  The Juilliard Theater

Huckleberry Finn [musical]

Libretto: Judah Stampfer and Hall Overton
Director: William Woodman

Music: Hall Overton
Costumes: Jeanne Button
Sets and Projections: Douglas W. Schmidt
Dancers: David Briggs, Jennifer Douglas, Margaret Fargnoli, Pamela Fialla, William Holcomb, Linda Levy, Dalienne Majors, Greg Mitchell, Marc Stevens

- November 12, 1971
  Juilliard Concert Hall, New York
  Juilliard Dance Ensemble

  Scenes from the Music of Charles Ives
  I. "Halloween"
  II. "Central Park in the Dark"
  III. "The Pond, in the Cage, the Pond"
  IV. "The Unanswered Question"

  Music: Charles Ives
  Costumes: John David Ridge
  Dancers: Pamela Fiala, Hannah Kahn, Linda Levy, Jane Lowe, Dalienne Majors, Risa Steinberg, Evan Williams, Angeline Wolfe, David Briggs, Gregory Mitchell, Marc Stevens, Christopher Pilafian, John Wohl, Richard Caceres

- June 12, 1971
  American Shakespeare Festival
  Stratford, Connecticut

  Merry Wives of Windsor [stage play]

  Writer: William Shakespeare
  No other information available

- August 5, 1971
  Loeb Theater, Harvard University, Cambridge, Massachusetts
  Players Project

  Metamorphosis [revision]

  Writer: Franz Kafka, adapted by John White
  Director: Anna Sokolow
  Music: Kenyon Hopkins, Robert Schumann, Beethoven
  Costumes: No credit listed
  Cast: Antonio Azito, Anne Hegira, James Kiernan, Jim May, Lorry May, Linda Rubinoff, Henry Smith

A Short Lecture and Demonstration on the Evolution of Ragtime as Presented by Jelly Roll Morton [revision]

Music: Jelly Roll Morton
Narrator: Antonio Azito
Piano: Henry Smith
Costumes: No credit listed
Dancers: Lorry May, Jim May

- February 23, 1972
  Virginia Commonwealth University, Richmond, Virginia
  Anna Sokolow's Players Project

Magritte, Magritte [revision]
    I. "The Lovers"
   II. "The Great War"
  III. "Discovery"
  IV. "The Troubled Sleeper"
   V. "The Ideas of the Acrobat"
  VI. "The Month of Harvest"
 VII. "The Threatened Assassin"
VIII. "The Red Model"

Music: Scriabin, Ravel, Liszt, Satie, Bal Musette
Poetry: John White, Paul Éluard, Edgar Allan Poe
Costumes: No credit listed
Dancers: Margaret Fargnoli, Charles Sumner Hayward, Henry Smith, Antonio Azito, Tonia Shimin, Jim May, Lorry May

- May 1973 [exact date unknown]
  Cubiculo Theatre, New York
  José Coronado and Phoebe Neville

Baile

Poetry: Federico García Lorca
Music: Silvestre Revueltas
Costumes: No credit listed
Dancer: José Coronado

- May 23, 1973
  Juilliard Concert Hall, New York
  Juilliard Dance Ensemble

Three Poems

Music: Joel Thome
Costumes: Guus Lighthart
Dancers: Dianne Hulbert, Patrice Regnier, Evan Williams, Debra Zalkind, Ann Crosset or Dian Dong, Jennifer Douglas, Jane Hedal, Yaeko Sasaki, Catherine Sullivan, Teri Weksler, Phillip Bond, Roderic Cranston, Robert Swinston, William Belle

- July 24, 1973
  Teatro del Ballet Folklorico de Mexico, Mexico City
  Ballet Independiente

  Homenaje a Federico García Lorca [Homage to Federico García Lorca]
    I. "Baile"
   II. "Duelo"
  III. "Son"

  Music: Silvestre Revueltas
  Poems: Federico García Lorca and Pablo Neruda
  Costumes: No credit listed
  Dancers: Bernardo Benitez, Raul Flores Canelo, Graciela Henríquez, Graciela Gonzalez, Eloisa Greene, Herminia Grootenboer, Patricia Infante, Anadel Lynton, Mario Malpica, Efrain Moya, Gladiola Orozco, Mario Rodriguez, Luis Zermeño

- December 3, 1973
  Nachmani Theatre, Tel Aviv
  Batsheva Dance Company

  Poem

  Music: Charles Ives
  Costume: No credit listed
  Dancer: William Louther

  In Memory of No. 52436

  Music: Tadeusz Baird
  Costume: No credit listed
  Dancer: Rina Schenfeld

- February 22, 1974
  ANTA Theater, New York
  José Limón Dance Company

Homage to Federico García Lorca [revision, a tribute to Federico García Lorca, Sylvestre Revueltas, and José Limón]
   I. "Baile"
  II. "Duelo"
 III. "Son"

Music: Sylvestre Revueltas
Poetry: Federico García Lorca
Costumes: José Coronado
Dancers: Rob Besserer, Robyn Cutler, Ronald Dunham, Laura Glenn, Ryland Jordan, Gary Masters, Fred Mathews, Carla Maxwell, Aaron Osborne, Marjorie Philpot, Jennifer Scanlon, Louis Solino, Risa Steinberg, Clay Taliaferro, Ann Vachon

- April 5, 1974
Juilliard Concert Hall, New York
Juilliard Dance Ensemble

Come, Come Travel With Dreams

Music: Alexander Scriabin
Costumes: Guus Lighthart
Dancers: Pierre Barreau, William Belle, Richard Caceres, Hsueh-Tung Chen, Ann Crosset, Dian Dong, Mary Lou Fager, Anthony Ferro, Jane Hedal, Joyce Herring, Mercie Hinton, Dianne Hulburt, Jaynie Katz, Nancy Mapother, Gregory Mitchell, Patrice Regnier, Andrew Roth, Linda Spriggs, Robert Swinston, Shelley Washington

- April 26, 1974
American Theatre Laboratory, New York
Annabelle Gamson solo concert

Quartertones

Music: Charles Ives
Costumes: No credit listed
Dancer: Annabelle Gamson

- May 18, 1974
Brooklyn Academy of Music, Brooklyn
Paul Sanasardo Dance Company

Ecuatorial [Equatorial]

Music: Edgard Varèse

Costumes: Alan Madsen
Dancers: Dominique Petit, Jacques Patarozzi, Diane Germaine, Willa Kahn, Joan Lombardi, Christine Varjan, Michelle Rebeaud, Gerri Houlihan, Judith Mercer

- August 8, 1974
  The Filene Center, Wolf Trap Farm Park for the Performing Arts, Vienna, Virginia

  A Cycle of Cities

  Music: Elie Siegmeister
  Dancers: Students of the Wolf Trap / American University Academy for the Performing Arts summer session

- February 1975 [exact date unknown]
  Portland, Maine
  Solo Concert

  Song

  Music: Gustav Mahler
  Costumes: No credit listed
  Dancer: Jane Kosminsky

- April 26, 1975
  Juilliard Theater, New York
  Juilliard Dance Ensemble

  Ride the Culture Loop

  Direction: Anna Sokolow
  Music: Teo Macero
  Costumes and Projections: Robert Yodice
  Dancers: Deborah Allton, Marilyn Banks, Yael Barash, Leslie Brown, Shirley Brown, Trude Cone, Helen Castillo, Yveline Cottez, Dian Dong, Thelma Drayton, Martina Ebey, Elizabeth Fisher, Mary Ann Golick, Nancy Hill, Janell Hollingsworth, Lisa Kerr, Ann Kohn Mare Lind, VV Dachin Matsuoka, Elizabeth McCarthy, Andrea Morris, Rosemary Newton, Valencia Ondes, Maria O'Neill, Revei Paul, Patrice Regnier, Ayala Rimon, Robin Somers, Linda Spriggs, Elizabeth Sung, Jill Wagoner, Anthony Balcena, Pierre Barreau, William Belle, Sam Berman, Hsueh-Tung Chen, Mercie Hinton, John Jackson, Allen Maniker, Andrew Miller, John Seaman

- May 15, 1975
  Theatre of the Riverside Church, New York
  Solo Concert

  Dreaming

  Music: Alexander Scriabin
  Costumes: No credit listed
  Dancer: Ze'eva Cohen

- May 18, 1975
  Kreeger Theater, Washington, D.C.
  Arena Stage

  The Dybbuk [stage play]

  Writer: S. Ansky
  Director: Gene Lesser
  Music: Robert Dennis
  Cast: Terrance Currier, Carl Don, Stanley Anderson, Max Wright, Leonardo Cimino, Howard Witt, Richard Bauer, Zviah Igdalsky, Elena Rimson, Michael Mertz, Dianne Wiest, Leslie Cass, Susan Stone Appleton, Ralph Glickman, Mark Hammer, Philip Mandelkorn, Robert Zukerman, Ruth Sadler, Halo Wines, David Garrison, Valorie Grear, Glenn Taylor, Gary Bayer, Robert Shilton, Robert Prosky, Max Jacobs, Bob Harper

- July 10, 1975
  The Place, London
  Student Group

  Remembrances

  Music: Franz Schubert
  No other information known

  Ode to Varèse

  Music: Edgard Varèse
  No other information known

- December 2, 1975
  American Place Theatre, New York
  Contemporary Dance System

  Moods

  Music: Gyorgy Ligeti

Costumes: No credit listed
Dancers: Pierre Barreau, Randall Faxon, Laura Glenn, Hannah Kahn, Victor Vargas, Teri Weksler, Ko'Yukihiro

- July 19, 1976
  Jerusalem Theatre
  Inbal

The Song of Songs

Music: Ben-Zion Orgad
Costumes: Shraga Weill
Dancers: Sara Shikarchi, Sion Nuriel, Amos Vituri, with Dalia Nadav, Drora Vitzman, Tamar Cohen, Ofra Flaksman, Aharon Sekarchi, Menashe Yakovian, Shimon Vitzman

- February 27, 1976
  Music Hall Center, Detroit

Seven Deadly Sins [revision, stage play]

Libretto: Bertolt Brecht
English Version: W.H. Auden and Chester Kallman
Director: Anna Sokolow
Music: Kurt Weill
Costumes: No credit listed
Cast: Cleo Laine and Mary Hinkson with Christopher Barron, Barbara Boyd, Drusilla Cagnoni, Mitzi Carol, Russ Cataldo, Barbara Early, Sabrina Jordon, Theresa Kowall, Charles Krause, Antoine McCoy, Gregg Radtke, Steve Raptis

- May 8, 1976
  Juilliard Theater, New York
  Juilliard Dance Ensemble

Ellis Island

Direction: Anna Sokolow
Music: Charles Ives
Poem: Emma Lazarus
Costumes and Sets: Robert Yodice
Dancers: Susan Allair, Marilyn Banks, Yael Barash, Teresa Coker, Trude Cone, Carolann Cortese, Yveline Cottez, Ann Crosset, Martina Ebey, Betsy Fisher, Jane Hedal, Janell Hollingsworth, Mary Ittelson, Ann Kohn, Jane Maloney, VV Dachin Matsuoka, Andrea Morris, Rosemary Newton, Valencia Ondes, Maria

O'Neill, Laurie Reese, Ayala Rimon, Susan Salinger, Elizabeth Sung, Leith Symington, Kathleen Tirrell, Jill Wagoner, Hsueh-Tung Chen, Anthony Balcena, Sam Berman, John Jackson, Russell Lome, Allen Maniker, Offer Sachs, Jack Waters

- July 19, 1976
Nachmani Theatre, Tel Aviv
Batsheva Dance Company

Poem of Ecstasy

Music: Alexander Scriabin
Costumes: Anna Sokolow
Dancers: Rina Schenfeld and Derek Linton

- December 3, 1976
Mandell Theater, Drexel University (Philadelphia)
South Street Dance Co.

Two Memories

Music: Justin Della Joio, Joel Thome
Costumes: Susan Lunenfeld
Dancers: Ellen Forman, Alice Forner, Judith Silverman, Michael Freed, Tom Brown, Lovice Weller, Paula Sepinuck, Nini Melvin

- January 29, 1977
Kirby Theater, Amherst College, Amherst, Massachusetts
Contemporary Dance System

Homage to Alexander Scriabin

Director and Creator: Anna Sokolow
Music and Poetry: Alexander Scriabin
Costumes: Robert Yodice
Actors: Tom Demastri, Nita Angeletti
Dancers: Pierre Barreau, Randall Faxon, Laura Glenn, Peter Healey, Hannah Kahn, Jim May, Victor Vargas, Teri Weksler

- May 7, 1977
Juilliard Theater, New York
Juilliard Dance Ensemble

The Holy Place

Music: Ernest Bloch
Costumes: Robert Yodice
Dancers: Susan Allair, Naomi Browar, Jane Carrington, Teresa Coker, Julia Dubno, Ellen Field, Julie French, Nan Friedman, Elizabeth Gooding, Barbara Gordon, Susan Jones, Lisa Miller, Judith Muldoon, Maria O'Neill, Judith Otter, Pamela Risenhoover, Susan Salinger, Denise Stampone, Leith Symington, Benjamin Greenberg, Neil Greenberg, Walter Kennedy, V. Keith Martin, Joseph Rich, Offer Sachs

- May 18, 1977
  Riverside Church, New York
  Sophie Maslow Dance Company

La Noche de los Mayas [*The Night of the Mayans*]

Music: Silvestre Revueltas
Costumes: Zoe
Dancers: Diane Chavan, Kimberly Dye, Karen Lashinsky, Nedra Marlin-Harris, Liz Rosner, Glenn Ferrigiari, Elmore Cisco James, Theodore Pollen III, Jerome Sarnat, Perry Souchuk

- June 4, 1977
  Gaillard Municipal Auditorium, Charleston, South Carolina
  Spoleto Festival, U.S.A.
  Contemporary Dance System

Poem [revision of *Homage to Alexander Scriabin*, 1977]

Music and Poetry: Alexander Scriabin
Reader: Laurence Guittard
Dancers: Pierre Barreau, Peter Healey, Victor Vargas, Randall Faxon, Hannah Kahn, Teri Weksler, Laura Glenn, Jim May

- June 29, 1977
  Colorado State College, Fort Collins, Colorado
  Repertory Dance Theatre (formerly Utah Repertory Dance Theatre)

Untitled [later *Poe*]
  I. "Alone"
  II. "Eureka"
  III. "Annabel Lee"
  IV. "Poe"

Music: Jacob Druckman, Frederic Chopin, Lou Harrison, Amadeo Roldan [added later]

Costumes: Marina Harris
Narrator: Michael Sloata
Dancers: Ellen Bromberg, Michael Kelly Bruce, Rich Burrows, Kay Clark, Martin Kravitz, Ruth Jean Post, Thom Scalise, Linda Smith, Karen Steele

- March 11, 1978
  Juilliard Theatre, New York
  Juilliard Dance Ensemble

  Songs Remembered

  Music: David Diamond
  Costumes: Judanna Lynn
  Dancers: Yael Barash, Brian Taylor, Maria O'Neill, Bruce Davis, Tzipora Levenboim, Jack Waters, Cynthia Morales, Rodney McGuire, Judith Otter, Jorge Trincheiras, Caroline Billings, Mary Duncan, Joan Karlen, Wendy Leo, Jennifer Lowe, Diane Simmons, Susan Allair, Teresa Coker, Julie French, Carol Lucas, Geraldine Meschino, Nina Ries, Nanette Ruggiero, Ann Westhoff, Amy Wynn, Yveline Cottez

- April 7, 1978
  Drama Theater, Juilliard Theater Center, New York
  The Theater Division Performance Project

  Poe [stage play]
    I. "Prologue"
    II. "Bells"
    III. "Annabel Lee"
    IV. "Alone"
    V. "Eureka"
  Director and Choreographer: Anna Sokolow
  Music: Frederic Chopin, Marianna Rosett, Sergei Rachmaninoff
  Text: Edgar Allan Poe
  Costumes: No credit listed
  Cast: Lisa Banes, Steve Bassett, James Curt Bergwall, Michael Butler, Sheila Dabney, William Deacutis, Janet DeMay, Kathryn Dowling, Boyd Gaines, Kathryn Grant, Anne Kerry, Steve Levitt, Mitch Litrofsky, Robert Lovitz, James Owen, Keith Williams, Denise Woods

- May 11, 1978
  The Music Hall, Boston
  The Boston Ballet

Visions of the Dark Night [revision of *Poe*, 1978]

Music: Tadeusz Baird
Costumes: Leslie Shaver
Dancers: Kathryn Anderson, Linda Bass, Carinne Binda, Lea Havas, Belinda Holt, Leslie Jonas, Pamela Royal, Rachel Whitman, David Drummond, Sheridan Heyns, Arthur Leeth, Clyde Nantais, James Reardon, Larry Robertson, Augustus Van Heerden

- September 2, 1978
  Jerusalem Theatre, Jerusalem
  Kibbutz Dance Company

Two Poems [also called *This Night*; inspired by the poetry of Leah Goldberg]
  I. "Remnants of Life"
  II. "With This Night"

Music: Mark Kopytman
Costumes: Bertha Kwartcz
Dancers: Timna Yeriel, Efrat Livni, Iris Frankel, Martha Reifeld, Zickri Dagan, Schlomo Zaga, Hagai Sortsky, Mike Levine

- October 12, 1978
  Nachmani Theatre, Tel Aviv
  Students of the Dance Department of the Jerusalem Rubin Academy of Music —
  on a program with Batsheva Dance Company

Homage to Gertrud

Music: Maurice Ravel
Costumes: No credit listed
Dancers: Dalia Barkai, Alice Cohen, Diana Eidelsztein, Daphne Einbinder, Liora Grossman, Miri Lavets, Talia Kadury, Liora Kusy, Evy Lifshitz, Anat Marnin, Michal Shahak, Nava Ziv, Anat Sharon

- February 16, 1979
  The Juilliard Theater, New York
  Juilliard Dance Ensemble

Así es la Vida en México [*This Is the Life in Mexico*]
  I. "La Noche de los Mayas" [revision]
  II. "Mercado" [premier]
     Baile
     Procession

Music: Silvestre Revueltas
Costumes: Daniel Michaelson
Dancers: Susan Allair, Caroline Billings, Jeanette Bolding, Kristen Borg, Teresa Coker, Jenny Coogan, Gregory DeJean, Jennifer Denham, Mary Duncan, Bambie Elmaleh de Buenos, Karen Ford, Julie French, David Fuerstenau, Joseph Garcia, Tanya Gibson, Stuart Gold, Robin Gray, Eloisa Greene, Elizabeth Harris, Barbara Hoon, Marilyn Johnson, Joan Karlen, Lilitte Knox, Francine Landes, Wendy Leo, Tzipora Levenboim, Carol Lucas, Elizabeth Maxwell, Dina McDermott, Rodney McGuire, Donna Miranda, Sylvia Morales, Donald Philpott, Madeleine Ribbing-Messihi, Kim Richardson, Nina Ries, Pamela Risenhoover, Michael Simon, Brian Taylor, Christopher Tuohy, Jack Waters, Julia Weitzer, Ann Westhoff, Lisa Woods, Amy Wynn

- February 18, 1979
  Colorado State University, Fort Collins, Colorado
  Theater Dance Trio

  Poem

  Music: Sergei Rachmaninoff
  Costumes: No credit listed
  Dancers: Lynda Davis, Clay Taliferro, Carol Warner

- April 21, 1979
  Chicago Dance Center, Chicago

  Opus '79

  Music: Teo Macero
  Costumes: Rod Johnston
  Dancers: Nolan Dennett, Danelle Helander, John Magill, Beth Pierce, Jesse Fred Shumway, Nana Solbrig, Mary Ward

- August 7, 1979
  YMCA Auditorium, Jerusalem — Seminar: "The Bible in Dance"
  Jerusalem Dance Workshop and students from the Jerusalem Academy

  From the "Song of Songs"

  Music: Sergei Rachmaninoff
  Costumes: No credit listed
  Dancers: Jacqueline Brailey-Marshall, Yaron Margolin, Atanasios Gadanidis, Tamara Melnik

  From the "Psalms"

Music: Gustav Mahler
Costumes: No credit listed
Dancers: Students of the Dance Department of the Jerusalem Rubin Academy
of Music

- October 6, 1979
  Haifa Municipal Theater, Haifa, Israel
  Haifa Municipal Theater with Batsheva 2 Dance Company

  Wings

  Text: Israel Eliraz
  Director and Choreographer: Anna Sokolow
  Music: Mark Kopytman
  Costumes: Gila Lahat
  Actors: Techia Danon, Rachel Marcus, Pinni Heller, Ezra Cafri, Ami Traub
  Dancers: Ron Ben-Israel, Atanasios Gadanidis, Irit Gold, Leora Grossman, Miri
  Javetz, Michal Israeli, Shai Levi, Shimson Kristal

- October 25, 1979
  Helen Carey Playhouse, Brooklyn Academy of Music, Brooklyn

  Homage to Scriabin

  Music: Alexander Scriabin
  Costumes: A. Christina Giannini
  Dancer: Naomi Sorkin

- November 14, 1979
  Camera Mart, Stage One, New York
  Dance Umbrella

  Kaddish [title used previously, but not a revision]

  Music: Olivier Messiaen
  Costumes: No credit listed
  Dancer: Naomi Sorkin

1980–1989

- March 14, 1980
  Juilliard Theater, New York
  Juilliard Dance Ensemble

Magritte, Magritte [revision]
   I. "The Lovers"
  II. "The Great War"
 III. "The Troubled Sleeper"
 IV. "The Ideas of the Acrobat"
  V. "The Threatened Assassin"
 VI. "The Red Model"

Music: Alexander Scriabin, Franz Liszt, Douglas Finch
Poetry: John White, Paul Éluard
Set: Calvin Morgan
Costumes: Judanna Lynn
Dancers: Elizabeth Maxwell, Morris Perry, Charles MacDonald, Joan Karlen, Michael Schumacher, Caroline Billings, Tzipora Levenboim, Stuart Gold, Ann Westhoff, Brian Taylor, Mark DeGarmo

• March 1980 [exact date unknown] Blackstone Theatre, Chicago
New York opening March 26, 1980

Clothes for a Summer Hotel [stage play]

Writer: Tennessee Williams
Director: José Quintero
Music: Michael Valenti
Dance Consultant: Anna Sokolow
Costumes: No credit listed
Cast (Principals): Geraldine Page, Kenneth Haigh, David Canary, Robert Black, Michael Connoly, Mary Doyle, Michael Granger

• May 8, 1980
Riverside Dance Festival, Riverside Church, New York
Rod Rodgers Dance Company

For Langston [Hughes]
   I. "My People"
  II. "Life Is Fine"
 III. "Tambourines"
 IV. "Feet o' Jesus"

Music: Teo Macero
Costumes: Vivian Jackson Jones
Dancers: Gina Ellis, Tamara Guillebeaux, Noel Hall, E. Laura Hausmann, Gregory Hinton, Craig Moore, Shirley Rushing, Edward Smith III, Broderick Wilson

- May 16, 1980
  Juilliard Theater Center, New York
  Students of Juilliard Theater Center

  From the Diaries of Franz Kafka [stage play]

  Director: Anna Sokolow
  Music: Robert Schumann, Gustav Mahler, Jewish liturgical Music, Arnold Schoenberg
  Costumes: No credit listed
  Cast: Kevin Bergman, David Bryant, James Eckhouse, Michele Farr, Barry Heins, Richard Howard, Robert Nadir, Pamela Nyberg, Jeffrey Rubin, Ascanio Sharpé, Neil Sims, Laura Smyth

- August 24, 1980
  Teatro de Estado, Jalapa, Mexico
  La Compania de Danza Contemporaria de la Universidad Veracruzana

  Llegada de la Primavera

  Music: Carlos Chavez
  Costumes: No credit listed
  Dancers: Contemporary Dance Company of University of Veracruz

- September 11, 1980
  National Institute of Fine Arts, Mexico City
  Compania de Danza, Raúl Flores Canelo, Director

  De los Diaros de Kafka [revision of *From the Diaries of Franz Kafka*]

  Director and Choreographer: Anna Sokolow
  Music: Robert Schumann, Arnold Schoenberg, Gustav Mahler, Ernest Bloch
  Text: Franz Kafka, Old Testament
  Costumes: No credit listed
  Dancers: Raúl Aguilar, Miriam Alerhand, Cecilia Baram, Blanca Gutiérrez, Benjamin Hierro, Jaime Hinojosa, Patricia Ladrón de Guevara, Araceli Maldonado, Socorro Meza, Efraín Moya, Dalia Próspero, Silvia Unzueta

- January 17, 1981
  University of California, Santa Barbara
  Repertory West Dance Company

  Preludes

  Music: Sergei Rachmaninoff
  Costume: Anna Sokolow
  Dancer: Tonia Shimin

- March 18, 1981
  The Concert Hall of the Abraham Goodman House, New York
  New Players' Project

Song of Deborah

Music: J. S. Bach
Costume: No credit listed
Performer: Aviva Davidson

Song of Songs

Music: Richard J. Neumann
Spoken by: Yossi Kipnis
Costume: No credit listed
Dancers: Dian Dong, Lynda Gudde, Leah Kreutzer, Michael Lengsfield, Tom d'Mastri, Jim May, Lorry May, Andrew Quinlan-Krichels, Kathleen Quinlan-Krichels, Stuart Smith

From the Diaries of Franz Kafka [revision]

Music: Robert Schumann, Gustav Mahler, Jewish liturgical music, Arnold Schoenberg
Costumes: No credit listed
Dancers: Entire company [see *Song of Songs*]

- April 3, 1981
  The Juilliard Theater, New York
  Juilliard Dance Ensemble

Los Conversos [*The Converted*]

Music: Richard J. Neumann
Costumes: Calvin Morgan
Dancers: Maria Alvarez, Hikari Baba, Anastasia Bain, Christopher Batenhorst, Jeanette Bolding, Bambie Elmaleh de Buenos, Mark DeGarmo, Sari Eckler, Linda Hubka, Margherite Johnson, Lilitte Knox, Jonathan Leinbach, Charles Mac-Donald, Clara Maxwell, Dina McDermott, Sylvia Morales, Sebastian Prantl, Nina Ries, Judy Schneier, Ann Emily Smith, Adrienne Stevens, George Wainwright, Megan Williams, Joseph Youngblood

- January 14, 1982
  Theatre Project, Baltimore
  Jeff Duncan Solo Concert

Three Preludes

Music: Sergei Rachmaninoff
Costumes: Gail Stewart
Dancer: Jeff Duncan

- March 18, 1982
  The Juilliard Theater, New York
  Juilliard Dance Ensemble

Everything Must Go

    I. "How ya doin?"
   II. "Honey, that's pretty"
  III. "Go for it!"
  IV. "Why?"

Music: Teo Macero
Costumes: James Bartek
Dancers: Anastasia Bain, Shell Benjamin, Gina Bonati, Diane Butler, Gregory Butler, Dennis Collado, Bambie Elmaleh De Buenos, Mark DeGarmo, Sari Eckler, Robbin Ford, Sandra Fuciarelli, Stuart Gold, Marilyn Johnson, Jonathan Leinbach, Charles Macdonald, Elizabeth Maxwell, Catherine Novak, Roberto Pace, Sebastian Prantl, Adrienne Stevens, George Wainwright, Charles Willett, Megan Williams

- March 19, 1982
  City College of New York
  Deborah Zall and Ze'eva Cohen shared concert

Kaddish [revision]

Music: Maurice Ravel
Costumes: No credit listed
Dancer: Deborah Zall

- April 22, 1982
  Bessie Schönberg Theater, Dance Theater Workshop, New York
  H. T. Dance Company (Chen Hsueh-Tung and dancers)

Nocturne

Music: Alexander Scriabin
Costumes: A. Christina Giannini
Dancers: Dian Dong, Chen Hsueh-Tung

- April 28, 1982
  Juilliard Theater, New York
  Juilliard Theater Center

  Love's Labor's Lost [stage play]

  Writer: William Shakespeare
  Director: Michael Langham
  Music: Craig Shuler
  Costumes: Mariann Verheyen
  Set: Kenneth Foy
  Cast: Marco Baricelli, Jack Stehlin, John Bunzel, Peter Crook, Nicholas Kilbertus, Paul Mackley, Timothy Monich, Jack Kenny, Gerald Gilmore, Penny Johnson, Leah Joki, Katherine Griffith, Megan Gallagher, Lili Flanders, Lorraine Toussaint, Joseph McGrath, Derek Hodel, Margaret Gibson, Tanya Pushkine

- May 20, 1982
  Marymount Theater, New York
  Mary Anthony Dance Theatre

  Elegy

  Music: Gustav Mahler
  Costumes: Gwendolyn Bye
  Dancers: Mary Anthony and Ross Parkes

- May 8, 1982
  Theresa L. Kaufmann Concert Hall, YM/YWHA, New York
  Jewish Opera at the Y

  Mikhoels the Wise [opera]

  Music: Bruce Adolphe
  Costumes: Mary Hayes
  Cast: Charles Abruzzo, David Anchel, Gerard Boyd, Ronald Corrado, Nancy Green, Marcy Jellison, Erie Mills, Joseph Penrod, Christine Radman, Michael Rosso, John West
  Dancers: Rae Ballard, Ron Hazard, Brooke Myers, John Proto

- July 6, 1982
  Bar Shira Auditorium, Tel Aviv
  Acting Studio Nissan Nativ [third year students]

  Los Marranos [dance/theater work]
    I. "The Secret Jews"

    II. "Lament"
   III. "Spinoza"
   IV. "Durme, durme" [Sleep, my beloved]
    V. "Survival"

Director: Anna Sokolow
Music: Ladino Folk-songs
Cast: Ilana Badash, Ofer Ben-Dor (guest), Yoav Dalal, Yael Feiler (guest), Orna Gelfand, Abraham Horowitz, Zippora Lichtenstein, Vicky Moran, Lior Nachman, Danny Roth

- September 6, 1982
  Mann Theatre, Tel Aviv
  Batsheva Dance Company

Les Noces

Music: Igor Stravinsky
Costumes: Yemima Kessler
Dancers: Sheli Shir, David Dvir, Nira Trifton, Oded Harari, Alice Dor-Cohen, Amir Kolban, with Haim On, Iris Gil, Nathan Gerda, Erez Levi, Gil Nagrin, Galia Fabin, Geri Feingold, Iris Frenkel, Retto Schleininger, Yossi Tmim

- October 6, 1982
  Bellas Artes Theatre, Mexico City
  Ballet Independiente [Homage to Anna Sokolow with works of her own creation]

Poema [Dedicated to Isadora Duncan]

Music: Sergei Rachmaninoff
Costumes: No credit listed
Dancers: Evelia Beristain, Jaime Hinojosa, Corenelio Laguna, Socorro Meza, Javier Romero, Sara Salazar, Carlos Tulosa, Silvia Unzueta

- January 27, 1983
  Harold Clurman Theatre, New York
  Players' Project

Hannah [dance/theater, revision of *Wings*, 1979]

Writer: Israel Eliraz
Director: Anna Sokolow
Music: Mark Kopytman

Costumes: Ruth Morley
Actors: Blanche Baker, Lois Smith, Stephen Lang
Dancers: Leah Kreutzer, Andrew Krichels, Jim May, Lorry May, Kathleen Quinlan, Stuart Smith, Susan Thomasson

- March 17, 1983
  The Juilliard Theater, New York
  Juilliard Dance Ensemble

Four Preludes

Music: Sergei Rachmaninoff
Costumes: John Lee
Dancers: Christopher Batenhorst, Laura Colby, Dennis Collado, Francie Huber, Margherite Johnson, Jonathan Leinbach, Charles MacDonald, Clara Maxwell

- November 16, 1983
  Joyce Theater, New York
  Eleo Pomare Dance Company

Transfigured Night

Music: Arnold Schoenberg
Costumes: Eleo Pomare
Dancers: Andrea Borak, Quentin Clark, Dyane Harvey, Roxane D'Orleans Juste, Monique Mannen, Deborah Redd, Thomas Reid, Peter Roche, Robert Todd, Leni Wylliams

- November 23, 1983
  Theater of the Riverside Church, New York
  Players' Project

Piano Preludes

Music: George Gershwin
Costumes: No credit listed
Dancers: Bill Cratty, Dian Dong, Andrew Krichels, Jim May, Lorry May, Kathleen Quinlan, Stuart Smith, Susan Thomasson

- January 5, 1984
  Riverside Church, New York
  Daniel Lewis Dance Repertory Company

As I Remember [revisions]
    I. "Lament for the Death of a Bullfighter"

    II. "Ballad in a Popular Style"
    III. "Kaddish"

Music: Silvestre Revueltas, Chick Corea, Maurice Ravel
Costumes: No credit listed
Dancers: Jane Carrington, Evelyn Shepard, Risa Steinberg

- September 25, 1984
  Palace of Fine Arts, Mexico City

  Homenaje a David Alfaro Siqueiros [*Homage to David Alfaro Siqueiros*]

  Conceived by Adriana Siqueiros
  Music: Silvestre Revueltas, Carlos Chávez, Rafael Elizondo
  Poems: Pablo Neruda, Rafael Alberti, Paul Éluard, Rodolfo Mier Tonche
  Costumes: No credit listed
  Dancers: Nallé-Li Cepeda, Magno Caballero, Margarita Dardón, Marcela Flores, Perla Fuentes, Pedro García, Eloisa Greene, Lorena Hernández, Martin Marmolejo, Ivón Muchoz, Verónica Patiño, Victor Hugo Paz, Claudia Suárez, Hilda Servin, Oscar Velázquez, Luis Gabriel Zaragoza

- December 5, 1984
  Theater of the Riverside Church, New York
  Players' Project

  Steps of Silence [complete revision]

  Text: Alexander Solzhenitsyn
  Music: Anatol Vieru
  Voice: Larry Robinson
  Costumes: No credit listed
  Dancers: Dian Dong, Larry Hahn, Andrew Krichels, Lorry May, John Passafiume, Kathleen Quinlan, Stuart Smith, Risa Steinberg, Susan Thomasson

- March 16, 1985
  The Juilliard Theater, New York
  Juilliard Dance Ensemble
  Magritte, Magritte [revision]
      I. "The Lovers"
      II. "The Great War"
      III. "The Troubled Sleeper"
      IV. "The Ideas of the Acrobat"
      V. "The Threatened Assassin"

VI. "The Red Model"

Music: Liszt, Satie, Scriabin, Thome, and French music hall ballads
Poetry and Script: John White
Set: Calvin Morgan
Costumes: Judanna Lynn
Dancers: Gina Bonati, Sara Bragdon, Vincent Brosseau, Chad Courtney, Amy Cypiot, Andrea Feier, Suzanne Harris, James Jeon, Jonathan Kane, Vernon Scott

- June 20, 1985
  The Place Theatre, London
  Dublin City Ballet

Homage to John Field

Music: John Field
Costumes: No credit listed
Dancers: Nicola Anthony, Tim Clarke, Kelvin Warren, Tara Syed

- July 9, 1985
  Peacock Theatre, Dublin
  Dublin City Ballet

Transfigured Night [revision]

Music: Arnold Schoenberg
Dancers: Anne E. Courtney, Nicola Anthony, Tim Clarke, Tracey Ellis, Tony Moss, Tara Syed, Fiona Quilligan, Kelvin Warren, John Scott, Donnachadh McCarthy, Mirune Bloomer, Penny Dormer, Aideen Gohery, Laura Macken, Adrienne Browne, Jackie O'Donoghoe

- October 3, 1985
  Kresge Theatre, Carnegie-Mellon University, Pittsburgh

One Who Cared: An Homage to Janusz Korczak [dance drama]

Libretto: Matti Megged
Direction by: Anna Sokolow
Music: Joel Thome
Backdrop: Projection of "The Warsaw Woodcuts" by Bruce Carter
Costumes: Terri Fluker
Cast: Anne Altieri, Shiras P. Beckwith, Deirdre Berry, Kevin Black, Anne Capron, Jill Christy, Judith Anne Conte, Orit Greenberg, Illyssa Haas, Mollie Halpern, Michael Hartson, Yossi Kipnis, Angela Pasqualino, Marcus Lovett,

Sydney Sidner, Lisa Siegel, Jason Turley, Craig Waletzco, Ming-Na Wen, Court Whisman, Tom Willmorth, Thomas Mills Wood, Robert A. Wornoff, Lisa Wurzel

- December 11, 1985
  Theater of the Riverside Church, New York
  Players' Project

Homage to Edgar Allan Poe [complete revision]

Music: Sergei Rachmaninoff
Costumes: Eiko Yamaguchi
Dancers: Dian Dong, Larry Hahn, Andrew Krichels, Jim May, Lorry May, Kathleen Quinlan, John Passafiume, Stuart Smith, Susan Thomasson

- May 18, 1986
  Jewish Community Center of Omaha
  Student Group "Young Dancers Workshop"

Two Poems

Music: Franz Schubert, Sergei Rachmaninoff
Dancers: Rikki Epstein, Dana Erman, Julie Gutnik, Andrea Kotok, Nicole Lerner, Sarah Malena, Leigh Mossman, Lisa Niederhaus, Amy Perlmeter, Kelly Pollard, Megan Sears, Ann Silverman, Angie Weaver, Lindsey Weinberg, Kari Wittman, Angela Yaffe, Rachel Bennett, Lisa Burns, Julie Challender, Rebecca Goldstein, Jill Hoover, Debbie Kirshenbaum, Jill Larson, Elizabeth Mellor, Miki Penner

- September 20, 1986
  Joyce Theater, New York
  A Gala Benefit Performance Honoring Anna Sokolow

Kaddish [revision]

Music: Maurice Ravel
Costumes: No credit listed
Dancers: Mor Eden, Lorry May, Dian Dong, Susan Thomasson

- November 26, 1986
  Riverside Church, New York
  Players' Project

Ellis Island [revision]

Music: Charles Ives

Costumes: No credit listed
Dancers: Dian Dong, Lorry May, Susan Thomasson, Solvieg Olson, John Passafiume, H.T. Chen, Jim May, Stuart Smith

* May 25, 1987
  Riverside Church, New York
  Joint Concert, Lori Belilove and Evelyn Shepard

Two Preludes

Music: Sergei Rachmaninoff
Costumes: No credit listed
Dancer: Evelyn Shepard

* May 30, 1987
  Gusman Center for the Performing Arts, Miami
  Ballet Concerto and Wolfson Campus of Miami-Dade Community College

Golda Meir: Ideals and Dreams [dance/drama]

Project Director: Vera Dubson
Libretto: David Eden
Music: Joel Thome
Choreography and Costumes: Anna Sokolow
Cast:

Golda	Velia Martinez
Little Golda	Susana Pernas
Golda's Grandmother	Tessie Arregui

Dancers: Carolina Cosculluela, Tania Diaz, Carlos Gonzalez, Elizabeth Lambert-Baker, Jorge Lugo, Hilda Maria Riera, Felix Romeo with Rina Estela Diaz, Martha Pujol, Janet Rodriguez, Andy Rosenfeld, Mitzouko Alvarez, James Arminio, Raul Concepcion, Ana Martha Curnow, Shirley Franco, Rita Martinez, Norma Mojicar, Vivian Narganes, Denise Pinera, Miriam Valiente

* December 10, 1987
  Florida International University, VH 100, Miami
  Momentum Dance Company

Poems of Scriabin

Music: Alexander Scriabin
Costumes: Marilyn Skow
Dancers: Andrea Seidel, Lee Brooke, Sheila Connelly, Delma Iles, Paul Mockovak

- January 4, 1988
  Buttenweiser Hall, YM/YWHA, New York
  Players' Project

  Kurt Weill

    I. "Youkali Tango"
   II. "Surabaya Johnny"
  III. "String Quartet No. 1, Op. 8"
   IV. "Moon-Faced, Starry-Eyed"
    V. "The Soldier's Wife"
   VI. "Matrosen-Tango"

  Music: Kurt Weill
  Costumes: Stuart Smith
  Dancers: Dian Dong, Lorry May, Susan Thomasson, Evelyn Shepard, Mary Gambardella, Jim May, Stuart Smith, John Passafiume, Hugh Murphy, Steven Beckon

- February 2, 1988
  Joyce Theater, New York
  José Limón Dance Company

  Poems

  Music: Sergei Rachmaninoff
  Costumes Supervised by: David Guthrie
  Dancers: Bambi Anderson, Michael Blake, Colin Conner, Roxanne D'Orleans Juste, Stuart Gold, Jonathan Leinbach, Gary Masters, Carla Maxwell, Carlos Orta, Nina Watt

- March 6, 1988
  St. Bartholomew's Episcopal Church, New York
  Juilliard Dance Ensemble

  The Stations of The Cross

  Music: Marcel Dupré
  Dancers: Brian Hawthorne as Jesus with Yoav Kaddar, Marc Kenison, Ronald Wright, Nancy Bannon, Laura Doughty, Rachael Durham, Fuensanta Gutierrez, Sarah Hedrick, Nanci Holden, Kristina Isabelle, Amy Kail, Christina Morrissey, Laura Staton, Sarah Suatoni, Sally Sullivan, Eryn Trudell

- May 18, 1989
  Triangle Theater, Brooklyn
  Diane Jacobowitz Dance Theater

Three Songs
  I. "Song of Lament"
 II. "Song of Joy"
III. "Song of Love"

Music: Gustav Mahler, Ernest Bloch
Costumes: Mary Catalina
Dancers: Felice Dalgin, Mohammed Drissi, Roberto Garcia, Diane Jacobowitz, Christine Jowers, Jill Marotta, Irene Morawski, Michael Moses, James Reedy, Sean Russo

• October 30, 1989
  Small Hall, Jerusalem Theatre, Jerusalem
  Presented by Amphi Center

Song of Machpelah [dance / theater]

Writer and Director: Philip Diskin
Music: Tsippi Fleischer, Ayal Meni
Costumes: No credit listed
Cast:
Dancers: Mordechai Abrahamov, Ofer Halaf, Hagit Raphaeli, Ziva Shohet, Albert Suisse
Speakers: Rosalind Gelcer, Arthur Ingram, Khalil Khaled, Hanna Yaffe, Robin Twyte

1990–1996

• February 22, 1990
  The Boston Conservatory Theater
  The Boston Conservatory
  The Seven Deadly Sins [revision]
  Music: Kurt Weill
  Libretto: Bertolt Brecht
  Costume and Set design: Roland Guidry
  Cast: Singing Anna   Lisa Lochart
  Dancing Anna   Marianne Kowalaski
  Dancers: Joe Abatecola, Scott Elliot, Liz Fasnacht, Joe Ferraro, Krissy Mulvaney, Andrea Salerno, Omayra Amaya, Gabriella Chiaravalla, Christopher DeNofrio, Joe Ferraro, Christine Jenks, James Keene

- April 13, 1990
  The Church of Our Savior
  Players' Project

  The Stations of the Cross [revision]

  Music: Marcel Dupré
  Costumes: No credit listed
  Dancers: Lorry May, Nancy Happel, Ghondra Dharmaperwira, Eleanor Bunker, John Passafiume, Alex Dolcemasculo, Eric Hess, Stephen Welsh, Shawn Gannon, Eric Hoisington

- October 31, 1991
  Marymount Manhattan Theater, New York
  Anna Sokolow's Players' Project

  Street

  Music: Joe Reiser
  Percussion: David Lewitt
  Engineer: Gary Horowitz
  Text: Langston Hughes
  Voice: Kenneth Barnes-French
  Dancers: Susan Thomasson, John Passafiume, Lauren Naslund, Gonda Dharmaperwira, Miles Everett, Clarence Brooks, Eleanor Bunker

- January 23, 1992
  The Juilliard Theater, Lincoln Center, New York
  Dance Workshop: The Juilliard School – Dance Division

  Reflections

  Music: Jacob Druckman, "Reflections On the Nature of Water"
  Dancers: Marcin Baczyk, Meng-Chen Chang, Jennifer McKelvey, Christina Paolucci

- May 30, 1992
  Harry Dujour Playhouse
  Henry Street Settlement, New York City

  Forgotten Melodies (Ode to Martha)

  Music by Nikolai Medtner (*Vergessene Weissen, op. 39*)
  Costumes: Anna Sokolow and Mino Nicolas
  "Meditation" — Mino Nicolas

"Primavera" — Randi Meares
"Romance" — Mino Nicolas and Julie Pollino
"Tragica" — Kacie Chang

- March 16, 1993
  HB Playwrights Foundation, New York City

  Homage to Edgar Allen Poe [Second complete revision]

  Music: Joseph Reiser
  Text: Fritz Weaver
  Scenic and Lighting Designer: Rick Martin
  Costumes: Tamar Cohn
  Technical Director: Wayne Kruse
  Dancers: Charles Black, Brett De Hart, Stacey Forsyth, Mari Mar Gomez, Julie Jin, Rebecca Milburn, Lauren Naslund, Rafael Quiles, Egypt Reale, Russell Rottkamp, Jon Shipley
  Principal Dancer: Jim May

- May 26, 1994
  Dia Center for the Arts, New York City

  Shir Hashirim (Song of Songs)

  Music: Arvo Part, Sergel Rachmaninov, Francis Poulenc, Bedrich Smetana
  Dancers: Lorry May, Jim May

- September 17, 1994
  The Sylvia and Danny Kaye Playhouse, New York
  A Dance Theater Concert; Poems, Proverbs, Prayers
  Bertram Ross, Deborah Zall with John Giudice
  The concert dedicated to Estelle Sommers

  Poem (from *Song of Songs*)

  Music: Ernest Bloch
  Costume: A. Christina Giannini
  Dancer: Deborah Zall

- March 2, 1995
  Playhouse 91, New York
  Anna Sokolow's Players' Project

September Sonnet [Revision of *Shir Hashirim*, 1994]

Linda Diamond and Company

Music: Arvo Part, Sergei Rachmaninov, Francis Poulenc, Robert Schumann
Costumes: Natasha Guruleva
Dancers: Lorry May, Jim May

- April 2, 1995
  92nd Street Y
  Perspectives in Motion — Ann Moradian Artistic Director

  Four Songs

  Music: Nocture — Paul Ben-Haim
  Polka — Marc Lavry
  Love Song — Traditional Ladino, Played and sung by Chaim Freiberg
  The Land of My Dreams — Naomi Shemer
  Dancers: Eleanor Bunker, Ann Moradian, Stephanie Nelson, Janet Wong

- May 3, 1995
  Home of Feliz and Fortuna Roth, New York City
  Linda Diamond and Company

  Como la Luna y el Sol

  Music: Sephardic Spanish music
  Dancers: Lois Silk, Max Gough, Linda Diamond and Brian Waite

- May 5, 1996
  Rubin Academy, Jerusalem
  Springboard Dance Camp

  Homage to Gertrud Krauss

- December 31, 1996
  Beyondance Company (New Jersey)

  Homage to Rachmaninoff

  Music: Rachmaninoff
  Dancers: Trish King, Coleen McArdle, Jo Ann Stugaard-Jones

- January 25, 1997
  Sephardic House, New York City

  Durme, durme

Music: Traditional, sung by Portuna; accompanied by Chaim Freiberg
Costumes: Linda Diamond
Dancers: Christianne Brown, Faith Hunter, Linda Diamond

Dedications and Homages

Through the years Anna has dedicated many of her works to people she has admired and felt a special kinship to:
Isadora Duncan; John Field; Anne Frank; Miguel Hidalgo; Louis Horst; Langston Hughes; Franz Kafka; Martin Luther King; Janos Korczak; José Limón; Federico García Lorca; René Magritte; Golda Meir; Vaslav Nijinsky; Bishop James Alber Pike; Silvestre Revueltas; Alexander Scriabin; Hannah Senesh; David Siqueiros; Edgard Varèse; and her parents, Sarah and Samuel Sokolow

Several years after she created *Lyric Suite* Anna dedicated the first two movements to Vaslav Nijinsky and Isadora Duncan. The Presto Delirando was also later dedicated to Franz Kafka.

FILM AND VIDEO RECORDINGS

Partial List

Dates refer to production dates, not necessarily when work was choreographed.

Act Without Words No. 1
(Television, 1/26/70, "Isolation—Two Views")

Writer: Samuel Beckett
Director and Choreographer: Anna Sokolow
Music: Joel Thome
Costumes: No credit listed
Dancer: Rex Bickmore

And the Disciples Departed
(Television, 3/24/67, WBZ-TV, Group W, Boston, Massachusetts)
Winner of Broadcast Media Award

Writer and Narrator: Barry Ulanov
Director: Thomas J. Knott
Music: Teo Macero
Choreography: Anna Sokolow
Costumes: No credit listed
Set Design: Lou Bortone
Dancers: Margaret Cicierska, Martha Clarke, Ze'eva Cohen, Ray Cook, Edward
David Krohn, Lenore Latimer, Clyde Morgan, John Parks, Trina Parks, Kathryn
Posin, Juan Antonio Rodea

Anna Sokolow, Choreographer
(Television, 11/27/77, CBS-TV, "Camera Three")
Tribute

Narrator: Uta Hagen

Anna Sokolow Directs—"Odes"
(Film, 1972, 38 min.)

Film: David Parker
Music: Edgard Varèse
Choreography: Anna Sokolow
Costumes: Charles Tomlinson
Dancers: The (Ohio State) University Dance Group with Susannah Newman and
James Payton

Así es la Vida en México
(Film, 1979, 16mm, b&w, MH/JS)
    I. La Noche de los Mayas
    II. Mercado
    III. Baile
    IV. Procession

Film: Dwight Godwin
Production and Filming Supervision: Martha Hill
Music: Silvestre Revueltas
Choreography: Anna Sokolow
Costumes: Daniel Michaelson
Dancers: Juilliard Dance Ensemble

Ballade
(Film, 1965, 12.5 min., 16mm, b&w, MH/JS)

Film: Dwight Godwin
Production and Filming Supervision: Martha Hill
Music: Alexander Scriabin
Choreography: Anna Sokolow
Costumes: Charles Tomlinson
Dancers: Juilliard Dance Ensemble

Bullfight
(Film, 1957, 9 min. color)

Film: Shirley Clarke
Music: Norman Lloyd
Choreographer and Dancer: Anna Sokolow
Costume: Rose Bank

The Celebrations
(Television, 1/15/67, CBS-TV, "Look Up and Live," 84 min., 16mm, b&w)
    I. Work
   II. Love
  III. Leisure

Writer: Ralph Moore
Director: Portman Paget
Music: Ed Summerlin
Choreography: Anna Sokolow
Narrator: Lawrence Pressman
Costumes: No credit listed
Dancers: Anna Sokolow Dance Company

Come, Come Travel With Dreams
(Film, 1974, 16mm, b&w, MH/JS)
Film: Dwight Godwin
Production and Filming Supervision: Martha Hill
Music: Alexander Scriabin
Choreography: Anna Sokolow
Costumes: Guus Lighthart
Dancers: Juilliard Dance Ensemble

Constructive Rebellion
(Television, 12/30/68, Channel 2—Pittsburgh, Pennsylvania, Group W) A juxta-position of dance and architecture with Anna's dancers at Frank Lloyd Wright's Falling Water

Director: Thomas J. Knott
Choreography: Anna Sokolow
Costumes: No credit listed
Dancers: Anna Sokolow Dance Company

Court of Pharoah [*La Corte de Faraon*]
(Film, 1945)

Director: Julio Bracho
Choreography: Anna Sokolow
Costumes: No credit listed
Dancers: "Las Sokolovas"

Dance: Anna Sokolow's "Rooms"
(Film, 1966, 30 min., 16mm, b&w, NET-TV, "USA: DANCE" Series #5)

Director: Dave Geisel
Introduction Written by Clive Barnes
Choreography: Anna Sokolow
Costumes: No credit listed
Dancers: Ze'eva Cohen, Jack Moore, Jeff Duncan, Peggy Cicierska, Martha Clarke, Kathy Posin, Ray Cook, Chester Wolenski

Dance: Robert Joffrey Ballet
(Videotape, NET-TV, "USA: DANCE" Series #3, 30 min.)
(Film, 1965, 30 min., 16mm, b&w)

Director: Charles S. Dubin
Choreography: Robert Joffrey, Gerald Arpino, Anna Sokolow
Costumes: No credit listed
Dancers: Robert Joffrey Ballet Company
Includes excerpts from *Pas de Déesses* and *Gamelan* (Joffrey), *Opus '65* (Sokolow), *Incubus* and *Viva Vivaldi* (Arpino)

Dance, New York Style
(Videotape, Show #5, 1976 [?])

No other information available

Deserts
(Film, 1983, 16mm, b&w, MH/JS)

Film: Dwight Godwin
Production and Filming Supervision: Martha Hill
Music: Edgard Varèse
Choreography: Anna Sokolow
Costumes: John Lee
Dancers: Juilliard Dance Ensemble

Desiertos
(Film, 1968, Mexico)

Film: Paul Le Duc
Choreographer: Anna Sokolow
Costumes: Raúl Flores Canelo
Dancers: Ballet Independiente

The Dove
(Film, 1970, 16 min., 16mm, b&w, MH/JS)

Film: Dwight Godwin
Production and Filming Supervision: Martha Hill
Music: Cristóbal Halffter
Choreography: Anna Sokolow
Costumes: No credit listed
Dancers: Juilliard Dance Ensemble

Dreams
(Television, 12/4/77, CBS-TV, "Camera Three")

Film: Roger Englander
Music: Bach, Macero, Webern
Choreographer: Anna Sokolow
Costumes: No credit listed
Dancers: Contemporary Dance System

The Dybbuk
(Television, 10/3–9/60, WNTA-TV, "Play of the Week")

Movement arranged by Anna Sokolow
Cast: Carol Lawrence and others

Echoes
(Film, 1969, 16mm, b&w, MH/JS)

Film: Dwight Godwin
Production and Filming Supervision: Martha Hill
Music: John Weinzweig
Choreography: Anna Sokolow
Costumes: No credit listed
Dancers: Juilliard Dance Ensemble

Ellis Island
(Film, 1976, 16mm, b&w, MH/JS)

Film: Dwight Godwin
Production and Filming Supervision: Martha Hill
Music: Charles Ives
Choreography: Anna Sokolow
Set and Costumes: Robert Yodice
Dancers: Juilliard Dance Ensemble

Everything Must Go
(Film, 1982, 16mm, b&w, MH/JS)

Film: Dwight Godwin
Production and Filming Supervision: Martha Hill
Music: Teo Macero
Choreography: Anna Sokolow
Set and Costumes: James Bartek
Dancers: Juilliard Dance Ensemble

Far Rockaway
(Television, 9/22/65, WNET-TV)

Music: George Rochberg
Choreographer: Anna Sokolow
Costumes: No credit listed
Dancers: Julie Arenal, Jeff Duncan, Jack Moore, Chester Wolenski,
Linda Tarnay

Four Preludes
(Film, 1983, 16mm, b&w, MH/JS)

Film: Dwight Godwin
Production and Filming Supervision: Martha Hill
Music: Sergei Rachmaninoff
Choreography: Anna Sokolow
Costumes: John Lee
Dancers: Juilliard Dance Ensemble

The Holy Place
(Film, 1977, 16mm, b&w, MH/JS)

Film: Dwight Godwin
Production and Filming Supervision: Martha Hill
Music: Ernest Bloch
Choreography: Anna Sokolow
Costumes: Robert Yodice
Dancers: Juilliard Dance Ensemble

In Rehearsal: The Cycle of Cities
(Videotape, 1974, documentary, 28 min.)

Director: Nancy Gleason
Music: Elie Siegmeister

Choreography: Anna Sokolow
Costumes: No credit listed
Dancers: Wolf Trap Summer Company

Lamp Unto My Feet
(Television, 1948, CBS)

Los Conversos
(Videotape, 1981, MH/JS)

Music: Richard J. Neuman
Choreography: Anna Sokolow
Costumes: Calvin Morgan
Dancers: Juilliard Dance Ensemble

Lyric Suite
(Videotape, 1974, 33 min., sd., b&w)

Music: Alban Berg
Choreography: Anna Sokolow
Costumes: Juilliard School
Dancers: Miguel Godreau, Hannah Kahn, Laura Glenn, Shelley Washington, Peter Sparling, Edward De Soto, Teri Weksler

Lyric Suite
(Film, 1972, 29.5 min., 16mm, b&w, MH/JS)

Film: Dwight Godwin
Production and Filming Supervision: Martha Hill
Music: Alban Berg
Choreography: Anna Sokolow
Costumes: No credit listed
Dancers: Juilliard Dance Ensemble

Magritte, Magritte
(Film, 1980, 16mm, b&w, MH/JS)

Film: Dwight Godwin
Production and Filming Supervision: Martha Hill
Music: Scriabin, Liszt, Douglas Finch
Choreography: Anna Sokolow
Costumes: Judanna Lynn
Dancers: Juilliard Dance Ensemble

Magritte, Magritte
(Film, 1972, Netherlands, Umbrella Productions)

Music: Scriabin, Lizst, Charles Summer Hayward, Hazel Masiello
Choreography: Anna Sokolow
Costumes: No credit listed
Dancers: Players Project

Memories
(Film, 1967, 22 min., 16mm, b&w, MH/JS)

Film: Dwight Godwin
Production and Filming Supervision: Martha Hill
Music: Teo Macero
Choreography: Anna Sokolow
Costumes: No credit listed
Dancers: Juilliard Dance Ensemble

A Moment in Love
(Film, 1957, 9 min., color)

Film: Shirley Clarke
Music: Norman Lloyd
Choreography: Anna Sokolow
Costumes: No credit listed
Dancers: Paul Sanasardo, Carmen Gutierrez

Night
(Film, 1966, 15 min., 16mm, b&w, MH/JS)

Film: Dwight Godwin
Production and Filming Supervision: Martha Hill
Music: Luciano Berio
Choreography: Anna Sokolow
Costumes: Ashley Bryan
Dancers: Juilliard Dance Ensemble

Odes
(Film, 1965, 21 min., 16mm, b&w, MH/JS)

Film: Dwight Godwin
Production and Filming Supervision: Martha Hill
Music: Edgard Varèse

Choreography: Anna Sokolow
Costumes: Charles Tomlinson
Dancers: Juilliard Dance Ensemble

Opus Op
(Film, 1967, King Screen, 20 min., color, documentary)
Includes a performance of *Opus '65* to rock music by Crome Syrkus and audience reaction

Director: Lazlo Pal
Choreography: Anna Sokolow
Costumes: No credit listed
Dancers: Robert Joffrey Ballet Company

Opus '63
(Film, 1963, 23 min., 16mm, b&w)

Film: Dwight Godwin
Production and Filming Supervision: Martha Hill
Music: Teo Macero
Choreography: Anna Sokolow
Costumes: No credit listed
Dancers: Juilliard Dance Ensemble

Queen Esther
(Television, 3/13/60, WCBS-TV, "Lamp unto my Feet")

Director: James MacAllen
Music: Robert Starer
Text: Bible
Costumes: Ann Eckert
Choreography: Anna Sokolow
Narrators: Dina Doronne, Arik Lavie
Costumes: No credit listed
Dancers: Juki Arkin, Schlomo Bachar, Avraham Elber, Kate Friedlich, Jack Moore, Nira Paaz, Noel Schwartz, Neima Zweil

The Question
(Film, 1965, 22 min., 16mm, b&w)

Film: Dwight Godwin
Production and Filming Supervision: Martha Hill
Music: Anton Webern

Choreography: Anna Sokolow
Costumes: No credit listed
Dancers: Juilliard Dance Ensemble

Ride the Culture Loop
(Film, 1975, 16mm, b&w, MH/JS)

Film: Dwight Godwin
Production and Filming Supervision: Martha Hill
Music: Teo Macero
Choreography: Anna Sokolow
Costumes: Robert Yodice
Dancers: Juilliard Dance Ensemble

Rooms
(Film, 1977, 16mm, b&w, MH/JS)

Film: Dwight Godwin
Production and Filming Supervision: Martha Hill
Music: Kenyon Hopkins
Choreography: Anna Sokolow
Costumes: No credit listed
Dancers: Juilliard Dance Ensemble

Scenes from the Music of Charles Ives
(Film, 1971, 23 min., 16mm, b&w)

Film: Dwight Godwin
Production and Filming Supervision: Martha Hill
Music: Charles Ives
Choreography: Anna Sokolow
Costumes: John David Ridge
Dancers: Juilliard Dance Ensemble

Session for Six
(Film, 1964, 9 min., 16mm, b&w)

Film: Dwight Godwin
Production and Filming Supervision: Martha Hill
Music: Teo Macero
Choreography: Anna Sokolow
Costumes: No credit listed
Dancers: Juilliard Dance Ensemble

Sokolow Choreographs Weill
(Videotape, 1988, documentary)

Video: Vicki Seitchik
Dancers: Players' Project

Sokolow Rehearses Charles Ives
(Television, 1/14/72, London BBC-2)
Music: Charles Ives
Choreography: Anna Sokolow
Dancers: London Contemporary Dance Theatre

The Song of Songs
(Film, 1959, 30 min., 16mm, b&w)
(Television, 4/26/59, *Look Up and Live*, WCBS-TV)

Director: Tim Kiley
Music: Ezra Laderman
Choreography: Anna Sokolow
Settings: Bob Markell
Costumes: Ann Eckert
Dancers: Anna Sokolow Dance Company

Songs Remembered
(Film, 1978, 16mm, b&w, MH/JS)

Film: Dwight Godwin
Production and Filming Supervision: Martha Hill
Music: David Diamond
Choreography: Anna Sokolow
Costumes: Judanna Lynn
Dancers: Juilliard Dance Ensemble

The Story of the Soldier
(Television, 3/10/57, CBS-TV, "Camera Three")

Music: Igor Stravinsky
Choreography: Anna Sokolow
Costumes: No credit listed
Narrator: Max Adrian
Dancers: James Mitchell, Annabelle Gold, Arthur Malet

"Technical essay"
(Film, 1966, 17 min., 16mm, b&w)

p. 18. "Louis Horst has…" Alice Lewisohn Crowley, *The Neighborhood Playhouse: Leaves from a Theatre Scrapbook* (New York: Theatre Arts Books, 1959), 242.

p. 19. "We all studied choreography…" Maslow, interview, 1980.

p. 19. "He was a fantastic teacher…" MM/LR.

p. 20. "A great deal…" Shurr, letter to the author.

p. 20. "In the first year…" David Pressman, personal interview, March 20, 1981, New York.

p. 21. "I could jump…" Anna Sokolow, personal interview, March 22, 1982, New York.

p. 21–2. "I can't do that…" Sokolow, interview.

p. 22. "I was a prostitute…" MM/LR.

p. 22. "Was I really awfully bad?" Sokolow, conversation with Ethel Butler and the author, October 20, 1979, University Park, Maryland.

3 Dance as a Weapon

p. 23. "Stokowski came to rehearsals…" Eleanor King, *Transformations* (New York: Dance Horizons, 1978).

p. 24. "…noteworthy contribution…" JM Quoted by King, 64.

p. 24. "Vaudeville by Woodstock Artists," Program, Woodstock Playhouse, July 22, 1930.

p. 26. "The unions were…" MM/LR.

p. 26. "Young dance students…" Anne L. Skalski, "Prelude to the WPA Federal Dance Project: Organization," Society of Dance History Scholars, New York, 1980.

p. 26. "Dance is a weapon in the class struggle." Program, Workers Dance League Recital: Leading Revolutionary Dance Groups, January 7, 1934.

p. 27. "…an organization of…" *New Dance*, January 1935. Article from Anna Sokolow's personal scrapbook; byline is missing.

p. 27. "At the same time…" *New Theatre*, September–October 1933.

p. 27. "Out of twelve conceptions…" Emmanuel Eisenberg, *New Theatre*, August 1934.

p. 28. "In our dances we…" Miriam Blecher, quoted by Joseph Mitchell, *New York World-Telegram*, December 13, 1934.

p. 28. "He was a shy pianist…" Anna Sokolow, personal interview, November 10, 1979, New York.

p. 29. "Yes, in some ways..." Alex North, personal interview, January 7, 1982, Pacific Palisades, California.

p. 29. "a time when nobody..." Rose Bank, personal interview, November 8, 1980, Pittsburgh.

p. 30. "When I lived with..." Ethel Butler, personal interview, April 24, 1982, University Park, Maryland.

p. 30. "For many years..." Bessie Schönberg, personal interview, September 28, 1980, Bronxville, New York.

4 Radical Theater/Radical Dance

p. 31. "5 Workers (Chanting)..." Mordecai Gorelik, *New Theatres for Old* (Binghamton, N.Y.: Vail-Ballou Press, 1948), 402.

p. 32. "...a mass development of..." Ben Blake, *The Awakening of the American Theatre* (New York: Tomorrow Publishers, 1935), 67.

p. 33. "I was riding..." Ethel Butler, personal interview, April 24, 1982, University Park, Maryland.

p. 33. "When I started with Anna..." Aza (Cefkin) Bard McKenzie, personal interview, January 5, 1982, North Hollywood, California.

p. 35. "Which side are you on?" Florence Reece (composer), libretto, 1931.

p. 35. "They took the entire..." LDN, August 1936.

p. 36. "While it was..." JM, AD, 280–281.

p. 36. "The outstanding exception..." Ralph Taylor, *Dance Observer*, February 1934.

5 Anna in the Promised Land: Russia

p. 39. "When you receive this..." Alex North, letter to Anna Sokolow, March 1934.

p. 39. "With all the progressive strides..." North, *Dance Observer*, May 1934.

p. 40. "Why not? I am a dancer!" Anna Sokolow, personal interview, November 10, 1979.

p. 40. "I enjoyed the dancing..." Sokolow, letter to Ronya Chernin, June 28, 1934. Rose Bank Collection.

p. 41. "Well I'm in Moscow..." Sokolow, letter to Rose Bank, June 14, 1934. Rose Bank Collection.

p. 41. "I kept wondering..." Sokolow, letter to Chernin.

p. 42. "We have been having..." Sokolow, letter to Sarah Sokolow, June 19, 1934. Rose Bank Collection.

p. 43. "...Anna Sokolova" Sokolow, interview, 1979.

p. 44. "The whole city marched..." Sokolow, letter to Bank, June 21, 1934. Rose Bank Collection.

p. 45. "We could make..." LDN, October 1934.

p. 45. "We were still..." MM/LR.

6 Landmarks

p. 47. "The first scene of *Lefty*..." Margaret Brenman-Gibson, *Clifford Odets, American Playwright: The Years From 1906 to 1940* (New York: Atheneum, 1981), 315.

p. 48. "...a 'spy' for Lincoln Kirstein." Don McDonagh, *Martha Graham* (New York: Popular Library, 1975), 108.

p. 49. "...like quicksilver." Muriel Stuart, personal interview, September 27, 1980, New York.

p. 49. "Anna Sokolov's *[sic] Histrionics*..." *Daily Worker* [New York]. Unsigned and undated article in Anna Sokolow's personal scrapbook.

p. 49. "[The revolutionary dancers] are learning..." JM, NYT, December 2, 1934.

p. 50. "His death emerges..." Unidentified article in Anna Sokolow's personal scrapbook.

p. 50. "When Anna Sokolow..." et seq. JM, NYT, June 30, 1935.

p. 50. "...a major work..." LDN, August 1935.

p. 51. "Certainly there is..." JM, AD, 279.

p. 51. "Anna always managed..." ML, BB, 216.

p. 51. "...first in the esteem..." LDN, August 1935.

p. 52. "...delightful satire..." JM, NYT, November 15, 1937.

p. 53. "She has taken..." Marjorie Church, *Dance Observer*, December 1937.

p. 53. "...to avoid art as social..." Thomas H. Dickinson (director), "Report of the Director: Arts in the Theatre," Triuna Island, Lake George, Summer 1936, 20.

p. 54. "I saw her perform..." Ben Belitt, *Bennington Review*, April 1980.

p. 54. "...a burning indictment..." Louise Mitchell, *Daily Worker* [New York], March 1, 1937.

p. 54. "Inspired by..." *Heart of Spain* (1937), by Frontier Film Group, who were radical militant filmmakers, working in a style similar to the *March of Time*. They also produced *People of the Cumberland* in 1938.

p. 54. "...a dance of perpetual motion." Santos Balmori, personal interview, May 17, 1981, Mexico City.

p. 55. "Her figure..." Edwin Denby, *New York Herald-Tribune*, December 12, 1943.

p. 56. "She travelled considerably..." Don McDonagh, *Martha Graham* (New York: Popular Library, 1975), 121.

p. 56. "It has been fun..." Anna Sokolow, letter to Rose Bank, April 1, 1937. Rose Bank Collection.

p. 56. "You had a summer..." Martha Hill, personal interview, June 12, 1980, New York.

p. 56. "I have a beautiful suite..." Sokolow, letter to Bank, July 1937. Rose Bank Collection.

p. 56. "[In] an exposition..." ML, BB, 217.

p. 57. "It's like a morgue in here..." Ethel Butler, personal interview, April 24, 1982, University Park, Maryland.

p. 58. "What Martha was saying..." Sokolow, personal interview, November 10, 1979, New York.

p. 58. "It was like..." ML, BB, 214.

p. 59. "She was very instrumental..." Alex North, personal interview, January 7, 1982, Pacific Palisades, California.

p. 59. "...from whom brilliant..." JM, NYT, February 28, 1939.

7 Mexico

p. 63. "...the rhythms of the city..." Ana Mérida, personal interview, May 26, 1981, Mexico City.

p. 63. "He asked if I would like..." MM/LR.

p. 64. "Our mothers packed roast chicken..." Rebecca (Rowen) Kramer, telephone interview, June 12, 1981, New York.

p. 65. "From the start..." Aza Bard McKenzie, personal interview, January 5, 1982.

p. 65. "As it happened..." McKenzie, interview.

p. 65. "Greetings to the Mexican People..." *El Popular* [Mexico], April 17, 1939. Signature on publicity photograph.

p. 66. *"Slaughter of the Innocents* is a…" *El Popular* [Mexico], April 17, 1939.

p. 66. "What was amazing…" Emmanuel Eisenberg, letter to John Martin, quoted in the *New York Times*, July 9, 1939.

p. 66. "Everyone from the peasants…" Kramer, interview, 1981.

p. 67. "Anna was a street kid…" McKenzie, interview, 1982.

p. 68. "If I did it…" Anna Sokolow, personal interview, January 18, 1989, New York.

p. 68. "Miss Sokolow will…" Summer 1939. Unidentified article from Anna Sokolow's personal scrapbook.

p. 69. "I was introduced…" MM/LR.

p. 70. "At first we could…" Rosa Reyna, Raquel Gutiérrez, Josephina Luna, and Alicia Ceballos, personal interview, May 20, 1981, Mexico City.

p. 71. "…the scenes are traced with…" Program, premier of *Don Lindo de Almería*, January 9, 1940.

p. 71. "…[you need] music for the eyes…" Frederico García Lorca, letter to José Bergamin, quoted in program, *Don Lindo de Almería*.

p. 71. "…such an effort…" Unnamed critic, quoted by Arturo Perucho, *Nuestra Muscia*, October 1947.

p. 72. "In a room…" Adolfo Salazar, *La Vida Musical*, October 16, 1939.

p. 73. "Landscapes of Goya…" Antonio Luna Arroyo, *Ana Mérida en la Historia de la Danza Mexicana Moderna* (Mexico City: Publicaciones de Danza Moderna, 1959), 94–97.

p. 73. "The stately beauty…" Carlos Gonzalez Pena, unidentified article from Anna Sokolow's personal scrapbook.

p. 73. "…this fine company…" *Jueves de Excelsior*, January 1940.

8 Finding a Fuller Expression

p. 76. "I knew when…" Ana Mérida, personal interview, May 26, 1981, Mexico City.

p. 76. "Her collaboration…" Ignacio Aguirre, personal interview, May 15, 1981, Mexico City.

p. 78. "Even in these seasoned…" Mary P. O'Donnell, *Dance Observer*, April 1940.

p. 78. "…destined to become…" Walter Terry, *New York Herald-Tribune*, March 4, 1941.

p. 78. "Anna Sokolow…is…" Terry, *New York Herald-Tribune*, April 20, 1941.

p. 78. "Miss Sokolow's present…" Edwin Denby, *New York Herald-Tribune*, December 12, 1943.

p. 78. "Apart from the Mexican…" ML, BB, 221.

p. 79. "…a haunting song of…" ML, BB, 221.

p. 79. "The Workers Dance League…" JM, NYT, January 21, 1934.

p. 80. "Why?" Anna Sokolow, personal interview, November 10, 1979, New York.

p. 80. "'Our lady' of the…" ML, BB, 221–222.

p. 81. "It was a solo…" ML, BB, 221.

p. 81. "Anna Sokolow…has improved…" Terry, *New York Herald-Tribune*, May 19, 1946.

p. 82. "Puncture the air…" ML, CSM, May 2 and 16, 1942.

p. 82. "I loved the work…" Sokolow, personal interview, January 18, 1989.

9 The Ups and Downs of Broadway

p. 83. "When Elia Kazan heard…" Anna Sokolow, interview by Barbara Newman, February 12, 1974. Oral History Archives, Dance Collection of The New York Public Library.

p. 83. "…musical play of…" Brooks Atkinson, NYT, January 10, 1947.

p. 84. "A dancer's business is…" Sokolow, quoted by Margery Dana, *Daily Worker* [New York], November 21, 1937.

p. 85. "Brooks Atkinson, who liked…" Atkinson, NYT, April 1, 1947.

p. 85. "In Germany…" Sokolow, personal interview, November 10, 1979, New York.

p. 86. "The big problem…" et seq. Richard Philp, *Dance Magazine*, May 1976. Copyright © 1997 Richard Philp.

p. 87. "I don't eat much…" Sokolow, personal interview, January 10, 1988.

p. 88. "…fresh and striking" Atkinson, NYT, June 4, 1948.

p. 88. "Under Mr. Lewis' direction…" Atkinson, NYT. Undated article from Anna Sokolow's personal scrapbook.

p. 88. "…an overdose." John Chapman, *Daily News* [New York], January 7, 1950.

10 Actors Studio

p. 91. "I had never been..." John Silvester White, personal interview, January 9, 1981, Sherman Oaks, California.

p. 91. "I was doing an arm movement..." Julie Harris, personal interview, October 18, 1988, Washington, D.C.

p. 91. "The floor is your friend..." David Garfield, *A Player's Place: The Story of the Actors Studio* (New York: Macmillan Publishing Co., 1980), 62.

p. 91. "What are you doing..." Aza Bard McKenzie, personal interview, January 5, 1982, North Hollywood, California.

p. 92. "There is an incident..." et seq. Vivian Nathan, personal interview, April 12, 1987, New York City.

p. 92. "As the months went by..." McKenzie, interview.

p. 93. "When I joined..." et seq. White, interview.

11 The Early Fifties

p. 95. "...a kind of self-induced..." Joseph North (ed.), *New Masses: An Anthology of the Rebel Thirties* (New York: International Publishers, 1969), 5.

p. 96. "Investigators did come..." et seq. John Silvester White, personal interview, January 9, 1981, Sherman Oaks, California.

p. 96. "I was never a member..." MM/LR.

p. 100. "That's the wrong way..." Anna Sokolow, conversation with the author, October 28, 1988, Washington, D.C.

p. 100. "My desire was..." Tennessee Williams, quoted by Richard Watts, Jr., *New York Post*, March 20, 1953.

p. 101. "...had set out..." Richard Watts, Jr., *New York Post*, March 20, 1953.

p. 101. "Williams is thinking..." Walter Kerr, *New York Herald-Tribune*, March 29, 1953.

p. 101. "One thing I'll..." Watts, *New York Post*, April 12, 1953.

p. 101. "If you think..." White, interview.

p. 102. "...une espèce de..." Igor Stravinsky, sleeve notes, *L'Histoire du Soldat* recording, Columbia.

12 Anna in the Promised Land: Israel

p. 103. "Your love affair..." Judith Gottlieb, speech, July 21, 1983, Tel Aviv. Anna Sokolow Collection.

p. 105. "didn't know..." MM/LR.

p. 105. "I drove out..." Carl Glaser, personal interview, June 25, 1983, Tel Aviv.

p. 105. "At the start of..." Anna Sokolow, "The Dance," in *Assignment in Israel*, edited by Bernard Mandelbaum (New York: Jewish Theological Seminary of America, 1960), 80.

p. 106. "The nearest I have..." et seq. Sokolow, "The Dance," 80–81.

p. 107. "We really didn't need her..." Inbal dancer, quoted in letter to the author, November 29, 1983.

p. 107. "We brought the raw materials..." Sara Levi-Tanai, *Duar Hashavuah* [Tel Aviv], September 2, 1954.

p. 109. "Miss Sokolow should not..." Ze'eva Cohen, personal interview, December 3, 1983, New York.

13 Building a Repertoire

p. 111. "Among the gifted..." Xavier Francis, personal interview, May 19, 1981, Mexico City.

p. 113. "In recent years..." Anna Sokolow, interview by Barbara Newman, February 12, 1974. Oral History Archives, Dance Collection, The New York Public Library.

p. 113. "Anna was no longer..." Jeff Duncan, personal interview, November 4, 1988, Baltimore, Maryland.

p. 114. "Now, Anna..." Anna Sokolow, conversation with the author, October 28, 1988, Washington, D.C.

p. 114. "Apparently they were..." JM, NYT, September 2, 1956.

"When group members..." Duncan interview.

p. 115. "My first memory..." Betty Walberg, taped interview, December 1988, Santa Barbara, California.

"At the premiere..." Duncan, interview.

p. 118. "Seeing them all together..." Marcia B. Siegel, *The Shapes of Change* (New York: Houghton Mifflin, 1979), 285.

p. 119. "Anna is uncanny..." Walberg, interview.

p. 120.. "Anna Sokolow's *Rooms* ..." Walter Terry, *New York Herald-Tribune*, May 16, 1955.

p. 121. "I know it is ..." et seq. La Conferencia, *Proceedings*, translated by Gabriel Houbard and Jose Coronado, Fall 1981. Collection of the author.

p. 121. "In an open letter ..." Waldeen, *Excelsior* [Mexico], July 20, 1956.

p. 122. "In one passage ..." Duncan, interview.

14 Working the Media

p. 123. "He noted that ..." JM, NYT, September 2, 1956.

p. 123. "Jeff Duncan remembered ..." et seq. Jeff Duncan, personal interview, November 4, 1988.

p. 124. "If it hadn't been ..." et seq. Douglas Watt, *Daily News* [New York], November 1, 1956.

p. 124. "According to Jeff Duncan ..." Duncan interview.

p. 125. "In September 1950 ..." Joan Peyser, *Bernstein: A Biography* (New York: William Morrow, 1987), 247.

p. 125. "Gentlemen, I cannot ..." *Nation*, May 31, 1952.

p. 125. "From the start ..." Tyrone Guthrie, *A Life in the Theatre* (New York: McGraw-Hill, 1959), 240–241.

p. 126. "According to an ANTA ..." et seq. *Chapter One*, March 1957.

p. 126. "If we are ever ..." JM, NYT, March 17, 1957.

p. 127. "Miss Sokolow has ..." Walter Terry, *New York Herald-Tribune*, March 17, 1957.

p. 128. "The star attractions ..." See cast of *The California Story* in Chronology, 1957.

p. 128. "Val Rosing, the director ..." Stage Manager Chris Mahan, letter to the author, April 15, 1989.

p. 128. "One day, for example ..." et seq. See *California Story* cast.

p. 130.. "Now about Anna ..." Leo Lerman, *Dance Magazine*, December 1967. Copyright © 1997 *Dance Magazine*.

p. 131. "The best view ..." Stephen Bank, personal interview, July 4, 1988, University Park, Maryland.

p. 132. "I was the negative one ..." John Silvester White, personal interview, January 9, 1981, Sherman Oaks, California.

p. 132. "Seemed to see himself ..." Larry Robinson, conversation with the author, October 8, 1988, New York.

15 The Juilliard Connection

p. 133. "Once you are taught..." Tony Azito, interview by Robert Berkvist, NYT, September 27, 1981.

p. 133. "You wouldn't catch..." Mary Chudick, observation of the author, November 15, 1985, New York.

p. 133. "I'll ask around..." et seq. Martha Hill, personal interview, November 15, 1985, New York.

p. 135. "That's very sweet,..." Eliot Feld, speech, "A Gala Benefit Performance Honoring Anna Sokolow," Joyce Theater, New York, September 20, 1986.

p. 135. "Motion comes from..." Ray Cook, personal interview, October 6, 1979, University Park, Maryland.

p. 136. "Her intensity..." Hill, personal interview, October 3, 1988, New York.

p. 136. "I like all..." Anna Sokolow, quoted by Christine Temin, *Boston Evening Globe*, May 7, 1978.

p. 137. "When she fights..." Hill, interview, 1988.

p. 137. "...how to direct..." Barbara Naomi Cohen, *Dance Scope*, 1981.

16 A New Era

p. 140. "to express..." Unidentified article in Anna Sokolow's personal scrapbook.

p. 140. "The gestures she..." et seq. Jose Coronado, personal interview, March 19, 1989, New York.

p. 141. "When I did..." Anna Sokolow, letter to Ana Mérida, October 14, 1960. Collection of the author.

p. 142. "In the 1970s..." Aurelio González, "Anna Sokolow: Rebeldía con disciplina." Unidentified article in Anna Sokolow's personal scrapbook.

p. 142. "The world is changing..." Unidentified article in Anna Sokolow's personal scrapbook.

p. 142. "Ninteen-sixty is..." José Alcaraz, *Excelsior* (Mexico), November 23, 1960.

p. 142. "The highly touted..." John Fealy, *Dance Magazine*, November 1960. Copyright © 1997 *Dance Magazine*.

p. 142. "I have always..." Anna Sokolow, quoted by Christine Temin, *Boston Evening Globe*, May 7, 1978.

p. 144. *"Dreams* gave one..." Doris Hering, *Dance Magazine*, November 1960. Copyright © 1997 *Dance Magazine*.

p. 144. "a deeply psychological..." Clive Barnes. Unidentified article in Anna Sokolow's personal scrapbook.

p. 145. "When we see..." Anna Sokolow, quoted by Ray Cook in notes for *Dreams* Labanotation score, Dance Notation Bureau, New York.

17 Lyric Theatre (Israel)

p. 147. "My plan is..." Anna Sokolow, "Suggestions for a New Dance Theatre in Israel," grant proposal to the America-Israel Cultural Foundation, July 6, 1961.

"was a revolution..." Judith Gottlieb, quoted by Nathan Mishori, *Israel Dance*, 1980.

p. 148. "I have formed..." Anna Sokolow, letter to Martha Hill, April 29, 1962. Martha Hill Collection.

p. 149. "We never thought..." Juki Arkin, personal interview, May 20,1989, New York.

p. 149. "Anna taught us..." Rina Shaham, personal interview, June 17, 1983, Tel Aviv.

p. 150. "The work goes..." Sokolow, letter to Martha Hill, July 1, 1962. Collection of the Juilliard School.

p. 150. "Gertrud Kraus soon..." Nathan Mishori, *Israel Dance*, 1980.

p. 151. "To aggravate..." Laurie Freedman Myers, letter to the author, October 25, 1983.

p. 151. "In the fall..." Shaham, interview.

Through the years a close relationship developed between Anna and Yossi, one that moved from a romantic involvement of two independent individuals to a symbiotic relationship of two adults, who at some point came to a silent understanding that their needs were inextricably linked. On the surface Yossi is a staunch supporter, willing on occasion to travel abroad with Anna, giving her his company and emotional support. As a cab driver, he has frequently taken her to and from airports. Sometimes he has performed for her when she needed an actor of his age and experience on stage. Anna, for her part, has been generous with financial help for Yossi's business ventures; too generous in the eyes of her family and close friends.

p. 153. "...when they announced..." Avraham Zouri, personal interview, June 23, 1983, Tel Aviv.

18 Other Ventures

p. 155. "...to force the actor..." Robert Lewis, *New York Times*, December 9, 1962.

p. 156. "...under Anna Sokolow's..." Robert Lewis, *Slings and Arrows*, 295.

p. 156. "My first aim..." Anna Sokolow, quoted by Walter Sorell, *Dance Magazine*, January 1964. Copyright © 1997 *Dance Magazine*.

p. 157. "Anna Sokolow's *The Question*..." Walter Terry, *New York Herald-Tribune*, December 6, 1964.

p. 157. "Where the American..." Terry.

p. 159. "In 1964. Duncan..." et seq. Jack Moore, personal interview, April 12, 1987, New York.

p. 169. "Art Bauman remembered..." Art Bauman, personal interview, March 18, 1989, New York.

p. 160. "For a time..." Bauman.

19 The Spirit of Rebellion

p. 164. "She hated it..." Anna Sokolow, interview by Alan M. Kriegsman, April 21, 1966, New York.

p. 165. "To have someone..." Rex Bickmore, personal interview, June 16, 1988, University Park, Maryland.

p. 165. "Miss Sokolow's lighthearted..." Clive Barnes, *New York Times*, October 8, 1976.

p. 166. *"Opus '65..."* Anna Kisselgoff, *New York Times*, October 28, 1976.

p. 168. "The lines, Anna..." John Silvester White, personal interview, January 9, 1981, Sherman Oaks, California.

p. 168. "There was an air..." Anne Warren, personal interview, June 5, 1987, University Park, Maryland.

p. 168. "What would you..." Warren.

p. 169. Courtesy Senta Driver, *Dance Scope*, and the American Dance Guild.

p. 171. "[*Deserts*] is..." Andrew Porter, *Financial Times* (London), July 26, 1967.

p. 171. "...like an explosion..." Unidentified article in Anna Sokolow's personal scrapbook.

p. 171. "The visit did not..." Jack Moore, personal interview, April 12, 1987, New York.

p. 171. "I wish I had..." Moore.

p. 172. "We never had..." Kei Takei, personal interview, January 13, 1981, Washington, D.C.

p. 172. "He recalls that..." Gerald Freedman, interview by Bill Rudman, "Broadway Melody," WCLV-FM, Cleveland, Ohio, October 3, 1987.

p. 172. "...non-book and lyrics." Ronald Gold, *Dance Magazine*, July 1968. Copyright © 1997 *Dance Magazine*.

p. 173. "The anger..." Lynda Gudde, personal interview, October 2, 1988, New York.

p. 173. "In the midst of..." Freedman, interview.

p. 174. "...he would come back..." Gerald Freedman, interview by Stephen E. Rubin, *New York Times*, April 22, 1973.

p. 174. "There seem to be..." Among the persons interviewed were James Rado, Gerome Ragni, Amy Saltz (Gerald Freedman's assistant), and Galt MacDermot.

p. 174. "...a spontaneous..." Unidentified article in Anna Sokolow's personal scrapbook.

p. 174. "...the sinewy toughness..." Doris Hering, *Dance Magazine*, December 1967. Copyright © 1997 *Dance Magazine*.

p. 175. "They picked my brains..." Anna Sokolow, personal interview, January 10, 1988, New York.

p. 175. "After all..." Julie Arenal, telephone interview, August 3, 1989, Los Angeles, California.

p. 175. "There will now be a spate of shitty rock musicals..." William Goldman, *The Season: A Candid Look at Broadway* (New York: Harcourt, Brace and World, Inc., 1969), 387.

20 Theater Danced and Danced Theater

p. 177. "...deserts suggests..." Program, Hunter College Playhouse, New York, March 10, 1967.

p. 178. "Each individual dance..." Jean Battey-Lewis, *Washington Post*, February 16, 1968.

p. 179. "...prophet of doom..." Clive Barnes, *New York Times*, November 14, 1968.

p. 179. "...apostle of darkness..." Deborah Jowitt, *Village Voice*, November 14, 1968.

p. 179. "Even after performing…" et seq. Ray Cook, personal interview, October 6, 1979, University Park, Maryland.

p. 181. "According to Lorry…" Lorry May, personal interview, April 15, 1989, New York.

p. 182. "I was only…" Rex Bickmore, personal interview, June 16, 1985, University Park, Maryland.

p. 182. "They spoke sometimes…" Bickmore.

p. 183. "For a while…" Lynda Gudde, personal interview, October 2, 1988, New York.

p. 183. "Mary Anthony commented…" Mary Anthony, telephone interview, April 16, 1989, New York.

p. 183. "Everywhere we went…" Bickmore, interview.

p. 183. "A few weeks after…" Bill Bales, personal interview, April 9, 1981, New York.

p. 184. "There was so little…" Jim May, personal interview, February 16, 1979, University Park, Maryland.

p. 184. "I just didn't know…" Anna Sokolow, conversation with the author, January 10, 1988.

p. 184. "I think some…" Anthony, interview.

p. 184. "Jim May remembers…" Jim May, interview.

p. 185. "I wasn't born…" George Tabori, script, *Pinkville*, 1971.

p. 185. "…a bellow of rage…" Jack Kroll, *Newsweek*, March 29, 1971.

21 The Seventies

p. 188. "Pierre Cardin, who…" Tonia Shimin, letter to the author, April 30, 1989.

p. 188. "We were a group…" Shimin.

p. 189. "There were problems…" Shimin.

p. 189. "This time the whole…" Doris Hering, *Dance Magazine*, January 1973. Copyright © 1997 *Dance Magazine*.

p. 189. "Lorry May remembers…" Lorry May, personal interview, April 15, 1989, New York.

p. 190. "It was the time…" Raúl Flores Canelo, personal interview, June 1981, Mexico City.

p. 190. "You will learn…" Flores Canelo.

p. 190. "I don't know…" Flores Canelo.

p. 190. "…they were like…" Flores Canelo.

p. 191. "The night is beautiful…" MM/LR.

p. 192. "…una epoca de oro…" Unidentified article in Anna Sokolow's personal scrapbook.

p. 193. "…literal, emotional…" Joan Cass, *Jerusalem Post*, December 12, 1973.

p. 193. "Rina Schenfeld…" Cass.

p. 195. "In her *Village Voice* review…" Deborah Jowitt, *Village Voice*, December 22, 1975.

p. 195. "…as technically proficient…" *eddy about dance, mostly*, April 1974.

22 Resurgence

p. 198. "It is a brisk…" Author's recollection, December 12, 1978, New York.

p. 198. "They just don't…" Author's recollection.

p. 198. "the Mayan piece…" Author's recollection, February 16, 1979, New York.

p. 200. "An incident that…" Author's observation, February 8, 1981, New York.

p. 200. "Jim May's first…" et seq. Jim May, personal interview, February 14, 1988, University Park, Maryland.

p. 201. "If she mentioned…" Author's observation, February 8, 1981.

p. 201. "The company…" Program, Abraham Goodman House, New York, March 18, 1981.

p. 202. "…the grain of optimism…" Jennifer Dunning, *New York Times*, March 23, 1981.

p. 202. "The dancers who are working…" Anna Sokolow, interview by Aaron Cohen, March 22, 1982, New York.

p. 203. "Recalling that period…" et seq. Jim May, interview.

p. 203. "New York's Joyce Theater…" Author's observation, September 20, 1986, New York.

p. 204. "I SALUTE ANNA…" Agnes de Mille, telegram, September 20, 1986. Collection of the author.

23 PS

p 207. "There was great dignity..." Jack Anderson, *New York Times*, March 2, 1995.

p 207. "A later article..." Jack Anderson, *New York Times*, April 2, 1995.

p 208. "Anna's work with actors..." Anna Kisselgoff quoting Uta Hagan, *New York Times*, February 17, 1995.

p 209. "Anna Sokolow is one..." Gerald Arpino speaking at Gala celebrating Anna's 85th birthday. The Sylvia and Danny Kaye Playhouse, Hunter College, New York City, February 15, 1995.

p 210. "Look at those children..." Anna Sokolow walking with the author in the West Greenwich Village section of New York City, April 22, 1996.

BIBLIOGRAPHY

Books

Anderson, Jack. *The American Dance Festival*. North Carolina: Duke University Press, 1987.

Arroyo, Antonio Luna. *Ana Mérida en la Historia de la Danza Mexicana Moderna*. Mexico: Publicaciones de Danza Moderna, 1959.

Benardete, Doris Fox. "The Neighborhood Playhouse in Grand Street," dissertation, New York University, 1952.

Blake, Ben. *The Awakening of the American Theatre*. NewYork: Tomorrow Publishers, 1935.

Brenman-Gibson, Margaret. *Clifford Odets, American Playwright: The Years From 1906 to 1940*. New York: Atheneum, 1981.

Brown, Jean (Ed.). *The Vision of Modern Dance*. Princeton: Princeton Book Co., 1979.

Brown, John Mason. *Dramatis Personae*. New York: Viking Press, 1963.

Cardona, Patricia. *Danza Moderna: Los Precursores*. Mexico: Universidad Nacional Autonoma de Mexico, 1980.

Chujoy, Anatole. *The Dance Encyclopedia*. New York: A. S. Barnes and Company, 1949.

—— and P. W. Manchester. *The Dance Encyclopedia*. 2nd ed. New York: Simon and Schuster, 1967.

Cohen, Selma Jeanne. *Doris Humphrey: An Artist First*. Middletown, Conn.: Wesleyan University Press, 1972.

—— (Ed.). *The Modern Dance: Seven Statements of Belief*. Middletown, Conn.: Wesleyan University Press, 1966.

Cook, Ray. *A Handbook for the Dance Director*. New York: Ray Cook, 1977.

Covarrubias, Miguel. *La Danza en Mexico*, edited by Raùl Flores Guerro. Mexico: Universidad Nacional Autonoma de Mexico, 1980.

Crawford, Cheryl. *One Naked Individual*. Indianapolis: Bobbs-Merrill, 1977.

Croce, Arlene. *Afterimages*. New York: Alfred A. Knopf, 1977.

Crowley, Alice Lewisohn. *The Neighborhood Playhouse: Leaves from a Theatre Scrapbook*. New York: Theatre Arts Books, 1959.

Dallal Alberto. *Femina-Danza.* Mexico: Universidad Nacional Autonoma de Mexico, 1985.

Flanagan, Hallie. *Arena, The History of the Federal Theatre.* New York: Benjamin Blom, 1965.

Fraleigh, Sandra Horton. *Dance and the Lived Body.* Pittsburgh: University of Pittsburgh Press, 1987.

Freedley, George and John A. Reeves. *A History of the Theatre.* New York: Crown Publishers, 1941.

Garfield, David. *A Player's Place: The Story of The Actors Studio.* New York: Macmillan Publishing Co., 1980.

Geisinger, Marion. *Plays, Players, and Playwrights: An Illustrated History of the Theatre.* New York: Hart Publishing Co., 1971.

Goldman, William. *The Season: A Candid Look at Broadway.* New York: Harcourt, Brace and World, 1969.

Gorelik, Mordecai. *New Theatres for Old.* Binghamton, N.Y.: Vail-Ballou Press, 1948.

Guthrie, Tyrone. *A Life in the Theatre.* New York: McGraw-Hill, 1959.

Higham, Charles. *Charles Laughton: An Intimate Biography.* New York: Doubleday, 1976.

Howe, Irving. *World of Our Fathers.* New York: Simon and Schuster, 1976.

Jowitt, Deborah. *Dance Beat: Selected Views and Reviews 1967–1976.* New York: Marcel Dekker, 1977.

———. *The Dance in Mind.* Boston: David R. Godine, 1985.

King, Eleanor. *Transformations.* New York: Dance Horizons, 1978.

Koegler, Horst. *The Concise Oxford Dictionary of Ballet.* London: Oxford University Press, 1977.

Lewis, Robert. *Slings and Arrows.* New York: Stein and Day, 1984.

Litvinoff, Valentina. *The Use of Stanislavsky Within Modern Dance.* New York: American Dance Guild, 1972.

Livet, Anne (Ed.). *Contemporary Dance.* New York: Abbeville Press, 1978.

Lloyd, Margaret. *The Borzoi Book of Modern Dance.* New York: Alfred A. Knopf, 1949; rpt. New York: Dance Horizons, 1974.

Lyle, Cynthia. *Dancers on Dancing.* New York: Drake Publishers, 1977.

Lynton, Anadel. *Anna Sokolow: 20 Cuadernos Cenidi-Danza José Limón.* Mexico: Instituto Nacional De Bellas Artes, 1988.

Mandelbaum, Bernard (Ed.). *Assignment in Israel.* New York: Jewish Theological Seminary of America, distributed by Harper, 1960.

Martin, John. *America Dancing.* rpt. New York: Dance Horizons, 1968.

———. *Introduction to the Dance.* rpt. New York: Dance Horizons, 1965.

Mazo, Joseph H. *Prime Movers: The Makers of Modern Dance in America.* New York: William Morrow and Co., 1977.

McDonagh, Don. *The Complete Guide to Modern Dance*. Garden City, N.Y.: Doubleday and Company, 1976.

——. *Martha Graham*. rpt. New York: Popular Library, 1975.

——. *The Rise and Fall and Rise of Modern Dance*. New York: Mentor, 1970.

Morgan, Barbara. *Martha Graham*. New York: Duell, Sloan and Pearce, 1941.

North, Joseph. *No Men Are Strangers*. New York: International Publishers, 1958.

—— (Ed.). *New Masses: An Anthology of the Rebel Thirties*. New York: International Press, 1969.

Palmer, Winthrop. *Theatrical Dancing in America*. 2nd ed. New York: A. S. Barnes and Co., 1978.

Peyser, Joan. *Bernstein: A Biography*. New York: William Morrow, 1987.

Riis, Jacob A. *How the Other Half Lives*. New York: Hill and Wang, 1957.

Rosenfeld, Lulla. *Bright Star of Exile: Jacob Adler and the Yiddish Theatre*. New York: Thomas Y. Crowell, 1977.

Schlundt, Christena L. *Tamiris: A Chronicle of Her Dance Career 1927–1955*. New York: New York Public Library, 1972.

Senesh, Hannah. *Hannah Senesh, Her Life and Diary*. New York: Schocken Books, 1972.

Siegel, Marcia B. *The Shapes of Change: Images of the American Dance*. Boston: Houghton Mifflin Company, 1979.

Stodelle, Ernestine. *Deep Song: The Dance Story of Martha Graham*. New York: Schirmer Books, 1984.

Terry, Walter. *I Was There*, edited by Andrew Mark Wentink. New York: Marcel Dekker, 1978.

Tibol, Raquel. *Pasos en la Danza Mexicana*. Mexico: Universidad Nacional Autonoma de Mexico, 1982.

Waldau, Roy S. *Vintage Years of the Theatre Guild 1928–1939*. Cleveland: Press of Case Western Reserve University, 1972.

Williams, Tennessee. *Memories*. Garden City, N.Y.: Doubleday and Co., 1975.

Articles

Alcaraz, José. *Excelsior* (Mexico City) November 23, 1960.

Allen, Patricia S. *American Dancer [Dance Magazine]* February 1938.

Anderson, Jack. *Dance Magazine* June 1966.

Atkinson, Brooks. *New York Times* January 10, 1947.

——. *New York Times* April 1, 1947.

——. *New York Times* June 4, 1948.

Balcom, Louis. *Dance Observer* January 1942.

Barnes, Clive. *Dance and Dancers* January 1969.

Barnes, Clive. *New York Times* November 14, 1966.

——. *New York Times* March 11, 1967.

——. *New York Times* March 12, 1967.

——. *New York Times* November 14, 1968.

——. *New York Times* October 8, 1976.

Barzel, Ann. *Dance News* March 1965.

——. *Dance News* May 1969.

Battey-Lewis, Jean. *Washington Post* February 16, 1968.

Beiswanger, George W. *Dance Observer* January 1944.

——. *Dance Observer* February 1957.

Belitt, Ben. *Bennington Review* April 1980.

Bernstein, Harry. *Dance Observer* June–July 1959.

Bissell, Robyn. *Dance Notation Journal* January 1983.

Blecher, Miriam. *New York World-Telegram* December 13, 1934.

Cass, Joan. *Jerusalem Post* December 12, 1973.

Chapman, John. *Daily News* (New York) January 7, 1950.

Church, Marjorie. *Dance Observer* March 1937.

——. *Dance Observer* April 1937.

——. *Dance Observer* December 1937.

Claire, William F. *Smithsonian* July 1977.

Cohen, Barbara Naomi. *Dance Scope* 1981.

Cohen, Selma Jeanne. *Dance Magazine* June 1959.

Daily Worker (New York). Unidentified article in Anna Sokolow's scrapbook.

Dal Negro, Leonard. *New Theatre* October 1934.

——. *New Theatre* August 1935.

——. *New Theatre* October 1939.

Dana, Margery. *Daily Worker* (New York) November 21, 1937.

Dance Magazine March 1947.

Denby, Edwin. *New York Herald-Tribune* December 12, 1943.

Driver, Senta. *Dance Scope* September 16, 1966.

Duncan, Kathy. *Dance News* January 1976.

Dunning, Jennifer. *New York Times* March 23, 1981.

Eisenberg, Emmanuel. *New Theatre* July–August 1934.

——. *New Theatre* May 1936.

El Popular (Mexico City) April 17, 1939.

Ellis, Rhoda Winter. *Impulse* April 1958.

Evan, Blanche. *Dance [Dance Magazine]* November 1939.

——. *New Theatre* April 1934.

——. *New Theatre* October 1934.

Excelsior (Mexico City) January 1940.

Fealy, John. *Dance Magazine* November 1960.

Felton, James. *Philadelphia Evening Bulletin* June 28, 1968.

Foster, Steven. *New Theatre* January 1935.

Galsworthy, John. *New York Globe* September 20, 1921.

Gilford, Henry. *Dance Observer* December 1934.

——. *Dance Observer* May 1936.

Gold, Ronald. *Dance Magazine* July 1968.

Gruen, John. *Dance Magazine* June 1975.

Haagsche Courant (The Hague) July 9, 1966.

Hering, Doris. *Dance Magazine* May 1951.

——. *Dance Magazine* May 1955.

——. *Dance Magazine* June 1955.

——. *Dance Magazine* July 1955.

——. *Dance Magazine* June 1956.

——. *Dance Magazine* November 1960.

——. *Dance Magazine* March 1962.

——. *Dance Magazine* May 1963.

——. *Dance Magazine* December 1967.

——. *Dance Magazine* January 1973.

Horst, Louis. *Dance* December 1929.

——. *Dance Observer* May 1954.

——. *Dance Observer* February 1955.

——. *Dance Observer* April 1958.

Jerusalem Post June 7, 1962.

Jowitt, Deborah. *Village Voice* December 22, 1965.

——. *Village Voice* November 14, 1968.

——. *Village Voice* June 21, 1976.

——. *Village Voice* June 28, 1976.

Kendall, Elizabeth. *Dance Magazine* May 1975.

Kerr, Walter. *New York Herald-Tribune* March 29, 1953.

Kisselgoff, Anna. *New York Times* October 28, 1976.

Kostakowsky, Lya. *El Popular* (Mexico City) April 27, 1939.

Kraus, Gertrud. Letter. *Jerusalem Post* July 4, 1962.

Kriegsman, Alan M. *Juilliard Review Annual* 1965/66.

Kroll, Jack. *Newsweek* March 29, 1971.

Lerman, Leo. *Dance Magazine* July 1953.

——. *Dance Magazine* December 1967.

Levi-Tanai, Sara. *Duar Hashavuah* (Tel Aviv) September 2, 1954.

Lewis, Robert. *New York Times* December 9, 1962.

Lloyd, Margaret. *Christian Science Monitor* (Boston) May 2 and 16, 1942.

Love, Paul. *Dance Observer* May 1934.

MacDonald. Anne Sprague. *Dance Observer* December 1938.

348   *Bibliography*

Manchester, Phyllis Winifred. *Dance News* May 1959.
Marks, Marcia. *Dance Magazine* March 1962.
——. *Dance Magazine* July 1963.
Martin. John. *New York Times* January 21, 1934.
——. *New York Times* December 2, 1934.
——. *New York Times* June 30, 1935.
——. *New York Times* November 15, 1937.
——. *New York Times* February 28, 1939.
——. *New York Times* September 2, 1956.
——. *New York Times* March 17, 1957.
MacDonald, Anne Sprague. *Dance Observer* December 1938.
Maskey, Jacqueline. *Dance Magazine* May 1966.
McDonagh, Don. *New York Times* February 25, 1972.
McLaughlin, Russell. *Detroit News* January 1, 1937.
Mishori, Nathan. *Israel Dance* 1980.
Mitchell, Joseph. *New York World-Telegram* December 13, 1934.
Mitchell, Louise. *Daily Worker* (New York) March 1, 1937.
Myers, Maryn. *New Theatre* October 1934.
Nation May 31, 1952.
Naslund, Erik. *dans* May 1975.
New Dance January 1935.
New Theatre September–October 1933.
North, Alex. *Dance Observer* May 1934.
O'Donnell, Mary P. *Dance Observer* April 1940.
Parks, Gary. *Dance Magazine* September 1986.
Perucho, Arturo. *Nuestra Musica* October 1947.
Philp, Richard. *Dance Magazine* May 1976.
Porter, Andrew. *Financial Times* (London) July 26, 1967.
Pratt, Lesley. *Dance News* September 1974.
Rubin, Stephen E. *New York Times* April 22, 1973.
Sabin, Robert. *Dance Magazine* June 1953.
——. *Dance Magazine* July 1968.
Saina, Arthur. *Village Voice* March 18, 1971.
Salazar, Adolfo. *La Vida Musical* (Mexico) October 16, 1939.
Sears, David. *Ballet Review* Summer 1984 (David Sears, ed.).
Shifren, David. *New American* December–January 1987.
Solomon, Susan. *The Load* [State University of New York] January 22, 1974.
Sorell, Walter. *Dance Magazine* January 1964.
——. *Dance Magazine* January 1970.
——. *Dance News* April 1972.
——. *Dance News* December 1972.

———. *Dance Scope* Spring–Summer 1976.

Soviet Art July 14, 1934.

Taylor, Ralph. *Dance Observer* February 1934.

Temin, Christine. *Boston Evening Globe* May 7, 1978.

Terry, Walter. *New York Herald-Tribune* March 4, 1941.

———. *New York Herald-Tribune* April 20, 1941.

———. *New York Herald-Tribune* May 19, 1946.

———. *New York Herald-Tribune* March 18, 1951.

——— . *New York Herald-Tribune* May 16, 1955.

———. *New York Herald-Tribune* March 17, 1957.

———. *New York Herald-Tribune* December 6, 1964.

———. *Saturday Review* September 30, 1967.

Theodores, Diana. *eddy about dance, mostly* April 1974.

Time May 16, 1938.

Time January 1981.

Todd, Arthur. *Dance Observer* March 1951.

Het Vaterland (Amsterdam) July 9, 1966.

Waldeen. *Excelsior* (Mexico City) July 20, 1956.

Watt, Douglas. *Daily News* (New York) November 1, 1956.

Watts, Richard, Jr. *New York Post* June 4, 1948.

———. *New York Post* March 20, 1953.

———. *New York Post* April 12, 1953.

Winter, Rhoda. *Impulse* 1958.

Other Sources

Brochure. Neighborhood Playhouse, 1928.

La Conferencia. Proceedings. Trans. by Gabriel Houbard and José Coronado, Fall 1981.

Cook, Ray. Notes. *Dreams* [Labanotation Score]. Dance Notation Bureau, New York.

De Mille, Agnes. Telegram. September 20, 1986.

Dickinson, Thomas H. (director). "Report of the Director: Arts in the Theatre." Triuna Island, Lake George, N.Y., Summer 1936.

Feld, Eliot. Speech. "A Gala Benefit Performance Honoring Anna Sokolow." Joyce Theater, New York, September 20, 1986.

Freedman, Gerald. "Broadway Melody," Interview by Bill Rudman. WCLV-FM Cleveland, Ohio, October 3, 1987.

Gottlieb, Judith. Speech. July 21, 1983.

Heart of Spain. Frontier Film Group, 1937.

Larson, Bird. Brochure. Neighborhood Playhouse, 1927.

Marinetti, F. T. "War Is Beautiful," excerpt of poem reprinted in recital program, 1937.

Program. Abraham Goodman House, New York, March 18, 1981.

Program. Hunter College, New York, March 10, 1967.

Program. Premier of *Don Lindo de Almería*, January 9, 1940.

Program. Woodstock Playhouse, July 22, 1930.

Program. Workers Dance League Recital: Leading Revolutionary Dance Groups, January 7, 1934.

Reece, Florence (composer). Libretto. 1931.

Skalski, Anne L. "Prelude to the Federal Dance Project: Political Organizing, 1932–1937." Dance History Scholars Conference, New York, 1980.

Sokolow, Anna. Interview by Aaron Cohen. Tape. New York, March 22, 1982.

——. Interview by Barbara Newman. February 12, 1974. Oral History Archives, Dance Collection, The New York Public Library.

——. Lecture. Lincoln Center library auditorium, New York, February 1968.

Stravinsky, Igor. Sleeve notes, *L'Histoire du Soldat* recording, Columbia.

Tabori, George. Script. *Pinkville*. New York, 1971.

Weidman, Charles. Panel Discussion: "What it means to be a dancer: one generation to another." New York University, February 10, 1975.

INDEX

Other titles in the Choreography and Dance Studies series:

This book is part of a series. The publisher will accept continuation orders which may be cancelled at any time and which provide for automatic billing and shipping of each title in the series upon publication. Please write for details.